Published by Liturgy Training Publications, 1800 North Hermitage Avenue, Chicago IL 60622-1101. Phone: 1-800-933-1800. Fax: 1-800-933-7094.

Cover design: Jill Smith.
Production artist: Mark Hollopeter

Printed in the United States of America
ISBN 1-56854-147-3
BCL2

1991 - 1995

BISHOPS' COMMITTEE ON THE LITURGY NEWSLETTER

INTRODUCTION

The Bishops' Committee on the Liturgy is a standing committee of the National Conference of Catholic Bishops with a history dating back to November 1958. It was then that the Bishops' Commission on the Liturgical Apostolate, taking a name which was suggested by Pope Pius XII's 1947 encyclical *Mediator Dei* (see no. 109), was established. Since 1965, the Bishops' Commission on the Liturgical Apostolate and since 1967, the Bishops' Committee on the Liturgy (its new name) has issued a monthly newsletter in order to communicate news and events of liturgical interest to bishops, diocesan liturgical commissions and offices of worship, and all who are interested in liturgical renewal. The *Newsletter* of the Bishops' Committee on the Liturgy also serves as a public record for the official and authoritative decisions of the Apostolic See and of the National Conference of Catholic Bishops concerning the liturgy.

Newsletters

In 1976 the issues of the *Newsletter* that were published from 1965–1975 were reissued in a single bound collection. In 1981 a second collection, which contained all issues of the Newsletter issued from January 1976 through December 1980, was published. It also contained a number of statements of the Bishops' Committee on the Liturgy originally issued separately: *The Sign of Peace* (1977), *A Call to Prayer* (1978), *Commemorative Statement on the Fifteenth Anniversary of the Constitution on the Sacred Liturgy* (1978) and *General Intercessions* (1979). A third collection, containing the issues of the *Newsletter* published from January 1981 through December 1985, was released in 1986. The fourth bound collection contained all the issues of the *Newsletter* of the Committee on the Liturgy published from January 1986 through December 1990 and marked the completion of the twenty-sixth volume of the *Newsletter*.

This fifth bound volume contains all the issues of the *Newsletter* published from January 1991 through December 1995, volumes twenty-seven through thirty-one. It should be noted that the first issue of the *Newsletter* was published in September 1965 and that September 1995 marked thirty years of uninterrupted publication of this resource.

1991

In March of 1991, the Congregation for the Clergy issued a decree on collective Mass intentions and indicated the circumstances when this is permitted. During the same month, confirmation was received for the addition of Blessed Miguel Augustín Pro and Blessed Juan Diego to the Proper Calendar for the Dioceses of the USA. The opening prayers for their Masses and for Blessed Katharine Drexel were also approved. The NCCB Committee on the Liturgy approved the *Lectionary for Masses with Children* at its June 1991 meeting. It also arranged for the final examination of the revised *Lectionary for Mass* by the Liturgy, Doctrine and Pastoral Practices Committees. The Liturgy Committee and Pastoral Practices Committee formulated a series of proposals relating to holy days of obligation in response to a survey of the bishops conducted by the Committees. The Liturgy Committee authorized a statement on the "unity candle" at weddings for publication in the July/ August *Newsletter* and invited readers to respond to it. The members of the NCCB at their November 1991 meeting approved the *Lectionary for Masses with Children*. They also approved the revised Psalms of the *New American Bible* and the *New Revised Standard Version* of the Bible for liturgical use. During the November meeting, there was a prolonged discussion of holy days of obligation, which resulted in a decision to remove the obligation for January 1, August 15 and November 1 when those days occur on a Saturday or Monday.

1992

In March 1992, the Liturgy Committee discussed the results of a survey conducted by its Task Group on the Adaptation of the *Roman Missal*. At the end of March the NCCB received the confirmation of the Apostolic See for its decision to change the acclamation at the end of the readings. April 1992 marked the publication by the International Commission on English in the Liturgy of its *Third Progress Report on the Revision of the Roman Missal*. As a result of confused reports in the press, fears were raised about possible changes in the Nicene Creed and the Lord's Prayer even though the Liturgy Committee had not even discussed the report. The Congregation for Divine Worship and the Discipline of the Sacraments confirmed the NRSV and the revised NAB psalms for liturgical use. It also confirmed *ad experimentum*, for three years, the *Lectionary for Masses with Children*. In June of 1992, the CDWDS confirmed the decision of the NCCB to provide alternative readings for the

Lectionary. Colossians 3:12–17 may be used in place of Colossians 3:12–21, and Ephesians 5:25–32 may replace the reading from Ephesians 5:21–32. The members of the NCCB approved the first volume of the *Lectionary for Mass* (Sundays and Solemnities) during their June 1992 meeting. In July the Apostolic See approved the decision of the NCCB to remove the obligation to participate in the celebration of the eucharist when January 1, August 15 or November 1 falls on a Saturday or a Monday. In November the members of the NCCB approved the second volume of the *Lectionary for Mass,* as well as the Mass in Thanksgiving for Human Life. The Congregation for Divine Worship and the Discipline of the Sacraments later informed the Conference that it was not expedient to confirm that Mass at the present time. In a rather rare voice vote, the bishops unanimously approved guidelines for the inclusion of saints and the blessed on the Proper Calendar for the Dioceses of the USA. These guidelines ensure that only persons with a true *cultus* in the USA are placed on the liturgical calendar for the United States.

1993

In March 1993, the Pontifical Council for Promoting Christian Unity published a revision of the *Directory for the Application of Principles and Norms on Ecumenism.* A number of the Directory's provisions touch on liturgical matters. At their June 1993 meeting the members of the NCCB voted to seek permission from the CDWDS for two new eucharistic prayers composed in English, one similar in length to Eucharistic Prayer II and the other similar to Eucharistic Prayer III. The Congregation for Divine Worship and the Discipline of the Sacraments later replied that the question of additional eucharistic prayers would have to be brought to a plenary meeting of the Congregation. As of the end of 1995, such a meeting had not taken place. The NCCB also approved an age range (between seven and eighteen years of age) for the reception of confirmation. During its June meeting, the Liturgy Committee discussed how there could be greater participation by the bishops in the approval process of the *Sacramentary.* This was in response to concerns raised by several bishops. The Liturgy Committee proposed a process which included a review of the ICEL texts by the chairmen of the Liturgy and Doctrine Committees and the Executive Directors of the corresponding Secretariats. The purpose of this review was to assure the members of the NCCB that there were no doctrinal errors in the liturgical texts. The procedure also provided for the possibility of remanding individual texts to ICEL. The process was ultimately approved by the members of the NCCB in November 1993. At the same meeting the bishops approved the Spanish translation of the *Order of Christian Funerals —*

Ritual de Exequias Cristianas. The bishops decided to postpone the voting on Segment One of the *Sacramentary* until November 1994. Finally, the NCCB did not approve the revised *Grail Psalter,* since a two-thirds majority of affirmative votes was not achieved even after a mail ballot.

1994

In January of 1994, the *Newsletter* carried a clarification concerning lectionaries for Masses with children. It stated that only the lectionary approved by the NCCB was authorized for use in the United States of America. The February issue of the *Newsletter* contained the complete text of the NCCB *Procedure for Approving the Revised Roman Missal* which had been approved by the members of the NCCB in November 1993. March 1994 marked the resolution of an issue that has caused much controversy for a number of years — whether or not females may be altar servers. As the result of an authentic interpretation of the Pontifical Council for the Interpretation of Legislative Texts, women may now serve at the altar. On March 18, 1994, the Congregation for Divine Worship and the Discipline of the Sacraments published the fourth instruction on the implementation of the Liturgy Constitution of the Second Vatican Council under the title: *Fourth Instruction for the Right Application of the Conciliar Constitution on the Liturgy.* The instruction is on the inculturation of the liturgy and explains how articles 37–40 of the *Constitution on the Liturgy* are to be interpreted and implemented. In May the NCCB received confirmation of the June 1993 decision of the bishops regarding the age of confirmation, i.e., between the ages of seven and eighteen. In June the Liturgy Committee provided the bishops with suggested guidelines regarding male and female altar servers. The text of these guidelines was published in the June/July issue of the *Newsletter.* The same issue of the *Newsletter* contained the address given on the Study Day on Liturgical Translations that was conducted during the June meeting of the NCCB. The purpose of the day was to deal with some of the issues about the translation of liturgical texts which were the concern of a number of bishops. At the end of the meeting there was a proposal that there be a forum on translation. This proposal was later approved at the June 1995 NCCB meeting. Also at its June meeting, the Liturgy Committee approved its proposed adaptations for the *Sacramentary.* The August/September *Newsletter* explains some of the proposed adaptations. It also decided to propose the Swiss Synod eucharistic prayer to the members of the NCCB for use in the USA. The members of the NCCB approved the ICEL provisional translation of the Eucharistic Prayer for Various Needs and Occasions at their November Plenary meeting. They also approved

Segments One and Two of the revised *Sacramentary:* Ordinary Time and Proper of Seasons. The approval of Segment Three: Order of Mass I was delayed until June 1995.

1995

The January/February 1995 issue of the *Newsletter* contained a detailed explanation of Segment Three: Order of Mass I of the proposed revision of the *Sacramentary.* At the March meeting of the Liturgy Committee, Bishop Trautman reported on the status of the *Lectionary for Mass* and discussions with the Congregation for the Doctrine of the Faith regarding inclusive language. The Committee spent a great deal of time going through motions on Segment Three and the USA adaptations. The Task Group on Televised Masses met for the first time in March 1995. The establishment of the Task Group was the result of a request made by the Federation of Diocesan Liturgical Commissions. The March, April and May issues of the *Newsletter* gave a description of the proposed USA adaptations for the Order of Mass, the *Pastoral Introduction to the Order of Mass*, the *Appendix to the General Instruction* and the *Appendix to the General Norms for the Calendar and the Liturgical Year.* In April the *Newsletter* reported the publication for study and comment of the ICEL *Liturgical Psalter.* This text has not been approved for liturgical use. On May 24, 1995, confirmation was received for the Eucharistic Prayer for Masses for Various Needs and Occasions. The June *Newsletter* contained the response of the Congregation for Divine Worship and the Discipline of the Sacraments to a number of questions about perpetual exposition of the eucharist. The response clarifies and corrects some of the practices that have arisen in this country. On June 19, 1995, Cardinal Ratzinger, Prefect of the Congregation for the Doctrine of the Faith, wrote to the presidents of episcopal conferences regarding the use of low-gluten altar breads and *mustum.* The new norms were published in the July/ August *Newsletter.* The Liturgy Committee, at its June meeting, reviewed the amendments submitted by the bishops on the Order of Mass, the *Pastoral Introduction to the Order of Mass*, and the USA adaptations. The members of the Committee approved the adaptations to the ordination rite and discussed a first draft of the guidelines on cremation and other burial practices. The Committee rejected a request to name the Second Sunday of Easter "Divine Mercy Sunday." The June meeting of the NCCB was occupied with the approval of Segment Three: Order of Mass I. The amendments approved by the Liturgy Committee were accepted. Due to a lack of a sufficient number of bishops being present, the actions went to a mail ballot. All the actions were approved by the required two-thirds majority of *de jure* Latin-rite bishops. In September the *Newsletter* completed thirty years of publication. In September of 1995, the Congregation for Divine Worship and the Discipline of the Sacraments confirmed the interim (provisional) translation of the Mass of the Blessed Virgin Mary, Star of the Sea. This Mass is intended for use by those engaged in the Apostolate of the sea. The month of October marked the Third Pastoral Visit of Pope John Paul II to the United States. The Liturgy Secretariat coordinated the liturgical celebrations and prepared the *Sacramentary* used by the Holy Father. The November meeting of the Liturgy Committee was devoted to a review of the resolutions and motions on the *Pastoral Introduction to the Order of Mass* and the texts of Segment Four: Prefaces, Solemn Blessings, and Prayers over the People. The members of the NCCB approved Segment Four and the *Pastoral Introduction to the Order of Mass*.

Chairmen

In November 1993, Bishop Wilton D. Gregory, Auxiliary Bishop of Chicago, completed his three-year term as Chairman of the Bishops' Committee on the Liturgy. He was succeeded by Bishop Donald W. Trautman, Bishop of Erie, who had been elected Chairman-elect of the Committee at the November 1992 meeting of the NCCB. In November 1995, Archbishop Jerome G. Hanus, OSB, Archbishop of Dubuque, was elected Chairman-elect of the Committee. He will assume the Chairmanship following the November 1996 meeting of the episcopal conference.

Chairmen of the Bishops' Committee on the Liturgy

1965 – 1966	Cardinal John F. Dearden
1966 – 1968	Archbishop Paul J. Hallinan
1968 – 1969	Archbishop Leo C. Byrne
1969 – 1972	Bishop James W. Malone
1972 – 1975	Bishop Walter W. Curtis
1975 – 1977	Archbishop John R. Quinn
1977 – 1978	Bishop Rene H. Gracida
1978 – 1981	Archbishop Rembert G. Weakland, OSB
1981 – 1984	Bishop John S. Cummins
1984 – 1986	Archbishop Daniel E. Pilarczyk
1986 – 1990	Bishop Joseph P. Delaney
1990 – 1993	Bishop Wilton D. Gregory
1993 – 1996	Bishop Donald W. Trautman

Staff

Staff changes took place during this five-year period: Father Ronald F. Krisman, after thirteen years of service to the Secretariat, was succeeded by Monsignor Alan F. Detscher. Father Kenneth F. Jenkins left the Secretariat to become Assistant General Secretary of the NCCB/USCC. From 1991 through 1994, Sister Linda L. Gaupin, CDP, served as an Associate Director in the Secretariat. In July 1995, Sister Ann F. Rehrauer joined the Secretariat staff as an Associate Director. Monsignor Frederick R. McManus, whose many years of association with the Bishops' Committee on the Liturgy has afforded both the Secretariat and Committee with invaluable insights and experiences, continued as staff consultant.

Executive Directors

1965 – 1975	Reverend Monsignor Frederick R. McManus
1975 – 1978	Reverend John A. Rotelle, OSA
1978 – 1981	Reverend Thomas A. Krosnicki, SVD
1981 – 1988	Reverend John A. Gurrieri
1988 – 1994	Reverend Ronald F. Krisman
1994 –	Reverend Monsignor Alan F. Detscher

Associate Directors

1968 – 1971	Reverend Joseph M. Champlin
1970 – 1975	Reverend John A. Rotelle, OSA
1972 – 1978	Reverend Thomas A. Krosnicki, SVD
1978 – 1981	Reverend John A. Gurrieri
1981 – 1988	Reverend Ronald F. Krisman
1987 – 1994	Reverend Monsignor Alan F. Detscher
1989 – 1991	Reverend Kenneth F. Jenkins
1991 – 1994	Sister Linda L. Gaupin, CDP
1995 –	Sister Ann F. Rehrauer, OSF

Administrative Assistant

1976 – 1980	Sister Luanne Durst, FSPA

Staff Consultants

1975 –	Reverend Monsignor Frederick R. McManus
1986 – 1987	Reverend Monsignor Alan F. Detscher

In Memoriam

It is appropriate to call to mind the names of those who died during this five-year period who faithfully sought to strengthen and develop the liturgical life of the Church in the United States: Dr. Thomas C. O'Brien whose service as the staff translator and editor for ICEL from 1979–1991 left his mark on the English editions of the reformed liturgical books prepared during this period; Monsignor Robert Hayburn, who served as the director of music for the Archdiocese of San Francisco from 1957–1977 as well as on the Board of Directors of the Federation of Diocesan Liturgical Commissions; Archbishop John F. Whealon, who served as the chairman of the Liturgy Committee's Subcommittee on the Lectionary; Father Robert Hovda, an editor and writer for the Liturgical Conference, author of "The Amen Corner" column in *Worship,* and one of the principal consultants on *Environment and Art in Catholic Worship;* Sister Theophane Hytrek, a nationally known composer, educator and concert organist and the first woman to receive the Berakah Award of the North American Academy of Liturgy; Sister Josephine Morgan, director of the Pius X School of Liturgical Music from 1951 to 1969; Dr. Mark Searle, who taught liturgical studies at the University of Notre Dame; Father Michael Joseph Marx, OSB, who taught systematic theology at Saint John's University in Collegeville and served as managing editor of *Worship* from 1963–1983; Father Edward J. Kilmartin, SJ, who taught liturgical and sacramental theology at Weston College, the University of Notre Dame, the Pontifical Oriental Institute and Boston College; and Father James B. Dunning, founder of the North American Forum on the Catechumenate.

COMMITTEE ON THE LITURGY

NEWSLETTER

1991
VOLUME XXVII
JANUARY

NATIONAL CONFERENCE OF CATHOLIC BISHOPS

Revised Edition of the Marriage Liturgy

The 1990 issue of Notitiae *(vol. 26, no. 6), published by the Congregation for Divine Worship and the Discipline of the Sacraments, contains the decree of promulgation for the second typical edition of the* Order for Celebrating Marriage (Ordo celebrandi Matrimonium) *and a commentary on the revised marriage rite. The Latin text of the revised edition of this liturgical book will be published in the early part of this year. An unofficial translation of the decree follows.*

ORDER FOR CELEBRATING MARRIAGE

Second Typical Edition

Prot. N. CD 1068/89

DECREE

The rite for celebrating marriage, formerly contained in the Roman Ritual, was revised by decree of the Second Vatican Council and promulgated by the Sacred Congregation of Rites in 1969 as the *Ordo celebrandi Matrimonium.*

In this second typical edition, the same Order is more richly presented in the introduction, in the rites and prayers, and in the emendations introduced in accord with the *Code of Canon Law* promulgated in 1983.

By special mandate of the Supreme Pontiff John Paul II, the Congregation for Divine Worship and the Discipline of the Sacraments now publishes this new edition of the Order. The Latin edition becomes effective as soon as it is published. A vernacular translation, once it has been confirmed by the Apostolic See, shall become effective on the date to be decreed by the conference of bishops.

All things to the contrary notwithstanding.

From the Congregation for Divine Worship and the Discipline of the Sacraments, March 19, 1990, the Solemnity of Saint Joseph.

> \+ Eduardo Cardinal Martinez
> Prefect
>
> \+ Lajos Kada
> Titular Archbishop of Thebes
> Secretary

New *Order for Celebrating Marriage*

The second typical edition (1990) of the marriage rite, as the above decree of promulgation indicates, is an enrichment and updating of the *Rite of Marriage* that was first published in 1969.

Introduction

The 1969 edition of the *Ordo Celebrandi Matrimonium* (*Rite of Marriage*), being one of the first of the revised liturgical books, contained a brief introduction (*praenotanda*) consisting of 18 paragraphs. The 1990 edition, by contrast, contains a totally new introduction of 44 paragraphs.

The first section of the new introduction treats the "Importance and Dignity of the Sacrament of Marriage" (nos. 1-11) by incorporating the insights of the Second Vatican Council's Dogmatic Constitution on the Church, *Lumen gentium,* no. 11, the Pastoral Constitution on the Church in the Modern World, *Gaudium et spes,* nos. 48-50, the revised *Code of Canon Law,* canon 1055, and the apostolic exhortation of Pope John Paul II, *Familiaris consortio,* nos. 13 and 51. In these texts, marriage is seen not merely as a contract, which is ordered toward procreation, but as a mutual covenant, "by which a man and a woman establish between themselves a partnership of the whole of life. . . ." This theological section of the introduction provides a brief summary of the Church's teaching on the nature of marriage and its importance in the life of the Church.

The second section, "Offices and Ministries," speaks of the essential role of the bishop, pastors, and the whole Christian community in the preparation of the couple and their families for the celebration of marriage. This preparation has several important components: preaching and catechesis for all the faithful concerning the Christian significance of matrimony, personal preparation of parties intending to marry, preparation for the fruitful celebration of the liturgy of matrimony, and ongoing support for married couples.

The role of the pastor and his associates is given special emphasis in this preparation. If one of the parties has not been confirmed, arrangements should be made for the completion of the sacraments of initiation before the marriage, if this is possible. The sacrament of penance should be received before the marriage ceremony, especially when the marriage takes place during Mass. The pastor is to insure that there is nothing that would make the celebration of marriage invalid or illicit.

Deacons with the proper faculties may preside at a marriage. With the prior approval of the episcopal conference and the confirmation of the Apostolic See, in special cases the diocesan bishop may designate laypersons to assist at marriages. Laypersons may take part in the spiritual preparation of couples and in the actual celebration of the marriage liturgy. The marriage may be celebrated in the parish of either party or, with the permission of the proper Ordinary or pastor, in another place.

The third section of the introduction, "The Celebration of Marriage," is concerned with the actual preparations required for the marriage liturgy and its celebration. Because of its relationship to a particular community, marriage should be celebrated with the participation of at least some of its members, and even at the Sunday liturgy. The marriage of two Catholics should normally take place during Mass, but it is up to the pastor to determine, in particular cases, whether it would be better to celebrate the sacrament outside Mass. The couple should be assisted by the priest to choose the readings and other texts that will be used in the marriage celebration. The music chosen for the celebration should reflect the faith of the Church. The couple should be advised of the penitential nature of Lent and how this will influence the celebration of marriage during this season. Marriages are entirely forbidden on Good Friday and Holy Saturday.

Provision is made for the celebration of marriage during Mass (chapter 1) and outside Mass during a liturgy of the word (chapter 2). The ritual Mass for marriage may be used except on those days listed in nos. 1-4 of the Table of Liturgical Days according to their Order of Precedence (see *General Norms for the Liturgy Year and the Calendar,* no. 60). During the seasons of Christmas and Ordinary Time, when marriage is celebrated during the Sunday Mass of the parish or community, the Mass used is that of the Sunday. On such occasions, one of the readings may by taken from the *Lectionary for Mass* for marriage. Normally the marriage between a Catholic and a baptized non-Catholic should take place outside Mass, but the local Ordinary may allow it to be celebrated during Mass. The norms for intercommunion are to be followed in these cases (canon 844). The marriage of a Catholic and a catechumen or an unbaptized person takes place during a liturgy of the word.

The final section of the introduction deals with "Adaptations prepared by the Conference of Bishops." The conference may decide on several adaptations indicated in the introduction, prepare and adapt vernacular versions of the introduction, prepare new texts and songs appropriate to particular local needs, and order the material so that it may be more easily used. The formulas of the prayers and other texts (even the questions and the exchange of consent) may be adapted or augmented. When the rite gives several formulas for a particular ritual text, similar ones may be composed.

Accommodations may also be made in the ordering of the elements of a rite. However, the acceptance of the consent by the minister must be retained. This consent may always be obtained through the questioning of parties. After the exchange of rings, other local customs, such as, crowning or veiling may be inserted. If the joining of hands and the blessing and exchange of rings are not appropriate in a particular culture, they may be omitted or replaced by other rites. Appropriate rites and customs of the people may be admitted into the marriage rites, but when such rites and customs are pre-Christian or non-Christian in origin, they must be purified of all error or superstition. In places where marriage rites customarily take place in the home, the conference of bishops may determine which rites may be used. The conference of bishops may also prepare its own proper marriage rite, which must include the exchange of consent and the nuptial blessing, and the introduction of the *Roman Ritual* must be included, except for those things that specifically refer to the rites.

Several additions to and changes of liturgical texts in the 1969 *Ordo* have been introduced in the revised typical edition of 1990. The rest of this commentary highlights these new elements.

Chapter I: Order for the Celebration of Marriage during Mass

Two brief introductions to the celebration are provided for use after the greeting, and the penitential rite is omitted. An unofficial translation of the second of these introductions reads as follows:

> N. and N., the Church takes part in your joy
> and with an open heart receives you,
> together with your parents and friends,
> on the day in which before God our Father
> you establish between yourselves a partnership of the whole of your lives.
> May the Lord exult you on this day of your joy.
> May the Lord send you help from heaven and watch over you.
> May the Lord grant the desires of your hearts
> and fulfill all your requests.

Five new readings have been added to those already provided in the *Lectionary for Mass*: Proverbs 31: 10-13, 19-20, 30-31; Romans 15: 1b-3a, 5-7, 13; Ephesians 4: 1-6; Philippians 4: 4-9; Hebrews 13: 1-4a, 5-6b.

An alternative formula is given for the reception of the consent by the minister. An unofficial translation of the text follows:

> May the God of Abraham, the God of Isaac, and the God of Jacob,
> God who joined our first parents together in paradise,
> confirm and bless in Christ
> the consent you have expressed before the Church.
> What God has joined, human beings must not divide.

There may be a brief acclamation after the exchange of consent and after the exchange of rings. The nuptial blessings, now provided with musical notation, have been revised to be more inclusive of the groom, and they include an invocation (*epiclesis*) of the Holy Spirit on the couple:

> . . . Send upon them the grace of the Holy Spirit,
> so that, with your love in their hearts,
> they may remain faithful in the marriage covenant.

Where it is customary, the signing of the marriage register may take place during the ceremony, but this is not to be done on the altar.

Chapter II: Order for the Celebration of Marriage outside Mass

The celebration begins with a greeting, brief introduction, and an opening prayer. The marriage rite continues with a liturgy of the word, the exchange of consent, and the blessing and exchange of rings. The general intercessions follow: invitation to prayer, petitions, Lord's Prayer, and the nuptial blessing. The rite for holy communion outside Mass may follow. In this case, the Lord's prayer is omitted from the intercessions and is said at the beginning of the communion rite. The celebration ends with a blessing.

Chapter III: Order for the Celebration of Marriage before an Assisting Layperson

In keeping with the *Book of Blessings* and the *Directory for Sunday Celebrations in the Absence of a Priest,* this chapter provides proper texts for use by a layperson. Unofficial translations of the greeting, introduction to the gospel, and the final blessing follow.

Greeting: Blessed be God, the Father of all consolation, who has shown us his great mercy.

Introduction to the Gospel: Brothers and sisters, listen to the words of the holy gospel according to N.

Final Blessing:
> May God fill us with joy and hope in believing.
> May the peace of Christ abound in our hearts.
> May the Holy Spirit enrich us with his gifts.

The nuptial blessing has a form similar to the blessing of baptismal water. It consists of three sections, addressed to the persons of the Trinity, to which the people respond: Blessed be God. The blessing concludes with a prayer by the lay person who is assisting.

Chapter IV: Order for the Celebration of Marriage between a Catholic and a Catechumen or a Non-Christian

This chapter is essentially that which appears as chapter III of the 1969 edition. Several modifications have been made to take better account of the fact that one of the parties may not be a Christian. The brief introduction provided at the beginning of the rite sets the tone of this form of the marriage liturgy.

> N. and N., the Church takes part in your joy
> and with an open heart receives you,
> together with your parents and friends,
> on the day in which you establish between yourselves
> a partnership of the whole of your lives.
> For those who believe, God is the source of love and fidelity,
> for God is love.
> For this reason let us listen attentively to God's word,
> and pray in supplication,
> that God may grant the desires of your hearts
> and fulfill all your requests.

During the exchange of rings the Trinitarian invocation ("In the name of the Father, and of the Son, and of the Holy Spirit") may be omitted.

On occasions when it may be appropriate to omit the nuptial blessing, a brief prayer taken from the *Leonine Sacramentary* may take its place.

Chapter V: Various Texts for Use in the Order of Marriage

As already indicated, five new readings have been included in the Lectionary. A new rubric notes that at least one reading should be chosen which speaks specifically about marriage. For this purpose, seven readings from the Old Testament, 2 readings from the Acts of the Apostles and three Gospels are marked with an asterisk. In addition to the four opening prayers contained in the previous edition, there are two additional prayers taken from the *Leonine* and *Gelasian Sacramentaries*. Proper intercessions for Eucharistic Prayers I, II, and III are given. No intercession is given for Eucharistic Prayer IV, which is not to be used during nuptial masses since the unchangeable preface cannot be replaced by one of the proper prefaces required for marriage.

Appendix

The Appendix contains two examples of General Intercessions and two blessings from the *Book of Blessings*: "Order for the Blessing of an Engaged Couple" and "Order for the Blessing of a Married Couple: Order of Blessing within Mass on the Anniversary of Marriage." This second blessing for use at a wedding anniversary has been supplemented by the addition of two forms for the renewal of marriage vows. The first form consists of the husband and wife, separately blessing God for the gift of each other and together thanking God for being with them in their marriage. This form concludes with a brief prayer by the priest. The second form consists of three questions addressed to the couple and a concluding prayer by the priest. Both of these forms are far superior to the previous unauthorized practice of having the couple repeat their marriage vows as if for the first time.

Once the Latin text of the new edition of the *Order for the Celebration of Marriage* is available, it will be translated by the International Commission on English in the Liturgy and presented to the episcopal conferences for their approval and the confirmation of the Apostolic See. The English translation will probably not be available until sometime in 1992 or 1993.

COMMITTEE ON THE LITURGY

NEWSLETTER

NATIONAL CONFERENCE OF CATHOLIC BISHOPS

1991
VOLUME XXVII
FEBRUARY

Chanting the Passion Narrative

On February 8, 1989 the Congregation for Divine Worship and the Discipline of the Sacraments published a new Latin typical edition of the passion narratives from the four Gospels. *Passio Domini Nostri Iesu Christi* (Prot. N. CD 143/89) provides two musical settings of the passion narratives for Passion (Palm) Sunday and Good Friday: the first setting uses the tradit: al tone, while the second uses a tone taken from the authentic collection of Gregorian chant. The Neo-Vulgate text of Scripture is used. An unofficial translation of the brief introduction to the musical settings of the passion narratives is given below. *Passio Domini Nostri Iesu Christi* is available from: Libreria Editrice Vaticana, 00120 Vatican City State, EUROPE. Cost: Lire 110,000.

Chanting the Passion Narrative

Introduction

1. The narrative of the passion of the Lord is sung by three persons who take the part of Christ (+), the narrator or historian (C), and the people (the "*synagogae*") (S).

The passion is sung by deacons, or, if they are not present, by presbyters, or, in their absence, by readers; in which case, the part of Christ must be reserved to the priest celebrant.

2. Three unadorned lecterns are placed on the floor of the presbyterium (sanctuary) for the singing of the passion.

3. Incense and candles are not used.

4. While the Verse before the Gospel is being sung, the deacons, each carrying a *Book of the Passion* before him, accompanied by two acolytes or servers, bow before the priest and ask for the blessing in a low voice, saying: *Father, give me your blessing.*

The priest in a low voice says: *The Lord be in your heart and on your lips that you may worthily proclaim his gospel. In the name of the Father, and of the Son, + and of the Holy Spirit.*

The deacons answer: *Amen.*

If the readers are not deacons, they do not ask for the blessing. However, in a Mass at which the bishop presides, the presbyters who, in the absence of deacons, sing or read the passion, ask for and receive the blessing from the bishop.

5. Then the deacons, together with the acolytes, after making the usual reverence, go to the lecterns. The deacon who takes the part of Christ stands in the middle, the one who takes the part of the narrator stands to his right, and the one who takes the part of the people stands to his left.

6. The passion of the Lord is begun directly: *The Lord be with you,* is not said, nor the response, *Glory to you, Lord.* When they begin to sing, the deacons sign neither the book nor themselves.

7. After the announcement of the death of the Lord, all kneel in place, and pause for a brief period.

8. At the conclusion of the singing the deacon who had the part of the narrator proclaims: This is the Gospel of the Lord, and all respond with the acclamation: *Praise to you, Lord Jesus Christ.*

9. The *Book of the Passion* is not kissed by anyone. The deacons, carrying the books, and accompanied by the acolytes, return to their seats. The lecterns are then removed.

Rereading the Constitution on the Liturgy (art. 41-46)

Articles 41-46 of the Constitution on the Liturgy treat the responsibility of bishops, dioceses, parishes, and episcopal conferences in promoting the reformed liturgy. General principles are provided for the bishop as the high priest of his flock, for liturgies at which the bishop presides, for liturgical life within parishes and other smaller groupings of the faithful within a diocese, and for structures, such as liturgical commissions and institutes, which assist the bishops as the moderators, promoters, and custodians of liturgical life in the dioceses.

The liturgical life of each diocese centers around its bishop. It is through the bishop's leadership, both in prayer and in direction, that the liturgical life of the entire diocese is to be promoted. This leadership is shown in various ways.

The Constitution rightly begins with the role of the cathedral church where the principal celebrations of the diocese and bishop are to take place. As no. 42 of the *Ceremonial of Bishops* [CB] states, the cathedral, the place of the bishop's chair, is to be a "sign of his teaching office and pastoral power in the particular Church, and a sign also of the unity of believers in the faith that the bishop proclaims as shepherd of the Lord's flock." The cathedral is to be a model for other churches, minimally in its adherence to liturgical norms, and ideally as an example of the high standard of celebration that enlivens the faith of all.

In the years since the promulgation of the Constitution on the Liturgy there have been many attempts both at renovating old cathedral churches and constructing new ones. While each project has enjoyed a measure of success, some basic issues still have not been resolved. The cathedra is be a chair which stands alone and is permanently installed and which, by its placement, makes it clear that the bishop is presiding over the whole community of the faithful [CB 47]. Yet it should be so constructed and arranged that it is clearly part of the one assembly of the faithful. This creates a tension which is not always balanced successfully in the liturgical design. Ideally the cathedra should be placed in the center of the apse behind the altar to show that the bishop presides over all the activities of the church, whether they be liturgical prayer, governance or teaching. But then the placement of another presidential chair for the priests who regularly celebrate at the cathedral needs to be carefully selected. Although these issues involve arrangement of liturgical furnishings, they point to deeper questions about the liturgical role of the bishop both in the cathedral church and in the diocese.

The cathedral church should be more than a center for exemplary celebration of the liturgy. Although the Constitution does not allude to the possibilities, it seems logical that if the cathedra is the symbol of the teaching office of the bishop and it is to be the center of diocesan life, bishops might consider using the cathedra, when appropriate, as the place where teaching occurs. Pastoral letters and issues of concern could be addressed from the chair. Public statements both to the church and the community could be made from the chair. The cathedral church could come to be recognized as the place from which the bishop speaks and where the Gospel is interpreted for the good of society.

The Constitution (no. 42) continues by recognizing that it is in the parish church, especially in the Sunday celebration of the Eucharist, that the Church is visibly represented. The parish priest, who takes the place of the bishop, is charged with encouraging the formation of a Christian community in which liturgical life is an essential element. Thus, it is at the level of the parish, celebrating the cycles of the Church year, Sunday after Sunday, week by week, that the success of the liturgical reform is most visible. Much of that success is due to the guidance and teaching of the bishops and priests who have labored in promoting liturgical life.

The initial enthusiasm for the work of the reform led to the creation of several bodies charged with various aspects of the liturgical renewal. The bishops of the United States established the Commission for the Liturgical Apostolate, which was renamed in February 1967 the Bishops' Committee on the Liturgy. As a standing committee of the National Conference of Catholic Bishops, this committee, which addresses the full gamut of liturgical issues, is assisted by a staff and advisors with expertise in the various areas of liturgy, as directed by the Constitution. It is within the staff, or Secretariat, that much of the ongoing work of the committee is accomplished. That work is defined in the Constitution. It is "to regulate pastoral-liturgical action throughout the territory and to promote studies and necessary experiments whenever there is a question of adaptations to be proposed to the Apostolic See" (no. 44).

This committee, the Constitution states, should also be assisted by "some kind of institute for pastoral liturgy, consisting of people who are eminent in these matters." Since the time of the Second Vatican Council six centers of liturgical research in the United States have received explicit recognition of the Bishops'

Committee on the Liturgy: the Woodstock Center for Religion and Worship, Woodstock College, New York, NY (1969); The Murphy Center for Liturgical Research (now the Notre Dame Center for Pastoral Liturgy), University of Notre Dame, Notre Dame, IN (1970); St. John's University, Collegeville, MN (1970); the Composers' Forum for Catholic Worship, Sugar Creek, MO (1971); the Mexican-American Cultural Center, San Antonio, TX (1974); The Center for Pastoral Liturgy, The Catholic University of America, Washington, DC (1976). Only two centers continue to function: the Notre Dame Center for Pastoral Liturgy and the Mexican-American Cultural Center. The Notre Dame Center for Pastoral Liturgy has recently outlined a five-year plan to rekindle as its primary purpose research for the benefit of the pastoral-liturgical life of the Church in the United States.

Each of these centers has made an important contribution in the promotion of the liturgy. The need for such centers of research continues, as does the need for scholars to pursue the discipline of liturgical studies.

Possibly the structure that has been the most influential in liturgical renewal during the past 25 years has been the diocesan liturgical commission, mandated for each diocese (or group of dioceses) by the Constitution (no. 45). These commissions have been invaluable in providing for liturgical formation, in establishing effective norms and guidelines for liturgical celebration, in the training of liturgical ministers, in short, in doing everything necessary to advance liturgical life in the diocese. Many bishops have also established full-time offices of worship in their dioceses to assist in directing the liturgical apostolate. Despite financial constraints, the need for trained and available liturgical personnel has not waned. Besides assisting in the training of liturgical ministers and in preparing diocesan and episcopal liturgies, an office of worship can provide a valuable service to the bishop in fulfilling his role as moderator-promoter-custodian of the Church's public prayer.

The Federation of Diocesan Liturgical Commissions (FDLC), first convened in 1969 by the Secretariat of the Bishops' Committee on the Liturgy, is a national organization of diocesan liturgical commissions and/or offices of worship in the United States. Although such a network of diocesan commissions is not explicitly called for by the Constitution, the FDLC has played an important role in coordinating the work of diocesan liturgical personnel, in offering advice and assistance to the Bishops' Committee on the Liturgy, and in articulating grass-roots liturgical concerns in the United States.

The Constitution gives major responsibility for the promotion of liturgical life to the diocesan bishop and to the territorial conference of bishops. In the dioceses of the United States there has been great initial success in the first stage of liturgical renewal, the implementation of the revised rites of the Church. But that renewal is far from complete. It fact, much effort still needs to be made in order that the reforms take firm root in the hearts of all the faithful. Article 43 of the Constitution expresses the hope that "the promotion and restoration of the sacred liturgy is rightly held to be a sign of the providential dispositions of God in our time, and as a movement of the Holy Spirit in his Church."

Clarification concerning Laypersons Presiding at Funerals

At the November 11-15, 1990 plenary assembly of the National Conference of Catholic Bishops [NCCB] the proposal that diocesan bishops be authorized to permit laypersons to preside at the Funeral Liturgy outside Mass, in accordance with the 1969 *Ordo Exsequiarum,* nos. 19 and 22:4, failed to receive the two-thirds majority vote of the *de iure* members necessary for approval. Since some misinterpretations of this action subsequently have appeared in the press, a clarification seems appropriate.

When the members of the NCCB approved the revised *Order of Christian Funerals* in November 1985, they accepted the pattern for funerals given in that liturgical book. The *Order of Christian Funerals* provides for three principal liturgical celebrations: the Vigil for the Deceased in the home or funeral home; the Funeral Liturgy at the church; and the Rite of Committal at the place of committal (cemetery, mausoleum, crematorium, etc.). The Funeral Liturgy normally takes the form of the Funeral Mass. But on those occasions when liturgical law prohibits a priest from celebrating the Funeral Mass (such as on Good Friday), when the celebration of the Eucharist is not considered appropriate in certain circumstances (such as when none of the mourners are Catholics), or when, because no priest is available, a deacon is to preside at the Funeral Liturgy, a "Funeral Liturgy outside Mass" has been provided.

The action item considered by the NCCB in November dealt solely with laypersons presiding at the Funeral Liturgy outside Mass. Although the proposal was not approved, the provision of no. 14 of the *Order of Christian Funerals* which permits, when no priest or deacon is available, a layperson to preside at the Vigil for the Deceased and its related rites as well as the Rite of Committal still remains in force. The effect of the bishops' action was to reaffirm the general norm for the dioceses of the United States that only a priest or a deacon may preside at the Funeral Liturgy outside Mass. Still, when there is a pastoral need, a diocesan bishop may request authorization directly from the Apostolic See to permit laypersons to preside at the Funeral Liturgy outside Mass in the diocese under his pastoral care.

The *Order of Christian Funerals,* while recognizing and providing for pastoral situations when it is not possible to have a priest or deacon present for one or more of the funeral rites, nevertheless affirms that priests, "as teachers of faith and ministers of comfort," have the primary responsibility of presiding at all the funeral rites.

Orbis Liturgicus

A volume is in preparation which will list researchers in the field of liturgical studies. The volume is part of a forthcoming series of a bio-bibliographical Directory of Liturgists from the year 1000 to the present day.

The work is already well advanced under the direction of Dom Cuthbert Johnson, OSB, and the Reverend Doctor Anthony Ward, SM. The title of the volume dealing with present day liturgists is: *ORBIS LITURGICUS, In Tempore Hodierno: Repertorium Peritorum Re Liturgica, Who's Who in Liturgical Studies, Repertoire des chercheurs en Etudes Liturgiques.*

Entries for researchers will appear in alphabetical order, the whole volume being completed by multiple indexes, multilingual where appropriate.

Material should be drafted in English, French, Italian, Spanish, or German, must be at least typewritten, and should, if possible, be sent both in hard copy and on computer disk (IBM compatible, disk 5¼" or 3½", WordPerfect/other compatible program or ASCII). Priority will be given to those entries submitted on disk. Material cannot be returned. Entries at present outstanding must be sent to arrive no later than September 15, 1991 (in time for publication in early 1992) to: Dom Cuthbert Johnson, OSB, Via della Traspontina 18, 00193 Roma, Italia (Tel. 6540841; Fax. 6892945).

Scheme for each entry:

A. Family name, first name, middle initial.
B. Professional address, telephone and fax number.
C. Professional posts, qualifications, honors, etc.
D. Editorship, membership on editorial committees, scholarly societies.
E. Main field of interest.
F. Publications in chronological order of appearance.
G. Publications in the press.
H. Publications in preparation.

The format for the presentation of bibliography must be complete and in accord with the accepted principles for bibliographical citations.

The volume will also contain information regarding liturgical institutes, and national and diocesan liturgical commissions.

Father Kenneth F. Jenkins Appointed NCCB/USCC Assistant General Secretary

On February 22, 1991 Monsignor Robert N. Lynch, NCCB/USCC General Secretary, announced the appointment of Father Kenneth F. Jenkins as NCCB/USCC Assistant General Secretary.

Father Jenkins, a priest of the Diocese of San Bernardino, has served as Associate Director of the Liturgy Secretariat since late-January 1989. In his new position he will assist the NCCB/USCC General Secretary and the three Associate General Secretaries in various aspects of Conference supervision, among them: the Conference Assessment Project-92; the planning and programming process of the NCCB/USCC; assessing the overall operations of the administrative and support staff of the General Secretariat; and supervising the administration of the priests' staff house.

The Liturgy Committee and its Secretariat staff congratulate Father Jenkins as he assumes his new position and wish him every success in his new responsibilities.

NATIONAL CONFERENCE OF CATHOLIC BISHOPS

COMMITTEE ON THE LITURGY

NEWSLETTER

1991
VOLUME XXVII
MARCH

Pope John Paul II Addresses CDWDS Plenary Assembly

On Saturday, 26 January 1991, Pope John Paul II received in audience the members of the Congregation for Divine Worship and the Discipline of the Sacraments, who had gathered in Rome for their plenary assembly. This meeting marked the first plenary of the Congregation since the reorganization of the Roman Curia as indicated in the apostolic constitution Pastor Bonus, *which went into effect on 1 March 1989. Following introductory remarks by Cardinal Martinez, Prefect of the Congregation, the Pope addressed the group in Italian. An excerpt from the translation of that address appears below. (For the complete text see the English-language edition of* L'Osservatore Romano, *February 4, 1991, p. 4.)*

. . . I consider that the topics being studied by your plenary can constitute a good experience for the work of the Congregation for Divine Worship and the Discipline of the Sacraments, especially the project of an Instruction for the adaptation of the Roman liturgy to diverse cultures and the project for the *Institutio Generalis Ritualis Romani* [General Introduction to the Roman Ritual].

3. The Instruction on adaptation has come to the plenary after a long journey of reflection which began with the Constitution *Sacrosanctum Concilium* [hereafter SC] itself. It is an important yet delicate topic: important in that it takes into account cultural dimensions which are part of liturgical activity; sensitive in that in presupposes a wise knowledge of the celebration of the Church's worship, which has been transmitted along with the Christian faith.

In the Apostolic Letter *Vicesimus Quintus Annus* (no. 16), I indicated that liturgical adaptation is one of the Church's current tasks. The meaning of this is not to suggest to the particular Churches that they have a new task to undertake following the application of liturgical reform, that is to say, adaptation or inculturation. Nor is it intended to mean inculturation as the creation of alternative rites. The Instruction which you have studied clearly indicates that the task consists in proceeding correctly in the application of what was foreseen by the council's constitution in numbers 37-40, and that it must be developed within the Roman rite. In effect, it is not a question of speaking in general of the inculturation of Christian liturgy, but rather of showing how the general principles are concretized in reference to the case for which the Church is legislating.

In every country the initial connection between evangelization and the rites in which they are celebrated is a fact which deserves the greatest attention. As a consequence, one cannot propose changes without a careful interdisciplinary study, thus avoiding improvisation and adapting them only when it is useful or necessary (SC 40).

On the other hand, belonging to the Roman rite means that the liturgy celebrated in the various particular Churches can be mutually recognized as the same Roman liturgy. The Constitution *Sacrosanctum Concilium* refers to this when it says that *"servata substantiali unitate ritus romani* [provided the substantial unity of the Roman rite is preserved]" (SC 38). This further justifies the close collaboration of Bishops' Conferences and the Holy See in all that concerns the whole inculturation process. Besides, it is a question of collaborating so that the Roman rite, maintaining its own identity, may incorporate opportune adaptations, in such a way as to allow the faithful of those Christian communities who, because of their culture, do not sense that a particular ritual is an adequate expression of themselves, to feel a part of the liturgical celebration. Such collaboration is necessary, and the failure to observe correct procedure in this matter would cause serious harm. The process of the fulfillment of the council's liturgical reform is, in fact, still under way, and cannot be compromised by turning back or by interventions which are not attentive enough to the religious feelings of the faithful. The Christian faithful are being offered the opportunity and the guarantee of authentically taking part in the Church's worship.

3211 FOURTH STREET NE • WASHINGTON, DC 20017

4. As for the project of the *Institutio Generalis Ritualis Romani,* we are dealing with a theological text with pastoral directives. It could not be otherwise, because the sacraments do not belong to the category of provisional instruments, but rather of fundamental realities, because the Church is built on the faith and the sacraments of the faith. The reason for this special case comes from the fact that the sacraments are actions of Christ in His glory, seated at the right hand of the Father, and yet present among His disciples in the world through His Spirit; they are Christ's actions which are made visible through the sacramental actions performed by the Church which celebrates the Paschal Mystery of the Lord as He Himself commanded. Through different signs, according to the various situations, the Christian is sanctified in the Church for worship in Spirit and truth.

We must insist on the eminently Christological and Trinitarian character of sacramental signs. True, it is the community of the baptized who celebrate them, but this takes place in giving thanks to the Father for the work of our salvation, which was brought about once and for all time by His Only-begotten Son—*opus Christi*—and in that from the Lord of glory it receives the strength of the Spirit, whom the Church never ceases to invoke.

For these reasons the sacraments are fundamentally acts of worship, in that in them is realized the sanctifying worship which Jesus Christ offered to the Father on the cross and perennially continues to offer for our salvation. In them Christ's action always takes precedence over the Church's activity: it is the grace of the Redeemer which is communicated to us, it is the communion coming from the Paschal Mystery which we received. It is the same Lord Jesus who is the main celebrant of the sacraments.

In this spirit I described the sacraments as "humble and precious" (cf. *Reconciliatio et Paenitentia,* no. 31), while the euchological texts of the Roman liturgy call them "ineffable" (*collecta, feria secunda Hebd. IV Quadr.*) and "heavenly" (*super oblata, feria tertia Temp. Nativ.*). In them we have a renewal in the present of what took place when people met Jesus of Nazareth (cf. Lk 4:22 ff). Those who see them merely as simple ritual actions can never manage to experience the "glorious exchange" (*super oblata, feria quinta Temp. Nativ.*) which takes place on behalf of mankind through the sacramental celebrations; like the inhabitants of Nazareth who, seeing only the "*fabri filius* [carpenter's son]" were unable to contemplate the Savior's wondrous deeds.

5. We are up against one of the causes which make sacramental apostolate difficult in our days which are known for the value they place on visible and effective efficiency. Only in faith is it possible to understand the sacraments. We must say the same of their celebration: only in the conviction that we are celebrating a mystery that is above us, can we act as ministers of the sacraments as "*alieni beneficii dispensatores* [stewards of otherworldly gifts]" (cf. *Conc. Trident. sess. XVI, cap. 6, DS* 1685), conscious that in the assembly of the faithful we are Christ's "*vicarii,*" "*in persona eius,*" His instruments and, at the same time, signs of the Church's dependence on her Lord.

The sacramental and liturgical pastoral care has the task of introducing the participants to the celebration in the mystery of God's free gift manifested in Christ and continually communicated in the Church's sacraments: from this derives its necessarily mystagogical character "*per visibilia ad invisibilia.*" Besides, all pastoral activity and the Christian life of each baptized person, beginning with the ministers, needs its center of unity and its fulfillment in a way that they can be lived under the influence of the Spirit, in harmony with the mystery celebrated.

Following Vatican II there was a great development in preaching the Word of God, an effort that should be maintained and strengthened. However, we cannot forgot what we proclaim in the Christian faith: "The Word was made flesh!" (Jn 1:14). This means that the Word which is proclaimed naturally leads to the celebration of the Sacrament. We are not merely Jesus' listeners or followers: we are members of His Body, in life-giving communion with Him! Rather, "the life of Christ is infused into believers who are united by the sacraments, in a mysterious but real manner, to Christ who died and rose" (*Lumen gentium* 7).6.

Taking up again what I wrote in the Apostolic Letter *Vicesimus Quintus Annus* (no. 14), it is not a matter of organizing liturgical reform, as it was 25 years ago, but rather of deepening our knowledge of and internalizing the liturgical celebrations as eminently spiritual realities. For this it is indispensable to know the texts published after Vatican II and every valid formation initiative in this field will always be welcome . . .

Lectionaries Approved for Liturgical Use

The Secretariat for the Liturgy is often asked about the requirements whereby a lectionary is approved for liturgical use. Since two lectionaries will shortly be submitted for the approval of the National Conference of

Catholic Bishops through its standing Committee on the Liturgy, this question is most timely.

The *Lectionary for Mass* is one of the liturgical books of the Roman rite. It remains a part of the revised *Missale Romanum,* even though it is now usually published separately from the Sacramentary. The Latin liturgical book which serves as the source for the approved editions of the *Lectionary for Mass* published in the United States is the *Ordo Lectionum Missae* (1969, second edition 1981 [hereafter OLM]), a listing or *cursus* of readings that are to be used at Masses on Sundays, weekdays, and the commemorations of saints, for ritual Masses, and on other occasions. It is the responsibility of the conferences of bishops to prepare and canonically approve vernacular editions of the *Lectionary* based on that *cursus* of readings and containing the complete text for each citation (OLM 112; see also 1983 *Code of Canon Law,* canon 838.3).

The conference of bishops must also approve *for liturgical use* the translation of Scripture which is to be used in a vernacular edition of the *Lectionary* (OLM 111). The approval of a Scripture translation for liturgical use must, in turn, be confirmed by the Apostolic See.

Approving a translation of Scripture for liturgical use is not the same as granting an *imprimatur,* which is the permission to *publish* a translation of Scripture. While a number of translations of the Bible or individual books of the Bible published in the United States bear an *imprimatur,* which guarantees fidelity to Catholic faith and morality, only certain biblical translations have been approved (in November 1968) by the members of the National Conference of Catholic Bishops for liturgical use: *New American Bible, Revised Standard Version-Catholic Edition,* and *Jerusalem Bible.* The *Grail* psalter received similar approval for liturgical use in November 1967. [The recently published *New Jerusalem Bible, New Revised Standard Version,* and the *Grail Psalter (Inclusive Language Version)* have yet to receive approval by the NCCB for liturgical use.]

Also affecting this matter is the fact that, *before* the 1983 Code of Canon Law obtained legal force, a diocesan bishop could grant an *imprimatur* for a vernacular translation of all or part of the Bible. Since November 27, 1983, only a conference of bishops or the Apostolic See may grant an *imprimatur* for a translation of Scripture (canon 825.1). Needless to say, a conference of bishops would not approve for liturgical use a translation of Scripture which did not first bear an *imprimatur.* Thus, the conference often must take two actions: granting the *imprimatur* (an action which perhaps may be delegated to another agent, for instance, one of the standing committees of the entire conference of bishops—the NCCB is presently studying this question), and authorizing the translation for liturgical use. Both actions would be necessary, for instance, if an edition of the *Lectionary for Mass* using the *New Revised Standard Version* were to be requested by the Bishops' Committee on the Liturgy.

A lectionary for Masses with children is an adaptation of the *Lectionary for Mass.* It too is a liturgical book of the Church. The preparation of such lectionaries is foreseen in the *Directory for Masses with Children,* no. 43: "It is recommended that the individual conferences of bishops see to the composition of lectionaries for Masses with children."

Since a lectionary for Masses with children will normally entail at least some modification of the usual cursus of readings given in the *Ordo Lectionum Missae,* such adaptations are to be approved by the conference of bishops and receive the confirmation of the Apostolic See before the lectionary may be used in liturgical celebrations.

The *Directory for Masses with Children,* no. 45, notes that special translations of the Scriptures may be used that are geared to the children's ability to understand: "In the biblical texts 'God is speaking to his people. . . and Christ is present to the faithful through his own word.' Paraphrases of Scripture should therefore be avoided. On the other hand, the use of translations that may already exist for the catechesis of children and that are accepted by the competent authority is recommended."

In summary, there are three principal "approvals" needed for a lectionary for Mass or a lectionary for Masses with children using a Scripture translation geared to the comprehension of children. The vernacular translation of Scripture must be granted an *imprimatur* by a conference of bishops or by the Apostolic See; the translation must be approved by the conference of bishops for use in the liturgy; adaptations to the cursus of readings presented in the 1981 *Ordo Lectionum Missae* must be approved by the conference of bishops. The second and third approvals must receive the confirmation of the Apostolic See.

Finally, before any translation of Scripture can be published in the form of a lectionary, it must be edited for liturgical use. A proper *incipit* (beginning) must be prepared for each reading (OLM 124). Pronouns will at times need to be replaced by the nouns to which they refer for the sake of clarity or facility in public reading. Without altering the meaning of the biblical text, some changes may need to be made for the sake of more inclusive language. And the readings will be arranged in sense-lines to assist proper proclamation.

For several years the Committee on the Liturgy has been preparing both a revised edition of the *Lectionary for Mass* as well as a children's lectionary, entitled *Lectionary for Masses and Other Celebrations with Children*. It is anticipated that in June the members of the Committee will be asked to approve these lectionaries. If that schedule is met, the lectionaries will then be submitted for the approval of the National Conference of Catholic Bishops in November of this year. For the *Lectionary for Masses and Others Celebrations with Children*, which uses the *Translation for Early Youth* of the American Bible Society, the NCCB must grant an *imprimatur,* approve the translation for liturgical use, and approve the adaptations to the normal *cursus* of readings. For the *Lectionary for Mass,* using the *New American Bible* which has already been approved for liturgical use, the NCCB must approve adaptations in the cursus of readings and review or approve changes introduced in the text of the *New American Bible* as pericopes were prepared for use in the lectionary.

The American Bible Society has been of great assistance in the preparation of the lectionary for children, and its translators have been very responsive to the Liturgy Committee's Task Group on the Lectionary for Children, as has the Federation of Diocesan Liturgical Commissions, which originally recommended this project to the Committee on the Liturgy.

Confirmation of Calendar Change and Additions

On January 24, 1991 the National Conference of Catholic Bishops received the decree of the Congregation for Divine Worship and the Discipline of the Sacraments, dated December 20, 1990, confirming the NCCB approval on November 13 of two additions to and one change of date in the Proper Calendar for the Dioceses of the United States. The following is an unofficial English translation of that decree. [The Opening Prayers for the Masses commemorating Blessed Juan Diego and Blessed Miguel Agustín Pro will be published in the next issue of the *Newsletter*.]

Prot. N. 885/90

At the request of His Excellency, the Most Reverend Daniel E. Pilarczyk, Archbishop of Cincinnati and President of the National Conference of Catholic Bishops, in a letter dated November 27, 1990, and by virtue of the faculties granted to this Congregation by the Supreme Pontiff, Pope John Paul II, we gladly concede that the following celebrations may be inserted into the Proper Calendar for the Dioceses of the United States of America with the rank of *optional memorial*:

> Blessed Juan Diego - December 9
> Blessed Miguel Agustín Pro, priest and martyr - November 23
> Saint Paul of the Cross, priest - October 20

In addition, we gladly approve, that is, confirm the English text of the Opening Prayer in honor of Blessed Juan Diego as it appears in the appended copy.

This decree, by which the requested confirmation is granted by the Apostolic See, is to be included in its entirety in the published text. Two copies of the printed text should be sent to this Congregation.

All things to the contrary notwithstanding.

From the Congregation for Divine Worship and the Discipline of the Sacraments, 20 December 1990.

> + Eduardo Cardinal Martinez
> Prefect
>
> + Lajos Kada
> Titular Archbishop of Thebes
> Secretary

COMMITTEE ON THE LITURGY

NEWSLETTER

NATIONAL CONFERENCE OF CATHOLIC BISHOPS

1991
VOLUME XXVII
APRIL/MAY

Decree on "Collective" Mass Intentions

The March 25, 1991 issue of L'Osservatore Romano *published the English translation of a decree recently issued by the Congregation for the Clergy concerning "collective" Mass intentions. The decree was approved by Pope John Paul II on January 22, 1991, and is signed by Antonio Cardinal Innocenti, prefect of the Congregation for the Clergy, and Archbishop Gilberto Agustoni, secretary of that congregation. The decree, along with a commentary written by Archbishop Agustoni, follow.*

Congregation for the Clergy

DECREE

It is the Church's constant practice, as Paul VI wrote in the motu proprio *Firma in Traditione* that "the faithful, desiring in a religious and ecclesial spirit to participate more intimately in the eucharistic sacrifice, add to it a form of sacrifice of their own by which they contribute in a particular way to the needs of the Church and especially to the sustenance of her ministers" (*AAS* 66 [1974], p. 308).

Formerly this contribution consisted predominately in gifts in kind; in our day it has become almost exclusively monetary. However, the motive and purpose of the faithful's offerings have remained the same and have also been sanctioned by the new Code of Canon Law (see canons 945.1 and 946).

Because the matter directly affects the Most Blessed Sacrament, even the slightest appearance of profit or simony would cause scandal. Therefore the Holy See has always followed the evolution of this pious tradition with attention, with opportune interventions to provide for adaptations to the changing social and cultural situations, in order to prevent or correct any eventual abuses connected with these adaptations, wherever they might occur (see canons 947 and 1385).

In recent times many bishops have appealed to the Holy See for clarification about the celebration of Masses for what are called "collective" intentions, according to a rather recent practice.

It is true that the faithful have always, especially in economically depressed regions, had the practice of giving the priest modest offerings, without requesting expressly to have a single Mass celebrated for a particular intention. In such cases it is licit to combine the various offerings in order to celebrate as many Masses as would correspond to the fixed diocesan stipend.

The faithful are also free to combine their intentions and offerings for the celebration of a single Mass for these intentions.

Quite different, however, is the case of those priests who, indiscriminately gathering the offerings of the faithful which are destined for the celebration of Masses according to particular intentions, accumulate them in a single offering and satisfy them with a single Mass, celebrated according to what is called a "collective" intention.

The arguments in favor of this new practice are specious and pretentious if not reflecting an erroneous ecclesiology. In any case this use can run the serious risk of not satisfying an obligation of justice toward the donors of the offerings and progressively spread and extinguish in the entire Christian people the awareness and understanding of the motives and purpose of making an offering for the celebration of the holy Sacrifice for particular intentions, therefore depriving the sacred ministers who still live from these offerings, of a necessary means of support and depriving many particular Churches of the resources for their apostolic activity.

3211 FOURTH STREET NE • WASHINGTON, DC 20017

Therefore, to execute a mandate received by the Supreme Pontiff, the Congregation for the Clergy, which has the jurisdiction for the discipline of this delicate subject, has carried out an extensive consultation on the matter, including the opinions of the conferences of bishops. After careful examination of the responses and the various aspects of the complex problem, in collaboration with other interested curial departments, this congregation has established as follows:

Article 1 (1) According to canon 948, "separate Masses are to be applied for the intentions for which an individual offering, even if small, has been made and accepted." Therefore the priest who accepts the offering for a Mass for a particular intention is bound *ex iustitia* to satisfy personally the obligation assumed (cf. canon 949) or to commit its fulfillment to another priest, according to the conditions established by law (see canons 954-955).

(2) Priests who transgress this norm assume the relative moral responsibility if they indistinctly collect offerings for the celebration of Masses for particular intentions and, combining them in a single offering and, without the knowledge of those who have made the offerings, satisfy them with a single Mass celebrated according to an intention which they call "collective."

Article 2 (1) In cases in which the people making the offering have been previously explicitly informed and have freely consented to combining their offerings in a single offering, their intentions can be satisfied with a single Mass celebrated according to a "collective" intention.

(2) In this case it is necessary that the place and time for the celebration of this Mass, which is not to be more than twice a week, be made public.

(3) The bishops in whose dioceses these cases occur are to keep in mind that this practice is an exception to the canonical law in effect; wherever the practice spreads excessively, also on the basis of erroneous ideas of the meaning of offerings for Masses, it must be considered an abuse which could progressively lead to the faithful's discontinuation of the practice of giving offerings for the celebration of Masses for individual intentions, thus causing the loss of a most ancient practice which is salutary for individual souls and the whole Church.

Article 3 (1) In cases described in Article 2.1, it is licit for the celebrant to keep the amount of the offering established by the diocese (see canon 950).

(2) Any amount exceeding this offering shall be consigned to the ordinary as specified in canon 951.1, who will provide for its destination according to the ends established by law (see canon 946).

Article 4 Especially in shrines or places of pilgrimage, which usually receive many offerings for the celebration of Masses, the rectors, bound in conscience, must attentively see to it that the norms of the universal law on the subject (see principally canons 954-956) and those of this decree are accurately applied.

Article 5 (1) Priests who receive a great number of offerings for particular intentions for Masses, e.g., on the feast of the Commemoration of All the Faithful Departed (All Souls) or on other special occasions, being unable to satisfy them personally within a year's time (see canon 953), rather than refusing them, and thus frustrating the devout intention of those making the offering and keeping them from realizing their good purpose, should forward them to other priests (see canon 955) or to their own ordinary (see canon 956).

(2) If in these or similar circumstances that which is described in Article 2.1 of this decree takes place, the priests must be attentive to the dispositions of Article 3.

Article 6 To diocesan bishops in particular falls the duty of promptly and clearly making known these norms, which are valid for secular and religious clergy, and seeing to their observance.

Article 7 It is also necessary that the faithful should be instructed in this matter through a specific catechesis, whose main points are as follows: the deep theological meaning of the offering given to the priest for the celebration of the eucharistic sacrifice, the goal of which is especially to prevent the danger of scandal through the appearance of buying and selling the sacred; the ascetical importance of almsgiving in Christian life, which Jesus himself taught, of which the offering for the celebration of Masses is an outstanding form; the sharing of goods, through which by their offering for Mass intentions the faithful contribute to the support of the sacred ministers and the fulfillment of the Church's apostolic activity.

On 22 January 1991 the Supreme Pontiff approved the norms of the present decree in their specific form and ordered that they be immediately promulgated and take effect.

From the Vatican, 22 February 1991.

+ Antonio Cardinal Innocenti
Prefect

+ Gilberto Agustoni
Titular Archbishop of Caorle
Secretary

COMMENTARY

The decree published above is the result of consultation with all the bishops' conferences, whose responses were elaborated by an interdepartmental committee of the Roman Curia. The Supreme Pontiff then approved, in its specific form, this decree which goes into effect according to the norm of canon 8.1 of the Code of Canon Law.

It responds to the repeated requests of many bishops who have asked the Holy See for clarification and directives in regard to the celebration of Masses which are commonly referred to as *multi-intentional* or *collective*.

The decree is divided into two parts: the first part, the introduction, expresses the reasons; the second part contains the dispositions.

First of all, it states the substantial identity of the motives and goals for which the faithful, following an uninterrupted tradition to be honored for its antiquity and meaning, ask the priest to celebrate a Mass for a particular intention, offering them a recompense—which in our day is almost exclusively monetary. In law this recompense is referred to as a *stipend*, but it is also commonly called an *offering*. The introduction always contains the salient point on which the practice which is the object of the document deviates from the norm that is in effect.

In fact, canon law stipulates that every priest who accepts the obligation to celebrate a Mass for the donor's intention must do so, under an obligation of justice, in person or by entrusting its fulfillment to another priest, regardless of the amount of the offering.

The anomalous practice consists in accepting or amassing indiscriminately the offerings for the celebration of Masses according to the intention of the donor, accumulating the offerings and intentions, and pretending to satisfy the obligation deriving from them through the celebration of a single Mass for an intention which is in reality *plurima* or "collective." Nor is it valid to claim that in these cases the intentions of those making the offering are specified during the celebration, because it cannot be seen in what way this procedure satisfies the obligation expressed in canon 948 of the Code of Canon Law to say as many Masses as there are intentions.

In order to illustrate more clearly the special nature of this anomaly, the decree makes reference to two cases which are apparently similar to a pluri-intentional Mass, but which in reality are very different and therefore are morally licit.

In one case it is a question of a practice which dates to time immemorial, in certain poor regions where the faithful give the priest modest offerings, sometimes still gifts in kind, not to request the celebration of Masses for their individual, particular intentions, but rather to contribute in general to the Church's public worship and the support of the priest himself, knowing quite well that he will then celebrate Mass for their intentions and needs, as canon law does in fact prescribe for bishops and priests with the Masses *pro populo* and which is also suggested by sensitivity and priestly charity.

The other case involves the faithful who spontaneously get together and agree to have one or more Masses celebrated for their common or various intentions, which in reality flow together voluntarily into a single intention, and offering the relative amount. No one can fail to see the radical difference between these practices and the "multi-intentional" Mass spoken of above.

The introduction also mentions the arguments given by those who support this new, illicit practice: it calls these arguments "specious and pretentious if not reflecting an erroneous ecclesiology." In fact, they often say that the Eucharistic celebration is an action of the Church and is therefore eminently communitarian, and that it would also be alien to the very nature of the Mass to "privatize it," affixing particular intentions, or to seek to channel its benefits for private purposes.

These arguments reveal the doctrinal confusion of a certain ecclesiology about the infinite merits of the one sacrifice of the cross, the celebration of the sacrament of that one sacrifice which Christ entrusted to the Church, and about the *thesaurus Ecclesiae* which the Church has at her disposal. Nor can we forget that Catholic doctrine has constantly taught that the fruits of the Eucharistic sacrifice can be attributed to various purposes: first of all to those whom the Church herself names in the "intercessions" of the Eucharistic Prayer, then to the celebrating minister (the so-called ministerial fruit), then to those making the offering, etc.

The priests who do not accept the commitment to celebrate Mass for particular intentions are not aware that they are precluding people from an excellent way of participating actively in the celebration of the memorial of the Lord, which Pope Paul VI himself recalled in the *motu propio "Firma In Traditione,"* precisely through an offering given to the priest. This is one of the spiritual harms to be avoided which the decree also speaks of (cf. art. 2.3).

There are also some people who theorize about the new and more adequate systems of clergy support which are, in fact, sanctioned by the new legislation. According to these people priests no longer need Mass intentions to satisfy their own material needs. Some of them even hold that the old system offends the dignity of the ministers of the altar.

This is one of the many illusions or utopian ideas that lack reference to reality. In fact, it has been demonstrated that the greater part of the world's priests, in contemporary society, too, still draw their own support from Mass offerings. Many other apostolic activities of the Church as well—from missions to parishes—are partially or totally supported from the income of the Mass "stipends" or "offerings." Only those who want to take offense, therefore, or those who are afflicted with a strange type of puritanism, can hold that the ancient traditional custom of using Mass offerings to support the clergy or the Church's works is anachronistic or improper.

The decree uses strong words and a severe tone in calling the attention of pastors to the incalculable damage which the practice of the "multi-intentional" or "collective" Masses can cause in the Christian people under various aspects. The multiplication of such celebrations, or a lack of attention to check them or stop their spread, could cause the faithful to turn against the custom of requesting the celebration of a Mass for a particular intention, which is also always a witness of a living faith. Rather it would do harm to a spiritually salutary Christian custom of great value: prayer for the deceased. To a large degree Mass intentions, or pious Mass associations—as is well known—are destined in suffrage for the faithful departed. Similarly there is the progressive growth of the Christian peoples' awareness that they participate in the Church's life through their Mass offerings which are destined for the support of the clergy and the Church's various activities of worship and charity.

The concern caused by this imprudent practice, and even more the danger that it could spread are repeatedly expressed in the decree, particularly in the dispositions. In it, in fact, some clauses or conditions of licitness are established for exceptional recourse to this improper method of celebration (art. 2). First of all, it requires the *explicit consent* of the person making the offering; currently, however, it is almost universally considered *presumed* or *implicit,* which is morally illicit. It is also necessary *to clearly, publicly* indicate the pla ȝe, day and hour in which these celebrations take place. And, since *in any case* it involves a practice which is *an exception to the norms in effect,* the Supreme Legislator has ruled that these celebrations *cannot take place more than twice a week in a given place of worship* (art. 2.3), in order to contain this practice as much as possible—even with conditions made to avoid abuses—and to prevent its spread.

The prompt and punctual execution of the decree is entrusted to pastors by the very nature of the dispositions. The seriousness of the commitment is due to the potential damage that this new manner—which must remain an exception—could bring about, particularly on the pastoral level. And since shrines furnish favorable conditions for ignoring the prescriptions of the present decree, a special warning is addressed to the rectors of shrines and sanctuaries making them aware of their responsibility, bound in conscience, for their observance.

It is also necessary to devote due attention to the pastoral content of the decree in that part (art. 7) which invites us to use the occasion of the promulgation of these norms to promote an appropriate catechesis with the intention of countering some preconceived ideas in this area which, because of ignorance or inaccuracy, recur in a certain pseudo-religious culture.

The last article indicates some of the points for such a catechesis: repropose and explain the true meaning of the offering which the faithful make to the priest for the celebration of Masses for a particular intention;

the value of almsgiving in Christian life, because of its great ability to make satisfaction; and lastly, the effective participation of the faithful in the Church's mission through a way of "sharing" represented by the offerings for the celebration of Masses which are distributed throughout the world.

For a proper reflection on this entire delicate topic it is good to recall also the directives given by the Second Vatican Council in the decree *Presbyterorum Ordinis:* "Priests, just like bishops, are to use moneys acquired by them on the occasion of their exercise of some ecclesiastical office primarily for their own decent support and the fulfillment of the duties of their state. They should be willing to devote whatever is left over to the good of the Church or to works of charity" (n. 17). Mass stipends fall into this category.

Opening Prayers for New Optional Memorials

The March 1991 issue of the Bishops' Committee on the Liturgy *Newsletter* (Vol. XXVII, page 12) contained the decree of the Congregation for Divine Worship and the Discipline of the Sacraments confirming two additions to the Proper Calendar for the Dioceses of the United States of America: the optional memorials of Blessed Miguel Agustín Pro, priest and martyr, on November 23, and Blessed Juan Diego on December 9. The approved English and Spanish opening prayers for use at Mass and in the Liturgy of the Hours on those two days, along with recently confirmed opening prayers for the optional memorials of Blessed Katharine Drexel (March 23) and Blessed Junipero Serra (July 1), are given below.

March 3

Blessed Katharine Drexel

MASS

Opening Prayer

Let us pray.

Ever-loving God,
you called Blessed Katharine Drexel
to teach the message of the Gospel
and to bring the life of the Eucharist
to the African American and Native American
    peoples.

By her prayers and example,
enable us to work for justice
among the poor and the oppressed,
and keep us undivided in love
in the eucharistic community of your Church.

Grant this through our Lord Jesus Christ,
    your Son,
who lives and reigns with you and the Holy
    Spirit,
one God, for ever and ever.

Oremos.

Dios siempre benigno,
que llamaste a la Bienaventurada Katharina
    Drexel
a ser misionera del Evangelio
y de la vida eucarística
entre los afro-americanos y los nativos de Norte
    América,
haz que por sus oraciones y ejemplo
estemos dispuestos a trabajar por la justicia
entre los pobres y oprimidos,
y concédenos que permanezcamos unidos por el
    amor
en la comunidad eucarística de tu Iglesia.

Por nuestro Señor Jesucristo, tu Hijo,
que vive y reina contigo
en la unidad del Espíritu Santo y es Dios
por los siglos de los siglos.

(English and Spanish texts confirmed by the Congregation for Divine Worship and the Discipline of the Sacraments for use in the dioceses of the United States on 13 April 1991: Prot. CD 775/90).

July 1

Blessed Junipero Serra

MASS

Opening Prayer

Let us pray.

God most high,
your servant Junipero Serra
brought the gospel of Christ to the peoples of
    Mexico and California
and firmly established the Church among them.

By his intercession,
and through the example of his evangelical zeal,
inspire us to be faithful witnesses of Jesus Christ,
who lives and reigns with you and the Holy Spirit,
one God, for ever and ever.

Oremos.

Altísimo Dios,
tu siervo Junípero Serra
trajo el evangelio de Cristo a los pueblos
    de Mexico y California
y estableció firmemente la Iglesia entre ellos.

Por su intercesión,
y por el ejemplo de su celo evangélico,
muévenos a ser fieles testigos de Jesucristo,
que vive y reina contigo
en la unidad del Espíritu Santo y es Dios
por los siglos de los siglos.

(English and Spanish texts confirmed by the Congregation for Divine Worship and the Discipline of the Sacraments for use in the dioceses of the United States on 13 April 1991: Prot. CD 774/90).

November 23

Blessed Miguel Agustín Pro

MASS

Opening Prayer

Let us pray.

God our Father,
you gave your servant Miguel Agustín
the grace to seek ardently your greater glory
and the salvation of your people.
Grant that, through his intercession
and following his example,
we may serve you and glorify you
by performing our daily duties with fidelity and joy
and effectively helping our neighbor.

We ask this through our Lord Jesus Christ, your
    Son,
who lives and reigns with you and the Holy Spirit,
one God, for ever and ever.

Oremos.

Dios y Padre nuestro,
que concediste a tu siervo Miguel Agustín,
en su vida y en su martirio,
buscar ardientemente tu mayor gloria
y la salvación de los hombres,
concédenos, a ejemplo suyo, servirte y glorificarte
cumpliendo nuestras obligaciones diarias con
    fidelidad y alegría,
y ayudando eficazmente a nuestros prójimos.
Por nuestro Señor Jesucristo, tu Hijo,
que vive y reina contigo
en la unidad del Espíritu Santo y es Dios,
por los siglos de los siglos.

(Spanish text confirmed by the Congregation for Divine Worship and the Discipline of the Sacraments on 30 September 1988: Prot. CD 1245/88. English text confirmed on 31 January 1989.)

December 9

Blessed Juan Diego

MASS

Opening Prayer

Let us pray.

Lord God,
through blessed Juan Diego
you made known the love of Our Lady of Guadalupe
toward your people.

Grant by his intercession
that we who follow the counsel of Mary, our
    Mother,
may strive continually to do your will.

We ask this through our Lord Jesus Christ, your
    Son,
who lives and reigns with you and the Holy Spirit,
one God, for ever and ever.

Oremos.

Oh Dios,
que por medio del beato Juan Diego,
quisiste manifestar a tu pueblo
el amor de Santa María de Guadalupe:
concédenos por su intercesión
que, dóciles al consejo de nuestra Madre,
nos esforcemos en hacer siempre tu voluntad.

Por nuestro Señor Jesucristo, tu Hijo,
que vive y reina contigo
en la unidad del Espíritu Santo y es Dios,
por los siglos de los siglos.

Rereading the Constitution on the Liturgy (art. 47-50)

Articles 47-50 of the Constitution on the Liturgy present doctrinal and pastoral considerations which serve to undergird the reform of eucharistic worship subsequent to the Second Vatican Council. The first article is primarily theological in nature. It begins by reflecting the teaching of the Council of Trent: " . . . Our Savior instituted the eucharistic sacrifice of his body and blood . . . in order to perpetuate the sacrifice of the cross . . . " It then goes on to describe the eucharist as " . . . a memorial of his death and resurrection: a sacrament of love, a sign of unity, a bond of charity, a paschal banquet . . . " This description, though far from new, broadens the sacrificial language which predominated the discourse on the eucharist since the Council of Trent.

In the early years of the liturgical reform one often heard of disputes over whether the Mass is a sacrifice or a banquet (meal); the Constitution, in but a few words, makes it clear that it is both. Neither description exhausts the reality of the eucharist, and both are essential for a full appreciation of this mystery. The challenge for the Church today is to resist the temptation of describing only one aspect of the eucharistic mystery to the exclusion of others. Following the lead of the Constitution on the Liturgy, all need to take advantage of the ancient theological language of the Church which sees the eucharist as sacrifice, banquet, paschal mystery of Christ's death and resurrection, sacrament of love, sign of unity, bond of charity, etc.

Pope Paul VI was aware that a thorough catechesis of the Christian faithful on the mystery of the eucharist was a necessary first step to their reception of the reform of the *Roman Missal*, particularly the Order of Mass. He prepared for this reform through both his own encyclical *Mysterium Fidei* on the doctrine and worship of the eucharist (3 September 1965) as well as the instruction of the Congregation of Rites *Eucharisticum mysterium*, issued on 25 May 1967. Both documents are "must reading," as they carefully present the principal aspects of the Church's teaching on the eucharistic mystery, the center of the whole life of the Church. Along with the effective celebration of the Eucharist itself, these two documents remain principal sources for proper catechesis on this central mystery of faith. Correctly understood, they close off the either-or "sacrifice or banquet" debate, which unfortunately still engages the energies of many persons in the Church today.

CSL 48 is a concrete application of the general principle of CSL 14 dealing with the active participation of the faithful. The faithful are not to be silent spectators who are merely present at Mass. Rather, "they should take part in the sacred service conscious of what they are doing, with devotion and full involvement." For most Catholic Christians, gone are the days when they attended what was perceived to be the Mass of the priest by silently following his prayers and actions in a missal, or by reciting the rosary, or engaging in other personal devotions. The Mass is not the prayer of the priest alone; it is the prayer of the whole community of the baptized.

A question that arises today, now that the people participate in the eucharistic celebration through prayer, song, gesture and posture, listening, and even silence, is whether this participation is purely external or has it been internalized by the liturgical assembly. Just because everyone is *doing something* is no guarantee that they are participating. True participation also involves silence and reflection: adequate time must be provided for them in liturgical celebrations. Consequently, the Mass should never be rushed just to empty the church parking lot before the people arrive for the next Mass. Nor should Masses be scheduled so close together that time is not provided for prayerful celebration.

CSL 48 serves as a reminder that in the Mass the Christian faithful are "instructed by God's word" and "nourished at the table of the Lord's body;" they give thanks to God; they join the priest in offering Christ, and learn to offer themselves as well; and through Christ they are united evermore closely with God and one another. The articles that follow (nos. 49-58) provide specific direction for the implementation of this theological perspective in the planned reform of rites and texts. Hence, article 49 says that the following decrees are made in order that the Mass, " . . . even in its ritual forms, may become pastorally effective to the utmost degree."

CSL 50 decrees that the Order of Mass is to be revised, so that the nature and purpose of its several parts and their interrelationships may be made more clear and enable the faithful to participate more fully in the Mass. This is to be done by the simplification of the rites, the removal of needless duplications, and by the restoration of those parts that have been corrupted through time. As a result of the implementation of this decree, the Church now possesses a revised Order of Mass that reflects the more ancient traditions of the Roman Church. The introductory rites have been simplified to some degree, the rites for the preparation of the gifts have been reformed to reflect the theological understanding that the true offering of the Mass takes place during the eucharistic prayer, and the communion rite has also been somewhat simplified.

CSL 51 identifies the second major change decreed for the revised *Roman Missal:* "the treasures of the Bible are to be opened up more lavishly, so that a richer share in God's word may be provided for the faithful." The revised *Lectionary for Mass,* one of the books of the *Roman Missal* (which also contains the Sacramentary and the Roman Gradual), has had a renewing effect on the Church since its publication in 1969. In the liturgy the Church searches the Scriptures and hears proclaimed a living, active word, a word in which Christ is always present, carrying out the mystery of salvation, sanctifying the Church through the power of the Holy Spirit, revealing the never-failing love of God, and offering perfect worship to the Father. The richer fare of God's word provided by the revised Lectionary for Mass is already seen as one of the greatest treasures flowing from the Second Vatican Council.

Finally, as Pope Paul VI stated in his apostolic constitution *Missale Romanum* (3 April 1969) promulgating the new Roman Missal, a third major change in the Missal—but one not specified in the degrees of the Constitution on the Liturgy—is the addition of three (and later, eight) new canons and a greatly enlarged collection of prefaces which have significantly enriched the eucharistic prayer of the Mass. Pope Paul refers to this change as "the chief innovation" in the reform of the Missal, and he defends this variety of anaphoras as consistent with Church tradition (particularly in Eastern liturgies) and as providing for more and richer forms for this central prayer of thanksgiving in the Eucharist.

For the most part this reform of the Roman Missal has been effective, particularly in the United States. Perhaps in the view of the majority of the Catholic faithful, it remains the greatest result of the Council. But further catechesis remains necessary, lest present successes in implementing and appropriating the reforms be disparaged in the zeal of some who may unreflectively think that novelty in the liturgy is all that counts.

COMMITTEE ON THE LITURGY

NEWSLETTER

NATIONAL CONFERENCE OF CATHOLIC BISHOPS

1991
VOLUME XXVII
JUNE

June Meeting of the Committee on the Liturgy

The Committee on the Liturgy of the National Conference of Catholic Bishops met in plenary session at Saint Thomas University in Saint Paul, Minnesota, from June 16-17, 1991.

Bishop Gregory welcomed Dr. Marchita Mauck, Sister Barbara O'Dea, DW, and Father Michael Witczak as new advisors to the Committee. Dr. Marchita Mauck is an art historian who teaches at Louisiana State University and in the liturgical studies program at the University of Notre Dame. Sister Barbara O'Dea is the Provincial Superior of the Daughters of Wisdom and has done extensive work on the Rite of Christian Initiation of Adults. Father Witczak is professor of liturgy at Saint Francis Seminary, Milwaukee.

The Committee discussed and took action on several items. It favorably reviewed *Praying Together*, a booklet containing slightly revised versions of the ecumenical common liturgical texts for the eucharist and the Liturgy of the Hours which was prepared by the English Language Liturgical Consultation (ELLC), a successor to the International Consultation on Ecumenical Texts (ICET). The International Commission on English in the Liturgy (ICEL) is studying these texts with a view toward their inclusion in the revised edition of the *Roman Missal,* and the Committee on the Liturgy voted to recommend their use to Archbishop Daniel E. Pilarczyk, the American representative on the ICEL Episcopal Board. The revised texts represent a greater use of gender-inclusive language and respond to criticisms of the previous versions.

Two lectionaries were considered by the Committee: the second edition of the *Lectionary for Mass,* and the *Lectionary for Masses with Children.* The Committee agreed to request the NCCB to approve for liturgical use the proposed new psalter of the New American Bible, once it has received the *imprimatur* of the Conference. It also reviewed the progress of the preparation of the new edition of the *Lectionary for Mass* and decided to request the members of the Committees on the Liturgy, Pastoral Practices, and Doctrine to review the Lectionary before it is presented to the NCCB. The *Lectionary for Masses with Children* was approved by the Liturgy Committee and it will be submitted to the NCCB for canonical approval at its November meeting. The Committee also decided to request the approval of the NCCB for the American Bible Society's *Contemporary English Version* (the complete New Testament and psalter and selected Old Testament passages) as a biblical translation for liturgical use. This translation has been used in the children's lectionary and was originally known as the *Translation for Early Youth.* The Committee on the Liturgy voted to simplify the title of the lectionary from *Lectionary for Mass and Other Celebrations with Children* to *Lectionary for Masses with Children.* In a related action, the Committee agreed to request the NCCB's approval for liturgical use of the *New Revised Standard Version* (NRSV) of the Bible once that translation has been granted the *imprimatur* of the Conference.

The Liturgy Committee agreed to reexamine the revised *Grail Psalter (Inclusive Language Version)* and will recommend to the publisher changes required by the *Criteria for the Evaluation of Inclusive Language Translations,* which the NCCB approved last November. Once this is done, the Committee will recommend that the NCCB authorize this version of the psalter for liturgical use.

The revised *Norms for Preaching by Lay Persons in Churches and Oratories,* prepared by the Committee for Pastoral Practices, were approved for submission to the NCCB in November.

The 1990 position statements from the National Meeting of Diocesan Liturgical Commissions were considered by the Committee. Position Statement 1990 A, dealing with the sequence (baptism-confirmation-eucharist) of the sacraments of initiation was discussed; the Committee asked Bishop Gregory to consult with the Committees on Education, Doctrine, Pastoral Practices, and Laity about a possible joint study of this question. P.S. 1990 C, on posture during the eucharistic prayer, will be forwarded to the Task

3211 FOURTH STREET NE • WASHINGTON, DC 20017

Group on the Adaptation of the Roman Missal. P.S. 1990 D, which treats the role of the liturgical assembly in the celebration of the rites of ordination, has already been addressed by an *ad hoc* task group on the ordination rites. The results of that group's meeting are given below. Finally, the Liturgy Committee took note of P.S. 1990 E on the use of a variety of images when speaking about God.

A revised version of a Mass in Thanksgiving for Human Life, prepared as a response to a *varium* submitted by Cardinal John J. O'Connor, was examined by the Committee; the members asked that further work be done on the text before approval is given.

The Committees on the Liturgy and for Pastoral Practices have prepared a series of proposals relating to holy days of obligation in response to the results of a survey of the bishops which was conducted in early 1991. The Committee on Liturgy agreed that, along with the Committee on Pastoral Practices, it would present five proposals to the NCCB plenary meeting in November: 1) transfer the solemnity of the Ascension to the Seventh Sunday of Easter as provided for in the General Norms for the Liturgical Year and the Calendar; 2) remove the canonical obligation to participate in the eucharist on August 15, the solemnity of the Assumption; 3) remove the canonical obligation to participate in the eucharist on November 1, the solemnity of All Saints; 4) remove the canonical obligation to participate in the eucharist on January 1, the solemnity of Mary, Mother of God; 5) remove the canonical obligation to participate in the eucharist when Assumption, All Saints, Mary, Mother of God, or Immaculate Conception falls on a Saturday; 6) remove the canonical obligation to participate in the eucharist when Assumption, All Saints, Mary, Mother of God, or Immaculate Conception falls on a Monday. If actions 1-4 are not approved by the bishops, actions 5 and 6 would be moved.

Proposals were made to place two saints and a blessed on the Proper Calendar for the Dioceses of the United States of America. The Liturgy Committee decided to defer action until guidelines can be prepared regarding diocesan calendars and the national calendar.

The Hispanic Liturgy Subcommittee requested that *Sunday Celebrations in the Absence of a Priest: Leader's Edition* be published only in a bilingual (English-Spanish) edition. The Committee approved this proposal, and the Secretariat staff will see that the Spanish texts are prepared.

At its March meeting the Committee on the Liturgy requested that the Secretariat prepare a statement on the use of the "Unity Candle" in the marriage liturgy. The Committee examined the statement and approved its publication in a future issue of the Newsletter.

As a result of a position statement approved by the delegates to the 1990 meeting of Diocesan Liturgical Commissions on the role of the liturgical assembly in the ordination liturgies, and also because the English translation of the second edition of the ordination rites is well advanced, a small task group met in May and prepared a series of proposed American adaptations to the ordination rites. The Liturgy Committee examined the texts, suggested some changes, and requested that a new draft be sent to the bishop members for approval. The texts will then have to be approved by the NCCB and confirmed by the Apostolic See.

Various information reports were given. Father Krisman spoke of the on-going work of the Secretariat and the departure of Father Jenkins from the Secretariat to work in the Office of the General Secretary. It is expected that a new Associate Director will be named shortly. Some initial concerns of the Task Group on Cremation and Other Funeral Practices have been forwarded to the Congregation for Divine Worship and the Discipline of the Sacraments, which is preparing to publish a new Latin edition of the funeral rites. The confirmation of the translation of the Mass into the Lakota language has been delayed because of some concerns raised by the Congregation for Divine Worship and the Discipline of the Sacraments. These have been addressed, and it is hoped that confirmation of the text will be received in the near future.

Monsignor Frederick R. McManus reported on the work of the International Commission on English in the Liturgy. He gave special emphasis to the revision of the *Roman Missal*, which is the major project of ICEL. English translations of the ordination rites and the marriage rite are in preparation, and ICEL hopes to begin work on a revision of the *Rite for Baptism of Children*. Work is nearing completion on the ICEL translation of the psalter.

Father Michael Spillane gave a report on the work of the Federation of Diocesan Liturgical Commission. Father Spillane indicated that the financial status of the Federation has greatly improved over the past several years. He then introduced Sister Anthony Poerio, the vice chairperson of the the FDLC board of directors. Sister Poerio was substituting for Father Richard Ward, chairperson of FDLC, who was unable to be present. Sister Poerio told the Committee members, consultants, and advisors of the plans for the next national meeting, which will take place in Phoenix, AZ on October 11-14, 1991.

Sister Rosa Maria Icaza, president of the Instituto de Liturgia Hispana explained the work of the Institute and noted that the next national conference of the IHL will take place at the University of Notre Dame on October 24-27, 1992.

Bishop Roberto O. Gonzalez informed the Committee that the Hispanic Liturgy Subcommittee had met in May and is completing its work on the draft Spanish translation of the *Order of Christian Funerals*. The subcommittee plans to translate the *Rite of Marriage* as well as the American blessings contained in the *Book of Blessings*.

Father Krisman reported that the Task Group on Cremation and other Funeral Practices has met and has asked him to prepare a position paper which will summarize the Task Group's discussions. Since the Congregation for Divine Worship and the Discipline of the Sacraments has begun the preparation of a revised Latin edition of the funeral rites, which includes liturgical provision for cremation, it asked Archbishop Pilarczyk to forward several concerns and comments to the Congregation.

Father Krisman also informed the Liturgy Committee that the Task Group on the Adaptation of the Roman Missal will meet in June under the chairmanship of Bishop Jerome Hanus, OSB. The Task Group will review all the present American adaptations in the *Sacramentary* and will determine what, if any, additional material needs to be prepared.

Finally, Father Krisman noted that the Task Group on Televised Masses has not yet been formed. This task group will be composed of liturgists, theologians, members of the USCC Communications Committee, and those engaged in broadcasting.

The next meeting of the members and consultants of the Committee on the Liturgy will take place on Sunday, November 10, 1991. The members, consultants, and advisors will have their next meeting together on June 18-21, 1992 at the University of Notre Dame.

Praying the Akathist Hymn

The following decree of the Apostolic Penitentiary was printed in the English edition of Osservatore Romano *and was signed by William Cardinal Baum. The decree grants a plenary indulgence to those who recite the Akathist hymn of the Byzantine Churches.*

The Akathist hymn is an ancient Greek hymn in honor of the Mother of God. The Greek word "Akathistos," meaning "not seated," was applied to the hymn since it is sung in the standing position at Matins of the fifth Saturday of Lent. It is also used separately as a devotion in honor of the Blessed Virgin Mary. It consists of twelve refrains (kontakion) and 12 canticles (ikos) divided into four parts and interspersed with psalms and litanies. The hymn was composed to commemorate the liberation of Constantinople in 626 after the invasion of the Persians. Pope John Paul II celebrated Matins with the Akathist hymn in the Byzantine-Slavic Rite on the Feast of the Annunciation during the Marian Year of 1988.

APOSTOLIC PENITENTIARY
DECREE

A plenary indulgence is granted to the faithful who recite the *Akathist* hymn in a church or oratory, as a family, in a religious community or in a pious association.

The Blessed Virgin Mary, Mother of Christ and the Church, "figured profoundly in the history of salvation and in a certain way unites and mirrors within herself the central truths of the faith. Hence when she is being preached and venerated, she summons the faithful to her Son and his sacrifice, and to love for the Father" (Vatican Council II, Dogmatic Constitution *Lumen gentium*, no. 65).

The Church has always and everywhere experienced this wondrous power of the Mother of God, whereby faith is enlightened and strengthened, and devotion increases in fervor. The Church has expressed this prerogative of Our Lady in prayer formulas and rites of worship, according to the different languages, sensitivities and cultural riches of nations.

Among the numerous documents of Christian wisdom which are also works of art distinguished for their radiant beauty, an eminent place is enjoyed by that truly sublime hymn of the Byzantine liturgy known as the *Akathist*. Indeed, in this hymn heartfelt fervor and a vision of mystical contemplation are joined to a prodigious literary perfection. In virtue of her catholicity, "each individual part of the Church contributes through its special gifts to the good of the other parts and of the whole Church" (ibid., no. 13) in regard to all the spiritual gifts of the divine generosity. As a result, the *Akathist* hymn has also become widespread among the faithful of the Latin rite, especially in recent years, and has been prayed both privately and publicly with no small advantage to religious devotion.

In order to strengthen in an appropriate way and spread this praiseworthy practice, which the Sovereign Pontiff John Paul II has encouraged by his own example by publicly praying this devotion on the solemnity of the Annunciation of the Lord during the 1988 Marian Year, so that the affection of the faithful for the Blessed *Theotokos* may grow, the bond of Catholic communion may be strengthened among brothers and sisters who, while belonging to different rites, still belong to one and the same Church, and the ability to perceive that spiritual comeliness which opens the way to God, the Supreme Beauty, may be sharpened, the Apostolic Penitentiary has decided to grant to this hymn the same plenary indulgence connected with recitation of Mary's Rosary, for the benefit of the faithful of any rite under the usual conditions, i.e., sacramental confession, Eucharistic communion and prayer for the intentions of the Sovereign Pontiff, if the *Akathist* hymn is prayed in a church or oratory, as a family, or in a religious community or pious association; a partial indulgence is granted in other circumstances (cf. *Enchiridion indulgentiarum*, concession no. 48).

His Holiness, Pope John Paul II, in an audience granted to the undersigned Cardinal Major Penitentiary on 25 May 1991, by his supreme Authority has approved the aforementioned resolution of the Apostolic Penitentiary and has ordered it to be published.

Given in Rome, from the office of the Apostolic Penitentiary, 31 May 1991, the feast of the Visitation of the Blessed Virgin Mary.

+ William Cardinal Baum
Major Penitentiary

Luigi De Magistris
Regent

Liturgical Calendar 1993

For nearly two decades the NCCB Liturgy Secretariat has annually prepared the official liturgical calendar for the dioceses of the United States which lists each day's celebration, rank, liturgical color(s), and lectionary citations. The manuscript each year is made available to commercial publishers of calendars, ordo's, etc. in the United States. For several years the USCC Office of Publications has published the information in the manuscript and supplemented it with notes concerning the daily celebration of the Liturgy of the Hours in its spiral-bound calendar and ordo.

The USCC has now discontinued publication of its annual calendar and ordo. Consequently, the Liturgy Secretariat will make available its manuscript directly to all who desire a copy. *Liturgical Calendar 1993* (8½ X 11 in., 32 pages) may be purchased from: Bishops' Committee on the Liturgy, 3211 Fourth Street NE, Washington, DC 20017-1194, Att: Ms. Rena Hinnant. All orders must be accompanied by a check made out to "Bishops' Committee on the Liturgy" in the amount of $5.00 to cover printing, postage, and handling.

COMMITTEE ON THE LITURGY

NEWSLETTER

1991
VOLUME XXVII
JULY/AUGUST

NATIONAL CONFERENCE OF CATHOLIC BISHOPS

Sister Linda Gaupin, CDP, Named BCL Associate Director

Monsignor Robert N. Lynch, General Secretary of the National Conference of Catholic Bishops, has announced the appointment of Sister Linda Gaupin, CDP, as an Associate Director of the Secretariat of the Bishops' Committee on the Liturgy.

A member of the Sisters of Divine Providence, Pittsburgh, Sister Gaupin for the past seven years has served as Director of Worship for the Diocese of Wilmington, where she had charge of directing liturgy, music, and the implementation of the *Rite of Christian Initiation of Adults* for the diocese.

Since 1986 Sister Gaupin has also served as an adjunct professor in the Graduate Religion Department of La Salle University, Philadelphia. Previously she served as chairperson of the Religious Studies Department of La Roche College in Pittsburgh and as an instructor in the Department of Religion and Religious Education at The Catholic University of America, Washington, DC.

Sister Gaupin holds a B.A. in Theology and History from La Roche College, an M.A. in Systematic Theology from Loyola University of Chicago, and an M.A. and a Ph.D. in liturgical studies from The Catholic University of America. Her 1985 doctoral dissertation was entitled "First Eucharist and the Shape of Catechesis in the Twentieth Century since *Quam Singulari.*" Several of her publications during the past five years have dealt with the sacraments of initiation, the first penance of children, and the *Rite of Christian Initiation of Adults*.

Sister Gaupin will assume her new position in Washington, DC, on September 3, 1991.

Immaculate Conception in 1991

In 1991 the Second Sunday of Advent occurs on December 8. In accordance with the recently emended norm no. 5 of the *General Norms for the Liturgical Year and the Calendar* (see *Newsletter*, September 1990) the celebration of the solemnity of the Immaculate Conception, whenever December 8 falls on a Sunday, is to be transferred to the *following* day, namely, to Monday, December 9. However, as was conceded by the Congregation for Divine Worship and the Discipline of the Sacraments when it promulgated this emendation in the law, the dioceses of the United States *will not* observe this change in December 1991 since all liturgical calendars and ordo's had already been published when the change was announced in April 1990. For this one last time only the observance of the solemnity of the Immaculate Conception will be on *Saturday, December 7.*

It should be noted that, even though the liturgical celebration is moved to December 7, according to sound canonical principles the obligation to attend Mass on that day is not transferred. Nevertheless, pastors should encourage the Christian faithful freely to observe this great solemnity in honor of the Blessed Virgin Mary by participating in the celebration of the Eucharist. An adequate number of celebrations at times convenient to the faithful should be offered in parishes.

In Memoriam: Dr. Thomas C. O'Brien

Dr. Thomas C. O'Brien, the staff translator and editor with the International Commission on English in the Liturgy (ICEL), died on June 18, 1991 after a long battle with cancer. A noted scholar of Saint Thomas Aquinas, Dr. O'Brien prepared the authoritative English translation of the *Summa Theologica* and was

3211 FOURTH STREET NE • WASHINGTON, DC 20017

the editor of the supplementary volume for the *New Catholic Encyclopedia*. He also served as a tutor in Thomistic studies at the Dominican House of Studies in Washington, DC. In his work at ICEL he was deeply involved in the preparation of a new edition of the *Sacramentary* and did extensive research into the Latin collects of the *Roman Missal*. In the process of his work on the collects, he compiled a lexicon of the terms used in the *Missale Romanum*, which has served as an invaluable resource for the translators of the Latin prayers.

Every English edition of the reformed liturgical books since 1979, when Dr. O'Brien joined the ICEL staff, bears the imprint of his painstaking scholarship. The *Rite of Christian Initiation of Adults*, the *Order of Christian Funerals*, the *Ceremonial of Bishops*, the *Book of Blessings*, and *Documents on the Liturgy, 1963-1979: Conciliar, Papal, and Curial Texts* all remain a tribute to his memory. Shortly before his death he finished work on a second volume of *Documents on the Liturgy* which brings the collection up to date. Dr. O'Brien is survived by his wife, Florence. He will be deeply missed by the ICEL staff and the community of scholars who assist in the work of ICEL. His death is a loss to the Church in the entire English-speaking world.

> O God,
> glory of believers and life of the just,
> by the death and resurrection of your Son, we are redeemed:
> have mercy on your servant Thomas,
> and make him worthy to share the joys of paradise,
> for he believed in the resurrection of the dead.

The Use of the "Unity Candle" at Weddings

In March 1991 the members of the Bishops' Committee on the Liturgy asked its Secretariat to address the issue of the use of the "Unity Candle" in the marriage liturgy. Accordingly, the following statement was prepared by the Secretariat staff and was approved for publication by the NCCB Liturgy Committee at its meeting in Saint Paul, MN, on June 17, 1991.

With the recent publication by the Congregation for Divine Worship and the Discipline of the Sacraments of a second revised edition of the *Rite of Marriage*, it is appropriate that a serious study of and reflection upon wedding practices and customs currently observed in the United States be undertaken with a view toward identifying those elements in the rite which require further catechesis of the Christian faithful. Similarly, practices which have arisen popularly during the past twenty years should be studied and, if found to be appropriate, they should be proposed as possible adaptations of the marriage liturgy for use in this country. The "unity candle" is one such practice which falls into this latter category.

Shortly after the first edition of the revised *Rite of Marriage* was published in English (1969), it was proposed that the ceremonial lighting of a large candle from two smaller candles, held by the bride and groom, be included in the marriage rite after the exchange of vows or after communion. In the ensuing years this practice, although never formally approved, has become fairly common. The rite apparently comes from an Eastern European context and has the intention of showing that the "two become one flesh" through the sacrament of marriage.

This popular practice raises several questions which call for reflection. The liturgical use of candles, other than for producing light itself, is most commonly related to seeing the lighted candle as a symbol of the light of Christ. This is epitomized in the Easter Vigil in the use of the paschal candle and in the lighting of the people's candles at the beginning of the liturgy. As the paschal candle is lighted, the priest prays: "May the light of Christ, rising in glory, dispel the darkness of our hearts and minds." The holding of lighted candles for the renewal of the baptismal promises harkens back to the rite of baptism when a lighted candle is given to a newly baptized adult or to the parents or godparents of an infant. As this is done, the minister says: "You have been enlightened by Christ. Walk always as children of the light . . ." This same symbolism is found in the rite for the dedication of a church when the deacon receives a lighted candle from the bishop so that he may light the candles at the altar; the bishop says: "Light of Christ, shine forth in the Church and bring all nations to the fullness of truth." Similarly, in popular celebrations of Evening Prayer, the use of the lucenarium service (lighting of a large candle and prayer of thanksgiving) recalls the Light of Christ in the darkness of the night.

Considering this liturgical usage of candles, what is the symbolism of lighting one larger candle from two smaller ones, which are then extinguished? If the larger candle does not represent Christ, what does it symbolize? The couple? If so, it seems to be at variance with liturgical tradition. And if the two smaller candles are meant to represent the individual baptized Christians entering this marriage, should not that symbolization be made explicit, such as, by the bride and the groom each carrying their candle in the entrance procession? And are those individual lives in some way "snuffed out" when the two who have become one in Christ extinguish their candles?

If the larger candle represents Christ, should it not be burning from the very beginning of the liturgy? The light of Christ does not come from the couple, but rather is shared with the couple. If this symbolism is the intended one, the couples' candles should be lighted from the "Christ candle" and stand next to it as a sign that the unity of the couple comes from Christ. For they are united with each other by being united in Christ.

One of the greatest criticisms of the "unity candle" is that it is not integrated into the liturgy and has to be explained in some detail when it is used. Its use should flow out of the very rites of the liturgy and not appear as something added on but not directly connected to the actions and prayers of the liturgy.

The Bishops' Committee on the Liturgy invites liturgical commissions and interested individuals to reflect upon the use of the unity candle, both its positive and negative features, and to communicate their thoughts to the Committee.

Rereading the Constitution on the Liturgy (art. 51-53)

Despite the reform of the Mass mandated by the Second Vatican Council and promulgated by Pope Paul IV, there still remains much to be done. Further revisions will be required. But more importantly, clergy and laity need ongoing formation to understand the present liturgy and fully implement it.

Indications that the reform of the eucharistic liturgy has not yet been appropriated by many persons in the Church abound. Some priests continue to celebrate Mass similar to the way they did before the Council. It may be that they lack an understanding of the principles of good communication, since they have not been taught their importance or how to use them effectively. Or perhaps they still see the Mass as "their" Mass and have not either accepted the teachings of the Council or understood them.

At the preparation of the gifts, for instance, some priests may wait for the singing to stop so that they may solemnly declaim the two prayers for the placing of the gifts on the altar. Some may elevate the chalice and paten to shoulder height as they say the prayers, even though the rubrics clearly indicate that they are to be raised only slightly above the altar before being placed on it. They may proclaim in a loud voice that they are sinners as they wash the tips of their fingers rather then their hands. Others, instead of using all the eucharistic prayers to enrich the liturgy, rely almost exclusively on eucharistic prayer II because it is the shortest.

Rarely does one hear the preface sung, and in many places the acclamations of the people during the anaphora are recited, not sung, with a boring monotony. Music is often not seen as a priority in good celebration; financial resources have not been dedicated to preparing competent musicians both at the diocesan and local levels. Parishes have not hired capable musicians nor sought to develop music programs that reflect the requirements of the revised liturgy, which presumes that music is integral to the celebration of Mass.

Priest celebrants may sometimes forget that they are addressing God in prayer, and by word and gesture act as if the eucharistic prayer were addressed to the congregation. Throughout the celebration, some priest celebrants recite the private prayers of the priest in a loud voice and even change them so as to include the people. The provision for communion under both kinds for the people is often ignored, with the excuse being given that it is too difficult, or that people don't want it (even though they often have never been asked).

In many parishes there was little attempt to explain the liturgical reforms to the people when they were first introduced, nor has this been remedied in the subsequent years. Some persons ignore liturgical legislation and the principles that underlie it and have embraced every new fancy which comes along. Celebrations based on such ideas quickly lose their attraction. Often one is given the impression that those who constantly must change the liturgy and conform it to their own ideas have not really assimilated the purpose and meaning of the liturgical reforms and the ecclesiology that is intrinsically related to those reforms. It would seem that an important phase of the liturgical reform and renewal, that of formation, must be repeated for both clergy and laity before the next English edition of the Missal is implemented.

These difficulties indicate that, even though a quarter of a century has passed since the Council, there continues to be a need for further liturgical education of the entire Church.

On the positive side of the picture, the vast majority of American clergy and laity have accepted the liturgical reforms. They have striven to implement the new liturgical books and have attempted to make the Sunday liturgy a time of prayer in which all fully, actively, and consciously participate. They are to be commended for their efforts; their hard work has paid off. Still, their challenge is to continue to deepen their understanding of the renewed rites and to celebrate them with the faith and vibrant enthusiasm that lead to a greater union with God and one another.

One of the most important reforms decreed by the *Constitution on the Liturgy* was that of the Lectionary. As was noted in the April-May *Newsletter,* the Council desired that the "treasures of the Bible... be opened up more lavishly, so that a richer share in God's word may be provided for the faithful. In this way a more representative portion of holy Scripture will be read to the people in the course of a prescribed number of years" (CSL 51). The concrete application of this article is found in the *Lectionary for Mass,* which was first published in 1969 and later revised in 1981.

The reform of the Lectionary was a massive undertaking, since it contains a collection of lectionaries or lists of readings for a variety of occasions. There is the Sunday lectionary which contains three readings and a responsorial psalm for each Sunday of the liturgical year. The Sunday readings are distributed over a three year cycle, each year of which uses one of the synoptic gospels: Matthew (year A), Mark (year B), and Luke (year C). The gospel of John is used in the Lenten and Easter seasons and at various times in year B as a supplement to the gospel of Mark, which is shorter than the other gospels. In the course of the three year cycle of the Lectionary the majority of the New Testament is proclaimed at the Sunday liturgy.

This Sunday Lectionary has been adopted by a large number of Christian Churches in the United States and Canada and adapted by them to their own particular needs and traditions, for example, the Presbyterian Church, Evangelical Lutheran Church in America, the United Methodist Church, the United Church of Christ, the Christian Church (Disciples), and many others. Since 1983 many of these Churches have been using an ecumenically agreed upon version of the Lectionary which was published by the North American Consultation on Common Texts under the title, *The Common Lectionary.* A revised version of this ecumenical lectionary will be published in 1992. The differences between the Roman *Lectionary for Mass* and the other adapted versions are mainly in the selection of Old Testament readings during Ordinary Time and a tendency of the other lectionaries to lengthen pericopes.

Other portions of the *Lectionary for Mass* contain readings for weekdays (with a two year cycle for the first reading and responsorial psalm), readings for solemnities, feasts, and memorials of saints, readings for ritual Masses (baptism, confirmation, ordination, etc.), readings for various needs and occasions, and readings for the funeral liturgy and Masses for the dead.

The Scriptures need to be explained and applied to people's lives, and so CSL 52 requires that there be a homily at Mass on Sundays and holydays of obligation. Since it is integral to the Sunday celebration of the eucharist, the homily "is not to be omitted except for a serious reason." The Constitution also indicates that a homily is strongly recommended at other times.

In the past, a sermon was usually given at Mass on Sunday. It might be related to the Scriptures, but often it was of a general nature or on a doctrine or practice of the Church. CSL 52 explains the meaning and purpose of the homily: "By means of the homily the mysteries of the faith and the guiding principles of the Christian life are expounded from the sacred text during the course of the liturgical year." Liturgical preaching is to be biblical preaching, that is, the word of God is the starting point and inspiration for the homily, which opens up God's word and applies it to our day to day experience of life.

The biblical renewal of the Mass provides us with some distinct challenges in the days ahead. Although we have restored the ancient liturgical role of the reader at Mass, we have not spent enough time in the formation of readers. The message of the Scriptures is often obscured by readers who are unable to proclaim the sacred texts well in public. Readers need to be afforded the opportunity to learn the basics of public speaking, and they should also be given at least a basic understanding of the structure and content of the Lectionary and of the Bible. Poor readers should be assisted in discerning another ministry which they are able to carry out in an effective manner.

When readers, deacons, presbyters, and bishops neglect to prepare the readings before Mass, it results in a failure to communicate the word of God effectively. Other common failures are the reading, rather than the singing, of the responsorial psalm, often in a hurried manner so that it ceases to be a reflection on the first reading: the mumbling of the Alleluia, rather than singing it as an acclamation of praise before the proclamation of the gospel; and the absence of silence, giving us the opportunity to reflect on God's word and to receive it into our hearts. These things alone give us ample material for reflection and action. However, there is an additional area that is critical for the future life of the Church and in many cases needs much improvement: the homily.

Although preaching has improved in the last two decades, there are still many bishops, presbyters, and deacons who preach poorly and with little if any preparation. "Canned" homilies, while useful in sparking the preparation of the homilist, do not really speak to a particular community. There is no substitute for the prayerful reflection on the Scriptures and the equally prayerful studying of biblical commentaries in the preparation of a homily.

Ordained ministers also need to be assisted in learning the basics of public speaking so that they can communicate the message of the Scriptures in a manner that invites their hearers to be attentive to the message of God's word. Many dioceses might consider continuing education programs for clergy in order to assist them to improve their preaching skills and to feel comfortable as preachers. Parish or diocesan programs for the education and preparation of readers are still needed. And musicians need to be assisted in understanding the place of music in the liturgy of the word, especially the responsorial psalm and the gospel acclamation.

In its final consideration of the liturgy of the word, CSL 53 speaks of the restoration of the "universal prayer" or "prayer of the faithful." This prayer, in which the people are to take part, is to take place after the homily on Sunday and holydays of obligation. Based on chapter 2:1-2 of Paul's first letter to Timothy, all present pray for the Church, civil authorities, those oppressed by various needs, all people, and the salvation of the entire world. The earliest mention of these prayers is found in the mid-second century *Apology* of Saint Justin Martyr. The name "prayer of the faithful" comes from the practice of restricting participation in this prayer to the baptized. It originally began only after the catechumens had been dismissed and was concluded by the exchange of peace.

The prayer of the faithful disappeared early in the history of the Roman liturgy and left vestiges at two places in the old Missal. The greeting (The Lord be with you) and the invitation (Let us pray) before the offertory verse marked the beginning of the prayer of the faithful. The nine-fold Kyrie eleison at the beginning of the liturgy was all that remained of the prayer itself. On weekdays the petitions of the prayer were transferred to the beginning of the liturgy, and ultimately the petitions were omitted, leaving only the responses of the people: Kyrie eleison . . . Christe eleison . . . Kyrie eleison. There is only one place in the pre-Vatican II Missal where the ancient Roman prayer of the faithful was preserved—on Good Friday. The Solemn Liturgy of Good Friday preserves the old Roman form of intercessory prayer. The Solemn Intercessions of that day consist of a series of intercessions, each containing an invitation to pray (Let us pray, dear friends . . .), a direction to kneel for silent prayer, an invitation to stand, and a concluding prayer. Prayers were offered for the Church, the pope, all the clergy, civil leaders, catechumens, particular needs, those seperated from the Church, for the Jewish people, and for non-believers. These intercessions for Good Friday are found in essentially the same form in the *Sacramentary* today. The restored form of the prayer of the faithful, found in the Order of Mass, bears the title: General Intercessions. This new name recognizes that these prayers, as CSL 53 reminds us, are not to be restricted to local concerns, but rather are for the entire Church and the world as well.

Although the General Intercessions are once again an established part of the liturgy, there are some aspects of pastoral practice that need to be addressed. The intercessions are one of the few parts of the Mass where no liturgical texts are prescribed (although several models are given in one of the appendices of the *Sacramentary*). Instead of taking advantage of this freedom, which allows the intercessions to be fully integrated into the particular celebration, some communities often use the same petitions at each Mass, often with no relationship to the other parts of the liturgy of the word. Other parishes slavishly use published resources that take no account of contemporary affairs or needs. Some priests reserve the announcing of the petitions to themselves rather than having the deacon, a reader, or another minister proclaim the individual intentions or petitions. And in some places the intercessions cease to be "general," i.e., "universal," because the petitions offered are resticted merely to local concerns. Properly prepared, and reflecting the needs of the whole Church and the world as well as the local community, the General Intercessions can be a most effective element of the reformed liturgy.

In Memoriam: Monsignor Robert F. Hayburn

Monsignor Robert F. Hayburn, pastor emeritus of Saint Brigid Church in San Francisco and a noted organist and liturgical musician, died on May 18, 1991 after a heart attack and automobile accident.

Monsignor Hayburn served as the director of music for the Archdiocese of San Francisco from 1957 to 1977. He was instrumental in the establishment of the San Francisco archdiocesan office of worship and had served on the Board of Directors of the Federation of Diocesan Liturgical Commissions. He was a life member of the Music Educators National Conference, a member of the American Guild of Organists, a founding member of the Church Music Association of America, and a member of the Consociatio Internationalis Musicae Sacrae. In 1979 his study of papal documents on liturgical music, entitled *Papal Legislation on Sacred Music: 95 A.D. to 1977 A.D.*, was published by The Liturgical Press, Collegeville, MN.

> May choirs of angels welcome you, Robert,
> and lead you to the bosom of Abraham;
> and where Lazarus is poor no longer
> may you find eternal rest.

Plenary Assembly of the Congregation for Divine Worship

The January-February 1991 issue of *Notitiae* reported on the plenary assembly of the members of the Congregation for Divine Worship and the Discipline of the Sacraments which took place in Rome from January 21-29, 1991. Joseph Cardinal Bernardin, Archbishop of Chicago, is a member of the Congregation and participated in the meeting, which was the first one held since the Congregation for Divine Worship and the Congregation for the Sacraments were united in June 1988.

The Congregation reviewed and approved two documents that will be published in the future: *Adaptation of the Roman Liturgy to Different Cultures* and *The General Instruction of the Roman Ritual.*

The instruction on adaptation has been in preparation for over a decade and seeks to explain the nature of adaptation and inculturation of the liturgy. When published, this instruction should be of assistance in the ongoing implementation of articles 37-40 of the Constitution on the Liturgy *Sacrosanctum Concilium* [=SC], which state that, while respecting the substantial unity of the Roman Rite (SC 38), conferences of bishops may specify the adaptations provided for by the typical editions of the liturgical books (SC 39) and may also seek more radical adaptation of the liturgy to local cultures, i.e., inculturation (SC 40). The conferences of bishops must weigh what elements of local tradition and culture may be appropriately incorporated into the liturgy, and this can be done only with the consent of the Apostolic See (SC 40). It is required that such traditional or cultural elements must not be indissolubly bound up with superstition and error (SC 37).

The second document approved by the Congregation is a general introduction to the *Roman Ritual.* The Roman Ritual no longer exists as a single book, but rather is a collection of various orders for the celebration of the sacraments and the other rites of the Church. Even the distinction that once existed between the *Roman Ritual* and the *Roman Pontifical*, the latter being the book for the sacramental and other liturgical celebrations of the bishop, is no longer clear-cut. In particular circumstances a priest may preside at several "pontifical" rites. The new *General Instruction of the Roman Ritual* attempts to unite the various orders for the sacraments and other rites by providing a synthesis or compendium of the liturgical theology of the sacraments and sacramentals. It is a general pastoral guide which gathers together all the norms of a general nature concerning the celebration of the various rites. Thus, this general instruction will not replace the individual introductions (*praenotanda*) of each of the liturgical books; rather, it will complement and enrich them. Once the instruction is published, there will be general instructions to the *Roman Missal,* the *Liturgy of the Hours,* and the *Roman Ritual.*

The Congregation also examined a proposal for a second typical edition of the funeral rites. In particular, the Congregation was interested in providing material for circumstances in which cremation is used rather then burial or entombment.

The Congregation now possesses the responsibility for granting dispensations from the obligations of ordination for both priests and deacons, and there was a discussion of the process that the Congregation would follow in granting these dispensations.

There was also some discussion of the liturgical provisions for those persons who have been beatified. It would seem that the Congregation wishes to limit the liturgical expression of the veneration of those who have been beatified but not canonized.

One of the most important matters discussed by the Congregation was the question of a possible third typical edition of the *Roman Missal*, including the *Lectionary for Mass*. In the context of the need for reprinting the second Latin typical edition of the *Missale Romanum*, the question was raised whether the Missal should be updated to include the various changes that have taken place since the 1975 second typical edition was first published, e.g., new feasts, changes in the General Instruction of the Roman Missal (GIRM) necessitated by the promulgation of the 1983 *Code of Canon Law*, musical needs, etc. Such a revision would not be a "new" Missal, but a revised edition of the Missal of Paul IV that would offer the clergy and laity in a fuller manner the nourishment of faith and piety that is necessary for human santification and the glorification of God.

In practical terms the third edition of the Missal would include a revision of the General Instruction of the Roman Missal and a revision of some of the liturgical texts and chants of the Mass. According to the Congregation, some consideration would also have to be given to the introductory rites and the rites for the preparation of the gifts. Certainly, some of the adaptations already approved for individual countries would have to be reviewed and possibly inserted into the Latin edition of the Missal.

In addition to the revision of the Missal, some changes are being considered for the *Lectionary for Mass* and the books of chant, i.e., *Graduale Romanum (Roman Gradual)* and *Graduale Simplex (Simple Gradual)*. The work on the Lectionary is already in progress, and plans have been made to publish a new Latin edition of the Lectionary that uses the Neo-Vulgate translation of Scripture.

The process of preparing new editions of these liturgical books will take some time, and the Congregation indicated that other interested parties will be consulted.

The Congregation has prepared a draft version of the rite of exorcism and will make it available to those episcopal conferences that request it. Work continues on the *Roman Martyrology* and the supplementary volume for the *Liturgy of the Hours*. The supplement will contain the psalm prayers and the alternate cycle of readings for the Office of Readings.

In Memoriam: Archbishop John F. Whealon

The Most Reverend John F. Whealon, Archbishop of Hartford, Connecticut, died suddenly on August 2, 1991 at the age of 70. A priest of the diocese of Cleveland, John Whealon was born in 1921 and was ordained to the priesthood in 1945. He received the STL in Scripture from the Pontifical Biblical Institute in Rome in 1950. Ordained a bishop in 1961, he served as an auxiliary bishop of Cleveland until 1967, when he was appointed bishop of Erie, PA. He was transferred to the Archdiocese of Hartford in March 1969.

Archbishop Whealon served on many committees of the National Conference of Catholic Bishops (NCCB) and gave extended service to the Committees on Ecumenism, Liturgy, and Pastoral Practices, the last of which he chaired at the time of his death. He also was the chairman of an *ad hoc* committee of the NCCB which reviewed the revised edition of the *New American Bible*.

For the past six years Archbishop Whealon had been the chairman of the Liturgy Committee's Subcommittee on the Lectionary. He personally reviewed all the revisions of the Lectionary and looked forward to the final approval and publication of the new edition.

> O God,
> from the ranks of your priests
> you chose your servant John Francis
> to fulfill the office of bishop.
> Grant that he may share
> in the eternal fellowship of those priests
> who, faithful to the teachings of the apostles,
> dwell in your heavenly kingdom.

National Meeting of Diocesan Liturgical Commissions

The 1991 National Meeting of Diocesan Liturgical Commissions will be held from October 11-14 in Phoenix, AZ. The meeting, cosponsored by the NCCB Committee on the Liturgy and the Federation of Diocesan Liturgical Commissions, will have as its theme "Ritual: The Language of Transformation" and will feature as speakers: Dr. Megan McKenna ("The Art of Communicating God"); Rev. Richard Fragomini ("Ritual: An Encounter with Mystery"); Rev. John Baldovin, SJ ("Ritual: A Language that Allows Symbols to Speak"); and Nancy and Graziano Marcheschi ("Ritual: the Rhythm of Rite and Life"). Several workshops, developing particular aspects of the theme, will also be offered.

For registration forms and additional information concerning the meeting, contact: Office of Worship Diocese of Phoenix, 400 East Monroe, Phoenix, AZ 85004. Telephone: 602/257-5551.

Resources

Several new publications have recently been received by the Liturgy Secretariat. Especially recommended are the following:

Alice Parker, *Melodious Accord: Good Singing in Church.* This book (122 pages) is an excellent resource for those who are concerned about liturgical music. The author is a composer and arranger, conductor, and teacher. She deals with a variety of important topics: The Need for Song; Good Singing Forges Good Congregations; Ear and Eye; Musical Space and Time; A Brief History of Melody; Studying and Teaching; A Different View of the Hymnal; The Song Leader; Collaboration in the Community; Sounding Space; Sacred Song. Order from: Liturgy Training Publications, 1800 North Hermitage Avenue, Chicago, IL 60622-1101. Cost: $5.95.

James Dallen and Joseph Favazza, *Removing the Barriers: The Practice of Reconciliation.* The authors of this small book (76 pages) examine the development of the Church's practice of sacramental reconciliation through the centuries to provide insight into contemporary pastoral issues and questions surrounding the sacrament. Emphasis is given to communal realities: conversion into community, commitment to community, celebration in community. A reconciling Church lives holiness in common. A thought- and action-provoking study. Available from Liturgy Training Publications (see above). Cost: $5.95.

Mary M. Shaefer and J. Frank Henderson, *The Catholic Priesthood: A Liturgically Based Theology of the Presbyteral Office.* (*Canadian Studies in Liturgy,* No. 4, 111 pages.) Published in 1990 by the Episcopal Commission for Liturgy, Ottawa, this book provides a broad treatment of the history and theology of the order of presbyters as found in the liturgical rites and texts of the Church. Such an approach is important since it derives the theology of the presbyteral office directly from the liturgies by which it has been conferred in the Latin Church, rather than from a sacramental theology that is not based on the rites. The individual chapters treat the following subjects: Christ, Church and Baptism; Trinity and Church; History of Ordained Ministry; The Presbyterate; The Sacramental Nature of Presbyteral Office; The Charism of Ministerial Priesthood; The Priest's Life in the Church and World; Theological Conclusions. Order from: Publications Service, 90 Parent Avenue, Ottawa, Ontario K1N 7B1, Canada.

Edward J. Kilmartin, SJ, with an appendix by Mary M. Shaefer, *Culture and the Praying Church: The Particular Liturgy of the Individual Church.* (*Canadian Studies in Liturgy,* No. 5, 125 pages.) This 1990 work is a revision of a series of lectures that Father Kilmartin delivered in 1986. In order to speak of the inculturation of the liturgy, the author first deals with the Church: its relation to the Trinity and to the Liturgy: Church of God; Church of God as Individual Church; Church of the Holy Trinity. In the second part he treats the Liturgy of the Church: Culture, *Cultus* and Religion; Inculturation of the Liturgy; Martyria - Diakonia - Leitourgia; Mystery of the Liturgy and Its Celebration. Available from Publications Service, Ottawa (see above).

COMMITTEE ON THE LITURGY

NEWSLETTER

NATIONAL CONFERENCE OF CATHOLIC BISHOPS

1991
VOLUME XXVII
SEPTEMBER

NCCB Administrative Committee Meeting

The Administrative Committee of the National Conference of Catholic Bishops met on September 10-12, 1991 at the NCCB/USCC headquarters building in Washington, DC. In the course of the meeting Bishop Wilton D. Gregory, Chairman of the NCCB Liturgy Committee, requested that three action items of the Liturgy Committee and one joint action item of the Liturgy Committee and the Committee for Pastoral Practices be placed on the agenda of the November meeting of the NCCB. The Administrative Committee approved each of these motions.

The first action item contains two proposals relating to the revised edition of the *Lectionary for Mass*: 1) that the NCCB approve for liturgical use the new psalter of the *New American Bible* so that it may be included in the revised edition of the Lectionary; 2) that the NCCB approve two shorter versions of readings for inclusion in the Lectionary as alternatives. The Liturgy Committee will add a third proposal to this action item, asking the members of the NCCB to approve a slightly abbreviated translation of the text "*Verbum Domini*," which follows all readings in the lectionary, namely, "The word of the Lord," and "The gospel of the Lord."

The second action item asks the NCCB to approve for liturgical use the *New Revised Standard Version* (NRSV) of the Bible so that an edition of the lectionary using this translation may be prepared in addition to the one which will use the *New American Bible*. The third action item seeks NCCB approval of the proposed *Lectionary for Masses with Children*, developed by a special Task Group of the Liturgy Committee and the Federation of Diocesan Liturgical Commissions. Four proposals are included in this action item: 1) that the NCCB approve the *Introduction* to the lectionary; 2) that the NCCB approve the *cursus* of readings in the lectionary; 3) that the NCCB grant the *imprimatur* for the translation of the psalms and the Old Testament readings of the *Contemporary English Version* (CEV) of the Bible used in the lectionary (the CEV New Testament has already received the *imprimatur*); 4) that the NCCB approve for liturgical use the *Contemporary English Version* of the Bible which is proposed for use in the lectionary.

Finally, the fourth action item, jointly submitted by the Liturgy Committee and the Committee for Pastoral Practices in response to some *varia* submitted by bishops, presents several proposals which address the number of holy days of obligation observed in the dioceses of the United States and the pastoral issue of concurrent Sundays and holy days.

In his information report to the Administrative Committee Bishop Gregory began by introducing Sister Linda Gaupin, CDP, the new associate director of the Liturgy Secretariat. He also acknowledged the dedicated work of the late Archbishop John F. Whealon and the late Father Stephen Hartdegen, OFM, on the *Lectionary for Mass*.

Rereading the Constitution on the Liturgy (art. 54-58)

Articles 54-58 of the Constitution on the Liturgy (CSL) conclude the Council Fathers' treatment of the celebration of the eucharist. CSL 54 applies the provisions of article 36 concerning the use of vernacular languages in the liturgy to the celebration of the Mass. It states that, although the use of Latin is to be preserved in the Latin rites (Roman rite, Spanish rite, Ambrosian rite, and the rites or uses proper to several dioceses and religious orders), the readings, the general intercessions ("universal prayer"), and the parts belonging to the people may be celebrated in the mother tongue of the people. If the conferences of bishops wish to expand the use of the vernacular to other parts of the Mass, they are to follow the principles and procedures for the more radical adaptation of the liturgy given in CSL 40. The article concludes by stating that the faithful should be able to say or sing their parts of the Ordinary of the Mass in Latin.

These first steps taken by the Council to permit the Mass to be celebrated in the languages of the people may appear to be strange to persons who have become accustomed to the liturgy being celebrated for more than 25 years now in the vernacular, and perhaps even stranger to young people who have only known the liturgy in their own language. It serves as a good example of how the liturgical reforms mandated by the Council sometimes provided the impetus for even further reforms in subsequent years.

In keeping with the provisions of the motu proprio *Sacram Liturgiam* of January 25, 1964, no. IX, and the first Instruction *Inter Oecumenici* of September 26, 1964, nos. 30, 40, and 57, the bishops of the United States of America approved the use of English for the readings at Mass, the parts of the Ordinary pertaining to the people, the Lord's prayer and its introduction, the invitation to communion and its response, the psalms and antiphons of the propers, the dialogues in which the people participate, and the prayer of the faithful. In the United States, the first edition of the Roman Missal containing these English texts was published at the end of 1964.

The next development took place in 1966 when the *Latin-English Sacramentary* was published. All the prayers of the Mass were given in English with the exception of the private prayers of the priest and the Roman Canon (the preface was authorized to be prayed in the vernacular in April 1965). On January 23, 1967 Pope Paul VI permitted the use of vernacular translations of the Roman Canon. Cardinal G. Lercaro, president of the Concilium for the Implementation of the Constitution on the Liturgy, explained to the presidents of the episcopal conferences on June 21, 1967, that the translation of the Roman Canon into the various languages was "the last step in the *gradual extension of the vernacular.*"

When the revised *Missale Romanum* was published in 1970 (the Order of Mass and the General Instruction of the Roman Missal were published separately in April 1969), the International Commission on English in the Liturgy (ICEL) was entrusted with the task of preparing a common translation of the missal for use in the various English-speaking countries. ICEL was established by the English-speaking conferences of bishops in conformity with no. 40 of the first Instruction on the orderly carrying out of the Constitution on the Liturgy (*Inter Oecumenici*) of September 26, 1964, which provides for joint effort by bishops of regions using the same language to arrive at a common translation.

ICEL quickly set about the task of translating all the liturgical books as they were issued by the Apostolic See. Liturgical, linguistic, biblical, patristic, and musical scholars were pressed into service to produce the new English liturgical books. With almost no past experience to rely upon, ICEL had to develop a contemporary style of liturgical language for use in the Catholic Church. This was a difficult task, since the translations had to satisfy a variety of cultures and nations. Translations were produced in a provisional form (called "Green Books" from the color of their covers), and, after one or more years of use, they were revised and submitted to the episcopal conferences for final approval (the so-called "White Books"). Over the past ten years, ICEL has engaged in a process of reviewing its earlier translations and producing a second generation of the revised liturgical books that take into account the various positive and negative comments that it has received about the rites.

ICEL is now engaged in a complete revision of the English translation of the missal. This work is expected to be completed within the next three years. The new translations which have been completed to date and which have been published in ICEL's progress reports on the revision are fine examples of the translator's art and reflect a maturity in the style of liturgical translation.

Critics of the present English liturgical texts sometimes complain that the texts don't say much. At times, the real problem may lie less with the critics' perceiving deficiencies in the English translations than with their not knowing the nature of the Latin originals. Latin prayer style tends to be brief and concise, frequently employing some often repeated basic themes. English prayer style, on the other hand, usually requires expansion of the compact Latin text and a greater use of imagery. A good translation will communicate the sense of the Latin original while respecting and reflecting the character and beauty of the vernacular language and the people who speak that language today. Viewed from this perspective, the work of the ICEL Secretariat staff, its translators, and its experts in liturgy, music, theology, scripture, and literature, deserves the deep thanks of the Church in all countries where English is spoken for making a significant contribution to the ongoing development of "liturgical English."

While English has been a liturgical language of the United States since 1964, it is not this country's only language approved for liturgical use. Mindful that Spanish is spoken by an increasingly large number of American Catholics, the members of the NCCB Administrative Committee on September 11, 1984 approved Spanish as a liturgical language in the United States. The Apostolic See confirmed this action on January 19, 1985 (see *Newsletter*, vol. XXI, February 1985). Since that time the Hispanic Liturgy

Subcommittee of the Bishops' Committee on the Liturgy has been preparing American editions of the liturgical books in Spanish which conform to those available in English. The *Rite of Christian Initiation of Adults* will soon be available in Spanish, the *Order of Christian Funerals* is in final preparation, and *Sunday Celebrations in the Absence of a Priest* will soon be published in a bilingual (English-Spanish) edition. Work is continuing on an American edition of the Sacramentary in Spanish, and several other translation projects are planned.

Several languages of Native Americans have also been approved for use in the liturgy: Navajo (November 19, 1983), Choctaw (October 1, 1984), Pima-Papago (October 16, 1987), and Lakota (December 12, 1989). And because of the growing number of refugees from Southeast Asia to the United States, it may one day be necessary to approve some of their languages for liturgical use in this country in order that Asian-American editions of liturgical books might legitimately be prepared.

The concern to introduce vernacular languages into liturgical celebrations in order to foster active participation may have led many to neglect the request of the Council that the people be able to say or sing together in Latin their proper parts of the Mass. It is not inappropriate, on occasion, for the Kyrie to be sung in Greek or the Sanctus or Agnus Dei or one of the more popular hymns (e.g. Rorate Coeli, Attende Domine, Pange Lingua, Adore Te Devote, Salve Regina) to be sung in Latin by the people. This will help to preserve the Church's Latin liturgical heritage and the venerable corpus of Gregorian chant.

The use of a vernacular language in the liturgy does not necessarily guarantee that the liturgy will be understood by all or that it will be more prayerful than a celebration in Latin. Understanding the liturgy means more than simply hearing the words in the vernacular. It also entails efforts to engage all the Christian faithful, clergy and laity alike, in liturgical, catechetical, and scriptural formation and renewal in order to achieve the full, conscious, and active participation of the liturgical assembly.

Careful preparation of the ritual texts, attentiveness to the quality and beauty of the Church's ritual symbols and gestures, and collaboration with trained liturgical musicians and artists all contribute to celebrations which can have a transforming effect in the lives the faithful. The suitable preparation of liturgical ministers so that they have a facility with the rites and skills appropriate to their ministry is also important in this regard.

CSL 55 states that the most complete form of participation of the faithful in the Mass is when they receive holy communion after the priest "from the same sacrifice." This first part of the article addresses several important points. The people participate most fully in the Mass when they receive holy communion. Fortunately, non-communicating attendance at Mass has become a rare occurrence. It is common today to see the majority of the congregation receiving communion at each Mass. However, all need to be reminded on occasion that spiritual preparation for the reception of the eucharist is essential, and communion should not be received merely out of habit.

The people are to receive communion after the priest has received the sacrament. The former practice of distributing communion at any time during the liturgy of the eucharist can no longer be justified. And, as the popes throughout this century have indicated, communion should be distributed from eucharistic bread consecrated at the Mass being celebrated. Every effort should be made to implement this clear instruction, with communion from the reserved sacrament becoming an increasingly rare exception to the rule. This is relatively easy to do at weekday Masses where the number of people remains basically the same day after day. Even on Sundays the number of communicants remains fairly consistent, and so no one should have to go to the tabernacle for eucharistic bread consecrated at another liturgy. Seasonal variations and special celebrations may require extra preparations, but those who minister as sacristans and ushers/greeters can be helpful in determining the amount of bread and wine needed for these situations.

The second paragraph of CSL 55 permits the distribution of holy communion under both kinds. Although the article gives only three examples, the list of circumstances when this may be done has been increased in the subsequent liturgical documents. In the United States, communion may be given under both kinds at virtually every Mass, Sunday or weekday. The document, *This Holy and Living Sacrifice*, which was prepared by the NCCB at the request of the Apostolic See, provides the theological background to this practice as well as the proper procedure for carrying out the rite. Consecrated wine is not to be reserved, except when it will be brought later to the sick (see *Pastoral Care of the Sick: Rites of Anointing and Viaticum*, no. 74). Nor is the blood of Christ which remains after communion to be poured into the sacrarium or onto the ground. In order to avoid the unsightly use of many cups on the altar which obscures the symbolism of the one bread and one cup, a flagon may be used for the wine.

The restoration of the cup to all the faithful in the rite of holy communion pertains to the fullness of the sign of the eucharist and should not be dismissed as "only an option." Communion under both kinds should more and more become the usual and expected practice. Needless to say, particularly in view of contemporary health concerns, care should be taken that the inner and outer rim of cup be wiped and the cup slightly rotated after each communicant has received. The minister of the cup should also use a different part of the purificator each time the cup is wiped. And eucharistic ministers need be be taught the proper signs of reverence and respect for the eucharist so that their handling of the eucharist will never appear to be routine or casual.

CSL 56 reaffirms that the liturgy of the word and the liturgy of the eucharist, the two parts of the Mass, are so intrinsically connected that they form but "one single act of worship." The Council directs that the faithful are to be given sufficient catechesis in this understanding. Rejected is the former popularly-held notion that missing Mass occurs only if one arrives after the "offertory." The obligation to participate in the celebration of the eucharist pertains to the entire celebration; the Christian community is nourished at both the table of God's word and at the eucharistic table when it assembles for Mass.

In CSL 57-58 the Council Fathers call for the restoration of a form of concelebration of the eucharist by several bishops or presbyters. They decree the preparation of a new rite for concelebration and for the extension of the permission to bishops and presbyters to concelebrate on particular occasions. Permission for concelebration has been extended to a number of occasions by the revised liturgical books.

It belongs to the bishop alone to regulate the practice of concelebration in his diocese. He is to indicate when it is permitted and appropriate. Church law gives the individual bishop and presbyter the right to *celebrate* an individual Mass, but it does not give the priest the right to *concelebrate* merely because he may wish to do so. In addition, the freedom of priests *not* to concelebrate is to be respected.

Several practical aspects about concelebration might be recalled. Once a concelebrated Mass has begun, priests who have arrived late are not to join in. A priest may not concelebrate without wearing the proper vestments and reciting (inaudibly) the appointed portions of the eucharistic prayer. The guidelines on concelebration prepared by the NCCB Liturgy Committee and approved by the NCCB Administrative Committee (see *Newsletter,* Vol. XXIII, September/October 1987) should be carefully studied by bishops and presbyters.

Careful reflection is needed on the positive and negative features of concelebration. The rite is intended as a sign of the unity of the bishop with his presbyters, deacons, and faithful around the altar. It should not be a matter of interest to clergy alone, nor is it meant to clericalize the Eucharist. It certainly should not be allowed to become a sign of division at the very time when the eucharist should unite the Church.

Often times concelebration is misunderstood as a "co-presidency" of concelebrating priests. To concelebrate is obviously not the same as to preside, and in ordinary circumstances there is only one presiding celebrant at the Eucharist. These issues, along with others arising from the practice of concelebration, illustrate the need for further theological, liturgical, and pastoral reflection on the rite.

Liturgical Resources for the Visually Impaired

The Liturgy Secretariat has recently received information concerning LARGE TYPE PRINT editions of the Gospel readings and presidential prayers (Opening Prayer, Prayer over the Gifts, Prayer after Communion, the four Eucharistic Prayers and Prefaces) for the Mass, along with the Rite of Viaticum, and the Rite of Baptism for Children. The texts are being made available to priests with visual impairment. Mass texts are available for Sunday and weekday celebrations. Font sizes range from 20 to 44 points in regular or bold print. Some materials are already on computer disk, and others will be created upon request. For more information contact: Mrs. Susan T. Woodward, 4704 Chevy Chase Boulevard, Chevy Chase, MD 30815-5342 or call (301) 652-9099.

COMMITTEE ON THE LITURGY

NEWSLETTER

NATIONAL CONFERENCE OF CATHOLIC BISHOPS

1991
VOLUME XXVII
OCTOBER

FDLC Address of Bishop Wilton D. Gregory

On October 11, 1991, the Most Reverend Wilton D. Gregory, Auxiliary Bishop of Chicago and chairman of the Bishops' Committee on the Liturgy addressed the delegates to the 1991 National Meeting of Diocesan Liturgy Commissions in Phoenix, AZ. The text of that address follows.

It is an honor and a great pleasure for me to be able to address the delegates to the 1991 National Meeting of Diocesan Liturgical Commissions. As you can see from the written report that has been provided for you and from the information contained in the monthly Newsletter, the Committee and its secretariat have been engaged in a number of time-consuming projects. I will mention only a few of them here; you can refer to our report for additional information.

The Lectionary for Masses with Children will be presented to the NCCB for approval in November. The Lectionary for Mass is nearing completion and will be presented to the bishops in June of this coming year. Sunday Celebrations in the Absence of a Priest will be published in a bilingual edition at the end of this year or early next year.

The tasks of the Secretariat are now being eased somewhat by the recent addition of Sister Linda Gaupin to the professional staff. Having served as director of the office for worship of the Diocese of Wilmington, DE, she is one of your own and is thoroughly acquainted with the liturgical needs and problems experienced in a diocese. I join Father Ronald Krisman and Monsignor Alan Detscher in welcoming her to the Secretariat.

You are all well aware of how far we have come in the renewal of the worship of the Church during the past quarter century. We have seen the revision, that is, the restoration and renewal, of nearly all the liturgical books, their translation into English, Spanish and, in some cases, one of the many languages of Native Americans. But it is clear that transforming liturgical rites does not necessarily guarantee the transformation of the lives of the baptized, especially their spiritual lives. We now have revised editions of the liturgical books, but the purpose of the liturgical reforms is not new books, but new lives, lives that are restored, reformed, and renewed.

We have a new Roman Missal (Sacramentary and Lectionary for Mass) and yet it is obvious that many persons, including a fair number of priests and deacons, unfortunately still do not understand the principles according to which these important liturgical books were revised. The time has come to begin once again a concerted effort at catechesis on the missal. The General Instruction of the Roman Missal and the Introduction to the Lectionary are not so much collections of rubrics as they are excellent sources of catechesis on the Mass and the reasons that underlie the reforms. As such, they must be read again and again by ministers. I know that each time I reread these foundational documents I find something new that gives me new insight into the reform of the Mass.

But a renewed catechesis is not just necessary for the clergy. There are too many parishes where there never was any real catechesis on the Mass and its reforms and even more where the introduction of the reformed rites was haphazard or even minimal. This task becomes even more urgent when we realize that within the next five years we will have a new edition of the Sacramentary. Hopefully, we will not repeat the errors of the past, and adequate catechesis will precede its introduction.

A second area that presents a challenge to us is that of worship for and with children. The publication of the Roman Directory for Masses with Children in 1973 provided for the adaptation of the rites and texts of the missal so that children might be able to enter more deeply into the celebration of the eucharist. Unfortunately, we have not always given the direction and assistance needed by those who plan and lead liturgies with children. One often gets the impression that religious educators have taken over children's

3211 FOURTH STREET NE • WASHINGTON, DC 20017

liturgies and are using them for catechetical purposes. Certainly there is nothing wrong with formation through the liturgy. However, the Mass is never to be reduced simply to a catechetical opportunity; it is worship.

The publication of the new Lectionary for Masses with Children, requested several years ago in a position statement approved by the delegates to another national meeting of diocesan liturgical commissions, will provide us with another opportunity to reemphasize the nature of Masses with children and the manner in which they are to be celebrated. There is much being written about so-called "lectionary based catechesis." We must ensure that the liturgy of the word at celebrations of the eucharist is not confused with such catechesis. The two should be complementary, and religious education should not replace a genuine experience of the Church's worship.

A third concern that must be addressed in the months ahead is that of the celebration of the Liturgy of the Hours. The Church's daily prayer must become just that. The Liturgy of the Hours is not the exclusive prayer of the clergy and religious; nor is it simply the prayer of single individuals; it is the prayer of the Church gathered in faith to praise God. Of course, clergy and religious have a special responsibility to pray with and for the Church, and there are times when the office, of necessity, must be prayed alone, but the Liturgy of the Hours remains the communal prayer of the Church. Many parishes have begun celebrating evening prayer during Lent, Holy Week, and the Easter Triduum, and this is a very good beginning. However, we need further efforts to extend the parish celebration of the hours to more and more occasions.

Serious study must be given to determine what changes need to be made in the Liturgy of the Hours to make parish celebrations more popular. The celebration of the hours in religious communities of women is also of vital concern today. The issue of inclusive language lies at the heart of the problem for many such communities. Various attempts to make the translation of the psalms and other texts more inclusive have resulted in alterations that are not approved and, in some cases, may even be heterodox and unpleasant to ears and spirits sensitive to beautiful poetry and prose. The newly revised psalter of the New American Bible should be of some assistance in resolving difficulties, since it deals in a careful manner with the use of inclusive language regarding persons and limits the use of masculine pronouns for God in accordance with the principles approved by the American bishops. ICEL is also in the process of revising many of the other texts of the divine office and intends to issue them in a resource collection for interim use until the complete revision of the translation of the Liturgy of the Hours can be undertaken after the publication of the Sacramentary.

One of the greatest concerns for our liturgical agenda in the days ahead is that of the inculturation of the liturgy. The liturgical books provide for various accommodations that can be made in the revised rites by the conferences of bishops and, in certain cases, by the presiding minister. The broader adaptation of the liturgy was foreseen by the Constitution on the Sacred Liturgy, art. 37-40. These articles of the Constitution, especially art. 40, make provision for the more radical adaptation of the liturgy to local cultures and customs provided they are not bound up with superstition or error (art. 37). In reality, little has been done to adapt the liturgy in this broader sense of inculturation or adaptation to local cultures.

In order to inculturate the liturgy we must first be able to identify those aspects of our life which truly reflect our American cultures and then decide if they are values which would contribute to the celebration of the liturgy. The problem is to identify the various elements that constitute our particular American cultures. Our nation manifests so many cultures that have blended together, and some that have remained quite distinct, that a great deal of work needs to be done before we can really speak of radical adaptation of the liturgy to make it fully American and still be faithful to the Roman rite. That is not to say that we should do nothing at the present time. Currently a task group is examining all of the American modifications in the present edition of the Sacramentary with a view toward their being incorporated into the long-awaited ICEL revision of the missal. The task group will have to deal with additional proposed variations in the Order of Mass and the other parts of the missal. In the process of doing this, the bishops and diocesan liturgical commissions will be consulted. Not all the ideas that will be surfaced will be good or helpful, but your cooperation is essential if the work of that task group is to be fruitful.

Surely the past twenty-eight years have provided the Church in this country with some definite ideas concerning the need for some distinctively American liturgical variations. But, at the same time, we should not lose sight of the larger scope of the revision as the quite serious business of fashioning a praying Church, a people who gather in faith to be nourished by Christ as His word is proclaimed and His eucharistic body and blood is shared.

In many ways, we are the liturgical "idea persons" in our dioceses. But it is very important that we do not lose contact with the legitimate needs and aspirations of our people. We must be fully grounded in the liturgical traditions of the Church with all of their breadth and variations. We must also seek to understand the often disparate longings of the people we hope to assist in praising God. Given the complexity of American society and the universal nature of the Church, this will be no easy task as we face the dawn of the Third Millennium of Christianity.

The first stage of the reform of the liturgy which began in 1963 may have been easy by comparison since it called for the revision of the texts of the liturgy based upon the restoration of the classical shape of the Roman liturgy. This primary stage was to give way to a secondary effort which would result in the adaptation of the revised books of worship to the living social and cultural circumstances of the people who use those texts in their praise of God. Finally, the Church in each of its local expressions is called to allow our worship to translate into action—right worship must result in right living. No one of these stages of liturgical reform is complete in itself; neither can any single stage of liturgical reform exist in isolation. Perhaps the most challenging task for the Church is to understand our liturgical reform as a process that is grafted to the very nature of the Church, which itself is a communion of people continually experiencing its own reform.

Those of us who are so centrally and regularly in contact with the Church's worship must be the very first people who admit of the change which the liturgy works in our own lives. We must be those who stand in awe and wonder and in humble submission to the transforming power of the worship of God. We cannot be afraid to admit hasty judgments, premature opinions, and those liturgical issues that are not yet ready for final decisions. We must be willing to allow the traditions of the Church to inform our work even as we probe the richness of our many cultures, customs, and aspirations as people of the 21st Century.

Speaking for the bishops of the United States of America, I want to thank you and your colleagues for all that you have done for our Church in helping us to worship God with grace and beauty. Thank you for your patience and faith and charity. We could not have accomplished so much without you, and we are confident that with you the liturgical life of the Church in America is bright indeed.

1991 National Meeting of Diocesan Liturgical Commissions

The annual national meeting of diocesan liturgical commissions and offices of worship was held in Phoenix, AZ from October 11-14, 1991. More than 230 delegates, representing over 120 dioceses, attended the meeting, which was jointly sponsored by the Federation of Diocesan Liturgical Commissions and the NCCB Committee on the Liturgy. They were joined by over 350 local parish liturgical ministers.

The general theme of the meeting was "Ritual: The Language of Transformation." Major presentation were given by Dr. Megan McKenna, Nancy and Graziano Marcheschi, Reverend John Baldovin, S.J, and Reverend Richard Fragomeni.

The delegates voted on several position statements which had been formulated at regional meetings of the delegates during the spring of 1991. Four statements received the requisite level of support needed for action to be taken on them by the FDLC Board of Directors at its next meeting in January. The delegates recommended the preparation of a Rite of Renewal of Commitment to Priestly Service which could be celebrated independent of the annual Chrism Mass. They supported concerted effort by all diocesan commissions and offices of worship to assign high priority to "the work of promoting the Eucharist as the culmination of Christian initiation." They authorized the development of a resource to assist parishes in eliminating the widespread practice of distributing Holy Communion to the faithful at Mass with hosts consecrated at a previous Mass, a practice strongly discouraged by the General Instruction of the Roman Missal and other revised liturgical books. And they asked the bishops of the United States to address "the urgent need to provide for the complete range of sacramental ministry and weekly celebration of the Sunday Mass by actively seeking means to broaden access to ordained ministry." Finally, the delegates approved a resolution of immediate concern, drafted in the course of the national meeting, which expressed support for an action to be considered by the bishops of the United States in November, namely, that the solemnity of the Ascension of the Lord be transferred to the Seventh Sunday of Easter.

During the business session of the FDLC Board of Directors which was held on October 11, Sr. Anthony Poerio, IBVM, of Phoenix was elected chairperson for the coming two years. Also elected as officers of the Board of Directors were: Reverend James P. Moroney (Worcester), vice-chairperson; Reverend Richard Butler (Boston), treasurer; Mr. Peter Ghiloni (Milwaukee) and Reverend Daniel Vogelpohl (Covington), delegates-at-large.

Newsletter Subscription Renewals

All subscribers to the Bishops' Committee on the Liturgy *Newsletter* will be sent computerized renewal notices in late November for the upcoming 1992 calendar year. To avoid interruption in service, the completed forms should be returned promptly. (Subscriptions which have not been renewed by the time of the January 1992 *Newsletter* goes to press will be placed on an inactive list and reinstated once payment is received.) Because of recent postage increases, individual subscription rates for 1992 have increased by one dollar to $10.00 domestic mail and $12.00 foreign mail. Bulk rates have increased 5 percent.

In order that subscribers' accounts may be properly credited, the instructions accompanying the renewal forms should be followed. The "renewal coupon" portion of the invoice must be included with payment. Coupon and payment should be returned in the self-mailer envelope which has been provided. This envelope is preaddressed for direct deposit to the bank. Payment should not be sent to the NCCB Secretariat for the Liturgy because it needlessly slows the renewal process.

Subscribers who have not received a renewal notice by December 13, 1991, should contact the Liturgy Secretariat so that a duplicate invoice can be sent. (*Newsletter* recipients whose subscription number is 205990, 205995, or 205999 are receiving gratis copies and therefore, will receive no renewal notice.)

The gratitude of the Liturgy Secretariat is extended to all subscribers for their cooperation in the *Newsletter* renewal process.

Resources

Plenty Good Room: The Spirit and Truth of African American Catholic Worship is the companion document to *In Spirit and Truth: Black Catholic Reflections on the Order of Mass.* A joint statement of the Secretariats for the Liturgy and for Black Catholics, *Plenty Good Room* is written with a particular view toward the African American Catholic community. The first three chapters, however, set out the basic principles for the relationship between culture and religious experience and are applicable to any culturally distinct community. The final four chapters focus directly on the African American religious experience. Publication No. 385-X, cost $9.95 (plus $1.50 postage and handling). Order from USCC Publishing Services in writing or by calling their toll free number: 1-800-235-USCC. *Plenty Good Room* is also available through the Josephite Fathers and the Federation of Diocesan Liturgical Commissions.

Gathered in Steadfast Faith: Statement of the Bishops' Committee on the Liturgy on Sunday Worship in the Absence of a Priest addresses the pastoral issues associated with the phenomenon of Sunday assemblies deprived of the celebration of the Mass. The publication of this statement, approved by the Liturgy Committee in 1989, coincides with the late fall release of the bilingual (English-Spanish) ritual edition of *Sunday Celebrations in the Absence of a Priest: Leader's Edition.* The statement reviews the tradition of Sunday as the Lord's day and also discusses the selection, training, commissioning, and continuing formation of ministers for these Sunday celebrations, the general principles of liturgical prayer which are applicable, and the structure which such celebrations should take. Publication No. 361-2, cost $1.95. Order from USCC Publishing Services.

Book of the Names of the Dead may be used to benefit by churches which have the custom of giving a place of honor to a book in which parishioners write the names of deceased relatives and friends. The size and dimensions of the book are large enough to guarantee its use for several years. The right side of each page includes graphics as well as texts from the *Order of Christian Funerals.* Pages are unlined, providing the freedom to write large or small anywhere on the page. Order from Liturgy Training Publications, 1800 North Hermitage Avenue, Chicago, IL 60622-1101. Telephone: 1-800-933-1800. Cost $49.95.

COMMITTEE ON THE LITURGY

NEWSLETTER

1991
VOLUME XXVII
NOVEMBER/DECEMBER

NATIONAL CONFERENCE OF CATHOLIC BISHOPS

November Plenary Assembly of the NCCB

The National Conference of Catholic Bishops met in plenary assembly from November 11-14, 1991, at the Omni Shoreham Hotel, Washington, DC. During the course of their meeting, the bishops approved several liturgical action items presented by the Committee on the Liturgy.

The items approved by the required two thirds majority vote of the *de iure* members and which now require confirmation by the Apostolic See are: the Introduction to the *Lectionary for Masses with Children*; the cursus of readings for inclusion in the *Lectionary for Masses with Children*; the *Contemporary English Version* of the Bible, prepared by the American Bible Society, approved for use in the liturgy in the dioceses of the United States of America in the *Lectionary for Masses with Children*; the new Book of Psalms of the *New American Bible,* approved for use in the liturgy in the dioceses of the United States of America; the addition of two alternative (shorter) readings for incorporation into the revised *Lectionary for Mass*; the *New Revised Standard Version* of the Bible, approved for use in the liturgy in the dioceses of the United States. The bishops by a simple majority vote granted the *imprimatur* for the psalms and Old Testament readings taken from the American Bible Society's *Contemporary English Version* (CEV) which will be used in the approved *Lectionary for Masses with Children*.

The Committee on the Liturgy and the Committee for Pastoral Practices jointly submitted for discussion and voting by the members of the NCCB six motions dealing with the observance of holy days of obligation in the dioceses of the United States. The following motions failed to receive a two thirds majority vote from the *de iure* Latin rite members: approval to transfer the celebration of the solemnity of the Ascension to the Seventh Sunday of Easter; and the three (3) separate motions to remove January 1, August 15, and October 1 respectively from the list of holy days of obligation in the dioceses of the United States. Voting on the motions that January 1, August 15, and November 1 will not be observed as holy days of obligation in the dioceses of the United States when they fall either on a Saturday and/or on a Monday remains inconclusive pending the reception of the mail-in votes of *de iure* Latin rite members of the NCCB who were not present at the time of the balloting during the meeting.

Rereading the Constitution on the Liturgy (art. 59-63)

Articles 59-63 of the Constitution on the Liturgy (CSL) introduce chapter 3 ("The Other Sacraments and the Sacramentals") by providing the foundational theological and pastoral principles for the comprehensive revision and adaptation of the rites for celebrating the sacraments and sacramentals of the Church.

CSL 59 reflects the growth in liturgical and biblical scholarship during the course of the last century. It departs from the structural language used to describe sacraments in preconciliar times and uses language that is liturgical and more dynamic in nature. Whereas scholastic theology perceived sacraments in terms of "objective realities", CSL 59 describes them in terms of lively expressions whose purpose is "to make people holy, to build up the Body of Christ, and, finally, to give worship to God."

During the first millennium before the Church settled on a precise definition and number of sacraments, there existed hundreds of rites which were referred to as "sacraments." When the Second Council of Lyons (1274) determined seven of these as the number instituted by Christ that signified what they effect, these various other rites and objects came to be known as sacramentals.

CSL 60 reaffirms the importance of sacramentals in daily life. Sacramentals "resemble" sacraments. They differ in the sense that they cause grace primarily through the faith and devotion of those who are

3211 FOURTH STREET NE • WASHINGTON, DC 20017

using, receiving, or celebrating them (*ex opere operantis*). Their value exists in the fact that they help to nuance the particular dimensions of our "daily" Christian lives. Through them we are able to see our daily human experiences as holy. In the process we become better disposed to "receive the chief effect of the sacraments." Sacraments and sacramentals, then, mutually enrich each other.

CSL 61 situates sacraments at the core of the Christian life. Not only are they integral to Christian living, they are necessary for the nourishment of Christian life. They sanctify almost every event of our lives "by the divine grace that flows from the paschal mystery of Christ's passion, death and resurrection." This sacramental vision is a radical departure from past notions of sacraments as "rewards" for righteous living or things "we" earn for proper behavior. Rather they are meant to transform all our basic human experiences: birth, life, ministry, love, sickness, sin and reconciliation, death, etc. "There is hardly any proper use of material things that cannot thus be directed toward human sanctification and the praise of God." Ritual plays a vital role in all of this. CSL 61 states that it is the "liturgy" of the sacraments and sacramentals that sanctifies. Ritual is the medium used to realize formally the meaning of the sacrament and to relate it to our contemporary human experience.

CSL 62 acknowledges the need for the revision of the Church's sacramental rites. The lack of clarity in ritual expression has "made their nature and purpose less clear to the people of today." It is interesting to note that the proposed text for this section included a statement that this has had a "detrimental effect on the faithful." Even though these words were not included in the final text, the concern for revision of the rites so that they have meaning for the faithful is nevertheless evident.

In the course of time, particularly during the middle ages, many rites took on certain features that not only obscured their meaning but in some instances actually altered it as well, for example, the gradual transformation of the anointing of the sick to a sacrament of the dying or extreme unction. In addition, adaptations were sometimes made to the rites which took into account the historical situation and the needs of the people of a particular cultural and historical era but which no longer address the realities and human experiences of our own times and culture.

Thus CSL 62 calls for changes in the sacramental rites that are "necessary as adaptations to the needs of our own times." The revisions envisioned here are twofold. First, they must take into account the revisions already called for in CSL 34 and 50. Article 34 directs that the changes made in the rites be distinguished by a noble simplicity and that they be short, clear, and free from useless repetitions; and article 50 directs that those parts which were duplicated or added with little advantage be omitted and other parts which suffered loss through accidents of history be restored to the vigor they had in the days of the holy Fathers as may seem useful or necessary. Secondly, CSL 62 calls for the sacramental rites to be adapted to address the present-day needs of the faithful. The task of revision includes those things which pertain to correcting, updating, or improving the rites in terms of their classical shape in the Roman liturgy. Adaptation requires a further step in the process whereby the rites are also changed to address the needs of the local Churches.

CSL 63 sets forth the parameters for change in terms of the language and the preparation of the rites. Although it is taken for granted today that the liturgy is celebrated in the vernacular, such was not the case at the time of the council. CSL 63 (a) permits the use of the vernacular in the celebration of the sacraments and sacramentals according to the norms set forth in CSL 36.

CSL 63 (b) deals with the preparation of the particular rituals. The process for liturgical reform was envisioned to take place in two phases. The process begins with the preparation of the *editio typica*, a liturgical model which serves as a norm for the preparation of particular rituals by bishops' conferences. The second phrase is the adaptation of the *editio typica* to the needs of the local Churches. This is done by competent, territorial ecclesiastical authority, or conferences of bishops, who do so by virtue of their right to preside over the liturgical life of the local Churches. These rituals must be submitted to the Apostolic See for approval.

The preparation of particular rituals realizes the conciliar concern to adapt the rites to the present day needs of the local Churches. Thus they are not intended to be a word for word translation of the *editio typica*. On the other hand they should not be prepared in isolation from the Latin edition but are to preserve the substantial unity of the Roman rite. This latter norm guarantees that the principles and criteria for liturgical reform, safeguarded in the Roman rite, will be integral to the particular rites as well.

The *editio typica* of a liturgical book allows for considerable freedom and room for creativity in the preparation of particular rituals. The general introduction of each liturgical book contains a heading entitled "Adaptations by the Conferences of Bishops." The purpose of this section is to promote and foster cultural adaptations of the rite.

Adaptations of particular rituals may take place in the introductions to the liturgical books, the rearrangements of parts of the rite, and the composition of new liturgical texts when optional formularies are permitted according to the fundamental norms set out by the *Constitution on the Liturgy*. CSL 40 even permits more radical adaptation. CSL 63 (b) points out, however, that "those who draw up these rituals or particular collections of rites must not leave out the prefatory instructions for the individual rites in the Roman Ritual, whether the instructions are pastoral and rubrical or have some special social bearing."

The issue of adaptation of the rites has often times been misunderstood. On the one hand there are those who do not realize that liturgical adaptation is seen as a value in the Church and that norms promoting and governing adaptation are set out in the *Constitution on the Liturgy*. Contrary to some expectations this means that in the course of time changes will continue to be made in our liturgical books both for the *editio typica* as well as for particular rituals. On the other hand some persons interpret liturgical adaptation to mean the freedom to change any part of the rite (or not to use the rite at all) based on what they perceive the people's "need" or "want." CSL 63 (b) cites the general norms for the reform of the sacred liturgy as found in CSL 22. Part three of this article states: "Therefore, no other person, not even if he is a priest, may on his own add, remove, or change anything in the liturgy." This does not mean that the minister may not make any variations in the rite. Occasions where this can be done are listed in the introductions to the liturgical books in the sections "Adaptations by the Minister" and are contained in the rubrics of each rite as well. There is sufficient latitude in each of the revised rites to allow for adaptation to the needs of the assembly. The criteria for such, however, is the fostering of full, conscious, and active participation of the faithful.

To make full and proper use of the options offered in the liturgical books, it is important that ministers and those who assist in the preparation of liturgical celebrations have a *thorough knowledge of the rite*. Liturgical preparation begins with the ritual text itself. Familiarity with the ritual options and careful liturgical preparation *in advance* of the celebration and/or season goes a long way to promote a fruitful celebration of the rites. It allows the rites to speak to the human experiences of the assembly gathered to worship together as the Body of Christ.

November 1991 Liturgy Committee Meeting

The NCCB Liturgy Committee met in Washington, DC, on November 10, 1991. The Committee reviewed the liturgical action items on the agenda of the NCCB plenary meeting and also discussed: 1) a survey on possible adaptations to the Roman Missal for the dioceses of the United States; 2) comments received on the use of the wedding candle at marriages; 3) proposed American adaptations to the revised rites of ordination; 4) position statements from the 1991 National Meeting of Diocesan Liturgical Commissions; and 5) first draft of proposed procedures for including saints or blessed on the proper calendar for the dioceses of the United States.

Reports were made on the status of various projects of the subcommittees and task groups of the Liturgy Committee, including future publications; the status of the *Lectionary for Mass*; the work of the Hispanic Liturgy Subcommittee; and the work of the Task Group on Cremation and Other Funeral Practices.

Resolutions of the 1991 National Meeting of Diocesan Liturgical Commissions

The following position statements were adopted by the delegates to the 1991 National Meeting of Diocesan Liturgical Commissions, held in Phoenix, Arizona, October 11-14, 1991. The degree of commitment to each statement is indicated in parentheses. The voting scale is graded from +3 (highest degree of commitment) to -3 (complete opposition to the statement). A commitment of +1.5 is required for acceptance. Resolutions P.S. 1991 A, 1991 B, and RIC 1991 E, are directed to the Committee on the Liturgy.

Renewal of Priestly Commitment

P.S. 1991 A

It is the position of the delegates to the 1991 National Meeting of Diocesan Liturgical Commissions that the Bishops' Committee on the Liturgy in the Revised Edition of the Roman Missal to be approved for use in the dioceses of the United States develop an independent rite for the Renewal of Commitment to

Priestly Service; and further that the focus of the Chrism Mass be restored with a new preface and presidential prayers. (Passed +2.5 —Submitted by the FDLC Ministry Committee)

We request that a time-line and procedure for implementation of this resolution be set by the FDLC Board of Directors at the January 1992 Board Meeting.

Actively Seeking Solutions for the Expansion of Ministerial Roles

P.S. 1991 B

It is the position of the delegates to the 1991 National Meeting of Diocesan Liturgical Commissions who believe that in an increasing number of communities the limited number of presbyters makes it difficult if not impossible to provide adequate sacramental ministry, that the FDLC request the Bishops' Committee on the Liturgy to bring to the attention of the NCCB the urgent need to provide for the complete range of sacramental ministry and weekly celebration of the Sunday Mass by actively seeking means to broaden access to ordained ministry in order that all communities of the faithful as well as the large numbers yet to be evangelized in compliance with the Bishops' National Plan and Strategy for Catholic Evangelization in the United States may be adequately served.

We request that a time-line and procedure for implementation of this resolution be set by the FDLC Board of Directors at the January 1992 Board Meeting. (Passed +2.08 —Submitted by Region X)

Focus for a National Agenda

P.S. 1991 C

It is the position of the delegates to the 1991 National Meeting of Diocesan Liturgical Commissions that the FDLC accept as a national agenda the work of promoting the Eucharist as the culmination of Christian initiation which "enables us to carry out the mission of the entire people of God in the Church and in the world" (Christian Initiation, GI, par. 2), and that Diocesan Liturgical Commissions and/or offices of worship promote that agenda.

We request that a time-line and procedure for implementation of this resolution be set by the FDLC Board of Directors at the January 1992 Board Meeting. (Passed +2.27 —Submitted by Region VIII)

Practice of Communicating the Assembly from the Reserved Eucharist

P.S. 1991 D

It is the position of the delegates to the 1991 National Meeting of Diocesan Liturgical Commissions that the Eucharist and Liturgical Year Committee of the FDLC compile appropriate documentation and provide a resource for diocesan liturgical commissions to assist parishes in eliminating the widespread practice of communicating the assembly at Mass from the reserved Sacrament.

We request that a time-line and procedure for implementation of this resolution be set by the FDLC Board of Directors at the January 1992 Board Meeting. (Passed +2.78 —Submitted by Region VI)

Holy Day of Obligation

R.I.C. 1991 E

WHEREAS the NCCB Secretariat for the Liturgy has issued a memorandum (September 20, 1991) to all bishops concerning November action items on Holy Days of Obligation;

WHEREAS six action statements regarding Holy Days of Obligation are present on the November 1991 agenda of the NCCB meeting;

It is the position of the delegates to the 1991 National Meeting of Diocesan Liturgical Commissions that we support an affirmative response of our Bishops to the question: Do the de iure members of the National Conference of Catholic Bishops approve transferring the celebration of the solemnity of the Ascension to the Seventh Sunday of Easter, as is provided for in the General Norms for the Liturgical Year and the Calendar, no. 7b?

We request that the Board of Directors of the FDLC relay our affirmative vote on said action item to the BCL before the November gathering of the NCCB. (Passed +2.23 —Submitted by Region V)

Lectionary for Masses with Children

At the November 1991 plenary meeting of the National Conference of Catholic Bishops, the *Lectionary for Masses with Children* [*LMC*] was approved for liturgical use by the requisite two-thirds majority vote of the *de iure* Latin rite members. Once the requested confirmation of the Apostolic See has been granted, the LMC will be the first such lectionary approved for use in the liturgy in the dioceses of the United States of America.

History of the Lectionary

In 1983 the Bishops' Committee on the Liturgy accepted the request of the Board of Directors of the Federation of Diocesan Liturgical Commissions (FDLC) to prepare a *Lectionary for Masses with Children* for use in the dioceses of the United States. This action was taken in conformity with the *Directory for Masses with Children,* prepared by the Congregation for Divine Worship and approved by Pope Paul VI on 22 October 1973, which "recommend(s), moreover, that the individual conferences of bishops see to the composition of lectionaries for Masses with children" (no. 43).

The FDLC request originated with a position statement approved by the diocesan delegates attending the 1982 National Meeting of Diocesan Liturgical Commissions in Buffalo, NY. The position statement noted that "1. There is at present no approved text of the Scriptures for use at liturgies with children. 2. Many catechetical texts settle for paraphrases of the Scriptures in their liturgical services. 3. Many catechists have experienced a frustration with the long absence of texts that allow children to experience the liturgy of the word on their own level and according to their own ability."

At the time of its acceptance of this request, the Liturgy Committee asked the National Office of the FDLC to coordinate a working group consisting of representatives of the Liturgy Committee, the Federation of Diocesan Liturgical Commissions, and experts in catechetics for young children to formulate plans for the lectionary.

Since that time the Task Group conducted a survey (135 respondents) to determine the contents of the lectionary, the targeted age group, and the occasions for its use. The survey produced these results, which were subsequently approved by the Liturgy Committee in June 1986:

1. The lectionary will contain the complete three-year cycle of readings for Sundays and major feasts.

2. One set of readings will be developed for each week of the year (seasons as well as ordinary time).

3. The lectionary will be geared to children in the lower primary grades, with the third grade (8 year-olds) being targeted as the primary though not exclusive group.

4. The readings for Sundays and major feasts will follow the *cursus* of readings from the Roman *Lectionary for Mass.* When all three readings are suitable to the comprehension of the targeted age group, they will be included in the *Lectionary for Masses with Children.* The Gospel will always be included, although at times it will be shortened. However, if either the Old Testament or the Epistle reading is beyond the comprehension of third graders, it will be omitted. If both readings need to be omitted for this reason (which proved to be the case only twice), another reading will be suggested.

5. The readings for weekdays will correspond to various liturgical/theological motifs of the major liturgical seasons (Advent, Christmas, Lent, Easter, Ordinary Time).

6. A section containing selected readings from the common of saints will be included. A complete listing of sanctoral solemnities, feasts, and memorials will provide references to the common of saints.

7. A final section will contain readings for sacramental occasions and needs, various celebrations during the course of a school year, etc.

In June 1987 the Task Group presented to the Liturgy Committee the complete listing of readings for inclusion in the proposed *Lectionary for Masses with Children.* The list was accepted by the Committee on the Liturgy, with the request that various outside consultants be asked to study the list for possible further refinement.

The Liturgy Committee also approved the recommendation of the Task Group that the translation of Scripture intended for early youth (children aged 5-9) being prepared by the American Bible Society be chosen as the translation to be used in the *LMC*.

At the September 1989 meeting of the NCCB Administrative Committee the Liturgy Committee requested the acceptance of the new ABS translation for inclusion in this project because the American Bible Society had indicated that, upon such approval, it would modify its own schedule in preparing the *Translation for Early Youth* (later renamed *Contemporary English Version*) and make available to the Liturgy Committee over the course of the next two years new translations of all of the pericopes to be included in its *Lectionary for Masses with Children*. The Administrative Committee authorized the Liturgy Committee to work with the American Bible Society on this project, but it preserved the right of the entire membership of the National Conference of Catholic Bishops to accept or reject the translation for liturgical use in the *LMC* once the completed text had been presented to the NCCB for the requisite approval.

The norms governing the preparation of vernacular lectionaries are contained in the 25 May 1969 decree *Ordo Lectionum* of the Congregation for Divine Worship. That decree states that "it is the responsibility of the conferences of bishops to prepare the complete vernacular texts, following the norms in the Instruction on the translation of liturgical texts (Consilium for the Implementation of the Constitution on the Liturgy, 25 January 1969). Vernacular texts may be taken from bible translations already lawfully approved for individual regions, with the confirmation of the Apostolic See. If newly translated, they should be submitted for confirmation to this Congregation."

Since the *Contemporary English Version* is a new translation, its use in the LMC required the 2/3 approval of the *de iure* members of the National Conference of Catholic Bishops with subsequent confirmation of the Apostolic See. The bishops granted such approval at their November 1991 meeting.

Introduction to the Lectionary

The 27-page Introduction to the lectionary was composed by the Task Group developing the *Lectionary for Children*. During the past two years its several drafts were carefully reviewed by the Liturgy Committee. It incorporates the many suggestions made by the Liturgy Committee and other consultants who examined it. The text presents the context for the *Lectionary for Masses with Children*; however, it does not repeat everything that is found in the *Directory for Masses with Children*, nor does it obviate the need for those who will use the *LMC* to be conversant with the Introduction to the *Lectionary for Mass*. When the *LMC* becomes available for use, it will be important that dioceses provide formation on its use with due consideration given to its relationship to the *Directory for Masses with Children* and the Introduction to the *Lectionary for Mass*. It is only within this broader context that the *Lectionary for Masses with Children* is properly understood.

The Introduction is divided into four parts. The first part is entitled "The Liturgical Celebration of the Word of God" and provides the context for understanding the use of the *LMC*. It emphasizes the *ritual nature* of proclamation of the word within a liturgical celebration.

Part two treats "The Celebration of the Word of God with Children." This section details basic principles that govern celebrations of the word with children: 1) biblical readings should never be omitted; 2) all integral ritual elements pertaining to the Liturgy of the Word should be preserved in celebrations with children; 3) liturgical dismissals are to be used in separate liturgies of the word; 4) the full Sunday assembly remains the goal towards which all children are to be led; and 5) a homily or biblical reflection is to be given at Masses with children.

Part Three provides directives for understanding and using the LMC. It emphasizes the lectionary's primary intent to lead children into active participation "in the worship of the whole assembly, *but not to establish a different rite for children.*" Directions are given for when the LMC may be used. The principles which governed the adaptation of the LMC are provided in this section under the topics of the 1) age level; 2) number of readings; 3) omission of readings; 4) length of readings; 5) replacement of readings; and 6) responsorial psalms. It also includes an extensive section on the relationship of the lectionary to the liturgical year.

Part Four highlights "Particular Issues" that pertain to the liturgy of the word when it is celebrated with children. It examines the place of celebration, objects used in the celebration, and the full use of music in the liturgy of the word. It emphasizes that the Mass is not an historical reenactment of events of salvation history and admonishes not to treat the liturgy of the word as a "play." Finally, it affirms the desire of the Church to assist children to participate in the worship of the entire community; therefore, "the basic shape of the ritual used with children, its symbols, gestures, and language" must be similar to that of the full assembly.

Cursus of Readings

The readings in the *LMC* are based on the *Lectionary for Mass* (1981 *Ordo Lectionum Missae*). The Sunday readings follow the cursus of the *Lectionary for Mass*. All three readings are given when they do not pose any difficulty in the comprehension of children in early primary grades, the target group for the *Lectionary for Masses with Children*. In many cases a reading has been omitted (usually the second reading) when it has been judged to be beyond the comprehension of such children. In general, the gospel readings have been kept as they are in the *Lectionary for Mass*, but in some individual cases, one or more verses have been omitted. There is always at least one reading given in addition to the gospel. Extensive consultation was conducted with liturgists and religious education experts regarding the readings contained in the *LMC*.

Imprimatur and Approval for Liturgical Use

The Administrative Committee of the NCCB granted an *imprimatur* to the New Testament of the American Bible Society's *Contemporary English Version* [CEV] at its meeting in March 1991. The American Bible Society published the New Testament of this version of the Scriptures in May of this year. The psalms and Old Testament readings of the CEV which are included in the *LMC* were not ready for inclusion in the *ad interim imprimatur* process approved by the NCCB in November 1990, and so the NCCB Administrative Committee was not empowered to grant the *imprimatur* for these texts. These texts were favorably reviewed by censors appointed by the Committee for Pastoral Practices. At their November 1991 plenary meeting the members of the NCCB, by voice vote, granted the *imprimatur*. Following this the NCCB also approved the *Contemporary English Version* of Scripture *for liturgical use* so that it might be used in the *Lectionary for Masses with Children*.

Search for FDLC Executive Secretary

The Federation of Diocesan Liturgical Commissions has begun a search for a new Executive Secretary for its national office, located in Washington, DC. The position will become available in October 1992. Applicants must have liturgical, administrative and computer skills. Resumes should be sent to: Reverend Richard E. Ward, 1607 Greentree Road, Pittsburgh, PA 15220. Telephone: 412/563-3189. Applications will not be accepted after March 1, 1992.

Solemnity of Christmas

The recent discussion by the members of the National Conference of Catholic Bishops on holy days has given rise to a consideration of the broader issue of how well the Catholic faithful prepare for and celebrate *all* the solemnities in the liturgical calendar and not just those designated as days of obligation. Even the celebration of the solemnity of Christmas, the most popular holy day of obligation in terms of participation in the Eucharist, should be studied in this context.

There is an increasing number of people participating in the Vigil Masses of Christmas with a corresponding decline in the number who are participating in the Masses on Christmas day. To accommodate these shifts, parishes are scheduling more Vigil Masses and discovering that they need to eliminate Masses on Christmas day. "Children's Liturgies" or "Family Liturgies" are scheduled for Vigil Masses so that people (and, in some cases, clergy) do not need to be inconvenienced on Christmas morning. Gospel readings are changed so that the faithful can listen to the Christmas readings at the Vigil in place of the account of Christ's genealogy. Lastly, in many instances, the care and solemnity given to the celebration of the Vigil Mass(es) is often absent from Masses during the day.

These trends need to be given critical attention by all who are involved in liturgical preparations for the Christmas season. All too often practices become enshrined as "tradition" or "custom" without a careful and serious consideration of how they may impact on the liturgical life of our communities.

Stations of the Cross

During the past year many inquiries have been received at the Secretariat for the Liturgy regarding the devotion known as the "Stations (or Way) of the Cross." These questions arose partly from news stories that indicated that Pope John Paul II used a new form of the stations of the cross containing only stations which are found in the New Testament at the annual Good Friday celebration at the Coloseum in Rome.

In the first centuries Christians who went to Jerusalem visited the sites of the various events recorded by the Scriptures and ancient tradition. This practice is recounted in the letter of the fourth century pilgrim Egeria. However, it is not until the twelfth and thirteenth centuries, when emphasis on the passion of Christ became popular, that we see the beginnings of the stations of the cross as a devotion. The modern devotion with fourteen stations is first seen in Spain in the first half of the seventeenth century and was spread by the Franciscans. Saint Leonard of Port Maurice (d. 1751) erected stations of the cross in the Roman Coloseum. Pope Clement XII formally established the devotion in 1731.

Chapter 42 of the *Book of Blessings* provides the Order for the Blessing of the Stations of the Cross and indicates that the erection and blessing of the stations of the cross is done by the rector (pastor) of the church or a priest deputed by him (no. 1400). The stations consist of fourteen images with crosses or simply crosses that are set up in the church or in a place of their own, and in a manner convenient to the faithful (*Book of Blessings,* no. 1401).

From 1979 to 1990 a variety of versions of the stations of the cross have been used for the papal Good Friday celebration of this devotion at the Coloseum. They have always included the fourteen traditional stations: Jesus is condemned to death; Jesus takes up the cross; Jesus falls the first time; Jesus meets his mother; Simon carries the cross for Jesus; Veronica wipes the face of Jesus; Jesus falls the second time; Jesus consoles the women of Jerusalem; Jesus falls the third time; Jesus is stripped of his clothing; Jesus is nailed to the cross; Jesus dies on the cross; Jesus is taken down from the cross; Jesus is placed in the tomb.

The 1991 celebration of the stations of the cross at the Coloseum provided a new list of the stations which are all based on the events recorded in the passion accounts of the New Testament. The three falls of Jesus (stations III, V, VII) and the encounters of Jesus with his mother (station IV) and Veronica (station VI), all of which are not found in the Scriptures, have been replaced by scriptural stations: Jesus in the Garden of Olives; Judas' betrayal of Jesus and his arrest; Denial of Jesus by Peter; Jesus is judged by Pilate; Jesus is scourged and crowned with thorns; Jesus promises his kingdom to the good thief; The mother of Jesus and his disciple at the cross. These revised stations are actually not new, since many of them were given in the *Book for Pilgrims* which was prepared for the Holy Year of 1991. This revised version of the stations of the cross continues the tradition of fourteen stations. In many places an additional station has been added, either before the altar or the blessed sacrament to commemorate the resurrection, and so situate the stations of the cross in the context of the whole paschal mystery of Christ's passion, death, and resurrection.

In recent years the Congregation for Divine Worship and the Discipline of the Sacraments has authorized various versions of the stations of the cross for use on different occasions as alternatives to the traditional forms. The 1991 papal version of the stations of the cross falls within the practice of allowing a variety of texts for use in this devotion. Monsignor Piero Marini, Master of Liturgical Celebrations of the Pope, in the introduction to the 1991 booklet containing the Good Friday stations of the cross, notes that the new version does not intend to change the traditional text, which still remains valid. In practice, this means that the number of stations remain the same and the traditional designation of the individual stations has not been changed.

Resources

Those familiar with the *Liturgy Documents: A Parish Resource* will be glad to know that a third edition of this book has been published. This 395-page work contains all of the previous liturgical documents and has added the following: *Fulfilled in Your Hearing, This Holy and Living Sacrifice,* and excerpts from the *Ceremonial of Bishops.* Father John Huels has carefully introduced the whole collection, and other scholars have added overviews for each document. The index has been reworked and expanded. Cost $9.95. Order from Liturgy Training Publications, 1800 North Hermitage Avenue, Chicago, IL 60622-1101.

COMMITTEE ON THE LITURGY

NEWSLETTER

1992
VOLUME XXVIII
JANUARY

NATIONAL CONFERENCE OF CATHOLIC BISHOPS

Recent Liturgical Decisions of the NCCB

At the November 11-14, 1991 plenary assembly of the National Conference of Catholic Bishops, balloting on two action items dealing with the holy days of obligation observed in the United States was inconclusive pending the receipt of the mail-in votes of the *de iure* Latin rite members who were not present at the time of the balloting. After a tally of those mail-in votes, the two action items were declared as having been approved by the NCCB. Approval of the motion that January 1, August 15, and November 1 will not be observed as holy days of obligation in the dioceses of the United States when they fall on a *Saturday* received the required 180 yes votes, with 184 votes in favor and 68 opposed. Approval of the motion that January 1, August 15, and November 1 will not be observed as holy days of obligation in the dioceses of the United States when they fall on a *Monday* also received the required 180 yes votes, with 180 votes in favor and 71 opposed. Both action items require the confirmation of the Apostolic See.

The approval of the revised English translation of *Verbum Domini* as "The word of the Lord" (after a first or second reading) and as "The gospel of the Lord" (after a reading from one of the four gospels) in the revised *Lectionary for Mass* (as well as in the *Lectionary for Masses with Children*, the *Collection of Masses of the Blessed Virgin Mary*, and the lectionaries of ritual books) also received the required 180 votes, with 195 in favor and 66 opposed. The approval requires the confirmation of the Apostolic See.

New Advisors to the Committee

The Most Reverend Wilton D. Gregory, chairman of the Bishops' Committee on the Liturgy, has announced the appointment of three new advisors to the Committee to replace outgoing advisors Fathers John Huels, OSM, Catholic Theological Union, Chicago, and Andrew Ciferni, O Praem, Washington Theological Union, both of whom completed their terms this past summer, and Sister Linda Gaupin, CDP, who became Associate Director of the Secretariat of the Bishops' Committee on the Liturgy in September.

Sister Madlyn Pape, CDP, Helotes, TX, and the Reverend Samuel J. Aquila, Denver, have received appointments as advisors at-large, and Father Joseph Levesque, CM, of Philadelphia will become an *ex officio* advisor to the Committee, serving as liaison with the Conference of Major Superiors of Men (CMSM).

Sister Madlyn Pape serves as General Councilor of the Congregation of Divine Providence in San Antonio, TX. She has received an MM degree from Westminster Choir College in Princeton, NJ, with a major in choral conducting and a minor in voice. Her other academic degrees include an MM in music literature and an MS in clinical counseling. Part of her role as an advisor to the Committee will be to serve as liaison between the Committee and the Leadership Conference of Women Religious (LCWR). Father Samuel Aquila is director of the Office of Liturgy for the Archdiocese of Denver. He also serves as Assistant Secretary for Catholic Education and Director for Continuing Education of Priests. Father Aquila received his STL in sacramental theology from San Anselmo's in Rome in 1987. Father Levesque is the provincial superior of the Congregation of the Missions in Philadelphia, PA. He received his STD in 1977 from The Catholic University of America in systematic theology with a concentration in sacramental theology.

The Bishops' Committee on the Liturgy and its Secretariat wish to express their appreciation for the assistance and advice given by Father John Huels and Father Andrew Ciferni during their three years as advisors and look forward to the collaboration of the newly appointed advisors.

Rereading the Constitution on the Liturgy (art. 64-66)

The Constitution on the Sacred Liturgy (CSL) contains fifteen articles (nos. 64-78) dealing with the reform of the rites of the sacraments other than the Eucharist. CSL 64-66 treat the restoration of the catechumenate and the reform of the rite of baptism for adults. Need for such reform was evident from a study of the history of the rite for adult baptism. In the course of time the elaborate preparatory stages of the rite were compressed together to form the liturgy for infant baptism. At the end of the Middle Ages a scanty rite for adult baptism was again created by using elements taken from the rite for the baptism of children.

CSL 64 requires as a first step the revival of the catechumenate divided into several stages. Restoring the catechumenate was not viewed as a novel idea. Attempts to revive the catechumenate were already taking place in several countries prior to the Second Vatican Council. For example, the success of the experiments of the Church in African near the mid-point of this century roused the Churches of Europe to undertake similar attempts at restoring the catechumenate. In France, these efforts in the early 1950's resulted in most dioceses having implemented some form of the catechumenate by 1965. Furthermore, prior to the Council the Sacred Congregation of Rites published a decree on April 16, 1962, restoring a rite of baptism of adults *in stages*. Although the new ritual did not depart greatly from the former rite for the baptism of adults, it did change the process of catechetical instruction given to adults involving the Church community.

The decree did, however, make the need for reform of the ritual, the *Ordo Baptismi adultorum,* all the more obvious. Thus CSL 64 calls for the revival of the catechumenate "sanctified by sacred rites to be celebrated at successive intervals of time." Other conciliar texts add further specifications regarding the catechumenate. The Decree on the Church's Missionary Activity *Ad gentes* states: "Those who through the Church have accepted from the Father faith in Christ should be admitted to the catechumenate by means of liturgical ceremonies . . . By means of sacred rites celebrated at successive times, they should be led gradually into the life of faith, liturgy, and charity belonging to the people of God (no. 14). The Decree on the Pastoral Office of Bishops *Christus Dominus* places on the bishop the responsibility to reestablish or to modernize the adult catechumenate (no. 14). The Dogmatic Constitution on the Church *Lumen gentium* addresses the ecclesial relationship of catechumens "who, moved by the Holy Spirit, desire with an explicit intention to be incorporated into the Church, (and) are by that very intention joined to her. With love and solicitude mother Church already embraces them as her own" (no. 14).

CSL 65 recalls the norms of adaptation previously stated in CSL 37-40 and applies them to the specific case of adult baptism: the Church in mission lands may admit initiation elements of the people's culture and traditions into the liturgy provided they are in keeping "with the Christian rite of initiation."

CSL 66 concerns the entire rite of the baptism of adults. It calls for the revision of "not only the simpler rite, but also the more solemn one, with proper attention to the restored catechumenate." The solemn form provides for different stages of the catechumenate with rites celebrated at successive intervals of time. Its intention is to serve the catechumens in their gradual conversion to Christ and his Church, a conversion which culminates in the life-giving waters of baptism and admittance to the Christian eucharistic assembly. The restoration of the catechumenate reestablishes the solemn form of initiation as the normal practice.

The revision of the liturgical books was undertaken by the Consilium, the postconciliar commission established by Pope Paul VI through his motu proprio *Sacram liturgiam* (25 January 1964). After conducting a consultation with the various particular Churches, the commission proposed outlines of the work to be undertaken for the revision of the rite for the baptism of adults. In 1966 the commission drew up a provisional ritual and distributed it for experimentation to the different Churches throughout the world. A second draft was formulated based on the responses to the 1966 text. This second draft was distributed in 1969 for further comments and suggestions. The responses to this second draft formed the basis for the typical edition (*editio typica*) of the revised rite, published under the title *Ordo Initiationis Christianae Adultorum* on 6 January 1972 by the Congregation for Divine Worship. The revised rite replaced the 1962 *Ordo Baptismi adultorum* of the Roman Ritual.

In 1974 the International Commission on English in the Liturgy (ICEL) issued the first English translation of the Latin editio typica. Like most translations of liturgical books prepared by ICEL, the English *Rite of Christian Initiation of Adults* was issued as a "provisional text," meaning that the translation was open to further refinement after it had been used for a number of years. Provisional translations are issued by ICEL in books with green covers, while the revised final translations appear in books with white covers; hence the designations of "green book" and "white book" translations.

Use of the term "provisional" for the first ("green book") English translation of the *Rite of Christian Initiation of Adults* led to the erroneous understanding that the revised rite was optional, which, of course, was not the case. The decree promulgating the Latin edition states that the rite replaces "the rite of baptism of adults now in the Roman Ritual" and "that this new rite may be used in Latin at once and in the vernacular from the day appointed by the conference of bishops, after it has prepared a translation and had it confirmed by the Apostolic See." The Congregation for Divine Worship confirmed the first English translation on September 23, 1974, and the *Rite of Christian Initiation of Adults* (RCIA) was published by the United States Catholic Conference for immediate use in the United States.

In 1984 the NCCB Liturgy Secretariat issued *Christian Initiation of Adults: A Commentary,* volume 10 in its Study Text series on the revised rites of the Church. The purpose of this volume was to prepare for the final ("white book") translation of the RCIA, then being prepared by ICEL, and to promote the rite's continual implementation. A revised edition of this commentary was published in 1988; it reflects the final English translation of the rite.

On November 11, 1986, the National Conference of Catholic Bishops approved for use in the dioceses of the United States the final ("white book") English translation of the *Ordo Initiationis Christianae Adultorum* prepared by ICEL. The NCCB also approved a number of supplementary rites and liturgical texts for use in the dioceses of the United States. These actions were subsequently confirmed by the Apostolic See by decree of the Congregation for Divine Worship on February 19, 1987. The mandatory effective date for implementation of the final text of the ritual was set for September 1, 1988.

The *Rite of Christian Initiation of Adults* fully implements the norm set forth in CSL 64 for the restoration of the catechumenate divided into several stages sanctified by sacred rites celebrated at successive intervals of time. Part I presents the rite "in its complete and usual form" (RCIA 3). The spiritual journey of the adult catechumen includes the four periods of inquiry, catechumenate, purification and enlightenment, and mystagogia. Three principal liturgical celebrations mark the progress of the catechumen: Rite of Acceptance into the Order of Catechumens, Rite of Election or Enrollment of Names, and Celebration of the Sacraments of Initiation.

In accord with CSL 37-40 and 65, the *General Introduction to Christian Initiation,* nos. 30-33, and the particular Introduction to the *Rite of Christian Initiation of Adults,* nos. 32-33, prescribe the instances when conferences of bishops may adapt the rites of Christian initiation. The American edition reflects the implementation of these norms. It incorporates the wisdom and experience gained from twelve years' use of the 1974 English translation in the United States.

In November 1986 the National Conference of Catholic Bishops approved several ritual decisions authorized by RCIA 33. These include: 1) leaving to the discretion of the diocesan bishop the inclusion of a first exorcism and a renunciation of false worship in the Rite of Acceptance into the Order of Catechumens; 2) establishing as a norm for that same rite the tracing of the cross on the forehead, while leaving to the discretion of the diocesan bishop the substitution of another symbolic gesture for those persons in whose culture the act of touching may not seem proper; 3) establishing as the norm that there is to be no giving of a new name, while leaving to the discretion of the diocesan bishop the giving of a new name to persons from those cultures in which it is the practice of non-Christian religions to give a new name; 4) inclusion of an optional presentation of a cross while leaving to the discretion of the diocesan bishop the inclusion of additional rites that symbolize reception into the community; 5) establishing the use of the anointing with the oil of catechumens during the period of the catechumenate as a kind of "rite of passage"; 6) permitting the early celebration of the presentations, the ephphetha rite, and the recitation of the creed when appropriate; 7) reserving the anointing with the oil of catechumens to the period of the catechumenate and to the period of purification and enlightenment and omitting it in the preparation rites on Holy Saturday and in the celebration of initiation at the Easter Vigil or at another time; 8) establishing as the norm that the formularies of renunciation should not be adapted, while leaving to the discretion of the diocesan bishop the matter of making more specific and detailed formularies of renunciation in the Rite of Acceptance into the Order of Catechumens and in the celebration of baptism in those cases where false worship is widespread in the culture of catechumens.

At the same national meeting the bishops also approved a number of additional texts to be combined with the "white book" translation of the Latin text to form the *Rite of Christian Initiation of Adults* for the dioceses of the United States of America. The first of these was the optional rite of Sending of the Catechumens for Election to be included in Part I under rites belonging to the period of the catechumenate. Composed in response to requests for a such a rite, the Sending of the Catechumens for Election allows for recognition of catechumens in the parish prior to the celebration of election (usually in the cathedral) by the bishop. At times this rite has been misunderstood. It was intended as a *parish* celebration to allow the local community to send the catechumens forth "to the celebration of election assured of the parish's care and support" (RCIA 108). The rite is not meant to be a second election rite, and every effort was made to avoid all appearances of such.

The second text to be added was an optional Rite of Election or Enrollment of Names to be included in Part II, Chapter 1, entitled "Christian Initiation of Children Who Have Reached Catechetical Age." This particular rite is not found in the Latin *editio typica*. It was initially included in the American edition because the experience of the Church in the United States was that more and more children of an advanced age were approaching the Church for initiation. Subsequently, the rite has proven valuable even for the very young, who in many cases participate in diocesan celebrations of the Rite of Election with adults and other older children.

The bishops also approved the inclusion of four chapters of optional rites designated for Part II, Chapter 4, entitled "Preparation of Uncatechized Adults For Confirmation and Eucharist." Pastoral experience evidenced a need for rituals that would mark the spiritual journey of baptized Christians seeking to complete their initiation with Confirmation and Eucharist. The liturgical rites of Part I, designated for catechumens, address the reality of the non-baptized person seeking baptism and were never meant to be celebrated with persons who had already been baptized. Thus the inclusion of these four ritual celebrations permitted baptized persons seeking to complete their initiation—especially those who had previously received little formation in the Christian life—an opportunity to ritualize their own unique spiritual journey that was different from that of catechumens. These four rites are: 1) Rite of Welcoming the Candidates; 2) Rite of Sending the Candidates for Recognition by the Bishop and for the Call to Continuing Conversion; 3) Rite of Calling the Candidates to Continuing Conversion; and 4) Penitential Rite.

The pastoral experience in the United States for the years 1974-1986 also indicated a need for "combined" rites to be celebrated at those times when both catechumens (unbaptized) and candidates (baptized) are present. The bishops approved three rites that were included along with the "Celebration at the Easter vigil of the Sacraments of Initiation and of the Rite of Reception into the Full Communion of the Catholic Church." This latter rite, already in the ICEL "white book," had been prepared at the request of all the English-speaking conferences of bishops.

Another American addition to the *Rite of Christian Initiation of Adults* can be found in Appendix III, entitled "National Statutes for the Catechumenate." These statutes were presented to the bishops for approval in virtue of the power of the conferences of bishops acknowledged in canon 788:3, which states: "It is the responsibility of the conference of bishops to issue statutes by which the catechumenate is regulated; these statutes are to determine what things are to be expected of catechumens and define what prerogatives are recognized as theirs." For the most part the statutes simply organize and restate the existing law governing the catechumenate and the rites of initiation found in the 1983 Code of Canon Law and in the liturgical books.

The national statutes address a number of pastoral issues and challenges pertaining to the implementation of the rite in the United States. As such all those involved with the catechumenate should be familiar with them. Four norms contained in the national statutes constitute particular law for the United States. Statute 6 addresses the length of the catechumenate. It states that, in the United States, the length of the catechumenate "should extend for at least one year of formation, instruction, and probation." This one year time period begins at the acceptance into the order of catechumens and includes the catechumenate proper and the period of purification and enlightenment.

(To be continued in the February 1992 issue.)

COMMITTEE ON THE LITURGY

NATIONAL CONFERENCE OF CATHOLIC BISHOPS

NEWSLETTER

**1992
VOLUME XXVIII
FEBRUARY**

New Officials Appointed for Vatican Congregation

On January 24, 1992, Pope John Paul II appointed His Eminence Antonio Maria Cardinal Javierre Ortas as prefect of the Congregation for Divine Worship and the Discipline of the Sacraments. Cardinal Javierre replaces Spanish Cardinal Eduardo Martinez Somalo, who served as prefect since July 1988 and who has now been appointed to head the Vatican Congregation for Institutes of Consecrated Life and Societies of Apostolic Life.

Cardinal Javierre Ortas was born in Sietamo in northeastern Spain on February 2, 1921. Ordained a Salesian priest in 1949, he developed an academic career as a theology professor, ecumenist, and university rector before beginning his work at the Vatican Congregation for Education and the Vatican's Apostolic Library and Secret Archives. He was an ecumenical consultor to the Spanish bishops during the Second Vatican Council. He also served as a member of the Faith and Order Commission of the World Council of Churches for three years and has written several books on ecumenical and theological topics. Cardinal Javierre Ortas was elected to the College of Cardinals in 1988.

In September 1991 Pope John Paul II appointed Archbishop Geraldo Majella Agnelo of Londrina, Brazil, as the new secretary of the Congregation for Divine Worship and the Discipline of the Sacraments, replacing Archbishop Lajos Kada, who had become apostolic nuncio to Germany. Ordained a priest in 1957, Archbishop Agnelo was named bishop of Toledo, Brazil, in 1978 and archbishop of Londrina in 1982. Before 1978 he taught philosophy and liturgical and sacramental theology in several Brazilian seminaries.

The Bishops' Committee on the Liturgy expresses its deep support and cooperation to Cardinal Javierre Ortas and Archbishop Agnelo in their new positions as promoters of the liturgical life of the Church.

Time for the Celebration of the Easter Vigil

The Roman Missal states that the entire celebration of the Easter Vigil takes place at night: the vigil should not begin before nightfall, and it should end before daybreak on Sunday. Yet this norm often goes unobserved. The *Circular Letter Concerning the Preparation and Celebration of the Easter Feasts,* issued by the Congregation for Divine Worship in 1988, notes that "the very concept of the vigil has almost come to be forgotten in some places, with the result that it is celebrated as if it were an evening Mass, in the same way and at the same time as the Mass celebrated on Saturday evening in anticipation of the Sunday."

The *Circular Letter,* no. 78, repeats the norm provided in the Roman Missal and adds that "this rule is to be taken according to its strictest sense. Reprehensible are those abuses and practices that have crept into many places in violation of this ruling, whereby the Easter Vigil is celebrated at the time of day that it is customary to celebrate anticipated Sunday Masses."

Liturgical law leaves no doubt as to when the Easter Vigil should be celebrated. This year Easter occurs after clocks in most parts of the United States have been moved ahead one hour for daylight savings time. Pastoral planners should contact a local weather station for the time *sunset* will occur on April 18, 1992. To that time another 45 minutes or one hour should be added to determine the approximate time of *nightfall.* For example, if sunset occurs at 7:43 p.m. DST in a given location, the celebration of the Easter Vigil should not begin before 8:30 p.m.

Particular Calendars

From time to time the Bishops' Committee on the Liturgy receives requests, often from religious communities, to include the commemoration of a saint or blessed in the proper calendar for the United States. Requests of this kind give rise to several concerns. Is there a danger that the *Proper Calendar for the Dioceses of the United States of America* might eventually become overloaded with commemorations? Does the particular saint or blessed whose commemoration is requested have significance for the entire nation or only for a particular group or region of the country? Does the saint or blessed truly enjoy a genuine *cultus* in the United States?

Part of the difficulty lies in the fact that there has been little development of diocesan, regional, and religious calendars in the United States. The *General Norms for the Liturgical Year and Calendar* (GNLYC) states: "Although it is reasonable for each diocese to have its own calendar and propers for the Mass and office, there is no reason why entire provinces, regions, countries, or even larger areas may not have common calendars and propers, prepared with the cooperation of all the parties involved (51). Thus the General Roman Calendar, which is observed by the entire Roman Rite, contains the celebrations of saints having universal significance for the Church. Particular calendars contain "more specialized celebrations, arranged to harmonize with the general cycle" (GNLYC 49).

In 1970, following the publication of the GNLYC, the Congregation for Divine Worship issued the instruction *Calendaria particularia* (CP). It was written to fulfill the directive of the Constitution on the Sacred Liturgy, art. 111: "Lest the feasts of the saints take precedence over the feasts commemorating the very mysteries of salvation, many of them should be left to be celebrated by a particular Church or nation or religious family; those only should be extended to the universal Church that commemorate saints of truly universal significance." *Calendaria particularia* responds to the many questions which had been proposed to the Congregation regarding the development of these particular calendars.

Calendaria particularia (CP) begins with a statement regarding the nature and purpose of particular calendars. Appropriate celebrations of saints not included in the General Calendar "should be observed only in those places where special reasons justify their being honored, that is, in the individual countries, dioceses, and religious institutes to which these saints more properly belong." For this purpose, the preparation of particular calendars for provinces and regions, dioceses, and religious institutes as well as for an entire nation is urged.

CP 8 lists the proper celebrations that may be observed in a province, region or nation. They are the feast of the principal patron; the memorial of the secondary patron; and other celebrations of saints or the blessed who are duly listed in the Roman Martyrology or its Appendix and who have a special relationship to the province, region, nation, or a wider geographical area. To date the *Proper Calendar for the Dioceses of the United States of America* lists the following celebrations:

January 4	Elizabeth Ann Seton, religious	memorial
January 5	John Neumann, bishop	memorial
January 6	Blessed Andre Bessette, religious	optional memorial
March 3	Blessed Katharine Drexel, virgin	optional memorial
May 15	Isidore	optional memorial
July 1	Blessed Junipero Serra, priest	optional memorial
July 4	Independence Day	optional Mass for a Special Occasion
July 14	Blessed Kateri Tekakwitha, virgin	memorial
August 18	Jane Frances de Chantal, religious	optional memorial
September 9	Peter Claver, priest	memorial
October 10	Blessed Marie Rose Durocher, virgin	optional memorial
October 19	Isaac Jogues and John de Brebeuf, priests and martyrs, and companions, martyrs	memorial
October 20	Paul of the Cross, priest	optional memorial

November 13	Frances Xavier Cabrini, virgin	memorial
November 18	Rose Philippine Duchesne, virgin	optional memorial
November 23	Blessed Miguel Agustin Pro, priest and martyr	optional memorial
Fourth Thursday in November	Thanksgiving Day	optional Mass for a Special Occasion
December 9	Blessed Juan Diego	optional memorial
December 12	Our Lady of Guadalupe	feast

Although much work has gone into the preparation of the proper calendar for the United States, little has been done to develop calendars for provinces and regions, dioceses, or religious institutes. Attention should now be given to these.

Provincial and regional calendars would include special celebrations which have particular importance to the people of a given ecclesiastical province or region, but which do not have the same importance for an entire nation or country.

This does not minimize the importance of these commemorations. Often people are not aware that, although the Proper of Seasons is shared universally, the sanctoral cycle has never been the same everywhere. A provincial or regional calendar allows people to express and celebrate their local heritage through celebrations of saints and the blessed that bear a special relationship to their region. They may include saints or the blessed associated with the first settlement of the area, evangelization of the region, the catechetical and/or educational ministry with the people, or who addressed the various social justice needs of the local area.

Along with provincial, regional, and national calendars all of the documents cited above speak of the development of calendars for dioceses and religious institutes. The purpose of these is the same. They allow for celebrations of special significance for a particular diocese or religious institute which may not have the same importance beyond their local area or institution.

CP 9 lists the proper celebrations of a diocese. These include the feast of the principal patron (for pastoral reasons this commemoration may be observed as a solemnity); the feast of the anniversary of the dedication of the cathedral; the memorial of the secondary patron; and celebrations of saints or the blessed who are duly listed in the Roman Martyrology or its Appendix and who belong to the diocese in a particular way, for example, because it was their place of origin, long-time residence, or place of death or because of a *cultus* from time immemorial that still continues.

Along with celebrations for a diocese are those for a town or city as well as for an individual church within the diocese. CP 10 lists the proper celebrations belonging to a town or city. They include the solemnity of the principal patron and the memorial of the secondary patron. Those proper to an individual church include the solemnity of the anniversary of its dedication, the solemnity of its title, and the memorial of a saint or a blessed listed in the Roman Martyrology or its Appendix whose burial place is in that church (CP 11).

Religious institutes are also encouraged to prepare a proper calendar to observe celebrations of significance for their entire institute and individual provinces. CP 12 (a) lists the following proper celebrations as belonging to the entire religious institute: the solemnity or feast of its title; the solemnity or feast of its canonized founder; the solemnity or feast of the principal patron of an order or congregation; the feast of a beatified founder; the memorial of a secondary patron; and celebrations of saints and the blessed who were members of the order or congregation keeping with the rule in no. 17 (a). Those proper to an individual province include: feast of the title or principal patron; memorial of the secondary patron; and celebrations of saints and the blessed who had some special connection with the province, in keeping with the rule in no. 17 (b).

In 1974 the Sacred Congregation for Divine Worship issued a letter to bishops and general superiors of religious asking them to speed up their preparation of the particular calendars of dioceses and religious institutes. This was followed by another reminder in 1977, when the Sacred Congregation for the Sacraments and Divine Worship issued *Calendaria et Propria*, noting that the work of revising the calendars and propers of both dioceses and religious institutes had still not been completed. In spite of this urging, few diocesan and religious calendars were prepared in the United States.

Recent requests to include saints and the blessed in the national calendar indicate the growing desire to recognize in a special way those celebrations that have significance in the lives of people. The GNLYC recognizes, however, that not all these commemorations are important to an entire nation. For this reason the development of calendars for regions, dioceses, and religious institutes is of utmost importance. It is a way of assigning proper celebrations to the appropriate calendars without overloading the proper calendar of the United States with celebrations that are not of national significance. Calendars for regions, dioceses, and religious institutes help to foster the religious and cultural identity of a given group or area and express and promote the local religious heritage.

Rereading the Constitution on the Liturgy (art. 64-66)

(continued from the January 1992 issue)

Four norms contained in the National Statutes for the Catechumenate constitute particular law for the United States. Statute 6 addresses the length of the catechumenate. It states that, in the United States, the length of the catechumenate "should extend for at least one year of formation, instruction, and probation." This one year time period begins at the acceptance into the order of catechumens and includes the catechumenate proper and the period of purification and enlightenment.

Statute 6 is important in light of pastoral practices that have emerged over the years. First, it raises a challenge to the nine month "school year" model for the catechumenate, in which the precatechumenate begins in September and acceptance into the order of catechumens occurs sometime around the beginning of Advent. In some cases this practice has become so enshrined that some people presume that the rite itself calls for the celebration of the first liturgical step during the Advent season. Second, this statute only governs catechumens. It is not intended to regulate the length of formation required for one who is already baptized. The length of catechesis required for baptized adults seeking reception into the full communion of the Catholic Church is governed by statute 30, which states: "Those who have already been baptized in another Church or ecclesial community should not be treated as catechumens or so designated. Their doctrinal and spiritual preparation for reception into full Catholic communion *should be determined according to the individual case,* that is, it should depend on the extent to which the baptized person has led a Christian life within a community of faith and been appropriately catechized to deepen his or her inner adherence to the Church" (emphasis added).

Statute 16 restates a ritual decision made by the bishops which is included in various places throughout the rite. It calls for omitting the rite of anointing with the oil of catechumens in the baptism of adults at the Easter Vigil. Like statute 6, this statute is also important for pastoral implementation of the rite. Omission of the anointing during the Easter Vigil is based on the intention that the anointing of catechumens is to take place during the periods of the catechumenate and purification and enlightenment. Ideally the pastoral practice for this American adaptation would be to have the anointing of the catechumens several times during these periods.

Statute 20 reinforces RCIA 331-333. It leaves to the determination of the diocesan bishop those individual and exceptional cases when the abbreviated catechumenate may be permitted. The statute also notes that moving from one parish or diocese to another, on that account alone, does not warrant the use of the abbreviated catechumenate.

Finally, statute 24 establishes an extended period of mystagogy for the Church in the United States. Following the period of mystagogia set out in the rite, it requires that the neophytes continue to gather at least monthly until the anniversary of their Christian initiation.

The English edition of the *Rite of Christian Initiation of Adults* also includes an editorial rearrangement of the *editio typica.* However, this reordering omits nothing from the Latin original.

The restoration of the catechumenate and the revision of the rites anticipated by CSL 64-66 are fulfilled in the *Ordo Initiationis Christianae Adultorum.* The American edition of the *Rite of Christian Initiation of Adults* reflects the principles and norms of liturgical adaptation and inculturation as set forth in CSL 37-40 and 65. The success of this endeavor can be attributed to the pastoral experience gained from the implementation of the 1974 ICEL provisional translation of the rite. The incorporation of additional texts, rites, and statutes reflects the American experience with initiation and initiatory practices over a twelve year period (1974-1986). The Church in the United States, however, is only beginning to appreciate the implications of these liturgical adaptations. It has not even been four years since this edition of the *Rite of Christian Initiation of Adults* was made mandatory in the dioceses of the United States of America. It should be expected that as the rite continues to be implemented and appropriated in the United States, pastoral experience will give voice to the need for further liturgical adaptation and inculturation.

COMMITTEE ON THE LITURGY

NEWSLETTER

NATIONAL CONFERENCE OF CATHOLIC BISHOPS

**1992
VOLUME XXVIII
MARCH/APRIL**

Third Progress Report on the Revision of the Roman Missal

The *Third Progress Report on the Revision of the Roman Missal* was published in early April by the International Commission on English in the Liturgy (ICEL). The report treats the present work of four ICEL subcommittees, those dealing with Translations and Revisions, Original Texts, Music, and the Presentation of Texts. A copy of the report was sent to each bishop in the United States as well as to each diocesan liturgical commission or office of worship.

Similar to the first and second progress reports, published in March 1988 and November 1990 respectively, the *Third Progress Report on the Revision of the Roman Missal* deals principally with the revised translation of texts of the Order of Mass, including the eucharistic prayers and prefaces. Also included are several original texts composed for the Order of Mass, including some new prefaces and solemn blessings. A section from the pastoral introduction to the Order of Mass and a note of clarification on the translation of *pro multis* in the eucharistic prayers complete the report.

The report contains revised translations of the first greeting at Mass, the first form for the blessing of water, the conclusion to the readings, the *Orate, fratres,* the introduction to the memorial acclamations, and the invitation to communion. Revised translations of texts used in common with other English-speaking Churches are also included. These texts have been prepared by the English Language Liturgical Consultation (ELLC), the successor body to the International Consultation on Common Texts (ICET), which was responsible for preparing the versions of the Gloria, Creed, Sanctus, etc., presently in use. Slight revisions have been made in the Nicene Creed, the preface dialogue, and the ecumenical version of the Lord's Prayer.

The section on prefaces includes the revised translation of several preface openings, 15 complete preface texts (two of them with music), and an explanation of the preface musical formulary tone and how the translation had to take into consideration the fact that the preface is, of its nature, a sung text.

The four Roman eucharistic prayers, the Eucharistic Prayer for Masses of Reconciliation I, and the Eucharistic Prayer for Masses with Children I are given in their revised translation. And the texts of 7 solemn blessings are provided to demonstrate the new translation which, by rhythm and cadence, more easily invites the liturgical assembly's response.

The revised Missal will be presented to the English-speaking conferences of bishops in two volumes in June 1994.

March Meeting of the Liturgy Committee

The bishop members of the NCCB Committee on the Liturgy met in Washington, DC, on March 23, 1992. The principal agenda item of the meeting was the Committee's plans and programs for 1993, which will be submitted for approval at the November 1992 plenary meeting of the National Conference of Catholic Bishops.

The ongoing work of the Secretariat in 1993 will include the publication of the *Newsletter*, preparation of liturgical books for approval and publication, response to liturgical inquiries, preparation of the liturgical calendar, and review of participation aids and other liturgical materials. The Secretariat will also work on the following: preparation of the revised edition of the *Sacramentary* in collaboration with the International Commission on English in the Liturgy (ICEL); preparation of American variations in that revised English translation of the *Sacramentary*; study of the need for and possible development of ritual books for

3211 FOURTH STREET NE • WASHINGTON, DC 20017

Southeast Asian-American Catholics; development of guidelines to address several areas of pastoral concern: sacristans and others who prepare the liturgy, and the liturgical roles of priests, deacons, and lay ministers; collaboration with the Federation of Diocesan Liturgical Commissions on position statements approved at national meetings; participation in ecumenical liturgical consultations, such as the North American Consultation on Common Texts (CCT), the English Language Liturgical Consultation (ELLC), the North American Academy of Liturgy (NAAL), and the Commission on Worship and the Arts of the National Council of Churches of Christ (NCC).

The Secretariat will be involved in the preparation, publication, implementation, and/or promotion of the following in 1993: *Lectionary for Mass* (second typical edition), the *Lectionary for Masses with Children*, the *Order for Celebrating Marriage*, the *Ordination of a Bishop, Presbyters, and Deacons*, the *Sacramentario* (the Spanish-language Sacramentary), *El Bendicional* (specifically, the Spanish translation of the U.S. additions to the *Book of Blessings*), the Spanish-language translation of the *Order of Christian Funerals*, the *Order for the Solemn Exposition of the Holy Eucharist, Guidelines for Cremation and Other Funeral Practices*, and additions to the *Study Texts* and *Liturgy Documentary Series*.

The Committee will participate in the work of the special *ad hoc* committee established to study of the age for the sacrament of confirmation in the dioceses of the United States. In collaboration with other NCCB committees, the Liturgy Committee will also continue to study liturgical/sacramental issues, including the initiation of a process for studying the effectiveness of liturgical texts and celebrations in the catechesis of young children.

The Committee concluded its meeting by examining a report containing the initial results of the survey on American variations in the English translation of the *Roman Missal*. It suggested points for inclusion in its review of the first draft of the proposed NCCB pastoral letter on stewardship, and it reviewed revised texts of a proposed Mass in Thanksgiving for the Gift of Human Life.

Update on the Revised Lectionary for Mass

The Bishops' Committee on the Liturgy will present the first volume of the revised edition of the *Lectionary for Mass*, containing the *New American Bible* translation of Scripture, at the June 1992 meeting of the National Conference of Catholic Bishops at the University of Notre Dame. Volume I includes all readings assigned for Mass on Sundays, solemnities, and feasts of the Lord.

Work on the revised lectionary began in 1983, when the NCCB Committee on the Liturgy established a Lectionary Subcommittee under the chairmanship of Des Moines Bishop William H. Bullock, then Auxiliary Bishop of Saint Paul and Minneapolis, to implement the changes which were contained in the second Latin edition of the *Ordo Lectionum Missae*, published by the Congregation for the Sacraments and Divine Worship on January 21, 1981. The first meeting of the subcommittee, composed of biblical, liturgical, and patristic scholars, was held on December 3, 1983.

The subcommittee began its task by first making a thorough study of the 1981 revised Order of Readings for Mass as well as the variation of that order of readings prepared in 1982 by the ecumenical North American Consultation on Common Texts (CCT). (In November 1982 the members of the National Conference of Catholic Bishops had approved a controlled experimental use of the CCT Order of Readings, but that action failed to receive the required confirmation of the Apostolic See.)

In 1985 the late Archbishop John F. Whealon of Hartford was appointed chairman of the Lectionary Subcommittee. Several issues relating to the ultimate completion of the lectionary were then underway within the NCCB. Archbishop Whealon himself was involved in reviewing the translation of the revised New Testament of the *New American Bible*. Several other bishops from the Committees on Doctrine and on the Liturgy were studying the issue of inclusive language in Scripture translations. Archbishop Whealon directed the Lectionary Subcommittee to begin preparing the text of the revised lectionary even while these other concerns were still unresolved.

The various components of the lectionary were approved by the NCCB as they were completed. In 1986 the NCCB Administrative Committee approved the revised New Testament of the *New American Bible*. In November 1990 the full body of bishops approved the principles for preparing the pericopes from the *New American Bible* which would be contained in the lectionary. They also approved *Criteria for the Evaluation of Inclusive Language Translations of Scriptural Texts Proposed for Liturgical Use*, a document formulated by a Joint Committee of the Liturgy and Doctrine Committees to provide guidance to the bishops when they were asked to approve any new inclusive-language Scriptural translations proposed for use in the liturgy.

In November 1991 the NCCB approved a new translation of the Book of Psalms for the *New American Bible* and a slightly revised translation of "*Verbum Domini,*" which concludes every reading in the lectionary (see below). Vatican confirmation is still awaited for the new psalter translation.

All the components of the revised lectionary have now been approved by the NCCB, and the Sunday readings have been prepared. Proofreading of the entire text by individual members of the Liturgy, Doctrine, and Pastoral Practices Committees is now underway. Every page of the manuscript is being reviewed by three persons. The Sunday volume of readings will be presented for the approval of the NCCB in June. Volume II, containing all weekday readings, ritual Masses, etc., is expected to be presented for approval in November.

Revised Translation of *Verbum Domini* Confirmed

On March 27, 1992, the Most Reverend Daniel E. Pilarczyk, Archbishop of Cincinnati and President of the National Conference of Catholic Bishops, notified the members of the NCCB that the Congregation for Divine Worship and the Discipline of the Sacraments had confirmed the Conference's action approving a slightly revised translation of "*Verbum Domini*" when used in the liturgy. The revised text is "*The word of the Lord.*" (after a first or second reading) and "*The gospel of the Lord.*" (after a reading from one of the four gospels). Approval of this change of translation was given by the Latin rite members of the NCCB at their November 1991 plenary meeting and in the subsequent mail-in balloting of members who were absent during the voting at the plenary meeting.

The new translation is being incorporated into the manuscript of the revised *Lectionary for Mass*. It will also be used in the *Collection of Masses of the Blessed Virgin Mary, Vol. II: Lectionary*, which is soon to be published by The Catholic Book Publishing Company and by The Liturgical Press, and the lectionary sections of the several books contained in the *Roman Ritual*, whenever any of these need to be reprinted by publishers.

A decree issued by Archbishop Pilarczyk on March 25 states that the new translation is to be incorporated into all approved liturgical books, whenever they are published or republished in the future. The translation is also to be incorporated into missalettes and other popular participation aids, beginning with the issues containing the liturgy for the First Sunday of Lent in 1993, and it will become *mandatory* in the dioceses of the United States on that date. However, it may be used in celebrations of the Eucharist prior to that date once the appropriate instruction has been given. The text of Archbishop Pilarczyk's decree follows:

NATIONAL CONFERENCE OF CATHOLIC BISHOPS
UNITED STATES OF AMERICA

DECREE

By authority of the National Conference of Catholic Bishops the translation of the versicle "*Verbum Domini*" as "*The word of the Lord*" (after a first or second reading) and "*The gospel of the Lord*" (after a reading from one of the four gospels) is declared to be the approved English translation for use in the liturgy in the dioceses of the United States of America.

This translation of *Verbum Domini* was canonically approved for use in the liturgy by the National Conference of Catholic Bishops on 17 December 1991 and was subsequently confirmed by the Apostolic See by decree of the Congregation for Divine Worship and the Discipline of the Sacraments on 27 February 1992 (Prot. N. CD 1257/91).

Henceforth the new translation is to be used in all publications of approved liturgical books. It may be used in celebrations of the Eucharist after appropriate instruction has been given to the Christian faithful, particularly those who exercise the liturgical ministry of reader. And it is to be published in monthly and seasonal participation aids beginning with the issues containing the liturgy for the First Sunday of Lent, 28 February 1993, on which date its use in all liturgical celebrations in the dioceses of the United States of America will become mandatory. From that day forward no other English version may be used.

Given at the General Secretariat of the National Conference of Catholic Bishops, Washington, DC, on 25 March 1992, the solemnity of the Annunciation of the Lord.

+ Daniel E. Pilarczyk
Archbishop of Cincinnati
President
National Conference of Catholic Bishops

Robert N. Lynch
General Secretary

Rereading the Constitution on the Liturgy (art. 67-70)

Articles 67-70 in the Constitution on the Sacred Liturgy (CSL) call for the reform of the rite of baptism of infants and the preparation of a new rite for receiving already baptized adult Christians into the full communion of the Catholic Church. Revision of the rite of baptism was to focus on three principal areas: the need for a rite that would address the condition of those being baptized; the importance of clearly setting out the role and obligations of the parents and godparents; and the development of rituals that would address a variety of pastoral circumstances encountered in infant baptism.

CSL 67 orders the preparation of a rite "suited to the fact that those to be baptized are infants." Before 1963 no rite had ever been prepared specifically for infants. At the time of the Council infants were directly addressed and questioned in the rite of baptism as though they were capable of response. For this reason the Council's preparatory commission made a double proposal that was approved by the Council Fathers: the child should not be addressed as an adult who answers through the godparents, and the godparents and parents should have a definite place in the rite. These two proposals were incorporated into CSL 67.

The Consilium prepared the revised rite based on principles which emphasized the communal nature of baptism. These included the possibility of regularly celebrating a liturgy of the Word at the beginning of the rite; the value of the ceremony of naming the child; and the need to adapt the formula of renunciation to modern conditions. Another important aspect of the reform was to clarify the relationship of infant baptism to the Christian initiation of adults.

The *Rite of Baptism for Children* (RB) was published by decree of the Congregation for Divine Worship on May 15, 1969. It contains two introductions. The first is a General Introduction to Christian Initiation which sets forth the fundamental doctrinal and pastoral principles underlying each of the sacraments of initiation: baptism, confirmation, and eucharist. It also describes the ministries for the celebration of baptism, requirements for the celebration of baptism, and adaptations which conferences of bishops and the minister of baptism are permitted to make in the rite.

The inclusion of the General Introduction to Christian Initiation in the *Rite of Baptism for Children* is significant. It indicates that the *Rite of Christian Initiation of Adults* is the premier rite of initiation from which all other initiatory rites take their meaning and form. In other words the baptism of children is no longer to be viewed as paradigmatic for adult initiation, as was the case in the years prior to the Council.

The second introduction is more specific and pertains to the baptism of children. It sets forth the nature of the revised rite, treating the proper subjects of the rite, the active role of parents and godparents in the celebration, the preference for communal celebration of the rite in the parish church, the emphasis on baptism as a sacrament of faith, and the paschal character of the rite.

The reforms incorporated into the rite are significant and reflect the ecclesial, sacramental, and liturgical principles that permeate the conciliar documents. Foremost among them is the preference for communal celebration. The *Rite of Baptism for Children* emphasizes that "the people of God, that is, the Church, made present by the local community, has an important part to play in the baptism of both children and adults" (RB 4). Not only do the people of God have an active role in the rite, but they play an important part in the life of the child both before and after baptism. "In this way it is clear that the faith in which the children are baptized is not the private possession of the individual family, but the common treasure of the whole Church of Christ" (RB 4).

CSL 67 also requires that the roles and obligations of the parents and godparents be brought out more clearly in the revised rite. The primary role is given to the parents. The rite states that the parents have "a ministry and a responsibility in the baptism of infants more important than those of the godparents" (RB 5).

Parents are to take an active role in the preparation for the sacrament, and their presence at the celebration is vitally important. Their duties are ritually set out in the questions, exhortations, and general intercessions during the celebration. Their primary task, however, is forming their child in the faith. This responsibility is so important that the rite stresses the necessity of faith in the parents and the importance of their preparation before the baptism of their child.

The revised *Rite of Baptism for Children* even speaks of delaying the celebration of the sacrament to "within the first weeks after birth" (RB 8) so that the mother may be present and to allow sufficient time for the preparation of the parents and the proper preparation of the sacrament. This is a departure from the speedy administration of the sacrament that was encouraged in the past and urged by the 1917 Code of Canon Law (can. 770). Although the godparents are no longer the focus of attention, they nevertheless have an active role in the rite, as well as the responsibility to support the Christian formation of the child, especially in those instances where parental responsibility is lacking.

CSL 68 offers a solution to two pastoral concerns that were raised at the Council by those from mission countries (although the circumstances are present in other places as well). The Rite of Baptism for a Large Number of Children (Chapter III in the revised ritual) was prepared at the request of Latin American bishops, whose clergy were often faced with the baptism of hundreds of children on a given Sunday. The structure of the rite is the same as that for the baptism of several children, but the rites are simplified and contain other modifications designed to address the pastoral needs of the situation. CSL 68 also addresses the situation in which neither a priest nor a deacon will be available for baptism; it decrees that a short rite be drawn up "especially in mission lands, for use by catechists but also by the faithful in general when there is danger of death and neither a priest nor a deacon is available."

The *Rite of Baptism for Children* provides two liturgical forms where none existed in the past for the particular occasions cited in CSL 68 when an ordained minister is lacking. They are the Rite of Baptism for Children Administered by a Catechist when no Priest or Deacon is Available (Chapter IV), and the shorter rite, The Baptism of Children in Danger of Death when no Priest or Deacon is Available (Chapter V). The former contains all the components integral to the baptismal liturgy, including the liturgy of the word and the liturgy of the sacrament, although these are abbreviated and in a somewhat simplified form. Omitted is everything a lay person would not do, such as the exorcisms, the anointings, and the ephphetha rite. The Rite of Baptism for Children in Danger of Death When no Priest or Deacon is Available (Chapter V) is a simple rite to be used when there is time to gather only a few people and an ordinary minister is lacking. The purpose of the rite is to maintain at least the essential elements of the baptismal ritual in order to give expression to the faith of the participants and to provide for an effective celebration. The rite also dispenses with all other ceremonies when there is urgency because of imminent danger of death; it mandates only the pouring of water using the customary words.

Prior to the Council a child who recovered health after being baptized in danger of death was taken to the church for the "Order of Supplying What Was Omitted in the Baptism of an Infant." The origin of this rite can be traced back to the thirteenth century. Its purpose was to provide those ceremonies which were omitted at the baptism. In particular, since the exorcisms had not yet been performed, the popular impression was conveyed that the child was still in the grip of the devil. CSL 69 requires that an entirely new rite be drawn up to "manifest more clearly and fittingly that an infant who was baptized by the short rite has already been received into the Church." The Rite of Bringing a Baptized Child to the Church (Chapter VI) adds what is lacking at a baptism celebrated by the short rite, namely, the public reception into the church. It also includes all the ritual elements omitted in the shorter rite.

CSL 69 also calls for a new rite "to be drawn up for converts who have already been validly baptized; it should express that they are being received into the communion of the Church." Until this time the liturgical books had not contained a general rite for reception into full communion that affirmed the validity of baptism in a non-Catholic Church or ecclesial community. The Reception of Baptized Christians into the Full Communion of the Catholic Church, found in Part II, Chapter 5 of the *Rite of Christian Initiation of Adults* (RCIA), fulfills this decree. The phrase "into the communion of the Church" used in CSL 69 was deliberately changed to "into the full communion of the Catholic Church" in the new rite of reception. This was inspired by the Decree on the Eastern Churches.

Unfortunately this rite of reception is often misunderstood, even by those involved in implementing the *Rite of Christian Initiation of Adults*. RCIA 473 states that for those seeking full communion "no greater burden than necessary (see Acts 15:28) is required for the establishment of communion and unity." Yet, it is not uncommon that adults requesting reception into full communion are indiscriminately incorporated into the ritual celebrations and catechetical formation called for in the RCIA, Part II, Chapter 4: Preparation of Uncatechized Adults for Confirmation and Eucharist. This matter is further compounded when all baptized adult candidates, whether previously catechized in the Christian faith or not, are made to join the formation offered to (unbaptized) catechumens.

While some candidates preparing to be received into full communion may have had little or no catechesis in the Christian faith and, consequently, will require a more extensive formation prior to their reception, other candidates may have had a thorough and lifelong grounding in living the Christian life. What is most important, then, is that there be a careful discernment of the amount of formation necessary for each candidate for reception into the full communion of the Catholic Church. They should not be automatically required to participate in a year-long "catechumenate" before they may be received. Clearly this is not called for by the rite itself or the special statutes approved by the bishops of the United States in 1986.

CSL 70 makes provision for the blessing of baptismal water during the rite of baptism except during the Easter season. The reason for this was twofold. The condition of baptismal water preserved for a whole year had been a growing concern in many areas. Members of the Council's preparatory commission deplored "the miserable and indecorous condition of the baptismal water found very often in smelly baptismal fonts, especially in warm climates." It was also deemed important to restore the richness of the sacramental sign, so that through frequent blessings, the liturgical and catechetical dimensions of the rite would be more clearly realized. The *Rite of Baptism for Children* includes the Blessing and Invocation of God over Baptismal Water as an integral part of the rite. The prayer is rich in biblical imagery and highlights the dimensions of spiritual rebirth.

The English translation of the *Rite of Baptism for Children* was approved by the National Conference of Catholic Bishops on November 13, 1969. The bishops also approved the following American adaptations: that the prebaptismal anointing with the oil of catechumens may be omitted, but only when the minister of baptism judges the omission to be pastorally necessary or desirable; that the two formulae in the Roman Ritual for the renunciation of Satan be retained, without the addition of a third formula; that the postbaptismal anointing be retained unchanged; and that the ephphetha rite may be performed at the discretion of the minister. These adaptations, along with the English translation of the rite itself, were confirmed by the Apostolic See on January 5, 1970, and the mandatory date for implementation of the rite in the United States was set for November 28, 1971.

The revised *Rite of Baptism for Children* has served the Church well, particularly in the United States. Much remains to be done, however, to realize its full potential in the life of the Church. Greater consideration needs to be given to the presence of the local community at baptismal celebrations. More work needs to be done to overcome a minimalistic approach to parental preparation. Further attention needs to be given to the quality of the primary liturgical symbols and gestures that enrich the rite.

Finally, it should be noted that the *Rite of Baptism for Children* is intended for infants and young children who have not yet reached catechetical age. Unbaptized children of catechetical age are to be initiated into the Church according to the RCIA, Part II, Chapter I: "Christian Initiation of Children Who Have Reached Catechetical Age." Such children who have attained the use of reason are not proper subjects for the *Rite of Baptism for Children*, since they are capable of receiving and nurturing a personal faith according to their age and ability. Accordingly, they are initiated according to the steps and periods of the *Rite of Christian Initiation of Adults*, including the reception of the three sacraments of initiation at one celebration.

In Memoriam: Father Robert Hovda

Father Robert Hovda, a leader in the liturgical movement in the United States before and after the Second Vatican Council, died on February 5, 1992, of heart failure. Ordained a priest in 1949, Father Hovda ministered in parishes in North Dakota, where he began writing articles on the liturgy. He taught at The Catholic University of America from 1960-1963, and from 1965-1978 he served as editor and writer for the Liturgical Conference. During those latter 13 years he edited the Liturgical Conference's monthly newsletter, *Living Worship*, and he authored the *Manual of Celebration*, a commentary on the revised texts of the *Sacramentary*, and *Strong, Loving, and Wise*, a book examining the art of presiding at worship. More recently he contributed a regular column for *Worship* entitled "The Amen Corner."

Father Hovda was widely regarded for his work as one of the principal consultants in the drafting of *Environment and Art in Catholic Worship*, the 1978 statement of the NCCB Liturgy Committee dealing with church art and architecture in the United States. Among his many contributions, however, Father Hovda was perhaps most influential as a speaker. Lecturing widely throughout the United States, he brought enthusiasm and unique insight to bear on the liturgy, inspiring those who heard him. His death is a loss to the Church.

> God of mercy and love,
> grant to Robert, your servant and priest,
> a glorious place at your heavenly table,
> for you made him here on earth
> a faithful minister of your word and sacrament.

Liturgical Calendar 1994

The NCCB Liturgy Secretariat recently prepared its 1994 edition of the liturgical calendar for the dioceses of the United States of America. The calendar lists each day's celebration, rank, liturgical color(s), and lectionary citations.

For many years the information in the annual calendars prepared by the Liturgy Secretariat was made available only to commercial publishers of other calendars, *ordines*, etc. in the United States. For the past two years it was been published in an inexpensive format and made available to anyone desiring a copy.

Liturgical Calendar 1994 (8½ X 11 in., 32 pages) may be purchased from: Bishops' Committee on the Liturgy, 3211 Fourth Street NE, Washington, DC 20017-1194, Att: Ms. Rena Hinnant. All orders must be accompanied by a check made out to "Bishops' Committee on the Liturgy" in the amount of $5.00 to cover printing, postage, and handling.

Presbyterian Liturgical Renewal

The Ministry Unit on Theology and Worship of the Presbyterian Church (USA) has recently published the last in a series of Supplemental Liturgical Resources in preparation for a new service book. *The Worshipbook - Services*, published in 1970, contains the last revision of the complete services of the Presbyterian Church. It was the first American Protestant liturgical book to contain a version of the new Roman *Lectionary for Mass*.

Over the past two decades much of the material in *The Worshipbook* has become dated. In 1980 the various Presbyterian Churches that now constitute the Presbyterian Church (USA) and the Cumberland Presbyterian Church began the process by which "a new book of services for corporate worship" might be developed. The Supplementary Liturgical Resources were published as an *ad interim* means of providing for the trial use of liturgical materials before the new service book is prepared. It is anticipated that editorial work on that new service book will be completed by the end of this summer.

The last three Supplementary Liturgical Resources (SLR 5, 6, 7) are of particular interest to Roman Catholics. SLR 5, *Daily Prayer: The Worship of God*, is a 435-page book containing resources for the daily celebration of the divine office. The introduction gives the background of the daily office and speaks of its appropriate use by Christians from the reformed tradition. Extensive pastoral guidance is given for each part of the office and how it may be celebrated. An ordinary is provided for Morning and Evening Prayer as well as for Midday and Night Prayer. The hinge hours of Morning and Evening Prayer may be celebrated in the basic form, an expanded form, or an abbreviated form, depending on the circumstances. Morning Prayer, in its basic form, consists of opening sentences, morning psalm or hymn, psalm(s) which may be concluded by silence and a psalm prayer, Scripture reading, biblical canticle, prayers of thanksgiving and intercession, Lord's Prayer, and dismissal. Evening Prayer begins with the entrance of the lighted candle, opening sentences, hymn of light or evening hymn, thanksgiving for light, Psalm 141 and its related psalm prayer. The remainder of the service follows the pattern for Morning Prayer. The book contains extensive propers for the seasons of the liturgical year, refrains and psalm prayers for the psalms, a collection of biblical canticles, and music for many parts of the office. The use of the *Daily Prayer* has quickly caught on among Presbyterians and is a welcome recovery of the Churches' tradition of daily prayer.

SLR 6, *Services of Occasions of Pastoral Care*, contains services for use with the sick and dying and also a service of repentance and forgiveness. Much of the material contained in this book will be familiar to anyone who uses *Pastoral Care of the Sick*. Scripture verses (sentences) and readings and prayers are given for use with the sick. An abbreviated version of the service of holy communion is provided for celebration in the home of a sick person. A rite for the imposition of hands and anointing of the sick is given under the title of Service of Wholeness. This service has both a communal form and one for use with a individual.

Also contained in the book is the Service for Repentance and Forgiveness for Use with a Penitent Individual. The rite consists of an invitation to confession, prayer of confession, declaration of pardon, sign of peace, and a dismissal. The introductory rubric states: "A penitent person who seeks an unburdening of conscience may seek the counsel of a minister. After counsel, the minister may suggest concluding the session with the following." The rite then follows.

The final sections of the book contain a form of renewal of baptismal vows for the sick or dying (similar to the provision in *Pastoral Care of the Sick* in the rite of viaticum) and a section of prayers at the time of death. SLR 6 has an extensive introduction which traces the history of pastoral care, its theology, and the role of worship in pastoral care.

The final volume of the series is SLR 7, *Liturgical Year: The Worship of God*. This resource of 428 pages provides an extensive treatment of the liturgical year. The introduction treats of liturgical time; the shape of the liturgical calendar; the Easter cycle: from the ashes of death to the fire of the Spirit; the Christmas cycle: from the darkness of the world to the light of Christ; Ordinary Time; and liturgical color. Both the shape of the calendar and the terminology used are familiar to Catholics. All the necessary liturgical resources for each season are provided: opening sentences, prayer of the day (collect), confession, great prayer of thanksgiving (eucharistic prayer), and a prayer of thanksgiving for occasions when the eucharist is not celebrated. Of special interest to Catholics is the recovery of liturgies for Ash Wednesday, Palm Sunday, and the Easter Triduum. Texts are given for the lighting of the Advent candles, for a service of lessons and carols, and the O Antiphons. An extensive commentary is given on the various special services of the liturgical year, and musical resources for the refrains of the responsorial psalms and for the Exsultet are also provided.

The Reverend Harold M. Daniels, who serves as the staff Associate for Liturgical Resources of the Theology and Worship Ministry Unit of the Presbyterian Church (USA), and the various committees that have worked with him are to be congratulated for their fine work. When incorporated into the proposed service book, these resources will provide rich liturgical fare for Presbyterians throughout the United States.

The Supplemental Liturgical Resources series is published by Westminster/John Knox Press, Louisville, KY.

Liturgical Programs/Conferences

National Association of Pastoral Musicians

Regional Conventions of the National Association of Pastoral Musicians will be held in Omaha, NE, July 8-11 (Blessed are Those . . . who Gather the Children), Albuquerque, NM, July 22-25 (Cantando la Fe del Pueblo - Singing the Faith of the People), Philadelphia, PA, August 5-8 (Break Forth! Renew the Renewal), and Nassau, Bahamas, Sept. 27-30 (The Cross and the Sword). NPM also offers a variety of summer programs and institutes throughout the country; these include week-long institutes on liturgical law and on Gregorian chant, and intensive programs for guitarists, organists, choir directors, and cantors and lectors. For further information contact: NPM Conventions, 225 Sheridan Street, NW, Washington, DC 20011-1492. Telephone: 202/723-5800.

Institute for Music and Liturgy

The first Institute for Music and Liturgy, sponsored by the Saint Lawrence Catholic Campus Center, University of Kansas, will be held on June 14-18, 1992. Faculty includes: Dr. Fred Moleck, Sr. Delores Dufner, OSB, Dr. Patrick Malloy, Dr. Michael Bauer, and Mr. Lynn Trapp, Executive Director of the Institute. For more information contact: Sally Hudnall, Saint Lawrence Catholic Campus Center, 1631 Crescent Road, Lawrence, KS 66044. Telephone: 913/843-0357.

COMMITTEE ON THE LITURGY

NEWSLETTER

1992
VOLUME XXVIII
MAY

New Revised Standard Version Confirmed

On May 15, 1992 the Most Reverend Daniel E. Pilarczyk, Archbishop of Cincinnati and President of the National Conference of Catholic Bishops, notified the members of the NCCB that the Congregation for Divine Worship and the Discipline of the Sacraments had confirmed the Conference's action approving the *New Revised Standard Version* (NRSV) of the Bible for liturgical use in the dioceses of the United States. The NRSV was approved by the Latin rite members of the NCCB at their November 1991 plenary meeting.

In a decree issued on May 14 Archbishop Pilarczyk states that the NRSV is to be incorporated into all approved liturgical books which contain the formerly approved *Revised Standard Version* (RSV), whenever those books are republished in the future. (Only a few liturgical books published in the United States have been issued in editions which incorporate the *Revised Standard Version*; most use the *New American Bible* for the Scripture texts.) The NRSV may be used in newly revised translations of liturgical books, once these have been approved by the National Conference of Catholic Bishops. The translation may also be used in an NRSV edition of the *Lectionary for Mass* once the date for the publication of the revised lectionary has been determined by the NCCB. The text of Archbishop Pilarczyk's decree follows:

NATIONAL CONFERENCE OF CATHOLIC BISHOPS
UNITED STATES OF AMERICA

DECREE

By authority of the National Conference of Catholic Bishops the *New Revised Standard Version* is declared to be approved for use in the liturgy in the dioceses of the United States of America.

Liturgical use of this translation of Scripture was canonically approved by the National Conference of Catholic Bishops on 13 November 1991 and was subsequently confirmed by the Apostolic See by decree of the Congregation for Divine Worship and the Discipline of the Sacraments on 6 April 1992 (Prot. N. CD 1261/91).

Henceforth the new translation may be used as a replacement for the earlier approved *Revised Standard Version* whenever any liturgical books containing that translation need to be reprinted. It may be used in newly revised translations of liturgical books, once these have been approved by the National Conference of Catholic Bishops. Finally, it may be used in an NRSV edition of the *Lectionary for Mass*, once the date for the publication of the revised second edition of the lectionary has been established, at which time its use as a replacement for the Revised Standard Version will become mandatory.

Given at the General Secretariat of the National Conference of Catholic Bishops, Washington, DC, on 14 May 1992, the feast of Saint Matthias, apostle.

+ Daniel E. Pilarczyk
Archbishop of Cincinnati
President
National Conference of Catholic Bishops

Robert N. Lynch
General Secretary

Rereading the Constitution on the Liturgy (art. 71)

Article 71 of the Constitution on the Liturgy (CSL) decrees the revision of the rite of confirmation. It follows the articles (64-70) devoted to the restoration of the catechumenate and to the revision of the rites of baptism for adults and for infants and manifests with them the conciliar vision of an integral process of initiation consisting of the three sacraments of initiation: baptism, confirmation, eucharist. Thus, it directs that the rite of confirmation is to be revised "in order that the intimate connection of this sacrament with the whole of Christian initiation may stand out more clearly."

CSL 71 includes two further directives that highlight the initiatory character of confirmation and more closely link it to baptism and eucharist. The first provides for the candidates to "renew their baptismal promises just before they are confirmed." The second states that "confirmation may be conferred within Mass when convenient."

At first glance the revisions mandated in CSL 71 seem simple enough; yet, the process of revision took several years. The complex history of the sacrament, the frequent changes in its ritual, prayers, and meaning throughout the centuries, and the theological controversies which surrounded the nature and purpose of confirmation down through the centuries made ritual revision a complicated enterprise. Questions concerning the minister of confirmation, the matter and form of the sacrament, and the age for its reception had to be examined. The diversity in theological and pastoral thinking compounded the problem.

The revised *Rite of Confirmation* (RC) is the result of much discussion and research by the Consilium and the Congregation for Divine Worship in consultation with the Congregations for the Doctrine of the Faith, for the Discipline of the Sacraments, and for the Evangelization of Peoples. The *Ordo Confirmationis* was approved by Pope Paul VI in the apostolic constitution *Divinae consortium naturae* on August 15, 1971, and was published by decree of the Congregation for Divine Worship on August 22, 1971.

The first step in the process of revision was to make the connection between confirmation and the whole of Christian initiation stand out more clearly, thus fulfilling the mandate of CSL 71. *Divinae consortium naturae* states that this was, in fact, the principal aim of the several years' work devoted to the revision of the rite and provides the basis upon which other decisions about the sacrament were made.

Since confirmation pertains to Christian initiation, the rite needs to be viewed in light of the *Ordo Initiationis Christianae Adultorum* and the *Ordo Baptismi Parvulorum*. The spirit and principles of initiation found in the adult rite are operative in the other rites of initiation and give continuity and meaning to them. This is evident in the *Rite of Confirmation* (RC). The opening paragraph of *Divinae consortium naturae* sets forth the initiatory character of confirmation when it states that "the faithful are born anew by baptism, strengthened by the sacrament of confirmation, and finally are sustained by the food of eternal life in the eucharist." This ordering presents confirmation as the second sacrament of Christian initiation, completing baptism and leading to participation in the eucharist. For this reason the Introduction to the rite states that "those who have been baptized continue on the path of Christian initiation through the sacrament of confirmation" (RC 1). And *Divinae consortium naturae* declares that the faithful are born anew in baptism, receive the Gift of the Holy Spirit, and "after being signed by baptism and confirmation, are incorporated fully into the Body of Christ by participation in the Eucharist."

Confirmation's close link with baptism and eucharist is set forth ritually in the revised *Rite of Confirmation*. The rite provides for the renewal of baptismal promises when confirmation is conferred on those who have been baptized in a previous celebration. Furthermore, the rite promotes the celebration of confirmation within Mass in order that the "fundamental connection of this sacrament with all of Christian initiation may stand out in clearer light" and so that the newly confirmed may participate in the eucharist, the sacrament "which completes their Christian initiation" (RC 13).

One of the more important reforms in the rite was providing a liturgical setting for the celebration of the sacrament of confirmation. The former rite had no Mass formulary, Scripture readings, or other liturgical rites to be used in the celebration of the sacrament. The *Rite of Confirmation* contains these proper texts, including a series of scriptural texts. Provision is made for confirmation to be celebrated within Mass (Chapter I) or, when this is not possible, outside Mass (Chapter II). Additional texts are provided for occasions when confirmation is celebrated by a minister who is not a bishop (Chapter III) and when the recipient of the sacrament is a person in danger of death (Chapter IV).

One of the more difficult issues dealt with in the revision process was specifying the essential rite of confirmation. The Eastern Churches give emphasis to the anointing with chrism, while the tradition of the Latin Church gradually linked the essence of the rite with the laying on of hands. Because this was a major issue of concern during the revision process and had ecumenical repercussions, the apostolic constitution takes care to demonstrate the continuity between the apostolic tradition of the laying on of hands and the signing of the forehead with chrism. It states that the "sacrament of confirmation is conferred through the anointing with chrism on the forehead, which is done by the laying on of the hand, and through the words: Be sealed with the Gift of the Holy Spirit." Thus, chrismation is the sacramental sign, but the action of anointing is by its nature a laying on of the hand. The Introduction to the rite provides a further explanation about the additional gesture of the outstretched hands of the minister prior to the anointing of those to be confirmed. It repeats the statement from the apostolic constitution but then adds: "The laying of hands on the candidates with the prayer, *All powerful God,* does not pertain to the valid giving of the sacrament. But it is still to be regarded as very important: it contributes to the complete perfection of the rite and to a more thorough understanding of the sacrament" (RC 9).

The *Rite of Confirmation* also contains a new sacramental formula that more suitably expresses the meaning of the sacrament. Those charged with the task of revising this formula made a careful study of the texts of the Western and Eastern traditions in order to find one that truly expressed the external action of signing as well as the effect of the sacrament, which is the imparting of the Spirit. They chose for the sacramental formula, "*N., accipe signaculum Doni Spiritus Sancti* (Be sealed with the Gift of the Spirit)". The wording is significant and deliberate. It expresses the fact that the gift which is given in confirmation is not merely *of* the Holy Spirit; the Gift is the Holy Spirit. The intention here was not to confuse this reality with the phrase "gifts of the Holy Spirit," which are distinct from the Holy Spirit.

The *Rite of Confirmation* also includes a significant change in the practice of who may serve as a godparent (sponsor) for confirmation. The previous rule, which did not allow the godparent at baptism to serve as the sponsor at confirmation, was abolished. In order to more fully express the relationship between baptism and confirmation the rite states that "it is desirable that the godparent at baptism, if available, also be the sponsor at confirmation" (RC 5). Although this is not mandatory, it nevertheless underscores the close connection of confirmation with baptism.

There are differing opinions today about sacramental preparation required for confirmation. The *Rite of Confirmation* itself does not place extraordinary demands for such preparation. RC 12 states that in addition to the requirement of baptism "those possessing the use of reason must be in the state of grace, properly instructed, and capable of renewing the baptismal promises." These requirements need to be kept in mind when assessing contemporary pastoral practices, some of which far exceed what is required by the rite.

This issue of catechetical preparation for the reception of a sacrament of initiation had been problematic in the Church in the past. Pope Saint Pius X dealt with the issue when, in his encyclical *Quam singulari*, he condemned the extraordinary demands required for first communion, citing them as examples of Jansenistic abuse.

The question of the appropriate age for confirmation was also taken up during the years devoted to the revision of the rite. Even while preparations were being made for the Second Vatican Council, bishops around the world were asking that answers be found to this question. In response to these requests, a special group was established in October 1964 to study the problem. The group, headed by Father Pierre-Marie Gy, OP, and Professor Balthasar Fischer, consulted with experts on the question. Their conclusion was to oppose the substitution of another age for the age of discretion. This did not resolve the matter, however, since there were pastors in the Latin Church requesting that the sacrament be delayed until the age of adolescence. Dom Bernard Botte, the relator of the study group in charge of the revision of the rite, held fast to the principle that the sequence of baptism-confirmation-eucharist must be respected and the tradition of the Roman Church specifying reception at the age of discretion be maintained. Botte's position concerning the age for confirmation was based on his firm belief that the essence of a sacrament could not be changed by modern theology and that the theory of confirmation as a sacrament of adolescence did not rest on any theological basis, but rather on psychological theories.

Nevertheless, the issue of age continued to come up at each of the Consilium meetings. Since the problem could not be resolved, the Congregation for the Doctrine of the Faith decided that the episcopal conferences should be given authority to decide, in light of the situation in each country, the age at which the sacrament of confirmation should be conferred. This suggestion was ultimately incorporated into the

Introduction of the new rite. RC 11 states that "with regard to children, in the Latin Church the administration of confirmation is generally delayed until about the seventh year. For pastoral reasons, however, especially to implant in the lives of the faithful complete obedience to Christ the Lord and a firm witnessing to him, the conferences of bishops may set an age that seems more suitable."

The age of confirmation is still problematic in the United States. In November 1984 the National Conference of Catholic Bishops voted to authorize diocesan bishops to determine the age at which the sacrament of confirmation is conferred in their dioceses. In June 1991 it was brought to the attention of the NCCB that, through an administrative oversight, they had failed to obtain the required *recognitio* of the Apostolic See for their action. On June 17, 1991 Archbishop Daniel Pilarczyk, President of the National Conference of Catholic Bishops, wrote to Cardinal Bernardin Gantin, Prefect of the Congregation for Bishops, and requested confirmation of the 1984 action. Cardinal Gantin responded that the congregation could not approve a norm that does not specify a particular age. Archbishop Pilarczyk subsequently appointed an *ad hoc* Committee on the Age for Confirmation to prepare a new proposal for action by the NCCB.

Whatever decision is made on the age of confirmation in the United States, the more important issue of maintaining the integrity and nature of the sacrament itself remains. The apostolic constitution *Divinae consortium naturae* and the *Rite of Confirmation* show that confirmation is a sacrament of initiation intimately connected with baptism and eucharist. Through confirmation those who have been born anew receive the gift of the Holy Spirit himself which endows them with special strength. Having received the character of this sacrament they are bound more intimately to the Church and are more strictly obliged to spread and defend the faith by word and deed as true witnesses of Christ. Nowhere in these documents is there to be found the suggestion that confirmation is a sacrament of adolescence, a sacrament of maturity, a rite of passage, or a time when the individual decides "for or against" the Church. The aim of the revision was to clarify the initiatory character of the sacrament and its intimate connection with the whole of Christian initiation. This was done for the most serious of theological and sacramental reasons: the signification of the unity of the Paschal Mystery.

Resources

New Parish Ministers: Lay & Religious Staffs, recently published by the National Pastoral Life Center in New York City, presents the findings of an extensive study—the first of its kind—of "new parish ministers," the nearly 20,000 lay people and religious employed at least twenty hours a week as "ministers" in half of the Catholic parishes in the United States.

The Center director, the Rev. Philip J. Murnion, along with the research team members David DeLambo, Rosemary Dilli, SNND, and Harry A. Fagan, surveyed more than 1,000 parishes and conducted on-site interviews with parish staff and parishioners in fifty-two of them to produce this report. The two-year study, commissioned by the Committee on Pastoral Practices of the National Conference of Catholic Bishops, was funded by Lilly Endowment of Indianapolis.

The book can be ordered directly from: The National Pastoral Life Center, 299 Elizabeth Street, New York, NY 10012-2806, (212)-431-7825; FAX (212)-274-9786. Cost for each is $11.95 plus $4.00 shipping and handling. Checks should be made payable to: The National Pastoral Life Center.

The Liturgy of the Hours Supplement: New Feasts and Memorials has recently been published by The Catholic Book Publishing Company, New York. It contains introductions and liturgical texts for the new feasts and memorials added to the *General Roman Calendar* and to the *Proper Calendar for the Dioceses of the United States of America* since 1976. It is available in paperback (4⅜ X 6¾ in., 48 pages) through Catholic bookstores. Cost: $1.25.

The *Handbook of Indulgences: Norms and Grants* is also available for purchase at Catholic bookstores. It is the authorized English translation of the third edition (May 1986) of the *Enchiridion Indulgentiarum: Normae et Concessiones.* The text was prepared at the request of the Apostolic See by the NCCB Liturgy Secretariat and has been approved by the Apostolic Penitentiary. It has now been published in hardback by The Catholic Book Publishing Company, New York (5½ X 8 in., 128 pages). Cost: $9.95.

COMMITTEE ON THE LITURGY

NEWSLETTER

NATIONAL CONFERENCE OF CATHOLIC BISHOPS

**1992
VOLUME XXVIII
JUNE/JULY**

Solemnity of the Assumption in 1992

The NCCB Secretariat for the Liturgy has received numerous inquiries concerning the canonical status of Saturday, August 15, 1992, as a holy day of obligation. In November 1991 the members of the National Conference of Catholic Bishops approved separate motions which stated that January 1, August 15, and November 1 will no longer be observed as holy days of obligation in the dioceses of the United States when they fall either on a *Saturday* or on a *Monday*.

For these decisions of the NCCB to acquire the force of law, the confirmation of the Apostolic See is required. At this time (July 3) the NCCB has not received the requisite confirmation of its decisions. Accordingly, Saturday, August 15, 1992, remains a holy day of obligation in the dioceses of the United States.

June Meeting of the Committee on the Liturgy

The Committee on the Liturgy of the National Conference of Catholic Bishops met at Notre Dame University, South Bend, IN, on June 21-23, 1992. Bishop Wilton D. Gregory, chairman of the Committee, welcomed Sister Madlyn Pape, CDP, and Father Samuel J. Aquila as new advisors to the Committee.

The Committee discussed and took action on several items: 1) procedures to be used for reviewing Volume II of the *Lectionary for Mass* before it is presented for approval at the November 1992 meeting of the NCCB; 2) liturgical implications and concerns pertaining to the use of prerecorded and computer-generated music in the liturgy; 3) the possible need to reexamine *Guidelines on Receiving Holy Communion* (approved by the NCCB Administrative Committee in November 1986) in light of several canonical, doctrinal, ecumenical, and liturgical concerns which have been raised in letters received by the Liturgy Secretariat.

The Committee also reviewed several ritual texts. It approved *Ritual de Exequias Cristianas*, the Spanish translation of the *Order of Christian Funerals*, and authorized its being submitted to the NCCB Administrative Committee for the requisite canonical approval. The Committee reviewed some adaptations which may be proposed for inclusion in a second U.S. typical edition of *The Book of Ordination: Ordination of a Bishop, of Presbyters, and of Deacons*. And the Committee gave its approval to the formation of a task group to work on American adaptations in the revised *Order of Celebrating Marriage*.

The Committee examined the results of a survey of bishops and of diocesan liturgical commissions and offices of worship dealing with possible American adaptations for inclusion in the revised *Roman Missal* (Sacramentary). The staff of the Secretariat will prepare an analysis of the results of the survey, and this will be sent to the bishops and to the diocesan commissions/offices. The Committee also spent time discussing the proposals which have been formulated to this time by its Task Group on American Adaptation of the *Roman Missal*.

The Committee considered two lectionaries. It discussed procedures for the publication of the *Lectionary for Mass* using the *New Revised Standard Version* (NRSV) of the Bible and approved the proposal by which the NRSV Lectionary will be reviewed for publication by the Secretariat for the Liturgy. A date for publication of the NRSV *Lectionary for Mass* will be determined once a similar date has been established for the publication of the lectionary using the *New American Bible*. The Committee also discussed the *Lectionary for Masses with Children*, approved by the NCCB in November 1991. Permission for a three-year experimental use of this lectionary was recently given by the Congregation for Divine Worship

3211 FOURTH STREET NE • WASHINGTON, DC 20017

and the Discipline of the Sacraments; following that three-year use, a renewal of the experimental use or definitive confirmation will be granted by the Congregation.

The Committee reviewed the revised draft of a proposed Mass in Thanksgiving for the Gift of Human Life. After making changes and corrections in the text, the Committee voted to present it for the approval of the NCCB in November 1992. The Committee also approved Norms for the Inclusion of Saints and the Blessed in the Proper Calendar for the Dioceses of the United States of America for presentation to the members of the NCCB in November 1992.

Various information reports were given. Father Michael Spillane presented a report on the work of the Federation of Diocesan Liturgical Commissions. He noted that 157 of the 176 dioceses in the United States are members of the Federation. The 1992 National Meeting of Diocesan Liturgical Commissions and Offices of Worship will be held in Miami, Florida, from October 2-5. Sister Anthony Poerio, chairperson of the Federation's board of directors, reviewed the position statements approved at the 1991 national meeting. The Committee discussed Position Statement 1991 B (on broadening access to ordained ministry in order that all communities of the faithful may be more adequately served) and Position Statement 1991 A (on the Renewal of Priestly Commitment and alternative prayers for the Chrism Mass). Sister Eleanor Bernstein, CSJ, and Dr. Mark Searle were invited to address the Committee. Sister Bernstein reported on the activities of the Notre Dame Center for Pastoral Liturgy, and Dr. Searle provided information on the liturgical studies program at the University of Notre Dame.

The next meeting of Committee members, consultants, and advisors will take place in New Orleans, LA, on June 20-21, 1993. The bishop members and consultants will meet on November 15, 1992, in Washington, DC.

Confirmation of Recent NCCB Liturgical Decisions

On June 10, 1992 the National Conference of Catholic Bishops received two letters from the Congregation for Divine Worship and the Discipline of the Sacraments, both dated 27 May 1992, which were related to the NCCB approval in November 1991 of several actions dealing with the revised *Lectionary for Mass* and the *Lectionary for Masses with Children*.

The same protocol number (Prot. N. 1259/91) was given to both letters, which were signed by Antonio Maria Cardinal Javierre Ortas, prefect of the congregation, and Archbishop Geraldo M. Agnelo, secretary. In the first letter, dealing with the revised *Lectionary for Mass*, the Congregation granted permission for the inclusion of Colossians 3:12-17 and Ephesians 5:25-32 as alternative readings to Colossians 3:12-21 and Ephesians 5:21-32 in the lectionary. It also confirmed the NCCB's decision to approve for liturgical use the revised Book of Psalms of the *New American Bible*.

In the second letter, dealing with the *Lectionary for Masses with Children*, the Congregation granted permission for a threeyear experimental use of the *cursus* of readings developed for the lectionary as well as the American Bible Society's *Contemporary English Version* of Scripture, the translation used in the lectionary. The Congregation stated that "after a three year period a full report of the experiment must be given and a renewal or definitive confirmation will be given."

Plans for the publication of the *Lectionary for Masses with Children* will be announced in a future issue of the *Newsletter*.

Rereading the Constitution on the Liturgy (art. 72)

The *Ordo Paenitentiae (Rite of Penance)* was the last of the revised rites for the sacraments to be approved. This was due in part to the theological and doctrinal controversies and political tension which prevailed during the process of revision.

Article 72 of the *Constitution on the Liturgy* (CSL) provided few guidelines for revision of the rite of penance when it stated: "The rites and formularies for the sacrament of penance are to be revised so that they more clearly express both the nature and effect of the sacrament." Thus the primary criteria for the liturgical reform of the rite of penance are found in other conciliar documents. These stress the social and ecclesial dimensions of the sacrament of penance, characteristics which had been virtually lost in the course of time. For example, *Lumen gentium* 11 situates the sacrament within the broader pastoral mission of the Church when it states that "those who approach the sacrament of penance obtain from God's mercy pardon for having offended him and at the same time reconciliation with the Church, which they have wounded by their sins and which by charity, example, and prayer seeks their conversion." *Presbyterorum ordinis* 5 speaks of the sacrament of penance as a means for sinners to be reconciled to both God and the Church. CSL 109 touches upon the social consequences of sin, and CSL 110 states that during Lent the practice of penance "should be not only inward and individual, but also outward and social."

The revision of the rite of penance was also guided by the general principles for the liturgical reform which are set out in the *Constitution on the Liturgy*. Foremost among these is the directive that liturgical celebrations are not private functions. Thus CSL 27 states that "whenever rites, according to their specific nature, make provision for communal celebration involving the presence and active participation of the faithful, it is to be stressed that this way of celebrating them is to be preferred, as far as possible, to a celebration that is individual and, so to speak, private. This applies with special force to the celebration of Mass and the administration of the sacraments, even though every Mass has of itself a public and social character." Other general norms which guided the revision included the integral role of scripture in liturgical celebrations (CSL 24 and 35), the primacy of active participation of the faithful (CSL 14 and 26), the inclusion of sacramental signs that can be easily understood (CSL 59), and the importance of liturgical adaptation (CSL 37-40). The emphasis on the social and ecclesial dimensions of the sacrament of penance in the conciliar documents along with the general principles of liturgical reform set out in the *Constitution on the Liturgy* combined to make the revision of the sacrament of penance one of the more radical reforms of the post-conciliar Church.

Such a reform was urgently needed in the Church. Even prior to the council there was evidence of growing dissatisfaction with the sacrament of penance and an increasing desire among many to restore its vitality. The "crisis" associated with the sacrament was seen in terms of its mechanical and privatized celebration, the reduction of its meaning to the confession of sins, and the general lack of awareness of the importance and role of conversion and reconciliation. As a result, the nature and effects of the sacrament had become obscured. Thus, the goal of the revision focused on the following: restoration of the ecclesial dimensions of the sacrament; a broadening of the sacramental dimension to include the mystery of reconciliation; greater emphasis placed on the interior disposition of conversion; recognition of both the personal and social dimensions of sin; and providing for communal forms for the celebration of the sacrament.

Almost ten years to the day that the *Constitution on the Liturgy* was promulgated, Pope Paul VI approved the Latin typical edition of the *Rite of Penance* (RP). It was published by decree of the Congregation of Divine Worship on December 2, 1973. In Advent 1975 this revised *Rite of Penance* in English became available in the United States. The effective date for implementation of the rite was extended to the First Sunday of Lent 1977. This was done for the most serious of reasons. Many of the essential aspects of the sacrament had been misunderstood or deemphasized throughout its history. By extending the effective date for implementation, it was hoped that dioceses and parishes would take time for adequate catechesis prior to the implementation of the new rite.

The title, *Ordo Paenitentiae*, refers to the fact that the ritual book contains both sacramental and non-sacramental rites. This is significant since the ritual addresses the spectrum for how the Church ritualizes conversion and reconciliation. The rite prefers the term "reconciliation" when speaking of sacramental liturgical actions, since this word better incorporates the reality that sacramental penance is an action of both God and a human being. Furthermore, the term "reconciliation" better expresses the reciprocal encounter that is proper to all the sacraments—God coming to meet human beings with the salvation that he given through Christ acting in his Church. The words "penance" or "confession," on the other hand, place greater emphasis on the actions of the individual person.

The *Rite of Penance* contains an introduction which is one of the most developed of all the reformed rites up until this time. It is divided into six sections. The first two sections provide theological background, and sections three to six detail elements pertaining to the rite itself.

Successful implementation of the *Rite of Penance* depends on a thorough understanding of the theological background provided in the first two sections. These contain the core insights of the new rite and bring many of the aspects of the sacrament that have been misunderstood and/or neglected throughout its history into clearer focus. One of the most important aspects found here is the emphasis placed on the concept of reconciliation; it includes much more than the confession and forgiveness of sins.

The Introduction begins by setting forth the Father's loving plan to reconcile the world to himself in Christ. Reconciliation is not something that just occurs at the sacramental moment, but a reality that sums up the whole of Christian life. Thus the Introduction situates the sacrament within the broader mission of the Church to call all people from sin to conversion. The Introduction also emphasizes the relationship of the sacrament of penance to baptism and eucharist. It restores Eucharist as the preeminent sacrament of reconciliation and the highlights the postbaptismal nature of penance as a renewal of baptism. Thus the Introduction presents the actual celebration of the sacrament of penance as a moment within the entire process of reconciliation which includes the whole life of the Church.

This theological understanding provides a sharp contrast to the presentation of the sacrament of penance found in the *Baltimore Catechism*. Of the fifty-five questions pertaining to the sacrament of penance, one remotely mentioned the history of salvation, forty-five were concerned with the acts of the penitent in the confessional or immediately before and after confession, and none dealt with the other signs by which God has manifested his love for sinners. This marked difference in context and understanding of the sacrament found in the revised *Rite of Penance* manifests the successful implementation of the conciliar mandate to fashion a rite that more clearly expresses the nature and effect of the sacrament.

Section III of the Introduction (RP 8-11) deals with offices and ministries in the reconciliation of penitents. It is appropriate that this section begins with the ministry of the community. Since the medieval period the sacrament of penance has rarely been seen within this context. This marked change reflects the overall thrust of the liturgical reform which begins any explanation of the offices and ministries in the community's liturgical life with the ministry of the community as a whole.

This ecclesial dimension is carried over in the treatment of the minister of the sacrament of penance. The rite states that "the Church exercises the ministry of the sacrament of penance through bishops and priests" (RP 9a). The minister's role is twofold: he calls the faithful to conversion through preaching God's word, and he ritually declares and grants forgiveness "in the name of Christ."

Finally the rite speaks of the penitent. The penitent's role as describe in RP 11 must be seen within the total context of the rite as well as within the whole process of continuing conversion. The rite emphasizes the importance of the active participation of the penitent in the celebration of the sacrament. It also highlights the ecclesial nature of the celebration when it states that the faithful "are with the priest celebrating the liturgy of the Church's continual self-renewal." Thus, even when the sacrament is celebrated with an individual penitent and minister, they should see themselves as the community of believers. But recovering this ecclesial understanding of the sacrament will not be easy, nor will it occur overnight.

Section IV of the Introduction (RP 12-35) deals with the celebration of the sacrament of penance. The rite provides for three sacramental celebrations: Rite for Reconciliation of Individual Penitents (Chapter I), Rite for Reconciliation of Several Penitents with Individual Confession and Absolution (Chapter II), and Rite for Reconciliation of Several Penitents with General Confession and Absolution (Chapter III). Although the Reconciliation of Individual Penitents appears first in the ritual book, the two communal rites for the celebration of the sacrament (Chapters II and III) have a priority. They more expressly fulfill the mandate of the *Constitution on the Liturgy* to bring out the public and communal dimension of every liturgical celebration.

The structure of the new Rite of Reconciliation of Individual Penitents is similar to the previous rite, but it has been given a better liturgical context. It provides for an opening rite, a reading of the Word of God, the confession of sins and acceptance of satisfaction, a prayer of the penitent, absolution by the minister, a proclamation of praise of God, and a dismissal. The ritual texts relate the sacramental encounter to the history of salvation, where God reconciles the world to himself through the death and resurrection of Christ. And they call attention to the ecclesial aspect of reconciliation effected through the ministry of the Church.

The Rite for Reconciliation of Several Penitents with Individual Confession and Absolution is the primary model for the ecclesial celebration of the sacrament. RP 22 states: "Communal celebration shows more clearly the ecclesial nature of penance." This ritual form brings out the public and communal nature of the sacrament, fosters the active participation of the faithful, and provides for an appropriate liturgical context for its celebration.

The introductory rites in this communal form of celebration are based on those of the eucharist and have a similar purpose of enabling the faithful to take on the form of community and prepare themselves to listen to God's Word. The rite states that the sacrament of penance should begin with hearing God's word, through which God "calls his people to repentance and leads them to a true conversion of heart" (RP 24). RP 51 provides for a choice of readings, and an entire scriptural repertoire can be found in Chapter IV. The rite sets out specific directions for the homily which reiterate many of the basic theological themes set forth in the Introduction to the rite. As such the homily becomes a primary liturgical moment for forming the faithful into the nature and spirit of the revised rite. The homily is followed by an examination of conscience and then the rite of reconciliation itself.

The Rite of Reconciliation consists of three parts: 1) the general confession of sins, litany or song, and the Lord's Prayer; 2) individual confession and absolution; and 3) proclamation of praise for God's mercy, concluding prayer of thanksgiving, and dismissal. The first part is a public and general confession of sins and prayer for God's pardon. This is followed by a litany or an appropriate song "to express confession of sins, heartfelt contrition, prayer for forgiveness, and trust in God's mercy" (RP 27).

Individual confession and absolution follow the praying of the Lord's Prayer. The sacramental formula provided in the ritual was the subject of much debate during the preparation of the rite. On the one side were those who believed that the declarative form ("I absolve you") of more recent tradition should be retained. Others preferred a return to the more ancient deprecative form which more clearly brings out the action of God and Christ ("May he absolve you"). The matter was ultimately resolved by the Congregation for the Doctrine of the Faith, which denied the use of the deprecative form.

Following the individual confession of sins and absolution, the community gathers for the Proclamation of Praise for God's Mercy. This is followed by the Concluding Prayer of Thanksgiving, and the Concluding Rite.

The rite contains many options for ritual texts as well as for scriptural readings. It also requires that the celebration be adapted to the "concrete circumstances of the penitents" (RP 40a). For these reasons it is necessary that careful attention be given to proper liturgical preparation of the rite. Appropriate consideration should always be given to the choice of ritual texts. The concrete circumstances of the faithful participating in the celebration may guide the choice of scriptural texts and various other ritual options permitted in the rite.

Chapter III provides for the communal celebration of the sacrament with general confession and absolution. This rite was formulated after extensive research on the part of the study group responsible for the revision of the rite. A ritual of general confession and absolution does not appear in the *Roman Ritual* of 1614, although it has precedence in the ancient Church and even in the *Roman Pontifical* of 1595. It appears in the *Rite of Penance* as a ritual on equal basis with the other two, yet its use is quite restricted. In 1972 the Congregation for the Doctrine of the Faith published a set of pastoral norms which set forth the doctrinal principles and practical guidelines for the use of this rite. These were included in the ritual, thus limiting the use of the rite to the conditions set down in these norms. Nevertheless, when the rite is celebrated, it is done so within the context of a fully developed rite with a liturgy of the word, general confession of sin, and a longer and somewhat more elaborate form of reconciliation and absolution.

Section V of the Introduction (RP 36-37) treats the nonsacramental penitential services that are included in the *Rite of Penance*. The ritual book gives nine models for such penitential celebrations. But for the most part these seem to have been overlooked in pastoral practice. This is unfortunate since their purpose is to promote and give communal expression to the Church's commitment to ongoing conversion and to better dispose the Christian community for the more fruitful celebration and reception of the sacrament itself. Given the concerns about the decline in the reception of the sacrament, it would seem that these penitential services would be more readily celebrated in parishes.

Non-sacramental penitential celebrations also serve an important function in those situations where a priest is not available to absolve penitents. Even though the faithful may not be able to receive the sacrament due to the absence of a priest, they are still bound to repent and be converted. This general call to repentance and conversion is one of the basic principles set forth in the ritual. Lastly the penitential services are excellent opportunities for developing a penitential attitude in children according to their age and ability.

Section VI of the Introduction (RP 38-40) provides for adaptations of the rite to various regions and circumstances. In November 1974 the National Conference of Catholic Bishops approved the following adaptations. The first concerned the place for the ordinary celebration of the sacrament of penance. Here the bishops approved the recommendation that it would be considered desirable that small chapels or reconciliation rooms be provided in which penitents might choose to confess their sins and seek sacramental reconciliation through an informal face-to-face exchange with the priest, with the opportunity for appropriate counsel. In addition they adopted the recommendation that it would also be desirable that such chapels or rooms be designed to afford the option of the penitent's kneeling at the fixed confessional grill in the usual way, but in every case the freedom of the penitent is to be respected.

Those familiar with ritual studies understand the importance of proper ritual space to better realize the nature and meaning of sacramental celebrations. Yet in many cases the place for sacramental reconciliation resembles more a liturgical "closet" than a chapel. (The very word "chapel" indicates the need for a worthy design that spatially sets out what is happening sacramentally.) Worse yet are those places where the old confessionals were barely renovated and are now used for the sacramental celebrations of the new rite or even as storage places for various objects when not being used for reconciliation. Even though the new rite is celebrated, the space reinforces the privatized notion of confession and undermines the ecclesial dimension restored in the *Rite of Penance*. Creating a worthy space for the celebration—one that fosters the ecclesial dimensions of the sacrament and reinforces the principles of conversion and reconciliation—needs to be given priority if the sacrament is ever to flourish and its vitality be restored.

The second adaptation approved by the National Conference of Catholic Bishops concerned the sign of penance which is to be used by the faithful in communal celebrations with general confession and absolution. Here the bishops approved the recommendation that in such circumstances the minister of the sacrament might determine and announce to the penitents the appropriate external sign of penance to be shown, e.g. kneeling, bowing of the head, bowing deeply, standing (if the penitents have been kneeling), a gesture such as the sign of the cross, etc.

Implementing the revised *Rite of Penance* does not guarantee that the Church's renewed understanding of reconciliation will be integrated into the lives of the faithful. Thus, revitalization of the sacrament will only happen when people recognize not only their sinfulness but also the basic Christian need for conversion and reconciliation in their lives.

Much more needs to be done to give priority to the communal celebration of the sacrament in parishes. And there is a long way to go before the individual penitent and minister see themselves as members of a community of believers when celebrating the Rite for Reconciliation of Individual Penitents. Initiation and reconciliation are closely connected. Thus reconciliation, as a post-baptismal experience of conversion, needs to be a primary consideration in catechesis. Given the needs of adolescents today, it is extraordinary that this sacrament has not emerged as a primary sacramental experience (along with eucharist) for dealing with the realities of the teenage years.

Clarification concerning Several Eucharistic Practices

The NCCB Secretariat for the Liturgy has received requests for clarification about a number of issues pertaining to proper eucharistic practice. The first of these concerns eucharistic reservation of the Precious Blood. *This Holy and Living Sacrifice: Directory for the Celebration and Reception of Communion Under Both Kinds* states that the consecrated wine may never be reserved, except for someone who is ill (no. 37). When this is done "the blood of the Lord is kept in a properly covered vessel and is placed in the tabernacle after communion." The Directory goes on to state that, if some of the precious blood remains after it has been given as communion for the sick, "it should be consumed by the minister, who should also see to it that the vessel is properly purified."

The approved procedure for dealing with the precious blood which remains after a eucharistic celebration is addressed in nos. 36 and 38 of the *Directory*. The consecrated wine is never to be poured into the ground or into the sacrarium. Rather, it is to be consumed by the ministers immediately at a side table before the Prayer After Communion. The sacred vessel are then purified, or they may be covered and then purified after Mass (see the *General Instruction of the Roman Missal*, no. 120).

Concerning the bread used for the celebration of the eucharist, the *General Instruction of the Roman Missal*, no. 283, states that, "The nature of the sign demands that the material for the eucharistic celebration truly have the appearance of food." The present discipline of the Latin Church is that bread for the eucharist be made only of wheaten flour and water. According to a statement made in 1980 by the Vatican Congregation for the Doctrine of the Faith, the addition or substitution of other ingredients can affect the validity of the sacrament.

It is possible to reconcile these two norms and produce larger loaves of bread made entirely of flour and water. When such bread is used in parish celebrations, catechesis should be given so that all of the faithful are aware that the bread used is in conformity to the norms established by the Congregation for the Doctrine of the Faith.

Concern is often raised about the continuing practice of communicating the assembly at Mass from the sacrament reserved in the tabernacle. The *Constitution on the Liturgy*, art. 55, states: "The more complete form of participation in the Mass by which the faithful, after the priest's communion, receive the Lord's body from the same sacrifice, is strongly endorsed" (emphasis added). This is supported in the *General Instruction of the Roman Missal*, no. 56-h, which states that "it is most desirable that the faithful receive the Lord's body from hosts consecrated at the same Mass and that, in the instances when it is permitted, they share in the chalice. Then even through the signs communion will stand out more clearly as a sharing in the sacrifice actually being offered."

The reason for which the Church reserves the eucharist outside Mass is, primarily, the administration of viaticum to the dying and, secondarily, communion of the sick, communion outside Mass, and adoration of Christ present in the sacrament (see *Holy Communion and Worship of the Eucharist outside Mass*, no. 5). Only under rare circumstances of necessity should the assembly at Mass communicate from the reserved sacrament in the tabernacle.

Ordination of Priests

The question is asked whether it is permissible to restore a practice that was found in the rite of ordination prior to the Second Vatican Council, namely, the binding of the newly ordained priest's hands with a white strip of cloth (sometimes called a "manutergium" = towel) after they have been anointed.

In the pre-conciliar ordination rite the prayer of consecration was followed by a series of rites intended to bring out the meaning of the laying on of hands and the prayer of ordination. After vesting the new priest in a stole and chasuble, the bishop said a long prayer which was originally an alternative prayer of consecration. The hymn *Veni, Creator Spiritus* was then sung. During the hymn the bishop anointed the hands of each new priest with the oil of catechumens (not chrism). The priest's hands were then bound together with a white strip of linen cloth. The bishop wiped his thumb on a piece of bread and then presented each priest with a chalice containing wine and water on top of which was a paten with a host. The new priest touched the chalice and host with the tips of his fingers (since his hands were bound together) while the bishop said: "Receive the power to offer sacrifice to God and to celebrate Mass for the living as well as for the dead in the name of the Lord." The bishop then washed his hands, and the gospel was read. While the offertory verse was being sung, the new priests washed their hands and dried them with the linen towel with which they were bound (manutergium).

The revised ordination rite for priests has greatly simplified these rites in order to show the centrality of the laying on of hands and the ordination prayer of consecration. The new priest is vested by another priest, and the bishop anoints the hands of the new priest using chrism. The new priest immediately washes his hands and then is presented with the chalice containing wine and water and the paten containing the bread for the eucharist. The bishop gives the kiss of peace to the new priest, and the celebration of the eucharist follows.

In the previous ordination rite the manutergium served a practical function. It kept the priest from unjoining his hands (and thereby getting oil on his vestments) until after the presentation of the chalice and paten. In the rite that is presently in use, as well as in the second Latin edition of the ordination rites published in 1990, no longer is there any need to bind the hands together, since the new priest washes his hands immediately after they are anointed and before the presentation of the offerings of the people. Accordingly, the use of the manutergium in the revised ordination rite has been abolished and no one on his own initiative may reintroduce the practice (see CSL 22, par. 3).

June Plenary Assembly of the NCCB

The National Conference of Catholic Bishops met in plenary assembly from June 18-20, 1992, at Notre Dame University, South Bend, IN. During the course of their meeting, the bishops voted on one item which had been presented by the Liturgy Committee: Volume 1 (Sundays, Solemnities, and Feasts of the Lord) of the revised *Lectionary for Mass* using the *New American Bible*.

This action item requires a two-thirds majority vote of the *de iure* Latin rite members of the NCCB and the subsequent confirmation of the Apostolic See. Voting on the action was inconclusive at the time that the meeting adjourned on June 20. The *de iure* Latin rite members of the NCCB who were not present at the time of the balloting during the meeting are now being contacted for their mail-in votes.

National Meeting of Diocesan Liturgical Commissions

The 1992 National Meeting of Diocesan Liturgical Commissions will be held from October 2-5 at the Eden Roc Hotel in Miami Beach, FL. The meeting, cosponsored by the Federation of Diocesan Liturgical Commissions and the NCCB Committee on the Liturgy, will have as its theme "Discovering Our Traditions," with a special focus on the Roman Missal. It will feature as speakers: Rev. Anscar Chupungco, OSB ("Tradition in Tension: Sources for the Roman Missal" and "Inculturation of the Liturgy"); Rev. Gilbert Ostdiek, OFM ("The Nuances of Liturgical Language"); and Sr. Kathleen Hughes, RSCJ ("Discovering our Traditions and Charting our Future"). Several workshops dealing with the Roman Missal or with liturgical inculturation will also be offered.

For registration forms and additional information concerning the meeting, contact: Ministry of Worship and Spiritual Life, Archdiocese of Miami, 9401 Biscayne Boulevard, Miami, FL 33138. Telephone: 305-757-6241, ext. 352.

United Methodist *Book of Worship*

At its Spring 1992 meeting, the General Conference of the United Methodist Church approved a new *Book of Worship* which as been in preparation since 1988. The *Book of Worship* represents the fruit of liturgical renewal that began in 1972 with the publication of the first volume of the *Supplemental Worship Resources Series*, the last of which was published in 1988. Along with the *United Methodist Hymnal*, published in 1989, the *Book of Worship* provides all the necessary prayers and services for the life of the United Methodist Church. The book contains a vast assortment of prayers and services that far surpass the number found in the previous edition of the *Book of Worship* (1965). The book is approximately 550 pages and is divided into 13 sections:

I. General Services (Services of Word and Table, Services of the Baptismal Covenant, Services of Christian Marriage, Services of Death and Resurrection)

II. Music as Acts of Worship

III. The Christian Year (Calendar; Calendar for Dating Easter and Related Holy Days; Colors for the Christian Year; Revised Common Lectionary; Advent; Christmas Season; Season after Epiphany; Lent; Easter Season; Season after Pentecost)

IV. Special Sundays and Other Special Days (Special Sundays of the United Methodist Church; Other Special Sundays)

V. General Acts of Worship (Ways of Praying; Greetings and Opening Prayers; Confession, Assurance, and Pardon; A Litany for the Church and for the World; The Ten Commandments; Prayers for Various Occasions; Blessing for Persons; Prayers of Thanksgiving; Dismissal, Blessings, and Closing Prayer)

VI. Daily Praise and Prayer

VII. Occasional Services

VIII. Healing Services and Prayers

IX. Services Relating to Congregations and Buildings

X. Consecrations and Ordinations

XI. Other Annual Conference and District Services

XII. General Church Services

XIII. Ecumenical Services

The general services have much in common with the corresponding rites of the Catholic Church and reflect the growing liturgical consensus among the Churches in the United States. The material in the Christian year section represents a restoration of many rites that were abandoned at the time of the Reformation: e.g., Ash Wednesday and the Holy Week liturgies. This section has much material taken from Part V of the American edition of the *Book of Blessings*: e.g., Blessing of the Advent Wreath, Christmas Trees, Nativity Scene. The blessings for Mother's and Father's Day are also included, as are the blessings for All Occasions, Birthdays, an Engaged Couple, a Victim of Crime or Oppression.

Congratulations are due to the Book of Worship Committee and to the Reverend Thomas Anderson Langford, III, the general editor, the Reverend Hoyt L. Hickman, worship services editor, and Dianna Sanchez, music editor. The *Book of Worship* will be published by Abingdon Press in the Fall.

COMMITTEE ON THE LITURGY

NEWSLETTER

**1992
VOLUME XXVIII
AUGUST**

Rereading the Constitution on the Liturgy (art. 73-75)

The reforms of the Second Vatican Council have gone a long way to restore the sacrament of the anointing of the sick to its original purpose and meaning. The reform of the rite focused on four primary areas referred in articles 73-75 of the *Constitution on the Liturgy* (CSL): the name and nature of the rite (CSL 73), the fitting time for its reception (CSL 73), the preparation of suitable rites when penance, anointing of the sick, and viaticum are celebrated on the same occasions (CSL 74), and the number of anointings (75).

In the Apostolic Constitution *Sacram Unctionem infirmorum* of November 30, 1972, Pope Paul VI established a new sacramental form of anointing and approved the *Ordo Unctionis infirmorum eorumque pastoralis curae*. The apostolic constitution also established January 1, 1974 as the date on which the use of the new rites became mandatory. The rites were issued by decree of the Congregation for Divine Worship on December 7, 1972.

In 1973 the International Commission on English in the Liturgy (ICEL) prepared a provisional translation of the Latin text. The purpose of the provisional ("green book") translation was to make the Latin typical edition immediately available and to use it as the basis for determining liturgical adaptations for the definitive ("white book") text. The *Rite of Anointing and Pastoral Care of the Sick* was approved for "ad interim" use in the United States by the Executive Committee of the National Conference of Catholic Bishops with an effective mandatory date of December 1, 1974.

The years during which the "ad interim" rite was used pastorally provided the opportunity for appropriate liturgical adaptations to be recommended. This was in conformity with CSL 63b, which states that "Particular rituals in harmony with the new edition of the Roman Ritual shall be prepared without delay by the competent territorial ecclesiastical authority mentioned in art. 22, par. 2 of this Constitution. These rituals are to be adapted, even in regard to the language employed, to the needs of the different regions."

Section IV of the General Introduction to the Latin edition lists the areas where liturgical adaptation may be made in the sacrament of the anointing of the sick. Responsibilities of the conferences of bishops in preparing particular rituals include: deciding on adaptations dealt with in CSL 39, determining what elements from the traditions and cultures of individual peoples may appropriately be admitted, preparing translations that are truly adapted to the genius of different languages and cultures, adapting and enlarging the Introduction in order to encourage the full, conscious, and active participation of the faithful, and arranging the materials in a format that will be as suitable as possible for pastoral use.

Accordingly the Bishops' Committee on the Liturgy asked for a broad consultation from all those who used the provisional translation of the rite. Areas of consultation included: the translation of the rite, the arrangement of the ritual texts, the selection/position of scripture readings, suggestions for additions to the rite or to the general introduction, suggested adaptations, suggestions concerning the use and presentation of options, and suggestions on how the rite might be more pastorally useful.

Following the consultation ICEL prepared a final translation of the rite, entitled *Pastoral Care of the Sick: Rites of Anointing and Viaticum*. This was approved by the National Conference of Catholic Bishops on November 18, 1982 and confirmed by the Congregation for the Sacraments and Divine Worship on December 11, 1982. The effective date for its implementation was the First Sunday of Advent, November 28, 1983.

Pastoral Care of the Sick: Rites of Anointing and Viaticum is a translation, adaptation, and expansion of the Latin *editio typica* of the *Ordo Unctionis Infirmorum eorumque pastoralis curae*. The attention given to the pastoral, liturgical, and theological responses to the consultation is evident in this definitive text. The material has been arranged to make a clear distinction between the Pastoral Care of the Sick (Part I) and the Pastoral Care of the Dying (Part II). Throughout the ritual distinctions are made between ordinary or normal celebrations and celebrations requiring adaptations because of particular pastoral circumstances. Original texts composed in English are found in almost every chapter. Most noteworthy is Chapter Two: Visits to a Sick Child. Here the Church's care for children is evident in the special attention given to enable a sick child to understand "that the sick are very special in the eyes of God because they are suffering as Christ suffered and because they can offer their sufferings for the salvation of the world" (63). Materials from other rituals, which address the sacramental needs of the sick and dying, are included in the rite in order to make it more pastorally useful.

Implementation of *Pastoral Care of Sick: Rites of Anointing and Viaticum* has been fairly successful in the United States. This is especially true in those places where communal celebrations have been given a priority in the parish and/or diocese. By means of them the entire parish community is led to understand that the sacrament addresses the human reality of sickness and is not merely reserved to those who are dying. In these instances, when liturgy functions as the primary formative experience of the Church, the faithful are led to see the sacrament "for what it is—a part of the prayer of the Church and an encounter with the Lord" (99).

Yet, much needs to be done in order to realize the full potential of the rite. One area that needs more attention is the development of an overall ministry to the sick in the parish. One of the hallmarks of *Pastoral Care of the Sick: Rites of Anointing and Viaticum* is that it situates the rites within the Church's overall pastoral care and concern for the sick in its midst. The rites do not limit this ministry to the priest or deacon. The importance of this ministry to the sick is stressed throughout the rite. The section on Offices and Ministries for the Sick in the General Introduction emphasizes the role of the Christian community. Paragraph 33 states, "It is thus especially fitting that all baptized Christians share in this ministry of mutual charity within the Body of Christ by doing all that they can to help the sick return to health, by showing love for the sick, and by celebrating the sacraments with them." Paragraph 42 in the introduction to Part I: Pastoral Care of the Sick states, "The concern that Christ showed for the bodily and spiritual welfare of those who are ill is continued by the Church in its ministry to the sick. This ministry is the common responsibility of all Christians, who should visit the sick, remember them in prayer, and celebrate the sacraments with them."

In other words ministry to the sick should not be limited to bringing them communion or anointing them. It should be expanded to include the ministry of visitation, works of charity, prayer etc. The rite even provides a liturgical setting for visits to the sick (and a sick child), thereby stressing the ministerial importance of this activity in the Church. These occasions are also to be used to prepare for future visits "during which the sick will receive the eucharist" (46). Sadly, there are too many instances where the homebound and those in hospitals or institutions receive communion only once a month, where clergy either are unable to or refuse to visit hospitals and nursing homes, where no concerted effort is given to visiting those who are ill, and where there is no social outreach in the parish which addresses the needs of the sick and their families.

The Church's broad ministry to the sick requires the involvement of the entire parish community. Laity and clergy, working together, each have their own special gifts to bring to this ministry. The involvement of the laity does not eliminate that of the clergy. And formation for clergy and laity alike is essential. It should be rooted in the ritual texts and take its inspiration from the prayers, introductions, scripture, gestures, and symbols which are elements of the rites. All those active in this ministry should have their own copy of the ritual book. Input and assistance from those involved in health care services and pastoral counseling bring additional insights and are important factors in formation.

A second area that needs further emphasis is that of catechesis. Liturgical catechesis in general is deficient in the Church. Paragraph 36 of *Pastoral Care of the Sick* points out that "it is important that all the faithful, and above all the sick, be aided by suitable catechesis in preparing for and participating in the sacraments of anointing and viaticum, especially if the celebration is to be carried out communally." A unique feature of the rites is their emphasis on the human experience of sickness. The General Introduction begins with this as its starting point and provides an excellent theology of sickness which needs to be the starting point for catechesis. Too often people perceive sickness as a punishment from God or as the absence of God in their lives. The rite, however, acknowledges sickness as a part of the human condition. As such, the human experience of sickness is an occasion to participate in the mysteries of salvation. Paragraph 1 states that "From Christ's own words they (Christians) know that sickness has meaning and value for their own salvation and for the salvation of the world. They also know that Christ, who during his life often visited and healed the sick, loves them in their illness."

This notion of sickness is essential to understanding the rite. Sickness is an occasion of conversion because it puts us in touch with the Paschal Mystery in a special way. Moreover, the one who is sick is seen as a Christ figure in our midst since "by their witness the sick show that our mortal life must be redeemed through the mystery of Christ's death and resurrection"(3). As such, the Church engages in a ministry to the sick which extends not only to those who are ill, but to those who are healthy as well. Within this context the sacramental acts of anointing and laying on of hands take on a new level of meaning.

Further catechesis needs to be given concerning Part II of *Pastoral Care of the Sick* which sets forth the rites that are used by the Church in its ministry to the dying. It is not uncommon that reference is still made to someone needing the "last rites" of the Church, as if these were one sacrament. Formation must begin to emphasize that the eucharist as viaticum is the sacrament proper to the dying Christian. The rite promotes the reception of viaticum within Mass and the full participation of the dying person and the community whenever possible in the liturgy. It also states that "priests and other ministers . . . should do everything they can to ensure that those in proximate danger of death receive the body *and* blood of Christ as viaticum"(176, emphasis added). This is the ordinary or normal celebration used for one who is dying. The rite points out that when the anointing of the sick is celebrated at the beginning of an illness, "viaticum, celebrated when death is close, will then be better understood as the last sacrament of Christian life" (175).

Misunderstanding sometimes arises with regard to cases of a sudden illness, accident, or any other situation that places a person in immediate danger of death. In these cases the rite provides for the celebration of the Continuous Rite of Penance, Anointing, and Viaticum. In keeping with the nature and purpose of each of these sacraments, however, the rite points out that if the circumstances are extreme, the priest should give viaticum immediately, without anointing. In this case the Rite for Emergencies is used.

It still bears repeating that if it is clear that a person has already died, the priest is not to administer the sacraments of penance or anointing. To this effect Chapter VII—Prayers for the Dead—points out that "sacraments are celebrated for the living, not for dead, and that the dead are effectively helped by the prayers of the living" (224).

Finally, more attention needs to be given to the relationship between sacramental and charismatic healing. Misunderstanding the distinction between the two has serious ramifications for the nature of the sacrament. Confusion often exists because both speak of bestowing the Holy Spirit, use similar gestures, involve the presence of the clergy, and take place within a liturgical context. The use of ambiguous language, such as "Healing Mass" and the anointing with oil, compounds the problem. Many laity and clergy are at a loss as to how to determine the difference between the two.

Pastoral Care of the Sick: Rites of Anointing and Viaticum provides an excellent example of liturgical adaptation at its best. Unfortunately the process of liturgical adaptation and preparation of particular rituals is still misunderstood. Some continue to find it disconcerting that our ritual texts continue to undergo revision. They find this process unsettling and often see it in terms of engaging in "faddish" liturgical tinkering or as a sign that the Church cannot make up its mind.

On the contrary, adaptation is integral to the liturgy if the liturgical celebration is to be an action of all God's people. Because of the fluidity of cultural expressions and the constant and growing needs of local Churches, adaptation will always be on the agenda of liturgical renewal. This is nothing new to the Church. It is the principle of adaptation that accounts for the varied rites and liturgical changes that the Church has known down through the centuries. It is for this very reason that the *Constitution on the Liturgy* provides that adaptations may be made in particular rituals and looks upon these rituals as the privileged place for adaptation.

The intent of CSL 63b is to say that the typical edition of a particular ritual book is to be adapted to the needs of the local Church. It is this adapted book that is meant to be the actual book for the liturgical celebration of the local Church. As evidenced in the *Pastoral Care of the Sick* the preparation of particular rites is governed by the norms set down by the *Constitution on the Liturgy* and the General Introduction (*praenotanda*) under the section "Adaptations by the Conferences of Bishops".

As we grow in our understanding of liturgy and the nature of ritual activity and become more attuned to the cultural and pastoral needs of local Churches, we will need to make further adaptations. This is true even of the Latin editions of the rites. For example, the time that elapsed between the first of the rites to be revised and the last major changes are evidenced by the style, arrangement of material, etc. The later rites were more detailed and complete. The introductions of the earlier rites were scantier, and differences are apparent in rubrics and guidelines. For this reason even the Apostolic See has issued an *editio typica altera* for the *Roman Missal,* for the *Ordination of a Bishop, of Presbyters, and of Deacons,* and for the *Order of Celebrating Marriage.* It is currently engaged in the process of preparing the third *editio typica* of the Roman Missal.

Pastoral Care of the Sick: Rites of Anointing and Viaticum reflects the cultural and pastoral needs of the Church in the United States. The years given to the pastoral use of the "ad interim" rite, the use of a process of consultation, and the pastoral sensitivity given to the English translation all combine to fulfill the spirit and goals of liturgical adaptation as set forth in the *Constitution on the Liturgy.*

Eucharistic Prayer for the Deaf

A eucharistic prayer for Masses with the deaf, approved for liturgical use by the bishops of English and Wales in 1977, was recently confirmed by Cardinal Javierre Ortas, prefect of the Congregation for Divine Worship and the Discipline of the Sacraments. The eucharistic prayer uses simplified language that is more easily signed than the present four eucharistic prayers. The introduction to the prayer notes that it to be used only in an assembly of the deaf and is to be signed by the celebrant himself. A rubric also notes that the celebrant must always pronounce all the words. It also states that when the celebrant signs while pronouncing the words, the liturgical gestures normally indicated in the rubrics are used or omitted as circumstances suggest and permit.

Resources

Deliver Those In Need is a book specially designed to receive the prayers of the faithful. The book is wire bound, covered in cloth and will lay flat on a table or writing stand in church. It contains 160 pages with space for people to write their intercessions. Each page has a verse from a psalm and is ornamented with images from everyday life. The general intercessions for the liturgy may also be inserted into a clear, acetate pocket which is bound into the book. The cost is $29.92. It may be purchased from Liturgy Training Publications, 1800 North Hermitage Avenue, Chicago, IL 60622-1101. Telephone: 1-800-933-1800.

Documents of the Marriage Liturgy, edited by Mark Searle and Kenneth W. Stevenson, is a collection of texts of the marriage liturgy throughout the centuries. Many of the texts are translated for the first time and are relatively inaccessible in their original form. Each text is situated within its historical context and is accompanied by historical and theological notes. The texts have been laid out to display the structure of the rites. The authors have also recast the prayer texts into sense lines to enhance their readability. Ritual sections, rubrics and prayers are numbered, and cross-referencing is provided where the same prayer recurs in different documents. Cost: $17.50 (paperback). Order from: The Liturgical Press, Saint John's Abbey, P.O. Box 7500, Collegeville, MN 56321-3299. Telephone: 612-363-2213.

In Memoriam: Sister Theophane Hytrek

Sister Theophane Hytrek, nationally recognized composer, educator, and concert organist, died on August 12 in her home in Milwaukee. A School Sister of Saint Francis, Sister Theophane taught at Alverno College for more than 50 of her 52 years in religious life. In 1990 she was honored as the first musician and the first woman to receive the annual Berakah Award of the North American Academy of Liturgy.

Composer of numerous compositions for liturgical use as well as for solo organ, Sister Theophane was perhaps best known for her "Pilgrim Mass," which was performed six times in one week by a 100-piece orchestra and a 2,000-voice chorus at the International Eucharistic Congress in Philadelphia in 1976.

> Lord, as we mourn the sudden death of our sister,
> show us the immense power of your goodness
> and strengthen our belief
> that Theophane has entered into your presence,
> there to rejoice with St. Cecilia
> and the chorus of angels the saints.

COMMITTEE ON THE LITURGY

NEWSLETTER

NATIONAL CONFERENCE OF CATHOLIC BISHOPS

1992
VOLUME XXVIII
SEPTEMBER

Rereading the Constitution on the Liturgy (art. 76)

The first of the revised liturgical books to be published after the Second Vatican Council contained the rites for the ordination of deacons, priests, and bishops. Revisions were made in both the ceremonies and the ritual texts. This was in accord with no. 76 of the *Constitution on the Liturgy*, which states that "both the ceremonies and texts of the ordination rites are to be revised. The address given by the bishop at the beginning of each ordination or consecration may be in the vernacular. When a bishop is consecrated, all the bishops present may take part in the laying on of hands."

The process for revising the rites of ordination addressed the major ritual and theological problems found in the preconciliar rites contained in the *Roman Pontifical*. Serious consideration was given to each rite of ordination so that the revised ritual would be clear in its organization, and that the words and gestures of the rites would be truly expressive of the teaching of the Church, especially as set forth in the conciliar documents.

Over the course of time, the preconciliar rites of ordination had undergone numerous changes which were the result of the doctrinal and cultural influences of particular periods of history. The allegorizing mentality and spirituality that marked the early Middle Ages, for example, came to be reflected in the formulas for ordination. The influence of the feudal period was responsible for the inclusion of certain gestures and several rites in the ordination ceremonies, e.g., the promise of obedience. The imposition of hands and its corresponding prayer of ordination, which form the core of the ordination rites, were gradually eclipsed by such secondary rites as the anointing of the hands of presbyters and the head of bishops, the presentation of the chalice and paten, the book of gospels, and the miter and pastoral staff of the bishop.

The revision of the ordination rites incorporated the doctrinal teaching of Vatican Council II, especially as set forth in *Lumen gentium*. The intention was to allow the rites to reflect the teaching of the Church on the sacrament of holy orders as well as to allow them to be a locus for the instruction of the faithful through the ritual celebration.

The revised ordination rites, which were published under the title *De Ordinatione Diaconi, Presbyteri et Episcopi*, were approved by Paul VI in the apostolic constitution, *Pontificalis Romani recognitio*, dated June 18, 1968. The Congregation of Rites decreed that their use should begin on Easter Sunday, April 6, 1969, although permission had already been given for experimental use in particular cases. A provisional English text was prepared by the International Commission on English in the Liturgy (ICEL). This was approved for use by the Executive Committee of the National Conference of Catholic Bishops and confirmed by the Apostolic See on December 16, 1971. In 1975 ICEL prepared the final translation, which was approved by the National Conference of Catholic Bishops in May 1976 and confirmed by the Apostolic See on August 12, 1977.

Like the other liturgical books that were revised in the earlier stages of the reform, the revised rites of ordination were warmly received, but in the course of time some deficiencies in them became apparent. The most significant of these were the lack of an Introduction comparable to those in liturgical books published after 1971; the continued used of the ancient ordination prayer for presbyters, which focused more on the Old Testament priesthood than on the priesthood of Christ; the lack of a rite of acceptance of celibacy in the rite of diaconal ordination; and the layout of the book, which placed the rite for the ordination of deacons first rather than that for bishops, thereby failing to highlight the order of bishops as the source of the other orders.

To address these deficiencies, a second *editio typica* of the rites of ordination was published by the Congregation for Divine Worship and the Discipline of the Sacraments on June 29, 1989. The book is entitled *De Ordinatione Episcopi, Presbyterorum et Diaconorum*. Based on the years of experience acquired from the liturgical reform as well as the pastoral use of the first typical edition, the *editio typica altera* contains elements that differ from the earlier edition.

It begins with a General Introduction, which is divided into three sections: I. Ordination (nos. 1-6); II. Structure of the Celebration (nos. 7-10); and III. Adaptations for Different Regions and Circumstances (no. 11). Each of the three orders of ministry are treated in separate chapters. Each chapter has an introduction divided into the following sections: I. Importance of the Ordination; II. Duties and Ministries; III. Celebration of the Ordination; and IV. Requisites for the Celebration. The first chapter contains the rite for the ordination of a bishop. This change from the first edition clearly demonstrates that it is the bishop who has the fullness of the sacrament of orders. It also more clearly communicates the notion that presbyters are the bishops' co-workers and that deacons are ordained for service.

The prayer of ordination of presbyters has been enriched with phrases from the New Testament and provides a better conception of the presbyterate as an order derived from the priesthood of Christ. A more extensive questioning takes place during the ordination of presbyters on the ministry of reconciliation and on the celebration of the eucharist. A rite of commitment to celibacy had earlier been included in the ordination of deacons, in light of the provisions set forth in the Apostolic Letter *Ad pascendum*, issued by Pope Paul VI in 1972. The discipline has now been changed so that even candidates who have pronounced perpetual vows in an institute of consecrated life are obliged, when being ordained to the diaconate, to make a commitment to celibacy as a distinct promise conjoined *de jure* to ordination. Provision has also been made for questioning members of institutes of consecrated life on their respect for the diocesan bishop and obedience to him in order to foster the unity of all the clerics in each local Church. And the Rite of Admission to Candidacy for Ordination as Deacons and Presbyters is included as an appendix.

In keeping with the teaching and spirit of the *Constitution on the Sacred Liturgy* for the preparation of particular rituals (CSL 63b), the second *editio typica* provides for adaptations for different regions and circumstances. Conferences of bishops have the authority to establish in what way the community, in keeping with regional customs, is to indicate its assent to the election of candidates in the ordination of bishops, of presbyters, and of deacons. They can direct that other questions be added to those provided in the various rites before the ordination. They have the authority to specify the form by which the elect for the diaconate and the presbyterate are to promise respect and obedience to the bishop. They may also direct the external manner in which the candidates manifest their resolve to accept the obligation of celibacy. Different songs may also be approved instead of those provided for in the book. Lastly, conferences of bishops may propose to the Apostolic See other adaptations that will be introduced with its consent.

Based on years of experience with celebrating the rites of ordination in the United States, it is possible to determine a number of areas where adaptation seems to be desirable. Greater attention needs to be given to the legitimate and active presence and participation of the laity at ordinations. In fact, this is stressed in the General Introduction of the second *editio typica*. Since ordination is the celebration of the whole community of the Church, the Introduction states that "ordination is to be celebrated within Mass, in which the faithful, particularly on a Sunday, take an active part 'at one altar at which the bishop presides, surrounded by his college of presbyters and by his ministers.' In this way the preeminent manifestation of the Church and the conferral of orders are joined with the eucharistic sacrifice, 'the fount and apex of the whole Christian life.'" It is easy to lose sight of this fact when large numbers of bishops, priests, and deacons overwhelm the presence of laity by sheer numbers, rendering their presence negligible.

The rites also need to be examined in light of the active participation of the laity during the ordination celebration, lest the impression be given that the laity are mere spectators. For example, adaptations could be made to include a formula which more clearly elicits the assent of the people before the election of presbyters and deacons and after the reading of the Apostolic Mandate at the ordination of a bishop. A question could be included in each of the rites directed to the people asking if they are willing to support the candidates. Lastly, directives may be necessary to ensure that the laity assume their proper roles in the ordination liturgy and are not excluded in favor of ordained ministers.

Other possibilities for adaptation include: a question in the promises of the elect for each of the orders regarding their willingness to consult or work with the laity; a better introduction to the question concerning celibacy in the rite of ordination for deacons that makes clear that the question is addressed to the unmarried candidates; a question in the same rite that refers to the ministry of charity; a petition for the wives (and families) of the married candidates in the ordination of deacons; an opportunity for testimony about the worthiness of the candidates in the rite of admission to candidacy; and provision for the promise of obedience to be made in a question and response form or directly without the question being posed by the bishop.

Consideration also needs to be given to the inclusion of pastoral notes that address particular issues that have emerged through the experience of the past twenty years in celebrating the rites. These would indicate that: concelebration may of necessity be limited in certain cases because of space considerations or other serious reasons; the sign of peace may be restricted to a representative group of presbyters when there are a large number of presbyters present; the entrance procession may be limited to the ministers of the liturgy, the candidates, selected concelebrants, and the bishop when there is a large number of presbyters or deacons present; the liturgical environment should be in keeping with the liturgical season, the nature of the rite and the liturgical space.

Revisions and adaptations will not resolve the problem of aberrations that periodically are introduced into the liturgical celebrations of the rites of ordination. One of the more common occurrences is the addition of a second or even a third homily and/or instruction. In spite of the norm specifying only one homily in the liturgy, lengthy addresses and expressions of thanks somehow get introduced into the liturgy even though they are more appropriately reserved to the reception after the ordination.

There are also instances when individuals reintroduce practices that have been abolished in the revised rites. A primary example of this is the re-introduction of the "manutergium", which has been abolished in the revised rite since the new priest washes his hands immediately after the anointing. Another is the retention of two "co-consecrators" on each side of the principal consecrator at an episcopal ordination. Although the consecrating bishops should sit near the principal consecrator, they should not take the place of the assisting deacons. Other practices include an elaborate expansion of the vesting of the newly ordained; the addition of songs and chants which lengthen the rite; presentation and vesting of candidates by family members or parishioners; the extension of the kiss of peace which concludes the ordination rite to family members or other laity in the assembly.

Currently the NCCB Liturgy Secretariat is assisting the International Commission on English in the Liturgy in the preparation of the English edition of the *editio typica altera*. The formatting of the book and the translation of the rubrics has been completed. The new liturgical texts are in the final stages of translation. A task group of the Bishop's Committee on the Liturgy has prepared several variations in the ordination rites for the United States. These will be proposed to the National Conference of Catholic Bishops at the same time as the ICEL translation.

In Memoriam

Sister Josephine Morgan, a Religious of the Sacred Heart of Jesus, died of cardiac arrest on July 3, 1992. A renowned musician who promoted the integration of liturgy and music, Sister Morgan studied Gregorian chant at Solesmes with Dom Gajard and taught music at Manhattanville College, Purchase, NY, for 43 years, serving also as director of Manhattanville's Pius X School of Liturgical Music from 1951 to 1969. Even after her retirement from teaching, Sister Morgan continued to lecture on liturgical music until her death. In an address at the time of Vatican Council II to musicians in St. Louis, she stated: "Musicians concerned with the liturgy require something in addition to their musical background and the scientific knowledge of church legislation, rubrics and ceremonial. Above all, they must have the spirit of the liturgy, enthusiasm for the true understanding of the liturgy."

> God of blessings,
> source of all holiness,
> the voice of your Spirit has drawn countless men and women
> to follow Jesus Christ
> and to bind themselves to you
> with ready will and loving heart.
>
> Look with mercy on Josephine
> who sought to fulfill her vows to you
> and grant her the reward promised to all good and faithful servants.
>
> May she rejoice in the company of the saints
> and with them praise you for ever.

Dr. Mark Searle, associate professor at the University of Notre Dame, died on August 16, 1992. Born in Bristol, England, he lived in the United States for the past 17 years. Mark studied at the Pontifical

Atheneum of St. Anthony in Rome and the Liturgical Institute in Trier. He wrote and edited numerous books and articles in the area of liturgy. His most recent research was in the area of ritual studies.

Mark is best known for his integration of the academic study of liturgy with its pastoral expression. He had a passion for encouraging the implementation of the liturgical reform, and was greatly respected both in academic and pastoral circles. He continued to teach liturgical courses until his death, and was in the process of preparing his fall course on the rites of death when he died. The Bishops' Committee on the Liturgy extends its prayers and expressions of sympathy to his wife, Barbara, and their three children, Anna, Matthew, and Justin.

> O God,
> you are water for our thirst
> and manna in our desert.
> We praise you for the life of Mark Searle
> and bless your mercy
> that has brought his suffering to an end.
> Now we beg that same endless mercy
> to raise him to new life.
> Nourished by the food and drink of heaven,
> may he rest for ever
> in the joy of Christ our Lord.

Resources

The *Collection of Masses of the Blessed Virgin Mary* has recently been published in separate editions by The Liturgical Press and The Catholic Books Publishing Company. Both editions contain two volumes: a Sacramentary (volume 1) and a Lectionary (volume 2). The Sacramentary contains the euchological texts, entrance and communion antiphons, the Order of Mass, and several formularies for solemn blessings at the end of Mass. The Lectionary provides the biblical readings for each Mass, together with the responsorial psalms and the alleluia verse or verse before the gospel reading.

The General Introduction of the *Collection of Masses of the Blessed Virgin Mary* includes a chapter entitled "Use of the Collection of Masses" (Chapter IV), which sets forth the norms for its use. It "is intended first of all for use in Marian shrines (nos. 29-33). The norms state that as long as the liturgical season is respected, the Masses provided in the Collection may be celebrated at such shrines on any day except those listed in no. 1-6 of the Table of Liturgical Days (no. 31a). This permission is granted *only* for priests who are part of a pilgrimage or for priests who celebrate Mass for the benefit of the members of a pilgrimage (no. 31b). The *Collection of Masses* is also intended for ecclesial communities for *ad libitum* use on Saturdays in Ordinary Time when there is no obligatory memorial, feast, or solemnity (nos. 34-36). Finally, the *Collection of Masses* may be used on days when, according to the *General Instruction on the Roman Missal*, the choice of Masses is left open. In these instances, a priest celebrating Mass, whether with or without a congregation, has the option of using one of the formularies in the Collection (no. 37).

The *Collection of Masses of the Blessed Virgin Mary* is the English typical edition of *Collectio Missarum de Beata Maria Virgine*, canonically approved for use *ad interim* in the dioceses of the United States by the Administrative Committee of the National Conference of Catholic Bishops on September 27, 1989, and confirmed by decree of the Congregation for Divine Worship and the Discipline of the Sacraments on March 20, 1990. The effective date for use of the Collection in the dioceses of the United States of America is December 8, 1992, the solemnity of the Immaculate Conception.

The *Collection of Masses of the Blessed Virgin Mary* is available from The Liturgical Press, Collegeville, MN (1-800-858-5450). The Sacramentary (Volume I) [hardcover, 8½ X 11, one color, 320 pages] costs $19.95, and the Lectionary (Volume II) [hardcover, 8½ X 11, one color, 256 pages] costs $19.95. The two volume set in hardcover costs $34.95.

The Collection is also available from The Catholic Book Publishing Company through Catholic bookstores. The Sacramentary (Volume I) [hardcover, 8½ X 11, two colors with tabs, 272 pages] costs $24.00, and the Lectionary (Volume II) [hardcover, 8 ½ X 11, two colors, 240 pages] costs $21.00. The two volume set costs $44.00.

NATIONAL CONFERENCE OF CATHOLIC BISHOPS

COMMITTEE ON THE LITURGY

NEWSLETTER

1992
VOLUME XXVIII
OCTOBER

1992 National Meeting of Diocesan Liturgical Commissions

The annual national meeting of diocesan liturgical commissions and offices of worship was held in Miami, FL from October 2-5, 1992. Two hundred ten delegates, representing over 100 dioceses, attended the meeting, which was jointly sponsored by the Federation of Diocesan Liturgical Commissions and the NCCB Committee on the Liturgy. They were joined by nearly 100 local parish liturgical ministers.

The general theme of the meeting was "Discovering Our Traditions" with a special focus on the *Roman Missal*. Major presentations were given by Anscar J. Chupungco, OSB ("The Tradition in Tension: Sources for the *Roman Missal*" and "Inculturation of the Liturgy"); Gilbert Ostdiek, OFM ("The Nuances of Liturgical Language"); and Kathleen Hughes, RSCJ ("Discovering our Traditions and Charting our Future").

The delegates approved five position statements which had been formulated at regional meetings of the delegates during the spring of 1992.

FDLC Address of Bishop Wilton D. Gregory

On October 2, 1992 the Most Reverend Wilton D. Gregory, Auxiliary Bishop of Chicago and Chairman of the Bishops' Committee on the Liturgy, addressed the delegates to the 1992 National Meeting of Diocesan Liturgical Commissions in Miami, FL. The text of that address follows.

It is an honor and a great pleasure for me once again to be able to address the delegates to the annual National Meeting of Diocesan Liturgical Commissions.

Last year, I spoke to you in some detail about the "second generation" of liturgical books presently being issued by the Apostolic See, by the International Commission on English in the Liturgy, and by our own Bishops' Committee on the Liturgy.

I will not spend a great deal of time looking again at those developments. But briefly, let me say that for the Bishops' Committee on the Liturgy this past year has been an important one for liturgical lectionaries. Last November the members of the National Conference of Catholic Bishops (NCCB) approved the *Lectionary for Masses with Children,* which uses the American Bible Society's *Contemporary English Version* of the Bible. They also approved for liturgical use the *New Revised Standard Version* of Scripture. These actions were confirmed by the Congregation for Divine Worship and the Discipline of the Sacraments in the spring of this year.

Then, at their June meeting at the University of Notre Dame, the members of the NCCB approved the Sunday portion of the revised *Lectionary for Mass* using the *New American Bible with Revised New Testament and Book of Psalms.* That action has been referred to the Apostolic See for the necessary confirmation. The final portion of the revised *Lectionary for Mass* will be presented for the approval of the bishops next month in Washington. Our Secretariat staff will be meeting with publishers later this month to formulate plans for the publication of these new lectionaries. And already, the lectionary volume of the *Collection of Masses of the Blessed Virgin Mary* incorporates the revised psalter and New Testament of the *New American Bible.*

While we await a revised English-language edition of the Sacramentary from the International Commission on English in the Liturgy in another two years, the Vatican Congregation for Divine Worship and the Discipline of the Sacraments is expected to continue to issue slightly-revised new editions of the

Missale Romanum, most of the books of the *Roman Ritual,* and a number of the rites contained in the *Roman Pontifical.* And, of course, the first typical edition of the *Roman Martyrology* is still anticipated.

But you undoubtedly have seen reports about all of these developments. And you are here for four days to devote some intense reflection specifically on the *Roman Missal.* What do we do as we await this revised Sacramentary? Just wait?

Last year I issued a challenge to you when I stated, "The time has come to begin once again a concerted effort at catechesis on the Missal. The *General Instruction of the Roman Missal* and the *Introduction to the Lectionary* are not so much collections of rubrics as they are excellent sources of catechesis on the Mass and the reasons that underlie the reforms. As such, they must be read again and again by all liturgical ministers..."

I continued by saying that, "catechesis is not just necessary for the clergy. There are too many parishes where there was never any real catechesis on the Mass and its reforms and even more where the introduction of the reformed rites was haphazard or even minimal."

Now I ask you today, what has been done during these past twelve months in response to this challenge? No doubt most of your spring regional meetings devoted a significant amount of time to a study of ICEL's *Third Progress Report on the Revision of the Roman Missal,* and perhaps the first and second progress reports as well. I hope you found your reflection on the work of ICEL—and that you will find this national meeting—important for your own knowledge about the *Roman Missal* and the ICEL revision.

But if this national meeting is to be termed a "success," it seems to me that a national strategy—or strategies—for catechesis on the *Roman Missal* needs to be articulated by the delegates assembled here.

What is at issue here at this meeting? It is this: liturgical catechesis is necessary; and catechesis on the *Roman Missal* is essential. Certainly, there will be some changes in the Missal as a result of the process of revision now being carried on by ICEL. But, for the people in the pews, these changes will not be that numerous. Some among you might be tempted to think that *only the priests* will need significant catechesis in light of this fact. Yet the whole reform of the Missal called for by the Second Vatican Council and implemented in Paul VI's 1970 edition of the *Missale Romanum* is still unknown to many of the Catholic people of our country, clergy and laity alike.

Perhaps there is some reluctance to invest precious time in preparing for a renewed effort at catechesis on the Missal because of some notion that we cannot *begin* until we have the completed revised Sacramentary in our hands. But such a position labors under a false understanding of catechesis as well as perhaps unrealistic expectations about the revised Sacramentary itself.

What *is* liturgical catechesis? We know that catechesis on the liturgy begins with the celebration of the liturgy itself. It follows from this that liturgical catechesis considers the *manner* in which we celebrate the liturgy as well as the *rites and texts* of the liturgy. And so, even as we await a revised Sacramentary, liturgical catechesis—for good or for ill—goes on as we *celebrate* the liturgy—*well, or not so well.*

We are able to see how effective our catechesis has been by carefully assessing our liturgical celebrations today. For instance, a foundational principle of the liturgical reform decreed by the Second Vatican Council is the full, conscious, and active participation of the Christian faithful who form our liturgical assemblies. Where such participation is half-hearted or almost altogether lacking we instinctively sense that catechesis has been ineffective. More than that, the celebrations themselves are continuing to *mis*-form such liturgical assemblies gathered for worship.

Our reformed liturgical rites call for a diversity of ministries, beginning with the ministry of the full liturgical assembly itself, in service to the Body of Christ. Furthermore, the rites are characterized by that "noble simplicity" which allows their symbolic ritual action to point clearly and forcefully to the unseen realities which are the heart of all our worship. When these principles of the liturgical reform are not actualized to their fullest, even a revised liturgical text will not help. The liturgical reform will continue to be frustrated, and the Christian faithful will not experience the transforming power of the liturgical rites.

We have heard a great many voices urge a more careful review of the texts that we already possess and the principles that continue to ground the liturgical reform. Today, I would like to propose a more careful liturgical catechesis of the clergy and the faithful laity. This is the same urgent task that Our Holy Father wrote of in his *Apostolic Letter on the 25th Anniversary of the Promulgation of Sacrosanctum concilium,* art. 15. Occasionally a particular dimension of the liturgy will demand more concentrated attention. We might be concerned about language and the related issues of inclusivity. At another moment we might be addressing the question of inculturation and the liturgy. The question of music and the impact of its technological development will occupy our attention at another time. We might even spend significant study addressing the question of the maturation of a contemporary liturgical aesthetic. But all of these components, as important as they are, remain parts of a larger concern, the total reality of the Church at prayer. We need to reintroduce a complete liturgical catechesis based upon a sound and renewed understanding of the Church, a theology that has been informed by the developments of the last thirty years and thoroughly grounded in the tradition of the Church.

Without such a solid theological foundation, all of our liturgical activity will lack cohesiveness and clarity and will render the individual components virtually ineffective in achieving their desired ends. Liturgical renewal by its very nature remains an expression of the spiritual renewal of the Church as both its source and its end. We need to continually remind our people of the importance of this fact. In the question of liturgical renewal, the whole is always greater than the sum of its parts. Perhaps, in the rush of our activity to address one or another element within the liturgy, we all may have lost sight of this important ecclesial reality at one time or another. Therefore we must invite our clergy and lay faithful to a renewed liturgical catechesis which will begin, not with any specific constitutive component of the liturgy, but with the full panorama of the Church in the sanctifying act of praise. Such liturgical catechesis will call to mind, once again, the significance of the Church standing in the awesome presence of the All-Holy God and the transforming power of that experience.

The Bishops' Committee on the Liturgy, co-sponsor of this national meeting along with the Federation of Diocesan Liturgical Commissions, is deeply committed to continuing liturgical catechesis. Our Secretariat staff has worked with the FDLC National Office and the Miami host committee in striving to guarantee that this meeting will be *informative* to you delegates as you prepare to receive the product of the ICEL revision of the Missal in a few years. Time has been allotted in the schedule for a thorough explanation of the work of ICEL, as well as our own Committee's Task Group on American Adaptation of the Roman Missal. You will have the opportunity to seek clarification about the revisions process and proposed U.S. adaptations. All aspects of the ICEL revision will be treated.

In your regional caucuses at this meeting you will continue to formulate the outlines of a national effort at effective catechesis on the *Roman Missal.* The Bishops' Committee on the Liturgy stands ready to support you in this task. May the important task of liturgical catechesis, entrusted to you by the bishops of your dioceses when they appointed you to the diocesan liturgical commissions and offices of worship, meet with every success in the months and years ahead.

Resolutions of the 1992 National Meeting of Diocesan Liturgical Commissions

The following position statements were adopted by the delegates to the 1992 National Meeting of Diocesan Liturgical Commissions, held in Miami, Florida, October 2-5, 1992. The degree of commitment to each statement is indicated in parentheses. The voting scale is graded from +3 (highest degree of commitment) to -3 (complete opposition to the statement). A commitment of +1.5 is required for acceptance.

Informational Materials for Revision of *Roman Missal*

P.S. 1992 A

It is the position of the delegates to the 1992 National Meeting of Diocesan Liturgical Commissions that, in addition to the three (3) ICEL progress reports on the revision of the *Roman Missal,* the Federation of Diocesan Liturgical Commissions (FDLC) and the Bishops' Committee on the Liturgy (BCL) collaborate in producing informational materials, such as teleconference, video, and other media technology, which promote the proposed revisions and additions. These materials are to be directed to our diocesan bishops to communicate to them our support of this project. Furthermore, we, the individual members of the FDLC, commit ourselves to work with our diocesan bishops as they prepare for this important vote.

We request that a time-line and procedure for implementation of this resolution be set by the FDLC Board of Directors at the January 1993 Board Meeting. (Passed + 2.39—Submitted by Region X)

Celebration of Initiation during Lent Inappropriate

P.S. 1992 B

It is the position of the delegates to the 1992 National Meeting of Diocesan Liturgical Commissions that the Bishops' Committee on the Liturgy recommend to the National Conference of Catholic Bishops that the sacraments of initiation (baptism, confirmation, and first reception of eucharist) normally should not be celebrated during the Lenten season. It is also recommended that the BCL propose appropriate directives to this effect to the NCCB, and that the FDLC provide catechetical materials on the appropriate seasons for the celebration of the sacraments of initiation.

We request that a time-line and procedure for implementation of this resolution be set by the FDLC Board of Directors at the January 1993 Board Meeting. (Passed + 1.53—Submitted by Region IX)

Discussion at National Meetings

P.S. 1992 C

It is the position of the delegates to the 1992 National Meeting of Diocesan Liturgical Commissions that the Board of Directors of the Federation of Diocesan Liturgical Commissions develop a component of the National Meeting to allow delegates' floor discussion of significant liturgical matters without requiring either action or a vote on the topic under discussion.

We request that a time-line and procedure for implementation of this resolution be set by the FDLC Board of Directors at the January 1993 Board Meeting. (Passed + 1.96—Submitted by Region II)

Confirmation at the Age of Discretion

P.S. 1992 D

It is the position of the delegates to the 1992 National Meeting of Diocesan Liturgical Commissions that the FDLC Board of Directors ask the Bishops' Committee on the Liturgy to communicate to the NCCB our support for the age of discretion as the governing norm for confirmation of those baptized in infancy, in order to preserve the original sequence of the sacraments of initiation.

We request that a time-line and procedure for implementation of this resolution be set by the FDLC Board of Directors at the January 1993 Board Meeting. (Passed + 2.12—Submitted by Region VIII)

The Position of Confirmation within the Sacramental System

P.S. 1992 E

It is the position of the delegates to the 1992 National Meeting of Diocesan Liturgical Commissions that the Board of Directors of the Federation of Diocesan Liturgical Commissions and the Bishops' Committee on the Liturgy urge the National Conference of Catholic Bishops to take the initiative to propose to the Apostolic See a discussion on the restoration of the ancient practice of celebrating confirmation and communion at the time of baptism, including the baptism of children who have not yet reached catechetical age, so that through connection of these three sacraments, the unity of the Paschal Mystery would be better signified and the eucharist would again assume its proper significance as the culmination of Christian initiation.

We request that a time-line and procedure for implementation of this resolution be set by the FDLC Board of Directors at the January 1993 Board Meeting. (Passed + 2.12—Submitted by the FDLC Sacraments Committee)

Resources

The Liturgical Press has published the *Book of Blessings: Abridged Edition.* This book contains all of the blessings that are celebrated outside Mass or outside of the church. (Rites of blessing during Mass and those celebrated in the church have been omitted.) The numbering for blessings in this edition varies from the unabridged, but the blessings remain essentially in the same order. The abridged edition is published in paperback (556 pages, 4 1/14 X 6 3/4) in the same color and design as the Liturgical Press ritual and study edition of the *Book of Blessings.* Cost: $14.95.

COMMITTEE ON THE LITURGY

NEWSLETTER

NATIONAL CONFERENCE OF CATHOLIC BISHOPS

1992
VOLUME XXVIII
NOVEMBER

November Plenary Assembly of the NCCB

The National Conference of Catholic Bishops met in plenary assembly from November 16-19, 1992, at the Omni Shoreham Hotel, Washington, DC. During the course of their meeting, the bishops approved three liturgical items presented by the Committee on the Liturgy.

Two action items were approved by the required two thirds majority vote of the *de jure* members and now require confirmation by the Apostolic See: 1) *Volume II: Weekdays, Saints, Commons, Ritual Masses, and Masses for Various Needs and Occasions* of the revised second edition of the *Lectionary for Mass,* using the *New American Bible with Revised New Testament and Book of Psalms;* and 2) a Mass formulary *"In Thanksgiving for the Gift of Human Life"* for inclusion in the section of the Sacramentary entitled "Masses for Various Needs and Occasions (*Missae et Orationes pro Variis Necessitatibus*)."

The membership also approved by unanimous voice vote *On the Inclusion of Saints and the Blessed in the Proper Calendar for the Dioceses of the United States of America,* a policy statement of the Committee on the Liturgy to guide it when responding to requests for the inclusion of various saints and the blessed on the national calendar.

In the balloting for Conference officers and Committee chairman, the Most Reverend Donald W. Trautman, Bishop of Erie, was elected Chairman-elect of the NCCB Committee on the Liturgy. Bishop Trautman will serve as a voting member of the Committee for the next twelve months and will assume the chairmanship of the Committee at the conclusion of the NCCB plenary assembly in November 1993.

Rereading the Constitution on the Liturgy (art. 77-78)

The rite of marriage was one of the first of the liturgical books to be revised after the Second Vatican Council. The revision took into account the directives set forth in the *Constitution on the Liturgy* (CSL, art. 77-78) as well as those detailed in the motu proprio *Sacram Liturgiam* and the instruction *Inter Oecumenici.* In light of these directives, the revision provided for the following: that the celebration of marriage should always take place within a Mass or a liturgy of the word; that the nuptial blessing should always be given to the spouses, even during closed times such as the season of Lent and even if one or both parties are contracting a second marriage; that the structure of the rite begins with a short instruction (not a homily), reading of the epistle, psalm, gospel, homily (based on the sacred text), celebration of the sacrament, prayer of the faithful and nuptial blessing; and that the readings are to be in the vernacular.

The *Ordo Celebrandi Matrimonium* was published by the Congregation of Rites on March 19, 1969. The National Conference of Catholic Bishops (NCCB) approved the English translation of the *Rite of Marriage* (RM) on November 13, 1969. Following confirmation by the Apostolic See on January 5, 1970, the effective date for its official use in the United States was set for November 28, 1971.

The *Rite of Marriage* contains four chapters. It begins with an Introduction which highlights the importance and dignity of the sacrament of marriage and recalls the teaching of the various conciliar documents on the subject (nos. 1-7). As is true for the other liturgical books revised in the early stages of the reform, this introduction is not as extensive and complete as the ones found in the liturgical books published later on.

Paragraphs 8-11 deal with the celebration of marriage during Mass and outside of Mass and the celebration of marriage between a Catholic and a non-baptized person. Accordingly the *Rite of Marriage* contains a Rite for Celebrating Marriage during Mass (Chapter I), a Rite for Celebrating Marriage outside

Mass (Chapter II), and a Rite for Celebrating Marriage between a Catholic and an Unbaptized Person (Chapter III).

The Introduction also includes norms for the preparation of particular rituals as called for in the *Constitution on the Liturgy,* art. 63b and 77 (RM 12-16). In the preparation of particular rituals the competent ecclesiastical authority may: adapt the formularies of the Roman Ritual or supplement them (including the questions before the consent and the actual words of consent); vary the arrangement of parts within the actual rite and omit the questions before the consent as long as the assisting priest asks for and receives the consent of the contracting parties; omit or substitute other rites whenever the exchange of rings does not fit in with the practice of the people; and consider marriage customs of nations receiving the Gospel for the first time whenever these are not bound up with superstition and error and harmonize with the true and authentic spirit of the rite.

In conformity with CSL 77 and 78 the Introduction also includes a section on the right to prepare a completely new rite (nos. 17-18). "Each conference of bishops may draw up its own marriage rite suited to the usages of the place and people and approved by the Apostolic See" (RM 17). According to the pastoral needs of the people, the conference of bishops may also allow the sacramental rite to be celebrated in the home among peoples where marriage ceremonies customarily take place there over a period of several days (RM 18).

In light of the above the National Conference of Catholic Bishops approved three resolutions at their plenary meeting in November 1969. These were subsequently approved by the Apostolic See and included in the ritual text. The conference approved the resolution that the wording of the existing form of consent be introduced as an alternative to the wording of the revised rite. Thus in the dioceses of the United States the form "I, N., take you for my lawful wife (husband), to have and to hold, from this day forward, for better, for worse, for richer, for poorer, in sickness and in health, until death do us part" may be used (see nos. 25, 45, and 60). The NCCB also determined that the disposition of the *Rite of Marriage* concerning the mode of exchanging consent be retained without change. Lastly, the NCCB delegated the Bishops' Committee on the Liturgy to prepare and include provisionally additional formulas or texts for the marriage service (and other rites) where this is expressly permitted by the norms of the Roman liturgical books in accord with art. 38 of the *Constitution on the Liturgy.* As a result the *Rite of Marriage* includes an additional solemn blessing that was previously included in the American edition of the *Collectio Rituum.*

In late 1990 the Congregation for Divine Worship and the Discipline of the Sacraments published a revised Latin edition of the *Ordo Celebrandi Matrimonium.* In contrast to the brief introduction of the first typical edition, the totally new introduction of the 1990 edition numbers 44 paragraphs. The new edition also contains several additions to and changes of liturgical texts found in the 1969 edition. It contains an Order for the Celebration of Marriage during Mass (Chapter I), an Order for the Celebration of Marriage outside Mass (Chapter II), an Order for the Celebration of Marriage before an Assisting Layperson (Chapter III), an Order for the Celebration of Marriage between a Catholic and a Catechumen or a Non-Christian (Chapter IV), Various Texts for Use in the Order of Marriage (Chapter V), and an Appendix which contains two examples of General Intercessions and two blessings from the *Book of Blessings:* the Order for the Blessing of an Engaged Couple and the Order for the Blessing of a Married Couple on the Anniversary of Marriage. (A description and a more complete outline of this revised ritual can be found in the January 1991 *Newsletter*).

The second typical edition also promotes the preparation of particular rituals by conferences of bishops who have the right to adapt the Roman Ritual to the customs and needs of their particular regions. The final portion of the Introduction to the *Order for Celebrating Marriage* concerns "Adaptations to be provided under the care of the Conferences of Bishops" (nos. 39-44). This section corresponds to the section on the preparation of local rituals found in the first typical edition (nos. 12-18).

The International Commission on English in the Liturgy (ICEL) is now preparing the English translation of the second edition of the marriage rite as revised by the Congregation of Divine Worship and the Discipline of the Sacraments. Included in the USA edition of the English translation will be the *Ecumenical Rite for Celebrating Marriage between a Catholic and a Baptized Member of Another Church or Ecclesial Community,* prepared by the North American Consultation on Common Texts and approved by the National Conference of Catholic Bishops in November 1987.

This is an appropriate time to consider the question of American adaptations. As noted above, the rite provides for a considerable number of possibilities where conferences of bishops may make adaptations to the rite even to the extent of preparing their own proper marriage rite within the limits set forth in the ritual text. Based on experience in this country with the 1969 edition, a number of issues have come to light that bear further consideration. For example, concerns have been raised about the formula for consent contained in the present *Rite of Marriage,* especially in light of the more developed understanding of matrimonial consent found in the teaching of the Second Vatican Council and in post-conciliar teaching. Greater attention and more prudent consideration needs to be given to the inclusion of appropriate symbolism within the rite. Also, the active participation of the assembly in the wedding ceremony needs to be examined. To this effect the Bishops' Committee on the Liturgy authorized the establishment of a task group to study the *Order for Celebrating Marriage* at their June 1992 meeting. It is expected that some particular adaptations for the United States will be presented with the ICEL translation of the revised rite for approval of the National Conference of Catholic Bishops.

It would be naive to think, however, that the publication of the second typical edition will resolve the pastoral liturgical problems that consistently emerge at the time of the celebration of marriage. Anyone who has assisted couples in marriage preparation is aware of the tensions that surface especially in reference to the liturgy. Disagreement arises at times over the choice of liturgical music, appropriate liturgical ministers, the inclusion of symbols, gestures and other elements into the rite that may be incompatible with the understanding of marriage as set forth in the ritual text. Furthermore, local customs sometimes have been introduced into the celebration without authorization and prudent and careful consideration. The form of the wedding "procession" that is still quite common in the United States does not correspond to the procession which is set forth in the ritual text. All of this is may be magnified when liturgical preparation is taken over by those who provide professional services and consultation for weddings.

Much of the above is the result of inadequate understanding of the rite on the part of both laity and clergy. Appropriate liturgical catechesis for marriage is necessary and must begin with the communal dimension of the sacrament. Marriage is a celebration of the entire Church. The significance of this is stressed in the second typical edition which states that "Marriage is meant to increase and sanctify the people of God and therefore its celebration has a communal character that calls for the participation even of the parish community" (no. 28). To this effect the rite even mentions that the "celebration of the sacrament may take place during the Sunday assembly" (no. 28).

Catechesis is also necessary because so many people are still unfamiliar with the *Rite of Marriage.* Since catechesis on the rite is generally limited to the couple at the time of immediate preparation, most are unaware of what the rite requires and the alternatives that it offers. Many presume that customs promoted by the media are included in or compatible with *Rite of Marriage.* Others come with a preconceived "vision" of what a wedding ceremony should look like, often bolstered by popular brides' magazines or the desires of parents.

The importance of catechesis is emphasized in the second typical edition of the *Order of Celebrating Marriage* and is not limited to the moments of immediate preparation. In fact the second typical edition states that the preparation and celebration of marriage concerns the entire ecclesial community. It encourages catechesis adapted to children, youth, and adults by methods that include the media of social communication, and promotes effective liturgical celebrations so that the significance and meaning of marriage stands out more clearly.

This latter point is very important. The preparation for and celebration of any sacrament is always a moment of conversion for those receiving the sacrament as well as for all those participating in the celebration. Marriage between two baptized people is considered a visible sign of the unfolding of the hidden mystery of God in this world and consequently is significant not only for the couple but for the community to which they belong. Proper celebration invites the community of believers to discover what we understand christian marriage to be.

Newsletter Subscription Renewals

All subscribers to the Bishops' Committee on the Liturgy *Newsletter* will be sent computerized renewal notices in early December for the upcoming 1993 calendar year. To avoid interruption in service, the completed forms should be returned promptly. (Subscriptions which have not been renewed by the time the January 1993 *Newsletter* goes to press will be placed in an inactive file and reinstated once payment is received.) Individual subscription rates are $10.00 domestic mail and $12.00 foreign airmail.

In order that subscribers' accounts may be properly credited, the instructions accompanying the renewal forms should be followed. The "renewal coupon" portion of the invoice must be included with payment. Coupon and payment should be returned in the self-mailer envelope which has been provided. This envelope is preaddressed for direct deposit to the bank. Payment should not be sent to the NCCB Secretariat for the Liturgy since this needlessly prolongs the renewal process.

Subscribers who have not received a renewal notice by the end of December 1992 should contact the Liturgy Secretariat so that a duplicate invoice can be sent. (*Newsletter* recipients whose subscription number is 205990, 205995, or 205999 are receiving *gratis* copies and will receive no renewal notice.)

The gratitude of the Liturgy Secretariat is extended to all subscribers for their cooperation in the *Newsletter* renewal process.

Alternative Reading for the Feast of the Holy Family

On June 10, 1992 the Congregation for Divine Worship and the Discipline of the Sacraments confirmed the decision of the National Conference of Catholic Bishops to include alternate readings to Colossians 3:12-21 and Ephesians 5:21-23 in the *Lectionary for Mass* (see June/July 1992 *Newsletter*). The Colossians reading is used on the feast of the Holy Family, which will be celebrated this year on Sunday, December 27, 1992. The alternate shorter reading of Colossians 3:12-17 may be used in place of Colossians 3:12-21.

Shorter forms of these two readings were requested because the present longer forms have been known to cause pastoral difficulties in some communities. It should be remembered that there are many instances in the lectionary where long and short forms of the same readings are provided. The shorter form of the reading from Colossians retains the verses which deal with the Christian qualities which are necessary for husbands, wives, and children, in fact, for all followers of Christ. Therefore it is appropriate for the feast of the Holy Family.

Rite of Christian Initiation of Adults

The Secretariat for Liturgy has received inquiries concerning the *Rite of Christian Initiation of Adults*. The first of these concerns the proper title of the rite. The title of the rite has *not* been changed to the *Order of Christian Initiation of Adults* (OCIA). The proper title of the English translation of the *Ordo initiationis christianae adultorum* is *Rite of Christian Initiation of Adults* (RCIA). Any change in the title of the English translation of liturgical books must be approved by the National Conference of Catholic Bishops and confirmed by the Apostolic See.

The second inquiry concerns the title of the rite celebrated with unbaptized children of catechetical age. There is no *Rite of Christian Initiation of Children* (RCIC). The Church has the *Rite of Baptism of Children* which is to be celebrated with all children under catechetical age who do not have the use of reason. The *Rite of Christian Initiation of Adults,* Part II Chapter I is celebrated with all unbaptized children who have attained the use of reason and are of catechetical age.

Resources

Advent Calendar: Fling Wide the Doors is a three-dimensional calendar that contains windows which allow light to pass through so that the calendar can be illuminated from within like a lantern. It includes saints days, the "O" antiphons, and the twelve days of Christmas. The calendar runs from November 30 to January 6. It is accompanied by a small booklet to be used each day when opening the doors and praying with the Church during Advent. The calendar is available from Liturgy Training Publications (1-800-933-1800) in family size (12 inches) for $10.00, or community size (18 inches) for $17.00.

A Promise of Presence, edited by Michael Downey and Richard Fragomeni, is a collection of studies on sacramental theology and practice presented by colleagues and students to noted theologian and teacher, David N. Power, OMI. Included in the work are chapters on *Lex Orandi, Lex Credendi* by Michael Downey; *The Sacraments, Interiority and Spiritual Direction* by Stephen Happel; *Devotio Futura: The Need for Post-Conciliar Devotions?* by Regis A. Duffy; *The Roman Catholic Response to Baptism, Eucharist and Ministry: The Ecclesiological Dimension* by Geoffrey Wainwright. The cost of the book is $24.95 (paperback, 325 pages) and can be ordered from: The Pastoral Press, 225 Sheridan Street, NW, Washington, DC 20011. Telephone: (202) 723-1254.

COMMITTEE ON THE LITURGY

NEWSLETTER

NATIONAL CONFERENCE OF CATHOLIC BISHOPS

1992
VOLUME XXVIII
DECEMBER

November 1992 Liturgy Committee Meeting

The NCCB Liturgy Committee met in Washington, DC, on November 15, 1992. The Committee reviewed the following liturgical items on the agenda of the NCCB plenary meeting: 1) the *Mass in Thanksgiving for the Gift of Human Life;* 2) Policy Statement of the Liturgy Committee *On the Inclusion of Saints and the Blessed in the Proper Calendar for the Dioceses of the United States of America;* 3) *Lectionary for Mass,* Vol. II. They also discussed the following topics: a proposal concerning the English formula for matrimonial consent; the issue of Holy Communion of persons with Celiac Sprue Disease; a Eucharistic Prayer for Masses with persons who are deaf; the liturgical spirit and ecclesial intent of the Paschal Triduum, particularly the Easter Vigil; and the question of communion hosts and contemplative orders of nuns. The Committee also reviewed the five position statements approved by the delegates to the National Meeting of Diocesan Liturgical Commissions held in Miami, Florida, October 2-5, 1992.

Reports were made on the status of various subjects of the subcommittees and task groups of the Liturgy Committee. These included the Hispanic Liturgy Subcommittee, the Task Group on Cremation and Other Funeral Practices, and the Task Group on American Adaptation of the Roman Missal.

Liturgy Committee Policy Statement on the USA Calendar Approved

During the June 1991 plenary meeting of the Committee on the Liturgy, the question of the inclusion of additional saints and the blessed in the Particular Calendar for the Dioceses of the United States of America was raised. Rather than adding more saints or beati *to the calendar at that time without any clear guidelines for doing so, the Committee directed its Secretariat staff to prepare a policy statement on this matter.*

The text which follows was approved by unanimous voice vote of the members of the National Conference of Catholic Bishops on November 18, 1992, as an internal policy statement of its standing Committee on the Liturgy to guide the Committee in responding to requests for the inclusion of various saints and the blessed on the national calendar.

ON THE INCLUSION OF SAINTS AND THE BLESSED IN THE PROPER CALENDAR FOR THE DIOCESES OF THE UNITED STATES OF AMERICA

In its Constitution on the Sacred Liturgy *Sacrosanctum Concilium* (hereafter SC), the Second Vatican Council decreed the revision of the liturgical year and the calendar (art. 106-111). The sanctoral calendar of the Church was to be revised in such a way that many commemorations "should be left to be celebrated by a particular Church or nation or religious family; those only should be extended to the universal Church that commemorate saints of truly universal significance" (SC 111).

In 1969 the *General Norms for the Liturgical Year and the Calendar* (hereafter GNLYC) were published along with the *General Roman Calendar for the Universal Church.* The *General Norms* note that the calendar consists of the *General Roman Calendar,* which is used by the entire Roman Rite, and of particular calendars used in a particular Church (nation or diocese) or in families of religious (GNLYC 48). (A "proper calendar" is the combination of the *General Roman Calendar* and one or more particular calendars.) Whereas the *General Roman Calendar* contains the celebrations of saints having a universal significance, the particular calendars "have more specialized celebrations, arranged to harmonize with the general cycle. The individual Churches or families of religious should show a special honor to those saints who are properly their own" (GNLYC 49). Particular calendars must be drawn up by the competent authority (conference of bishops, diocesan bishop, religious superiors) and be approved by the Apostolic See (GNLYC 49).

3211 FOURTH STREET NE • WASHINGTON, DC 20017

Particular calendars may be drawn up for entire provinces, regions, and countries as well as individual dioceses (GNLYC 31). As a result, we now have a particular calendar for the Dioceses of the United States of America as well as particular calendars for individual dioceses and religious communities. The Instruction, *Calendaria particularia* (hereafter CP), on the revision of particular calendars, of June 1970, indicates that in a region or nation the following celebrations may be observed: the feast of the principal patron, memorial of the secondary patron, other celebrations of saints or the blessed who are duly listed in the *Roman Martyrology* or its Appendix and who have a special relationship to the region or nation (see CP 8). The particular calendar for the Dioceses of the United States of America presently contains the following celebrations:

JANUARY

4   Elizabeth Ann Seton, religious - Memorial
5   John Neumann, bishop - Memorial
6   Blessed Andre Bessette, religious - Optional Memorial

MARCH

3   Blessed Katharine Drexel, virgin - Optional Memorial

MAY

15   Isidore - Optional Memorial

JULY

1   Blessed Junípero Serra, priest - Optional Memorial
4   Independence Day (Optional Proper Mass)
14   Blessed Kateri Tekakwitha, virgin - Memorial

AUGUST

18   Jane Frances de Chantal, religious - Optional Memorial

SEPTEMBER

9   Peter Claver, priest - Memorial

OCTOBER

6   Blessed Marie Rose Durocher, virgin - Optional Memorial
19   Isaac Jogues and John de Brébeuf, priests and martyrs,
      and companions, martyrs - Memorial
20   Paul of the Cross, priest - Optional Memorial

NOVEMBER

13   Frances Xavier Cabrini, virgin - Memorial
18   Rose Philippine Duchesne, virgin - Optional Memorial
23   Blessed Miguel Agustín Pro, priest and martyr - Optional Memorial
Fourth Thursday - Thanksgiving Day (Optional Proper Mass)

DECEMBER

9   Blessed Juan Diego - Optional Memorial
12   Our Lady of Guadalupe - Feast

In addition to these national celebrations, the calendar of a diocese will add the celebrations of its patrons, the anniversary of the dedication of the cathedral, and the saints and blessed who bear some special connection with that diocese (see GNLYC 52a), for example, because it was their place of origin, longtime residence, or place of death (see CP 9). The calendars of religious communities will also include the "celebrations of their title, founder, or patron and those saints and blessed who were members of that religious family or had some special relationship with it" (GNLYC 52b).

In order to determine which saints or blessed belong on the particular calendar of a nation or region, or on diocesan or religious calendars, some general norms are to be observed:

1) Care must be taken not to overload the national calendar or that of a diocese or religious institute (see GNLYC 53).

2) Saints and the blessed should be included on a particular calendar only if they have particular significance for the entire nation, diocese, or religious family (GNLYC 53b).

3) Other saints and blessed are to be celebrated only in those places with which they have closer ties (see GNLYC 53c).

When applied to particular circumstances, these norms need to be made somewhat more specific. It is frequently the case that a religious community asks that a saint or blessed of its community who was not born in the United States and who did not serve in this country be placed on the national calendar for the USA. In such cases the following guidelines are to be applied:

1) As a general practice, before being considered for inclusion on the national calendar, saints or the blessed of a religious community must first be included on diocesan calendars for a significant period of time (usually 5 to 10 years) in order to insure that they have a genuine *cultus* in the United States.

2) The *cultus* of the saint or blessed must exist in a significant number of dioceses throughout the country before the saint or blessed may be proposed for inclusion on the national calendar. This *cultus* must be broader than in a particular area or region of the country in order to demonstrate that the saint or blessed is of significance to the entire country.

3) Normally the saint or blessed must have served in the United States of America.

4) Such commemorations of saints or the blessed will ordinarily be given the rank of optional memorial.

Holy Days of Obligation

At their plenary assembly in November 1991, with follow-up mail balloting by absentees, the members of the National Conference of Catholic Bishops approved two motions which affect the observance of holy days of obligation in the dioceses of the United States. They decided that whenever January 1, the solemnity of Mary, Mother of God, or August 15, the solemnity of the Assumption, or November 1, the solemnity of All Saints, falls on a Saturday or on a Monday, the precept to attend Mass is abrogated. The next month, Archbishop Daniel E. Pilarczyk, president of the NCCB, requested confirmation of this decision from the Vatican Congregation of Bishops.

This action was confirmed by the Congregation for Bishops on July 4, 1992 (Prot. N. 296/84), after that dicastery had received the advice of the Congregation for the Clergy and the Pontifical Council for the Interpretation of Legal Texts. The letter of confirmation was signed by Bernardin Cardinal Gantin, Prefect, and Archbishop Justin Rigali, Secretary. Pope John Paul II approved and confirmed the same on the same date.

On November 17, 1992 Archbishop Pilarczyk announced this confirmation to the members of the National Conference of Catholic Bishops meeting in executive session. His decree promulgating this decision follows.

NATIONAL CONFERENCE OF CATHOLIC BISHOPS
UNITED STATES OF AMERICA
DECREE OF PROMULGATION

On December 13, 1991 the members of the National Conference of Catholic Bishops of the United States of America made the following general decree concerning holy days of obligation for Latin rite Catholics:

In addition to Sunday, the days to be observed as holy days of obligation in the Latin Rite dioceses of the United States of America, in conformity with canon 1246, are as follows:

January 1, the solemnity of Mary, Mother of God;
Thursday of the Sixth Week of Easter, the solemnity of the Ascension;
August 15, the solemnity of the Assumption of the Blessed Virgin Mary;
November 1, the solemnity of All Saints;
December 8, the solemnity of the Immaculate Conception;
December 25, the solemnity of the Nativity of Our Lord Jesus Christ.

Whenever January 1, the solemnity of Mary, Mother of God, or August 15, the solemnity of the Assumption, or November 1, the solemnity of All Saints, falls on a Saturday or on a Monday, the precept to attend Mass is abrogated.

This decree of the Conference of Bishops was approved and confirmed by the Apostolic See by a decree of the Congregation for Bishops (Prot. N. 296/84), signed by Bernardin Cardinal Gantin, prefect of the Congregation, and dated July 4, 1992.

As President of the National Conference of Catholic Bishops, I hereby declare that the effective date of this decree for all the Latin rite dioceses of the United States of America will be January 1, 1993, the solemnity of Mary, Mother of God.

Given at the offices of the National Conference of Catholic Bishops in Washington, DC, November 17, 1992.

+ Daniel E. Pilarczyk
Archbishop of Cincinnati
President of the National Conference of Catholic Bishops

Robert N. Lynch
General Secretary

Southwest Liturgical Conference 1993 Study Week

The Southwest Liturgical Conference will hold its 31st annual study week at the Hyatt Regency Hotel, Albuquerque, NM, on January 20-23, 1993. The theme of the conference is "Journey through the Sacraments."

Major topics and speakers include: "The Future of Our Rituals: Looking to the Year 2000 and Beyond" by Nathan Mitchell; "I Was Sick and You Visited Me" by Charles Gusmer; "RCIA: An Invitation into the Story" by Rita Claire Dorner, OP; "The Ethics of Liturgical Behavior" by Therese Koernke, IHM; "What the Sacramental Assembly Can Learn from 12-step Programs" by John Gallen, SJ; and "Reconciliation and Forgiveness: A Neglected Sacrament, A Forgotten Art" by Peter Fink, SJ.

For further information contact: 1993 SWLC Study Week, Archdiocese of Santa Fe Office of Worship, 4000 Saint Joseph Place NW, Albuquerque, NM 87120. Telephone: 503/831-8194.

National Conference On Preaching

The newly-formed Catholic Coalition on Preaching will sponsor its first National Conference on Preaching, entitled "Lord, Your Servant is Listening: Sunday Preaching Today." The conference will be held at the Hyatt Regency Woodfield Hotel in Schaumburg, Illinois on September 23-26, 1993. The coalition is made up of eleven national organizations with a deep interest in the continuing development of Catholic preaching. Resource persons for the conference will include Fred Baumer, Joan Delaplane, Most Reverend Kenneth Untener, J. Glenn Murray, Teresita Weind, Robert Schreiter, Robert Waznak, and Virgil Elizondo. For more information write to: Conference Services by Loretta Reif, P.O. Box 5084, Rockford, IL 61125.

Hispanic Music Composition Competition

The Southwest Liturgical Conference is currently presenting a competition for a new bilingual (Spanish-English) setting of the acclamations for the Mass and the litany for the Fraction Rite (Lamb of God). Texts used must truly be bilingual versions of the approved liturgical texts. The texts being sought include the Gospel Acclamation, the Santo/Holy, Memorial Acclamations A or C (Spanish and English texts), the Great Amen, and the Lamb of God/Cordero De Dios. To receive a copy of the rules and criteria for the competition, write to: Mary McLarry, chairperson, SwLC Hispanic Music Competition, 800 W Loop 820 S, Ft. Worth, TX 76108.

COMMITTEE ON THE LITURGY

NEWSLETTER

1993
VOLUME XXIX
JANUARY

New Chairman-Elect and Advisors to the Committee

At the November 1992 plenary meeting of the National Conference of Catholic Bishops (NCCB), the Most Reverend Donald W. Trautman, Bishop of Erie, was elected the next Chairman of the Bishops' Committee on the Liturgy. His term of office will begin after the November 1993 meeting of the NCCB.

Bishop Wilton D. Gregory has recently appointed two new advisors to the Committee on the Liturgy: Reverend Kevin W. Irwin, a member of the faculty of the School of Religious Studies at The Catholic University of America, and Reverend Jeremy Driscoll, OSB, a member of the faculty of Mount Angel Seminary in St. Benedict, Oregon. Reverend John Baldovin, SJ, has completed his term as an advisor to the Committee. The Bishops' Committee on the Liturgy and its Secretariat wish to express their appreciation for the assistance and advice which he gave during his term as advisor. The Secretariat for the Liturgy has also employed a new administrative secretary: Scott Obernberger.

Rereading the Constitution on the Liturgy (art. 79)

The *Constitution on the Liturgy* (CSL) gives renewed significance to the role of sacramentals in the life of the Church. CSL 60 defines sacramentals as "sacred signs bearing a resemblance to the sacraments: they signify effects, particularly of a spiritual kind, that are obtained through the Church's intercessions. They dispose people to receive the chief effect of the sacraments and they make holy various occasions in human life."

This definition provides the foundation for the revisions called for in CSL 79-82 and contains some notable advances from the classical definition of sacramentals found in the 1917 Code of Canon Law. The constitution speaks of sacramentals as signs; not mere objects of devotion, but liturgical activities and celebrations of the worshiping community. This does not discount objects from being called sacramentals, but they are referred to as such because they are destined for use in the celebration of worship. The constitution also more closely relates sacramentals to the sacraments. This is evident in chapter three, where sacraments and sacramentals are treated together in the same chapter. Sacramentals resemble sacraments and dispose the faithful "to receive the chief effect of the sacraments" (CSL 60). Finally, the constitution speaks of the sanctifying power of sacramentals pointing out that "for well-disposed members of the faithful, the effect of the liturgy of the sacraments and sacramentals is that almost every event in their lives is made holy by divine grace that flows from the paschal mystery of Christ's passion, death, and resurrection, the fount from which all sacraments and sacramentals draw their power" (CSL 61).

For these reasons CSL 79 calls for the revision of all sacramentals. It directs that they should be revised to take into account "the primary criterion that the faithful participate intelligently, actively, and easily." This is in accord with CSL 14, which states that "in the reform and promotion of the liturgy, this full and active participation by all the people is the aim to be considered before all else." As liturgical celebrations of the worshiping community, sacramentals should contain those dimensions that are integral to all liturgical activity in the Church. These would include symbols, gestures, scripture, formularies, as well as the full participation of the ecclesial community.

CSL 79 also issues three new norms pertaining to the revision of sacramentals. In accord with the principles set forth in CSL 63, new sacramentals may be added that address the needs of the time and the human experiences of the faithful. The number of reserved blessings is to be limited in order to make them more available to the faithful. And those blessings reserved to bishops should be those that are intimately connected with the life of the diocese. Lastly, CSL 79 directs that "provision be made that some

3211 FOURTH STREET NE • WASHINGTON, DC 20017

sacramentals, at least in special circumstances and at the discretion of the Ordinary, may be administered by qualified laypersons."

In response to the directives of CSL 79 a study group was placed in charge of revising the part of the Roman Ritual that contained the blessings. In the process of striving to uncover the authentic meaning of blessings, the study group began by determining a set of doctrinal and practical norms that were to guide their work. These included the following: 1) a prayer of blessing always includes acknowledgment and thanksgiving for benefits received from God and a petition for the needs of human beings; 2) God's blessing is invoked first and foremost on human beings and only secondarily on things that aid human beings in attaining their end; 3) the Church has always been on guard to prevent superstitious use of blessings; 4) provision should be made for lay persons to administer some blessings in accord with CSL 79; and 5) blessings can be differentiated as constitutive (blessings that make a person or thing sacred by destining a thing for use in worship or consecrating a person to a special state and are usually reserved to ordained persons), invocative (those which can be performed by lay persons in the absence of a priest or deacon), and blessings that have to do with family life and are more properly left to the laity.

Although the work of the study group began in 1970, the *Rituale Romanum: De benedictionibus* was not promulgated by the Congregation for Divine Worship until May 31, 1984. Two years previous to this the Bishops' Committee on the Liturgy had established a Subcommittee on Blessings to examine an earlier draft of the Latin text and its English draft translation prepared by the International Commission on English in the Liturgy (ICEL) and to formulate the various rites and blessings which were to be added to the English edition for the United States.

At the request of the Subcommittee the Secretariat for Liturgy sent a questionnaire to diocesan liturgical commissions and offices concerning the Latin draft prepared by the Congregation for Divine Worship and other matters arising from that draft. The respondents were asked to indicate the "degree of usefulness" for each blessing, to indicate those occasions not provided for in the Roman book for which there should be a blessing or rite, to suggest blessings which arise from popular or ethnic traditions and practices, and to provide suggestions on the eventual arrangement of the ritual book. The Committee on the Liturgy also approved the proposal of the Subcommittee to prepare and have published three separate books of blessings based on the Latin edition: 1) Book of Blessings, full ritual edition; 2) Book of Blessings, abbreviated minister's edition; and 3) Book of Blessings, home/family edition.

The preparation of a particular ritual for the United States was in accord with CSL 63b. And the mandate for this work is found in the *praenotanda* of *De benedictionibus* of the Roman Ritual which states that "in virtue of the Constitution on the Liturgy, each conference of bishops has the right to prepare a particular ritual, corresponding to the present title of the Roman Ritual, adapted to the needs of the respective region" (no. 39).

The English translation of *De Benedictionibus* was prepared by the International Commission on English in the Liturgy (ICEL). The *Book of Blessings* (BB) and the additional proper blessings for use in the United States were canonically approved for use *ad interim* by the Administrative Committee of the National Conference of Catholic Bishops on March 22, 1988, and this action was confirmed by the Apostolic See by decree of the Congregation for Divine Worship on January 27, 1989 (Prot. N. 699/88). The *Book of Blessings* was mandated for use beginning December 3, 1989, the First Sunday of Advent; from that day forward no other English version could be used.

In accord with the directives in Part V of the General Introduction, which concerns Adaptations Belonging to Conferences of Bishops, the United States edition of the *Book of Blessings* differs somewhat from the Latin *editio typica*. It contains all the material of *De Benedictionibus* as well as forty-two orders and prayers of blessing prepared by the Committee on the Liturgy of the National Conference of Catholic Bishops. The new blessings for use in the dioceses of the United States are designated "USA" in the margins. A new Part V: Blessings for Feasts and Seasons has been added to the *Book of Blessings* and consists mainly of newly composed blessings connected with the liturgical year. Part V of the Latin edition is numbered Part VI in the United States edition. It is entitled Blessings for Various Needs and Occasions and contains those blessings primarily related to the parish, its pastoral and liturgical ministries, and its organization. The *Book of Blessings* also includes two appendices. Appendix I: Order for the Installation of a Pastor complements the blessings of Part VI and was included for pastoral convenience. Appendix II: Solemn Blessings and Prayers over the People consists of solemn blessings and prayers over the people found in the *Sacramentary*.

The *Book of Blessings* (BB) is remarkably clear about the significance and importance of sacramentals in the life of the Church. There remains a considerable amount of work to be done, however, before this becomes a reality in the lives of all the faithful. On the pastoral level many laity and clergy still perceive blessings in terms of private actions and/or devotional practices. It is not uncommon that people consider persons, objects, or places blessed if the priest simply makes the sign of the cross over them and uses holy water. And there are too many people as yet unaware of the numerous blessings available to sanctify the various events of their human lives.

Liturgical catechesis is essential for the continued growth and development of liturgical renewal in the Church today. This is especially true as it pertains to the significance and role of blessings in the lives of the faithful. The need for catechesis in this area is affirmed in the General Introduction to the *Book of Blessings*, which states, "The participation of the faithful will be the more active in proportion to the effectiveness of their instruction on the importance of blessings. During the celebration of a blessing and in preaching and catechesis beforehand, priests and ministers should therefore explain to the faithful the meaning and power of blessings. There is a further advantage in teaching the people of God the proper meaning of the rites and prayers employed by the Church in imparting blessings: this will forestall intrusion into the celebration of anything that might replace genuine faith with superstition and/or shallow credulity" (BB 19).

The starting point for liturgical catechesis is good celebration. Since blessings are a part of the liturgy of the Church, priority should be given to communal celebrations which foster the active participation of the assembly. This principle is stressed throughout the *Book of Blessings*. No. 16 of the General Introduction states that "communal celebration is in some cases obligatory but in all cases more in accord with the character of liturgical prayer." The principle of communal celebration is so integral to the rite of blessing that the General Introduction states that even when there is no assembly present, "the person who wishes to bless God's name or to ask God's favor and the minister who presides should still keep in mind that they represent the Church in celebration" (BB 17).

The General Introduction also points out that catechesis needs to take into account the proper meaning of the rites and prayers employed by the Church in imparting blessings. This includes an understanding of the typical structure of a blessing and its essential components. The General Introduction explains that the typical celebration of a blessing has two parts: the proclamation of the word of God and praise of God's goodness and petition for his help. "In addition there are usually rites for the beginning and conclusion that are proper to each celebration" (no. 20). In other words the faithful should always experience the celebration of blessings within a liturgical context. Blessings are not private moments nor do they merely take place with the minister making the sign of the cross over the person, place, or object. To guard against this perception Part V on Celebration of a Blessing states that "to ensure active participation in the celebration and to guard against any danger of superstition, it is ordinarily not permissible to impart the blessing of any article or place merely through a sign of blessing and without either the word of God or any sort of prayer being spoken" (no. 27).

Catechesis for the rites of blessing should emphasize the proclamation of the word of God as a constitutive element of a blessing. The General Introduction states that the proclamation of the Word of God ensures that the "blessing is a genuine sacred sign" and is the central point of the first part of the rite of blessing (no. 21). As such it should not be omitted. The proclamation of the word of God transforms blessings into sacramentals and provides a blessing with its meaning and effectiveness. For this reason every blessing in the *Book of Blessings* has proposed biblical readings that suit the nature of the blessing.

The same holds true of the second central element in every blessing: "the blessing formulary itself, that is, the prayer of the Church, along with the accompanying proper outward sign" (no. 22). Although the outward signs are not essential to the rite of blessing, they bring to mind God's saving acts, express a relationship between the present celebration and the Church's sacraments, and in this way "nurture the faith of those present and move them to take part in the rite attentively" (no. 25). The traditional signs are enumerated in Part V and include "outstretching, raising, or joining of the hands, the laying on of hands, the sign of the cross, sprinkling with holy water, and incensation" (no. 26).

Since the conciliar reform more closely relates sacramentals to sacraments, a contemporary catechesis on the rites of blessing needs to take this relationship into account. It is given concrete expression in the *Book of Blessings*. Thus in some instances those blessings which have a special relationship to the sacraments are joined with the celebration of the Mass. In other cases some blessings may be joined with other liturgical celebrations. All blessings, however, should dispose the faithful to receive the chief effect of the sacraments.

CSL 79 also made a significant advance when it called for the provision to be made for qualified lay persons to administer some sacramentals. Such change, however, requires catechesis so that all understand that sacramentals are not reserved to clerics and that the Church can depute a lay person to give a blessing in the name of the Church. To this effect Part III, Offices and Ministries, explains that it belongs to the ministry of the bishop to preside at celebrations that involve the entire diocesan community; that it belongs to the ministry of a priest to preside at those blessings especially that involve the community he is appointed to serve; that it belongs to the ministry of deacon to preside at those blessings that are so indicated since the deacon is the assistant of the bishop and the college of presbyters; and it belongs to the acolyte or reader who by formal institution may impart certain blessings because of their special office in the church. Finally it states that "other laymen and laywomen, in virtue of the universal priesthood, a dignity they possess because of their baptism and confirmation, may celebrate certain blessings, as indicated in the respective orders of blessings, by use of the rites and formularies designated for a lay minister" (no. 18d).

A significant dimension of liturgical reform must include the integration of liturgical prayer with daily life. But this vision called for by CSL 61 will not be easily accomplished if no bond exists between liturgical prayer and the daily prayers of every Catholic. To this effect the Bishops' Committee on the Liturgy prepared a book of prayers and blessings for use by Catholic families and households. *Catholic Household Blessings and Prayers* was approved by the National Conference of Catholic Bishops' Administrative Committee in March 1988. The book enables the faithful to integrate the liturgical prayer of the Sunday assembly with the daily prayer learned at home.

The goal of *Catholic Household Blessings and Prayers* is to foster the full, active, and conscious participation of all the baptized. This will only be achieved, however, when "the people who assemble for the Sunday liturgy are people who know their part well, know it truly by heart, and know it because they know what it is to praise God, to attend to the Scriptures, to intercede, and to give thanks" (Introduction). Thus the book contains the prayers and rites of the baptized and is meant to do all that a book can do to remind us of our words, our texts.

The Foreword to *Catholic Household Blessings and Prayers* expresses the hope that this book "will find a place in every Catholic household." Diocesan and parish leaders need to seek ways to make this hope a reality. Liturgical catechesis must strengthen the bond between liturgical prayer and daily prayer. It must also contribute to the liturgical spirituality of the faithful. This is necessary if liturgical renewal is to become a reality in the Church. When this happens the words of CSL 61 can truly be fulfilled.

Time for the Celebration of the Easter Vigil

Each year the Secretariat for the Liturgy receives letters expressing concern regarding the erosion of the liturgical spirit and intent of the Paschal Triduum. One area of particular concern has been the celebration of the Easter Vigil late Saturday afternoon or early Saturday evening before nightfall.

The *Roman Missal* states that "the entire celebration of the Easter Vigil takes place at night. It should not begin before nightfall; it should end before daybreak on Sunday." Lack of adherence to this norm prompted the 1988 *Circular Letter Concerning the Preparation and Celebration of the Easter Feasts* to repeat this rubric from the *Sacramentary* and to add that "This rule is to be taken according to its strictest sense. Reprehensible are those abuses and practices which have crept in many places in violation of this ruling, whereby the Easter Vigil is celebrated at the time of day that it is customary to celebrate anticipated Masses."

Many of the abuses associated with the untimely scheduling of the Easter Vigil are due to a general lack of understanding regarding the nature of the celebration of the annual Pasch. It is incumbent upon diocesan liturgical commissions/offices of worship to provide catechesis on the Easter Vigil. This is best done far in advance of the celebration.

This year Easter will occur after clocks in most parts of the United States will have been moved ahead one hour for daylight savings time. Pastoral planners should contact a local weather station for the time sunset will occur on April 10, 1993. To that time another 45 minutes or one hour should be added to determine the approximate time of nightfall. For example, if sunset occurs at 7:41 p.m. DST in a given location, the celebration of the Easter Vigil should not begin before 8:30 p.m.

COMMITTEE ON THE LITURGY

NATIONAL CONFERENCE OF CATHOLIC BISHOPS

NEWSLETTER

**1993
VOLUME XXIX
FEBRUARY**

Feast of Our Lady of Guadalupe

In December 1993 the feast of Our Lady of Guadalupe (December 12) falls on the Third Sunday of Advent. The *General Norms for the Liturgical Year and the Calendar* (GNLYC) state that "because of its special importance, the Sunday celebration gives way only to solemnities or feasts of the Lord. *The Sundays of the seasons of Advent, Lent, and Easter, however, take precedence over all solemnities and feasts of the Lord"* (5) [emphasis added]. Accordingly, the Third Sunday of Advent takes precedence over the feast of Our Lady of Guadalupe. The readings and Mass formulary for that day will be those for the Advent Sunday. Our Lady of Guadalupe may be appropriately honored in one or more of the petitions of the general intercessions, in the homily, and perhaps in one of the hymns during the liturgy. The singing of the *Mananitas* early in the morning and the traditional Guadalupe procession later in the day should not detract from the character of the Advent Sunday.

In those places where the feast of Our Lady of Guadalupe has very special significance, the liturgical celebration may be transferred to Saturday, December 11, or Monday, December 13. This is in accord with the *General Instruction of the Roman Missal* which states that "in cases of serious need or pastoral advantage, at the direction of the local Ordinary or with his permission, an appropriate Mass may be celebrated on any day except solemnities, the Sundays of Advent, Lent, and the Easter season, days within the octave of Easter, on All Souls, Ash Wednesday, and during Holy Week" (332).

In light of the liturgical norms cited above, when December 12 falls on a weekday, the liturgical celebration of Our Lady of Guadalupe may not be transferred to a Sunday of Advent.

Rereading the Constitution on the Liturgy (art. 80)

In addition to its call for the revision of the blessings of the Church, the *Constitution on the Liturgy* (CSL) gave consideration to the rites pertaining to the consecration of virgins and to religious profession. CSL 80 decrees the revision of the rite of consecration to a life of virginity and directs that a rite of religious profession and renewal of vows "be drawn up with a view to achieving greater unity, simplicity, and dignity." This work was to be guided by the primary criterion for reviewing sacramentals contained in CSL 70 (see *Newsletter,* January 1993) as well as the fundamental liturgical principles set forth in the *Constitution on the Liturgy.*

The revision of the rite for the consecration of virgins was prepared by one of the study groups of the Consilium in consultation with superiors general of the religious orders of men and women, abbesses, the Congregation for Religious, and the Congregation for the Doctrine of the Faith. Although it had been included in the *Roman Pontifical,* the rite was unfamiliar even to the fathers on the Consilium. Thus, the preliminary work on the revision dealt with basic issues of intelligibility, relevance, and usage.

The *Ordo consecrationis virginum* was published by the Congregation for Divine Worship on May 31, 1970. The English translation, *The Rite of Consecration to a Life of Virginity* (RCLV), was prepared by the International Commission on English in the Liturgy (ICEL). It was approved by the National Conference of Catholic Bishops (NCCB) in May 1976 and confirmed by the Apostolic See on May 21, 1976.

In accord with the ancient practice of the Church the celebration of this rite constitutes the candidate as a sacred person, a "surpassing sign of the Church's love for Christ, and an eschatological image of the world to come and the glory of the heavenly Bride of Christ" (RCLV 1). The rite may be used not only for nuns, whose religious family "uses this rite because of long-established custom or by new permission of the competent authority" (RCLV 4c), but also for women living in the world who are called to this form of consecrated life in the Church. It is not intended for use by other women religious (RCLV 3-5). The celebration of the rite is reserved to the bishop (RCLV 6). The rite contains three chapters: The Rite of Consecration (Chapter I), Combined Rite of Consecration and Religious Profession (Chapter II), and Other Texts for the Rite of Consecration (Chapter III). An Appendix contains a sample formula of profession, but each religious community "may compose a formula of profession to be approved by the Sacred Congregation for Religious and for Secular Institutes."

Since the *Roman Ritual* did not have a rite of religious profession, a new rite of religious profession with renewal of vows was drawn up in accord with the directives given in CSL 80. The absence of any rite had resulted in some serious pastoral and liturgical practices that were not in accord with the liturgical reforms nor the theology of religious life presented by the Second Vatican Council. Some religious communities had simply adopted the rite for consecration of virgins. Others had based their celebrations solely on devotional practices. In many cases rites for religious professions lacked a definite liturgical orientation and order.

To address this lack of uniformity, the rite of religious profession which was drawn up establishes a common structure for the liturgical celebration while allowing each religious community to make adaptations according to the particular tradition, charism, and character of the institute. In this way the liturgical and ecclesiological principles promoted by the Second Vatican Council are preserved while attention may still be given to the particular character of each religious family.

The *Ordo professionis religiosae* was published on February 2, 1970 by the Congregation for Divine Worship. The ICEL prepared an interim English translation of the *Rite of Religious Profession* (RRP) in 1971 and a second revised edition in 1974. The *Rite of Religious Profession* was approved by the NCCB without any adaptations in May 1975 and was confirmed by the Apostolic See on May 16, 1975. On September 12, 1983 the Congregation for Sacraments and Divine Worship published *Emendations in the Liturgical Books following upon the New Code of Canon Law*. It directed that the Rite of a Promise be deleted from the text of the *Rite of Religious Profession* and that all references to it be removed from the Introduction. And so a revised edition of the *Rite of Religious Profession* was published in 1989; it contains the changes mandated by the *Emendations*.

The *Rite of Religious Profession* contains two distinct formulations, one for men religious and the other for women religious. Each section contains chapters pertaining to initiation (Chapter I), temporary profession during Mass (Chapter II), perpetual profession during Mass (Chapter III), renewal of vows during Mass (Chapter IV), and biblical readings and prayer formularies (Chapter V). An Introduction precedes these divisions.

The Introduction begins by treating the nature and meaning of religious life set forth in *Lumen Gentium* and *Perfectae Caritatis*. Here the connection between religious life and the mystery of Christ and the Church is clearly expressed. The Introduction states that "it is the Church that receives the vows of those who make religious profession, begs God's grace for them by its public prayer, puts them in God's hands, blesses them, and unites their offering with the eucharistic sacrifice" (RRP 2).

Part II of the Introduction concerns the rites for the different stages of religious life. The rites corrrespond to the various steps of religious life (novitiate, first profession or other sacred bonds, and final profession) and are constitutive of the step being taken. For instance, entry into the novitiate, which is a time of testing, is "marked by a rite in which God's grace is sought for the special purpose of the period. The rite should, of its nature, be restrained and simple, celebrated in the presence only of the religious community. It should take place outside Mass" (RRP 4).

In accord with CSL 80 religious profession, especially the rite of final profession, fittingly takes place within Mass in order to highlight its consecratory nature and more closely connect it with the mystery of Christ and the Church. The rite also provides guidelines and texts for the renewal of vows during Mass.

The *Rite of Religious Profession* introduced a number of changes that are marked departures from previous practices in the ceremonies of religious institutes. Investiture with the religious habit is removed from the ceremony celebrating entrance into the novitiate and placed in the Rite of Temporary Profession during Mass. The habit and other religious insignia are now reserved for this celebration, since the Rite of Temporary Profession celebrates religious commitment. The solemnity that once characterized the celebration of entrance into the novitiate is now replaced with simplicity and directness. The Rite of Initiation into the Religious Life may not be celebrated during Mass and is reserved to the religious community only. Changes in the Rite of Perpetual Profession emphasize the ecclesial nature of this celebration by marking the relationship between religious life and the mystery of Christ and the Church. Religious are encouraged to celebrate this rite on a Sunday or a solemnity of the Lord. It should take place at a time that allows the faithful to attend in greater number. It may be celebrated at the cathedral, a parish church, or some other notable place. And it is preferred that the Mass be concelebrated.

The most notable feature of the *Rite of Religious Profession* is its sensitivity to the spirituality, manner of life, and traditions of the various religious families. Although CSL 80 insisted on greater "unity, simplicity, and dignity" of the rites in light of the preconciliar situation of disorder and lack of liturgical orientation, the revised rite acknowledges the need for adaptation so that the rite "more closely reflects and manifests the character and spirit of each institute" (RRP 14). Adaptations that may be made to the rite are found in Part IV of the Introduction, entitled "Adaptations to be Made by Individual Institutes."

The process of implementing and adapting the *Rite of Religious Profession* was directed by several communications following its promulgation. On July 15, 1970 the Congregation of Divine Worship sent a letter to the superiors general of the religious institutes concerning adaptation of the rite. The letter reaffirms the conciliar intent to achieve greater unity in the rites of religious profession and states that "except for cases of particular law—it should become the rite universally used by all who make profession within Mass or would like to do so." This feature, however, is to be combined with a spirit of "broad openness to adaptation to the varying circumstances of the different communities."

In order to facilitate appropriate adaptation of the rite, the Congregation for Divine Worship issued guidelines on the adaptation of the *Rite of Religious of Profession* on July 15, 1970. The guidelines direct that: 1) adaptations must begin with the rite as the point of departure and not with the institute's former book of ceremonies; 2) an adapted version of the rite in a vernacular language must use the official translation of the *Ordo professionis religiosae* prepared by the respective conference of bishops; 3) elements incorporated into the adapted rite should reflect the conciliar principles found in *Sacrosanctum Concilium, Lumen gentium, Perfectae Caritatis,* and *Gaudium et Spes*; 4) any substitutions for a proper formulary of the rite (usually designated "in these or similar words") should reflect the same literary genre as well as the style, content, and doctrine of the prayers in the *Rite of Religious Profession*; 5) adaptations should not impoverish the Rite of Profession; 6) the habit needs no special blessing, but if it is to be blessed, it should be done outside Mass; 7) institutes should avoid introducing an excessive number of saints of their own in the Litany of the Saints; and 8) each institute must submit to the Congregation for Divine Worship its own work of adapting the *Rite of Religious Profession*.

Order of Processions

The Liturgy Secretariat frequently receives questions about the order for processions, especially when bishops are present. Although the *General Instruction of the Roman Missal* (GIRM) and the *Ceremonial of Bishops* (CB) are of great help in determining the order for a procession, they do not resolve all the questions that are frequently raised.

Procession when no bishop is present: The basic form for the entrance procession of the Mass is found in no. 82 of the GIRM: acolyte (server) with censer, crossbearer between two acolytes (servers) with lighted candles, other acolytes and ministers (e.g., special ministers of holy communion), reader (who may carry the Book of Gospels), priest celebrant. When a deacon is present for the Mass, he may carry the Book of Gospels and precede the priest; otherwise he walks at the priest's side (usually the priest's right side) (GIRM 128). When there are concelebrants present for the Mass, they walk ahead of the principal celebrant (GIRM 162). If the deacon carries the Book of Gospels, he walks before all the concelebrating presbyters (see CB 128), otherwise he walks with the principal celebrant. If deacons who will not assume a ministry at the Mass or non-concelebrating presbyters are present, they walk two by two after the crossbearer, with the deacons preceding the presbyters.

Procession when the bishop is celebrant: The bishop who presides at a liturgical celebration always walks vested and alone, following the presbyters, but preceding his assisting ministers, who walk a little behind him (CB 80). Accordingly, the procession at a Stational Mass of the diocesan bishop takes the following order: censerbearer carrying a censer with burning incense; acolyte carrying the cross between two (or seven) acolytes with lighted candles; clergy who are performing no ministry at the Mass walking two by two (deacons first, followed by the non-concelebrating presbyters and bishops); deacon with the Book of Gospels; ministering deacons (who would, for example, serve as ministers of communion); concelebrating presbyters; (other concelebrating bishops); diocesan bishop; two deacons who walk slightly behind the bishop on either side; ministers who assist with the book, miter, and pastoral staff (GIRM 128). When the bishop does not carry the pastoral staff because he is carrying something else (e.g., a candle, the blessed sacrament or a sacred object), the pastoral staff is carried by a minister who walks ahead of the bishop; the other ministers, as usual, walk behind him (see CB 1099-1101).

When the bishop presides over the liturgy of the word but does not celebrate the eucharist, the presbyter who is the celebrant of the eucharist walks directly before the bishop, who wears cope and miter and uses the pastoral staff. The bishop is assisted by two vested deacons or, in their absence, by two presbyters in copes (CB 176). The bishop follows the presbyter who will celebrate the eucharist. The deacons who assist the bishop and the ministers of the book, miter, and pastoral staff follow the bishop, as is indicated above for a Stational Mass (CB 177).

Procession when the bishop does not preside: When the bishop does not preside at a liturgical service wearing cope and miter, but merely attends in choir dress (mozzetta and rochet), he does not use the cathedra (see CB 186). He is assisted by two presbyters or deacons in cassock and surplice (CB 81). In this case, he walks as the last of the non-concelebrating clergy in the procession (in front of the deacon with the Book of Gospels). This procedure is also followed for other bishops, archbishops, and cardinals who are not concelebrating and is the practice followed at papal liturgies.

In summary, all members of the clergy who are not exercising a liturgical ministry in a particular celebration, walk in the first part of the procession according to their order and dignity (deacons, presbyters, bishops, archbishops, cardinals).

Symposium on Crossed Cultures

The Yale Institute of Sacred Music, in conjunction with the Department of Worship and the Arts of the National Council of Churches, is sponsoring Crossed Cultures, a symposium which will examine the crisis of the Christian tradition in relation to society today. With a focus on the shifting understanding of the role of Christian symbols in society, specifically the symbol of the cross, the Symposium will consider the relationship of Christian symbol, meaning, and message in contemporary cultures.

The symposium will be held April 23-25, 1993 at Yale University in New Haven, Connecticut. The registration fee is $125 per person. Meals and housing are not included in the cost of the registration. For further information call: (203) 432-5180 or (203) 432-5325. Brochures for the symposium are also available from the Secretariat for the Liturgy, 3211 Fourth Street NE, Washington, DC 20017. Telephone: (202) 541-3060.

Institute for Music and Liturgy

The Saint Lawrence Catholic Campus in Lawrence, Kansas, is sponsoring its Institute for Music and Liturgy on June 27-July 1, 1993. The theme of the Institute is "Music and the Word," and the institute experience will include education, music-making, and inspired prayer. Designed to support and nourish the talents of those who are engaged in the vocational ministry of expressing God's Word through music, the institute will focus on Scripture-based spirituality for the church musician, Scripture and liturgical preparation, liturgical ministry as an extension of the Word, the Psalms, the Canticles, choral repertoire, and choral singing. The faculty for the institute will consist of Dr. Fred Moleck, Sister Delores Dufner, OSB, Rev. John Allyn Melloh, SM, John Brooks-Leonard, Ph.D., and Lynn Trapp.

Registration fee for the institute, which is limited to 75 participants, is $175.00. For further information contact: Sally Hudnall, Program Coordinator, Saint Lawrence Catholic Campus Center, 1631 Crescent Road, Lawrence, KS 66044. Telephone: (913) 843-0357.

COMMITTEE ON THE LITURGY

NEWSLETTER

1993
VOLUME XXIX
MARCH

NATIONAL CONFERENCE OF CATHOLIC BISHOPS

Rereading the Constitution on the Liturgy (art. 81-82)

The final articles of Chapter III in the *Constitution on the Liturgy* (CSL) treat the rite of funerals and the rite for the burial of infants. The reform was guided by the norms set forth in CSL 81-82, which stress the paschal character of Christian death and encourage sensitivity to the circumstances and tradition of various regions.

The study group charged with the revision of the funeral rites carefully evaluated the rite being used before the conciliar reform. They determined that many of the ritual texts were too distressing and frightful and that the concept of death in the formularies did not adequately express the doctrine of hope and the paschal character of Christian death held by the Church and promoted by the Second Vatican Council. For this reason the study group recommended the inclusion of more texts that express the paschal dimension of Christian death; a greater variety of Mass formularies to nourish faith; fostering the active participation of the faithful; and respect for the funeral customs among various peoples.

The *Ordo Exsequiarum* was published by decree of the Congregation for Divine Worship on August 15, 1969. The English translation of the *Rite of Funerals* (RF) was prepared by the International Commission on English in the Liturgy (ICEL) and was approved by the National Conference of Catholic Bishops (NCCB) in November 1970. At this same meeting the NCCB also approved many adaptations to be included in the *Rite of Funerals* for the United States.

The adaptations approved by the NCCB in 1970 reflect the pastoral experience of extensive experimentation with the funeral rite in the United States which had been authorized by the Apostolic See. They are in accord with the section on "Adaptations by the Conferences of Bishops" (nos. 21-22) in the *Rite of Funerals*, which states that "in virtue of the *Constitution on the Liturgy* (art. 63 b), the conferences of bishops have the right to prepare a section in particular rituals corresponding to the present section of the Roman Ritual and adapted to the needs of the different parts of the world" (RF 21).

Adaptations approved by the NCCB included the following: 1) consent for a lay person to lead the station in the home and the cemetery in the absence of a priest or deacon and to lead the station in the church (liturgy of the word and the commendation) if deputed by the local Ordinary; 2) the use of holy water may not ordinarily be omitted and it should be explained with reference to Christian baptism; 3) white, violet, or black vestments may be worn at funeral services and at other offices and Masses for the dead; 4) additional forms for the Vigil or Wake Service; 5) additional formularies for the prayer before the body of the deceased person, the sprinkling of the body with holy water and the placement of the white pall on the coffin, and for the Invocations/Litany in place of the Song of Farewell; 6) the use of the paschal candle in the entrance procession; 7) the use of family or friends for the readings and the presentation of the gifts; and 8) a reading from scripture and a responsorial psalm may be said at the station at the grave or tomb. The *Rite of Funerals* was confirmed by the Apostolic See on January 31, 1971. It was mandated for use in the United States on November 1, 1971.

In 1981 ICEL began its process of preparing revised translations of the various ritual books issued by the Apostolic See between 1969 and 1974. This was in conformity with the 1969 Instruction of the Congregation of Rites entitled "On the Translation of Liturgical Texts." The Instruction directed that after "sufficient experiment and passage of time, all translations will need review" (no. 1). The *Rite of Funerals* was chosen to inaugurate this process since it was one of the earliest texts issued by ICEL. The rite also contained a relatively small number of texts and therefore allowed for a very controlled beginning for this extensive project.

The entire process of revision was collaborative in nature, and reflects the process ICEL continues to use in the preparation of revised translations. All members and associate member episcopal conferences were asked to participate in the study of the translation of the *Rite of Funerals*. ICEL devised a workbook for the project in which each text was presented in the original Latin and in the current ICEL translation. It also contained a brief set of guidelines on the preparation of English liturgical texts and a questionnaire which dealt with original texts needed for the rite, ways in which the rite might better be presented for pastoral use, and particular pastoral situations or local circumstances not taken into account in the rite. The questionnaire also invited comments on the translation of the Introduction and rubrics of the funeral rite and on the entire revision program inaugurated by ICEL.

In the United States each bishop was invited to use the workbook personally or to delegate the task to his diocesan liturgy office or commission or to other qualified persons. The respondents were also invited to send all comments to the Bishops' Committee on the Liturgy (BCL).

The consultation took place from February to October 1981. The revised translation of the *Ordo Exsequiarum* was completed in 1985. It included adaptations set forth in the *praenotanda* of the rite which permit conferences of bishops to arrange the material in a format deemed to be best suited to pastoral practice and to add different formularies of the same type whenever the Roman Ritual provides optional formularies. In light of these concessions, the newly named *Order of Christian Funerals* (OCF) included a revised translation of the decree of promulgation, praenotanda, texts and rubrics of the Latin *editio typica*; a pastoral rearrangement and presentation of the contents of the book; a number of supplementary texts to cover pastoral circumstances not addressed in the Latin, e.g., prayers for the interment of the cremated remains of a deceased person, prayers for a victim of accidental or violent death, prayers for a stillborn child, etc.; Morning and Evening Prayer from the Office for the Dead in the *Liturgy of the Hours*; and a General Introduction which presents the Christian theology of death within the pastoral context of the Church's liturgical and sacramental economy. These adaptations were made in response to the comments received in the consultation of 1981.

The National Conference of Catholic Bishops approved the *Order of Christian Funerals* on November 14, 1985 for liturgical use in the United States. The revised translation of the *Ordo Exsequiarum* (*Order of Christian Funerals*) was confirmed by the Congregation for Divine Worship on April 29, 1987. The letter from the Congregation was accompanied by "a somewhat extensive list of modifications which were to be incorporated into the approved text." These included altering selected ritual actions, retranslating, emending, and modifying various texts translated from the Latin, and reformulating several prayers composed in English and intended for pastoral situations not addressed in the Latin *editio typica* of the *Ordo Exsequiarum*.

The National Conference of Catholic Bishops along with other member conferences of bishops requested the assistance of the International Commission on English in the Liturgy in making the necessary modifications. These were approved by the ICEL Episcopal Board in July 1989 and were forwarded to the NCCB Executive Committee, which subsequently approved the changes for inclusion in the USA edition of the *Order of Christian Funerals*. The *Order of Christian Funerals* was mandated for use on All Souls Day, November 2, 1989.

The *Order of Christian Funerals* provides an exceptional example of the preparation of a particular ritual as envisioned by CSL 63.b. It also faithfully reflects the principles of inculturation promoted in articles 37-40 of the *Constitution on the Liturgy*. The translation as well as the original formularies splendidly capture the human sentiments caused by death and provide a rich context for expressing the theology of death of the Church. And the paschal character of death pervades throughout the rite thus fulfilling the norm set out in CSL 81.

The OCF is composed of five parts, an Appendix, and a Biblical Index. Part I, "Funeral Rites," provides those rites that are used in the funerals of Christians. It includes rites for the three principal ritual moments in Christian funerals (Vigil and Related Rites and Prayers, Funeral Liturgy, and Rite of Committal), and a section entitled "Vigil and Related Rites and Prayers" that includes rites celebrated between the time of death and the funeral liturgy. Part II, "Funeral Rites for Children," responds to the directive of CSL 82, which states that "the rite for the burial of infants is to be revised and a special Mass for the occasion provided." It adapts the principal rites in Part I for use in the funerals of infants and young children. It includes texts for use in the case of a baptized child and in the case of a child who died before baptism. Part III, "Texts from Sacred Scripture," contains Scripture readings and psalms for the celebration of funeral rites; Part IV, "Office for the Dead," includes Morning Prayer, Evening Prayer, and Additional Hymns; and

Part V, "Additional Texts," contains "Prayers and Texts in Particular Circumstances" and "Holy Communion outside Mass."

The General Introduction of the *Order of Christian Funerals* is a rich source for catechesis on the meaning of death and how the Christian community responds in faith to this experience. Its depths have yet to be fully plumbed in many parish communities. Catechesis needs to extend beyond merely familiarizing laity and clergy with the newly revised text. The OCF explicitly states that "as a part of the pastoral ministry, pastors, associate pastors, and other ministers should instruct the parish community on the Christian meaning of death and on the purpose and significance of the Church's liturgical rites for the dead. Information on how the parish community assists families in preparing for funerals should also be provided. By giving instruction, pastors and associate pastors should lead the community to a deeper appreciation of its role in the ministry of consolation and to a fuller understanding of the significance of the death of a fellow Christian" (OCF 9).

The section on "Ministry and Participation" promotes the full, active, and conscious participation of the community at every ritual step, because "those who are baptized in Christ and nourished at the same table of the Lord are responsible for one another" (OCF 8). As such members of the community are encouraged to console those who mourn, assist them in the routine tasks of daily living, and aid in the preparation of the funeral rites. The community's principle involvement is expressed, however, "in its active participation in the celebration of the funeral rites, particularly the vigil for the deceased, the funeral liturgy, and the rite of committal" (OCF 11). Parishes are encouraged to schedule these rites at times when the community can be present.

The Order introduces an entire section on the "Ministry for the Mourners and the Deceased." The development of this ministry in the parish is paramount. In essence it breaches the gap between our liturgical prayer and daily life by pointing out that the active participation in the liturgical rites naturally leads to consideration of the "spiritual and psychological needs of the family and friends of the deceased to express grief and their sense of loss, to accept the reality of death, and to comfort one another" (OCF 16).

An important contribution of the OCF is its section on Liturgical Elements. Here the integral elements of the liturgical celebration are set forth and explained in a manner not found in any other revised rite. The section is based on the premise that "since liturgical celebration involves the whole person, it requires attentiveness to all that affects the senses" (OCF 21). Special emphasis is given to all the elements of "The Word of God" so that all is "proclaimed or sung with understanding, conviction, and reverence" (OCF 21). In terms of the homily the OCF states that it is "based on the readings" and may be given after the gospel reading at the funeral liturgy or vigil service; *"but there is never to be a eulogy"* (OCF 27, emphasis added).

Music in the funeral rites is given special attention and warrants careful examination, since this is often a source of controversy in a parish. The rite is very specific about the selection of music for the funeral rites: "The texts of the songs chosen for a particular celebration should express the paschal mystery of the Lord's suffering, death, and triumph over death and should be related to the readings from Scripture" (OCF 30). It is expected that music will be provided "for the vigil and funeral liturgy and, whenever possible, for the funeral processions and the rite of committal" (OCF 32). Furthermore the presence of "an organist or other instrumentalist, a cantor, and, whenever possible, even a choir should assist the assembly's full participation in singing the songs, responses, and acclamations of these rite" (OCF 33).

There is also a section explaining the meaning and use of the Christian symbols associated with the funeral rites. The rite specifically notes that "only Christian symbols may rest on or be placed near the coffin during the funeral liturgy. Any other symbols, for example, national flags, or flags or insignia of associations, have no place in the funeral liturgy" (OCF 38). This also precludes teddy bears, toys, and other effects that are sometimes incorporated into the funeral liturgy for children.

Finally there is a section on the importance of "Ritual Gestures and Movement" appropriate to the funeral rites. Here processions are given greatest attention since they "can strengthen the bonds of communion in the assembly" (OCF 41).

The liturgical elements detailed in the OCF are integral to all liturgical celebrations. In fact if the parish community is accustomed to good liturgical celebration on Sunday, these elements should be commonplace at funeral rites. Obviously the best catechesis on the funeral rites occurs when they are properly celebrated. This does not, however, preclude other forms of remote catechesis that need to take place in the parish community separate from the immediate occasion of death.

Over and above the issues already mentioned, catechesis also needs to build up the community's understanding of the human experience of death within the Catholic Christian context. This understanding is set out in OCF 1-7, in which the Church confidently proclaims its belief in and understanding of the mystery of death and its paschal character. The understanding that the funeral liturgy mirrors "the journey of human life, the Christian pilgrimage to the heavenly Jerusalem" will enable the community to better appreciate the three principal ritual moments in Christian funerals as well as the "Related Rites and Prayers" that are used on occasions of prayer with the family.

Reservation of the Blessed Sacrament during the Paschal Triduum

Q. How is one to understand the directives of the *Roman Missal* concerning the reservation of the Blessed Sacrament after the Mass of the Lord's Supper on the evening of Holy Thursday?

R. The directives of the Roman Missal appear to be clear. Perhaps the problem in their correct interpretation is attributable to the fact that people remember what they did *before 1969,* and reading the present Missal in light of former practice causes the confusion.

The Missal states that the tabernacle is to be empty when the Mass of the Lord's Supper is celebrated. Hosts are to be consecrated for the Mass of the Lord's Supper and for Good Friday. After the prayer after communion, the blessed sacrament "is carried through the church in procession . . . to the place of reposition prepared in a chapel suitably decorated for the occasion." The ciborium (or several containers, if necessary) is *placed in the tabernacle* and "the tabernacle of reposition is then closed" after the incensation at the place of reposition. (Adoration does not take place before the *exposed* blessed sacrament.) This adoration continues for a suitable period of time, "but there should be no solemn adoration after midnight."

After the veneration of the cross is concluded at the Celebration of the Lord's Passion on the following day, "the deacon or, if there is no deacon, the priest brings the ciborium with the Blessed Sacrament *from the place of reposition* to the altar *without any procession*" (emphasis added). The place of reposition is the place of reposition from the preceding evening. The provision that the Eucharist be brought to the altar "without any procession" but "accompanied by two ministers with lighted candles" means that this liturgical action should be done very simply; it does not have the solemnity of the previous evening when the Eucharist was carried to the place of reposition.

The Missal states that, "When the communion has been completed (on Good Friday), a suitable minister may take the ciborium to a place prepared outside the church or, if circumstances require, may place it in the tabernacle." This takes place *before* the prayer after communion and the concluding prayer over the people.

Since no additional rubric is given about the disposition of the blessed sacrament after the Celebration of the Lord's Passion (except that on Holy Saturday "holy communion may be given only as viaticum"), one concludes that the Easter Vigil begins with this tabernacle in the church *empty* if, on Good Friday, the ciborium had been taken to a "place prepared outside the church," as is the prescribed ordinary practice. On the other hand, if circumstances had required that the ciborium be placed in the tabernacle in the church after communion on Good Friday because there was no other suitable place for reservation outside the church, one presumes that the reserved sacrament would still be there at the beginning of the Easter Vigil unless it had all been given as viaticum on Holy Saturday (recall that no one except the dying may receive communion that day).

There are some significant things to be noted about these rubrics. The place of reposition on Holy Thursday evening is a "chapel." It is either the chapel of reservation, if the church has one, or a chapel set up apart from the church. It is from that place of reposition that the deacon or priest brings the eucharist for the communion rite during the Good Friday liturgy. The place of reposition *after* the Good Friday liturgy ordinarily should *not* be a chapel or the tabernacle *in the church*. The blessed sacrament is reserved only for viaticum and ordinarily should be *absent* from the church—thus the rubric about taking the ciborium "to a place prepared outside the church." Only when it is required by circumstances should the blessed sacrament be placed in the tabernacle in the church after the communion rite on Good Friday.

COMMITTEE ON THE LITURGY

NEWSLETTER

1993
VOLUME XXIX
APRIL

NCCB Administrative Committee Meeting

The Administrative Committee of the National Conference of Catholic Bishops (NCCB) met on March 23-25, 1993 at the NCCB/USCC headquarters building in Washington, DC. In the course of the meeting Bishop Wilton D. Gregory, Chairman of the NCCB Liturgy Committee, requested that an action item of the Committee be placed on the agenda of the June meeting of the NCCB.

This action item asks that formal authorization be requested from the Congregation for Divine Worship and the Discipline of the Sacraments (CDWDS) for the preparation of two new eucharistic prayers in English. It arises from the survey on possible American variations in the revised English translation of the Roman Missal (*Sacramentary*) conducted in January 1992 when 80% of the bishops responded yes to the question on the need for additional eucharistic prayers. This request is in accord with the 1988 *Declaration concerning Eucharistic Prayers and Liturgical Experimentation,* which reaffirms the requirement of *Eucharistiae participationem* that a conference of bishops must first request permission of the Apostolic See before it may begin to prepare new eucharistic prayers. Once the permission is received, and under the conditions laid down by the CDWDS, the texts may then be prepared. Once the texts are prepared, they must be approved by the conference of bishops and submitted to the Congregation for the required *confirmatio.*

The Liturgy Committee also presented a motion that the Administrative Committee approve for liturgical use in the dioceses of the United States of America the *Ritual de Exequias Cristianas,* the Spanish translation of the *Order of Christian Funerals.* (Since it is the practice of the Liturgy Committee to seek only *ad interim* approval for Spanish-language liturgical books, the text only needed to be submitted to the NCCB Administrative Committee for the requisite canonical approval.) The Administrative Committee unanimously approved this motion.

The *Ritual de Exequias Cristianas* is based on the Spanish-language translation of the Latin *Ordo Exsequiarum* prepared by the Commission on the Liturgy of the Episcopal Conference of Mexico, published under the title *Ritual de Exequias.* Rubrics, pastoral notes, and all original English prayers prepared by the International Commission on English in the Liturgy for inclusion in the English-language *Order of Christian Funerals* were translated by the Hispanic Liturgy Subcommittee. All Scripture texts were taken from the Spanish-language *Leccionario.* When a particular reading was not found in the *Leccionario,* it was taken from the *Biblia Latinoamericana,* the translation used in the U.S. edition of the *Leccionario.* Since all materials used in the English *Order of Christian Funerals* have been translated, this Spanish-language version is a "mirror image" of the English edition of the *Order of Christian Funerals* already in use throughout the United States. The approval of the *Ritual de Exequias Cristianas* has been referred to the Congregation for Divine Worship and the Discipline of the Sacraments for the necessary confirmation.

March Meeting of the Liturgy Committee

The bishop members of the NCCB Committee on the Liturgy met in Washington, DC, on March 25, 1993. The principal agenda item of the meeting was the Committee's plans and programs for 1994, which will be submitted for approval at the November 1993 plenary meeting of the National Conference of Catholic Bishops.

The ongoing work of the Secretariat in 1994 will include the publication of the *Newsletter,* preparation of liturgical books for approval and publication, response to liturgical inquiries, preparation of the liturgical calendar, and review of participation aids and other liturgical materials. The Secretariat will also work on

3211 FOURTH STREET NE • WASHINGTON, DC 20017

the following: preparation of the revised edition of the *Sacramentary* in collaboration with the International Commission on English in the Liturgy (ICEL); preparation of American variations in the revised English translation of the *Sacramentary;* preparation of the English translation of the *Order for Celebrating Marriage* in collaboration with ICEL and the preparation of American adaptations of the revised *Order;* development of guidelines to address several areas of pastoral concern (televised Masses, sacristans and others who prepare the liturgy, etc.); collaboration with the Federation of Diocesan Liturgical Commissions on position statements approved at national meetings; participation in ecumenical liturgical consultations, such as the North American Consultation on Common Texts (CCT), the English Language Liturgical Consultation (ELLC), the North American Academy of Liturgy (NAAL), and the Commission on Worship and the Arts of the National Council of Churches of Christ (NCC).

The Secretariat will engage in the preparation, publication, implementation, and/or promotion of the following in 1994: *Lectionary for Mass* (second typical edition), the *Ordination of a Bishop, of Presbyters, and of Deacons,* the *Sacramentario* (the Spanish-language Sacramentary), *Guidelines for Cremation and Other Funeral Practices,* and additions to the *Study Texts* and *Liturgy Documentary Series.* It will also pursue several issues pertaining to the Christian initiation of children: evaluation of the effectiveness of liturgical texts and celebrations and related pedagogical issues in the catechesis of young children; the ICEL consultation on the revision of the rites for the Christian initiation of children; and a dialogue on the proposal to restore in the Latin rite the ancient practice of celebrating confirmation and Eucharist at the time of infant baptism.

The Committee also discussed the proposal approved by the NCCB at the November 1992 plenary meeting to study the question of inclusive language for those liturgical texts that have not been revised for inclusive language and to recommend some form of interim guidelines. This pertains specifically to texts in the *Sacramentary* and in the *Liturgy of the Hours.*

Rereading the Constitution on the Liturgy (art. 83-101)

The entirety of Chapter Four of the *Constitution on the Liturgy* (CSL) concerns the revision of the Divine Office. Here the Divine Office or the *Liturgy of the Hours* is emphasized as a form of liturgical prayer for the whole people of God. Although there had been other reforms of the divine office in this century, the one inaugurated by Vatican Council II was the most encompassing. Consequently, revising the office according to the principles and norms set out in CSL 83-101 was an enormous task; it was assigned to eight separate study groups, who worked on the revision from 1964 until 1971.

The *Constitution on the Liturgy* provides an extensive list of norms for guiding the revision. They include the following: 1) restoring lauds and vespers as the chief hours of the daily office (CSL 89 a); 2) composing Compline so that it will be a suitable prayer for the end of the day (CSL 89 b); 3) adapting Matins so that it may be recited at any hour and revising it so that there are fewer psalms and longer readings (CSL 89 c); 4) suppressing Prime (CSL 89 d); 5) observing the minor hours (terce, sext, and none) in choir, but allowing the choice of one of these hours outside choir (CSL 89 e); 6) adapting the ancient and venerable treasures of the office so that they may be more fully and readily appropriated (CSL 90); 7) distributing the psalms over a longer period of time (CSL 91); 8) revising the psalter so that it takes into account the liturgical use of the psalms, including their being sung (CSL 91); 9) arranging the Scripture readings so that God's word may be easily accessible in more abundant measure (CSL 92 a); 10) providing a better selection from the excerpted works of the Fathers, doctors of the Church, and ecclesiastical writers (CSL 92 b); 11) making the accounts of the martyrdom or lives of the saints to be in accord with historical fact (CSL 92 c); 12) restoring the hymns to their original form, dropping or changing hymns that conflict with Christian piety, and incorporating a better selection from the treasury of hymns (CSL 93); and 13) praying the hours at a time most closely corresponding to the true time of each canonical hour (CSL 94).

Along with ensuring that the revision was made in conformity to the approved norms, the Concilium also had to deal with a great diversity of opinions within its own ranks. Members disagreed on the length of the psalms, selection of psalms (eliminating the imprecatory psalms or using them only on certain occasions during the year), the integrity of the psalter, the format of the text, the length of the office, the structure of Lauds and Vespers, the text that would be used in the new translation of the psalter, and the selection of scripture readings for the office. Differences of opinion occurred between those more attached to tradition who did not want to seek any major changes, and those who felt it was necessary to provide the clergy and faithful with something vital and solid. Furthermore, there was division between those who understood the Breviary as a prayer of the Church and those who felt it should be reserved to certain categories of persons.

The apostolic constitution, *Laudis canticum,* promulgating the revised *Liturgia Horarum* was issued by Pope Paul VI on November 1, 1970, but it was not published until February 1971. It soon became apparent that more time was needed to complete the edition of the volumes for the divine office due to the magnitude of the work and other related problems. Thus, on February 2, 1971 the Congregation for Divine Worship issued the decree *Cum editi* (CE), which accompanied the prior and separate publication of the *Instructio generalis de Liturgia.* It expresses the hope that, by publishing the *General Instruction of the Liturgy of Hours* before any of the volumes, "priests, religious, and faithful, both individually and in groups meeting for study or prayer, will have ample opportunity to become familiar with the nature of this new book of the Church at prayer, the structure marking the liturgy of the hours, the norms regulating its celebration, and the spiritual treasures it will place in the hands of the people of God."

On April 11, 1971 the Congregation for Divine Worship issued the decree *Horarum Liturgia,* promulgating the *editio typica* of the liturgy of the hours. The new Office is comprised of four volumes. The issue of format was the source of considerable discussion throughout the revision process. It was ultimately resolved when it was determined that a two-volume Office would have been too cumbersome. The four volume plan was finally approved by the Secretariat of State on August 22, 1970. The four volumes of the Latin edition were published one after another during 1971 and 1972. The first volume contained the official documents: the decree of the Congregation for Divine Worship, the apostolic constitution *Laudis canticum,* and the General Instruction; but the distribution of the material was the same throughout all four volumes: Proper of the Seasons; Ordinary, with four-week Psalter; Compline for one week, with supplementary psalmody; Proper of Saints; Commons; and, in an appendix, the various introductory formulas for the Our Father, and shorter *preces* for Lauds and Vespers. A fifth volume was also envisioned for future publication. This was to include the two year cycle of Scripture readings, the hymns which had been omitted for reasons of space, and a more extensive selection of patristic readings.

(to be continued)

Liturgical Calendar 1995

The NCCB Liturgy Secretariat recently prepared its 1995 edition of the liturgical calendar for the dioceses of the United States of America. The calendar lists each day's celebration, rank, liturgical color(s), and lectionary citations.

For many years the information in the annual calendar prepared by the Liturgy Secretariat was made available only to commercial publishers of other calendars, *ordines,* etc. in the United States. For the past three years it has been published in an inexpensive format and made available to anyone desiring a copy.

Liturgical Calendar 1995 (8 1/2 X 11 in., 32 pages) may be purchased from: Bishops' Committee on the Liturgy, 3211 Fourth Street NE, Washington, DC 20017-1194. Att: Mr. Scott Obernberger. All orders must be accompanied by a check made out to "Bishops' Committee on the Liturgy" in the amount of $6.00 to cover printing, postage, and handling.

Solemnity of All Saints

At their November 1991 plenary meeting, with follow-up mail balloting by those absent during the voting session, the members of the National Conference of Catholic Bishops approved two motions which affect the observance of holy days of obligation in the dioceses of the United States. They decided that whenever January 1, the solemnity of Mary, the Mother of God, or August 15, the solemnity of the Assumption, or November 1, the solemnity of All Saints, falls on a Saturday or on a Monday, the precept to attend Mass is abrogated. This action was confirmed by the Congregation for Bishops on July 4, 1992 (see *Newsletter,* December 1992, vol. XXVIII).

This year the solemnity of All Saints will fall on Monday, November 1, 1993. The precept to attend Mass on this day is abrogated. Since this will be the first occasion when a holy day of obligation is effected by the decision of the NCCB, the faithful should be given proper catechesis on this action. Even though the obligation to participate in the celebration of the Eucharist has been removed, the preparation for and celebration of All Saints is still given priority in accordance with its nature as a solemnity in the liturgical calendar. The full celebration of the solemnity should be encouraged through the scheduling of the Eucharist at times when large numbers of the faithful will be able to participate.

Conference on Seminary Liturgical Formation

A conference on Seminary Liturgical Formation is planned for June 13-15, 1993 at the Clarion Hotel in St. Louis, MO. Sponsored by the National Association of Pastoral Musicians and its standing committee for seminary music educators, the conference is intended for seminary rectors, directors of liturgy and music, and those who teach liturgical studies in Catholic seminaries. Speakers include Rev. Michael Joncas, Rev. Mark Francis, Rev. Gil Ostdeik, Rev. Frank Quinn, and Rev. Edward Foley. For more information contact: NPM Seminary Liturgical Formation, 225 Sheridan Street NW, Washington, DC 20011. Telephone: 202-723-5800.

1993 NPM Convention

The sixteenth annual convention of the National Association of Pastoral Musicians is planned for June 15-19, 1993 in St. Louis, MO. The theme of the convention is "The Rhythm of Time . . . in Faith" and is open to musicians, clergy, liturgists, and all leaders of worship. Major speakers include Rev. J-Glenn Murray, Dr. Monika J. Hellwig, Rev. Edward Foley, Rev. Michael Joncas, Dr. Nathan D. Mitchell, Mr. John Romeri, and Rev. Bryan Hehir. For more information contact: NPM Seminary Liturgical Formation, 225 Sheridan Street NW, Washington, DC 20011. Telephone: 202-723-5800.

Resources

Sources of Confirmation from the Fathers through the Reformers by Paul Turner presents an overview of the many significant texts from Hippolytus to Robert Bellarmine which gradually shaped the practice of confirmation in the Church. A brief introductory note is given for each text. The excerpts from primary sources offer an excellent perspective on the divergent theological understandings of confirmation in the Catholic Church and in the writings and practices of the reformers. The book is available in paperback (6 X 9 in., 96 pages; $6.95) from: The Liturgical Press, Saint John's Abbey, Box 7500, Collegeville, MN 56321-7500. Telephone: 1-800-858-5450.

Fire and Light in the Western Triduum: Their Use at Tenebrae and at the Paschal Vigil, by A.J. MacGregor, identifies from a historical viewpoint the cultural and liturgical milieux from which the ceremonies of Tenebrae, the new fire, and the Easter candle emerged. It traces their development, incorporating the theological significance and pastoral aspects of each, relating them to the liturgical changes mandated by Pope Pius XII in the 1950's while offering reasons for those changes. *Fire and Light* is available in paperback (5 1/2 X 8 1/2 in., 157 pages; $22.95) from: The Liturgical Press, Saint John's Abbey, Box 7500, Collegeville, MN 56321-7500. Telephone: 1-800-858-5450.

Children in the Assembly of the Church contains the proceedings from the 1991 twentieth annual conference of the Notre Dame Center for Pastoral Liturgy. Dedicated to Mark Searle, it contains his address and those of others who explore questions concerning the inclusion of children in the proclamation of God's Word and handing on the faith to the young. The book is available in paperback ($8.95) from: Liturgy Training Publications, 1800 North Hermitage Avenue, Chicago, IL 60622-1101. Telephone: 1-800-933-1800.

The *Role of the Assembly in Christian Initiation* by Catherine Vincie is the first in a series of cooperative works between The North American Forum on the Catechumenate and Liturgy Training Publications. The author explores the issue of how the assembly is to see itself in the rites of initiation. Notes and appendices round out the booklet. It is available in paperback ($6.00) from: Liturgy Training Publications, 1800 North Hermitage Avenue, Chicago, IL 60622-1101. Telephone: 1-800-933-1800.

The *Handbook of Church Music for Weddings* was prepared by Mary Beth Kunde Anderson, the Director of Music for the Archdiocese of Chicago and her husband, David Anderson, the Director of Music for Ascension Parish in Oak Park, Illinois. It includes sound pastoral suggestions for preparing engaged couples and the liturgical ministers for weddings. It is available in paperback ($5.95) from: Liturgy Training Publications, 1800 North Hermitage Avenue, Chicago, IL 60622-1101. Telephone: 1-800-933-1800.

COMMITTEE ON THE LITURGY

NEWSLETTER

1993
VOLUME XXIX
MAY

Rereading the Constitution on the Liturgy (art. 83-101)

(continued from the April 1993 issue)

The International Commission on English in the Liturgy (ICEL) completed the English translation of the Latin *Liturgia Horarum*, subtitled "The Divine Office according to the Roman Rite," in 1974. The text was approved by the National Conference of Catholic Bishops (NCCB) by mail vote in October 1974. The NCCB also approved for liturgical use the English translation of the *Benedictus, Magnificat, Nunc Dimittis, Gloria Patri* and *Te Deum* prepared by the International Consultation on English Texts (ICET) and adopted by the International Commission on English in the Liturgy (ICEL). The *Liturgy of the Hours* was confirmed by the Apostolic See on December 6, 1974; and November 27, 1977 was set as the effective date for its use in the dioceses of the United States. It replaced all other interim breviaries (e.g., *Prayer of Christians*).

At their May 1973 meeting in Toronto, the ICEL Episcopal Board announced a policy recommending, where possible, the use of the Grail translation of the psalms in the *Liturgy of the Hours*. This decision was made in light of the fact that ICEL had not yet prepared a new English translation of the psalms for liturgical use. Although ICEL was given the mandate to prepare such a liturgical psalter, this project was put on hold because of the more urgent demand for English translations of a number of revised liturgical rites in a short period of time.

By 1974 four versions of the psalter had been approved for liturgical use in the United States. These were the Book of Psalms from the *New American Bible,* the *Jerusalem Bible,* the *Revised Standard Version* (Catholic edition), as well as the *Grail Psalter.* Ordinarily editors and publishers would have been free to include any of the four approved versions of the psalms in their editions of the *Liturgy of the Hours.* In order to encourage common celebration of the hours, however, the Bishops' Committee on the Liturgy determined that only one translation of the psalms would be permitted in the *Liturgy of the Hours.* The public and communal celebration of the *Liturgy of the Hours* was given primacy in judging the psalters for this particular use. After consultation with the members of the NCCB, the Bishops' Committee on the Liturgy recommended the Grail translation of the psalms. This decision was based on the following: 1) the Grail translation was widely accepted as the version most suited to singing; 2) liturgical tradition, as witnessed in the Gallican psalter and in the texts of the *Graduale Romanum,* has accorded priority to more popular versions of the psalter rather than the more literal translations based on critical texts; 3) the experience of many religious communities in the United States indicated that the Grail psalter was preferred; 4) there had been widespread use of the Grail psalter by parish and other congregations; and 5) the recommendations of the ICEL Episcopal Board reflected the acceptance of the Grail psalter by the various episcopal conferences of the English-speaking world.

In 1983 the Bishops' Committee on the Liturgy was asked to consider the request that other versions of the psalter approved for general liturgical use (namely, those from the *Jerusalem Bible,* the *New American Bible,* and the *Revised Standard Version*) be approved for use in the *Liturgy of the Hours.* In light of this the Committee proposed to the NCCB that the Grail psalter be retained as the only approved psalter for commercial publications of the *Liturgy of the Hours* but that the other versions of the psalms could be used in the praying of the *Liturgy of the Hours* whenever those psalms were sung. This proposal was approved by the members of the NCCB at their November 1983 plenary meeting.

In 1976 a one-volume edition of the *Liturgy of the Hours,* entitled *Christian Prayer* and containing morning, evening, and night prayer, was published. It was intended for use by religious and lay persons not bound to pray the full *Liturgy of the Hours* daily. In accord with the decision of the Episcopal Conference, all editions of this one-volume publication used the Grail translation of the psalms.

In order to promote the responsibility of the entire Church to pray the Office, the Bishops' Committee on the Liturgy prepared the statement "A Call to Prayer: The Liturgy of the Hours" (see *Newsletter*, October/November 1977, Vol. XIII). The statement was issued at the time of the official effective date for use of the *Liturgy of the Hours* in the United States. It contains an introduction on the conciliar reforms of the *Liturgy of the Hours*, a brief history of the revision, and sections on "The Prayer of the Church," "The Responsibility to Pray," "The Importance of the Various Hours," and a conclusion. It acknowledged that the "most difficult and challenging task is to make the liturgy of the hours in fact and practice, as well as in theory and doctrine, the prayer of the entire Church."

This challenge still confronts the Church sixteen years later. Although the conciliar revisions had restored the *Liturgy of the Hours* as a form of liturgical prayer for the entire people of God, there is still much that must be done before the conciliar vision for the celebration of the *Liturgy of the Hours* is fully appropriated. Efforts to implement this have already been initiated in many parishes, where the *Liturgy of the Hours* is celebrated during the seasons of Advent, Lent, and during the Triduum. Although this has been a good beginning, a concerted effort at catechesis on the *Liturgy of the Hours* is essential for its full and proper implementation and incorporation into the lives of the faithful.

Implementation of the *Liturgy of the Hours* in parishes has been unsuccessful for a variety of reasons. Too often energies are expended towards designing "prayer services" for those occasions when the faithful gather, thus neglecting or overlooking the celebration of one of the hours. In other cases people are unaware that the liturgical prayer of the Church takes many forms and includes more than eucharistic or sacramental celebrations. In addition, criticism have been expressed that the *Liturgy of the Hours* is inadequate for parish celebrations, thereby rendering the conciliar mandate that "pastors should see to it that the chief hours, especially vespers, are celebrated in common in church on Sundays and the more solemn feasts" (CSL 100) pastorally unpractical. More recently there have been concerns expressed about the non-inclusive language used in the ritual texts and psalmody.

As ICEL begins to prepare for the eventual revision of the *Liturgy of the Hours* in the latter half of this decade, it is imperative that dioceses and parishes embark on a concerted effort to restore the *Liturgy of the Hours* as the prayer of the whole people of God. Already an ICEL subcommittee on the *Liturgy of the Hours* has been established to prepare a study text entitled *Daily Praise: A Study of Morning, Evening, and Night Prayer*. Although it is not intended for ritual use, the book has as its primary purpose to assist parishes in reflecting on possible ways of celebrating the principal hours in the present *Liturgy of the Hours*. This study text will contain a pastoral introduction and extensive pastoral notes that explain in detail the significance of each of the ritual, structural, and textual elements that make up the principal hours of the Office. It will provide examples of how the rites of morning, evening, and night prayer may be celebrated in various settings: parishes, homes, religious communities. It will also suggest the possibility of adding elements to the hours that were not included in the post-Vatican II reform of the *Liturgy of the Hours*, for example, a *Lucernarium* service as an optional part of the introductory rite for evening prayer.

ICEL has recently completed work on a liturgical psalter. One of the principle charges given to ICEL in its mandate (approved in 1964) was the "provision of biblical texts used in the liturgy." ICEL's first response to this aspect of its mandate was the issuance in 1967 of *English for the Mass: Part II*, which contained a translation of four psalms (Psalms 25, 34, 85, and 130) and guidelines for the preparation of a liturgical psalter. It was also explained that ICEL would undertake this project because of the special need for a text for singing. Three basic principles were established to guide this work: 1) the best existing versions both critical and literary should be consulted; 2) greater freedom should be allowed in translating psalms than most books of the bible since they are poetry and must be such in English and because they are meant for the frequent and inspiring use of the people, choirs, and cantors in the liturgy; and 3) a rhythm suited to the English language should be used in the translation.

Unfortunately this project was delayed for another decade, due to the need for countless vernacular texts of the various rites in a short period of time. In the meantime other modern English Bible translations became available and the episcopal conferences of English-speaking countries authorized the psalter of one or more of these for liturgical use in their regions.

In 1978 ICEL's Advisory Committee (the general steering committee for all ICEL projects) received authorization from the Episcopal Board (ICEL's chief governing body made of a bishop-representative from the eleven English-speaking member conferences of bishops) to establish a subcommittee on the liturgical psalter (see *Newsletter,* January 1979, Vol. XV). In 1981 a consultation booklet was printed which included a translation of ten psalms, their musical settings, liturgical comments on their use, explanatory notes, and a questionnaire. During this first limited consultation the translation team continued its work on another set of texts, taking into account the response to the questionnaire.

By Easter 1984 twenty-two psalms (those most often used in the liturgy) were sent out for an extensive consultation to two thousand worship commissions, parishes, religious communities and schools in the English-speaking world (see *Newsletter,* April 1984, Vol. XX). The *Consultation on a Liturgical Psalter* contained an Introduction, a "Brief on the Lilturgical Psalter," "The Psalm Texts with Critical Notes," "The Psalms in the Liturgy," and various questionnaires and indexes. The *Consultation on a Liturgical Psalter, People's Edition* contained settings of all the antiphons and the complete printed texts of the twenty-two psalms. In the United States these were sent to all bishops, to each diocesan liturgical commission or office of worship, and to selected liturgical and biblical scholars for their separate evaluation.

In 1987 twenty-three psalms were published under the title *Psalms for All Seasons: From the ICEL Liturgical Psalter Project* by Pastoral Press in Washington, DC. At the same time the ICEL Episcopal Board authorized the completion of the full project. The translation of the remaining psalms and canticles was done by four working groups whose members possessed various specialties necessary for the scope of the project. Once texts were judged to be in presentable form, they were circulated to the other working groups for review and written comments. They subsequently were submitted to the Editorial Committee and ICEL Advisory Committee for review, comment and approval. The Editorial Committee would then arrive at a final draft of the text on the basis of these comments.

Those who worked on the project aimed at creating a translation that: 1) faithfully rendered into the English the best critical Hebrew and Greek texts available; 2) would be guided by liturgical use by the psalms and canticles, and be fitting for musical setting; 3) would be received by the reader or auditor as idiomatic English in contemporary poetic style; and 4) would be sensitive to evolving gender usage in English, for example, as described in the "Criteria for the Evaluation of Inclusive Language Translations of Scriptural Texts Proposed for Liturgical Use" of the NCCB.

The ICEL Psalter includes the translation of one hundred fifty psalms and fifty-six Old and New Testament canticles designated for use by the Church in its public prayer. In accord with canon 825 of the new Code of Canon Law, ICEL has submitted these texts to the NCCB *ad hoc* Committee for Review of Scripture Translations for the purpose of securing the *imprimatur.* It is hoped that once the *imprimatur* is granted, these texts will be published in various editions in order to make possible ongoing study and comment. Each edition will contain a questionnaire which will invite responses to the texts in accord with the consultation process used by ICEL. It is expected that after a study period of five years, a final draft of the texts will be prepared for the vote of the Episcopal Board and for the eventual submission to the conferences of bishops.

Although there is still a long way to go before the conciliar vision for the celebration of the *Liturgy of the Hours* becomes a reality, the preparations for an eventual revision of the *Liturgy of the Hours* provide a new opportunity to instill in the faithful an appreciation of this prayer as the public prayer of the Church.

Lectionary for Masses with Children

September 1, 1993 has been established as the publication date for the *Lectionary for Masses with Children.* It may begin to be used in the liturgy in the dioceses of the United States of America at that time. The First Sunday of Advent, November 28, 1993, has been established as the effective date for use of the lectionary. On that date "no other English lectionary for Masses with children may be used" (from the decree of promulgation).

It should be noted that the meaning of "mandatory effective date" for the *Lectionary for Masses with Children,* as well as for the *Collection of Masses of the Blessed Virgin Mary,* differs from its usual one for a liturgical book. Both of these books are used *ad libitum* in the liturgy. They *need not* be used at all; but if they are used, they must be in the approved versions. One may still use the *Lectionary for Mass* in Masses with children, a practice which has gone on for nearly 20 years by now. The advantage of using the *Lectionary for Masses with Children* in such celebrations is that it employs a translation of Scripture that uses a vocabulary and sentence structure geared for a third-grade reading level. Older elementary school children will still benefit from the simplicity of the translation in the *Lectionary for Masses with Children* but they should also be led to appreciate the more standard translations used in the *Lectionary for Mass*.

As with any liturgical book, catechesis will be essential to promote proper implementation of the *Lectionary for Masses with Children*. Diocesan liturgical commissions and offices of worship should ensure that such catechesis is provided. The Introduction to the *Lectionary for Masses with Children* is an excellent and enriching resource that should be a primary text for developing this catechesis. An explanation of the history of the Lectionary and its components is found in the November/December 1991 *Newsletter* (Vol. XXVII).

The *Lectionary for Masses with Children* will be published in different formats by Liturgy Training Publications, The Catholic Book Publishing Company, and The Liturgical Press.

Communion Under Both Kinds and Health Concerns

The Secretariat for the Liturgy has received several inquiries for current information concerning potential health hazards associated with the practice of communion under both kinds. On November 10, 1985 the Bishops' Committee on the Liturgy, under the chairmanship of Archbishop Daniel E. Pilarczyk, issued a statement entitled "Communion Under Both Kinds and Certain Health Concerns" (see, *Newsletter,* December 1985, Vol. XXI). Approved for publication by the Executive Committee of the National Conference of Catholic Bishops, the statement provides basic theological and liturgical principles which need to be taken into consideration when the issue of communion under both kinds and health concerns is raised. These principles remain as important today as they were in 1985.

Since 1985 the NCCB Liturgy Secretariat has contacted the Centers for Disease Control (CDC) in Atlanta on a regular basis to request their latest advisories concerning the possible health risks associated with drinking from a common communion cup. Each time the CDC, while not ruling out the fact that there are some risks involved in the practice of drinking from a common cup, has stated that with proper precautions (such as wiping both sides of the rim of the chalice after each communicant has received the Precious Blood) such risks are greatly reduced. The CDC has also responded that there is no clinical evidence that life-threatening pathogens such as the HIV virus have been transmitted through the Precious Blood. The CDC has not recommended to the Catholic Church that it abandon the practice of drinking from the cup because of these risks.

The 1985 statement of the Bishops' Committee on the Liturgy notes that the restoration of the fuller sign of holy communion under both forms, in obedience to the command of the Lord to "take, and eat" and "take, and drink," outweighs the risk that drinking from the same communion cup poses. Nevertheless, it counsels that communicants should use good common sense and not drink from the communion cup when they are more susceptible to being infected or to infect others even with the common cold, etc.

The Notre Dame Liturgy Conference

"The Rite Stuff: Bodies that Pray Words which Live" is the theme of the 21st Liturgical Conference, to be held at the University of Notre Dame on June 14-17, 1993. Sponsored by the Notre Dame Center for Pastoral Liturgy and the Institute for Church Life, the conference will address topics dealing with the Sunday Eucharist, occasional rites, alternative prayer forms, and children at worship. Four different focus sessions will be included under each topic. The general session presentations will be "Re-learning a Forgotten Way of Doing Things" (Gertrud Mueller Nelson), "The Ritual Crisis: Cultural Challenges" (Mary Collins), "The Ritual Crisis: Personal Obstacles" (Julia Upton), and "The Assembly as Ritual Performer" (Andrew Ciferni). For additional information, contact the Center for Continuing Education, Box 1008, Notre Dame, IN 46556. Telephone: (219)-631-6691; or FAX: (219)-631-8083.

COMMITTEE ON THE LITURGY

NEWSLETTER

NATIONAL CONFERENCE OF CATHOLIC BISHOPS

1993
VOLUME XXIX
JUNE/JULY

June Plenary Assembly of the NCCB

The National Conference of Catholic Bishops met in plenary assembly from June 17-19, 1993, at the Hyatt Regency New Orleans, New Orleans, LA. During the course of their meeting the bishops voted on one liturgical item which had been presented by the Committee on the Liturgy.

The action sought the approval of the members of the NCCB to seek permission from the Congregation for Divine Worship and the Discipline of the Sacraments to prepare two new English-language eucharistic prayers for general use in the dioceses of the United States, one a shorter composition (similar in length to Eucharistic Prayer II) and the other a longer prayer (similar in length to Eucharistic Prayer III), each to use the prefaces of the Roman Missal. The balloting on this action item was inconclusive when the NCCB meeting concluded, and the *de iure* Latin rite members who were not present at the time of the balloting were sent mail ballots subsequent to the meeting.

The NCCB ad hoc Committee for the Canonical Determination of the Age of Confirmation, comprised of the chairmen of the Committees on Pastoral Practices, Doctrine, Liturgy, and Education, submitted for discussion and vote by the members of the NCCB an action item dealing with the proper age for confirmation in the Latin rite dioceses of the United States which the NCCB is able to determine in accordance to canon 891. The action item was approved by the required two-thirds majority vote of the *de iure* Latin rite members and now requires confirmation of the Apostolic See. The norm states: "In accord with the prescriptions of canon 891, the National Conference of Catholic Bishops hereby decrees that the sacrament of confirmation in the Latin rite shall be conferred between the age of discretion, which is about the age of 7, and 18 years of age, within the limits determined by the diocesan bishop and with regard for the legitimate exceptions given in canon 891, namely, when there is danger of death or, where in the judgment of the minister grave cause urges otherwise."

June Meeting of the Committee on the Liturgy

The Committee on the Liturgy of the National Conference of Catholic Bishops met at Saint Mary's Dominican Conference Center, New Orleans, LA, on June 20-21, 1993. Bishop Wilton D. Gregory, chairman of the Committee, welcomed Fathers Jeremy Driscoll, OSB, and Kevin W. Irwin as new advisors to the Committee.

The Committee discussed and took action on several items, including: 1) procedures to be used for approving the revised *Roman Missal;* 2) interim guidelines for the use of inclusive language in liturgical texts which are not scheduled to be revised for several years; 3) the question of liturgical language and behavior in response to the concerns raised in *One in Christ Jesus;* and 4) a proposal for English and Spanish translations of the Mass formulary for the memorial of Saint Marguerite Bourgeoys for use in dioceses that have included her commemoration in their calendars.

The Committee reviewed a request for use of the Eucharistic Prayer for Masses with the Deaf, approved for use in the dioceses of England and Wales. In response to several issues raised by those who minister to the hearing impaired in the United States, the Committee voted to reject this proposal; it decided instead to pursue the recognition of American Sign Language as an approved liturgical language in the United States with subsequent development of liturgical texts in that language to follow.

The position statements approved by the delegates to the 1992 National Meeting of Diocesan Liturgical Commissions were considered by the Committee. Position Statement 1992 A, on information materials dealing with the revision of *Roman Missal,* was endorsed by the Liturgical Committee with the provision that the Federation of Diocesan Liturgical Commissions, in conjunction with the International Commission on English in the Liturgy, prepare the preliminary work for this project.

The Committee also heard several information reports. Father Michael Spillane reported on the work of the Federation of Diocesan Liturgical Commissions and highlighted the serious situation of the closing of offices of worship around the country. Bishop Roberto Gonzalez provided an overview of the projects of the Hispanic Liturgy Subcommittee, which include work on the Spanish-language Sacramentary. Bishop Jerome Hanus gave a report on the work of the Task Group on American Adaptation of the Roman Missal. Sister Rose Maria Icaza presented a report on the Instituto de Liturgia Hispana. And Father Krisman detailed the on-going work of the Secretariat for the Liturgy.

Rereading the Constitution on the Liturgy (arts. 102-111)

Chapter V of the *Constitution on the Liturgy* (CSL) deals with the reform of the liturgical year and calendar. The revisions called for in CSL 102-111 build on the reforms promoted by the liturgical movement and especially set forth by Pius X and Pius XII in our own century. These paved the way for the complete revision of the liturgical year and calendar in the decrees of the CSL.

The structure of the liturgical year was not radically altered in the conciliar reform. Rather the central goal of the revision was the unveiling of the paschal mystery as the center of all liturgical worship. The CSL restores Sunday as the original feast day and establishes it as the foundation and core of the whole liturgical year (CSL 106). It calls for the revision of the liturgical year to be centered on the paschal mystery, thereby giving precedence to the Proper of Seasons over the feasts of saints "in order that the entire cycle of the mysteries of salvation may be celebrated in the measure due to them" (CSL 108, see also art. 107). Particular attention is given to the reform of Lent, and the CSL requires that both the baptismal and penitential aspect of Lent "are to be given greater prominence in both the liturgy and liturgical catechesis" (CSL 109). Lastly the CSL mandates a revision of the sanctoral cycle "lest the feasts of the saints take precedence over the feasts commemorating the very mysteries of salvation" (CSL 111).

While the conciliar document formulated a vision for the reform of the liturgical year and calendar, it left the specific details of that revision to the postconciliar commission, the Consilium. Since the liturgical calendar was the foundation for organizing the celebrations of the Mass and the Liturgy of the Hours, the study group in charge of revising the calendar was put first in the list of Consilium committees.

The *motu proprio, Mysterii paschalis,* which promulgated the new calendar, was dated February 14, 1969, but was not published until May 9, along with the revised *Calendarium Romanum.* In addition to *Mysterii paschalis,* the volume contains the decree of the Congregation of Rites, the *General Norms for the Liturgical Year and Calendar* (GNLYC), the revised *General Roman Calendar,* the interim calendar for 1970, and the revised Litany of Saints. A second section contains a lengthy commentary on the calendar, in which the historical, liturgical, and pastoral reasons for changes are given along with a comparison of the new calendar with the old.

On June 29, 1969 the Congregation for Divine Worship issued an instruction on the interim adaptation of particular calendars for the year 1970 until the typical editions of the liturgical books were completed. Since the publication of the *Roman Missal* and the *Liturgy of the Hours* was still incomplete, the Congregation for Divine Worship issued a further notification on May 17, 1970, explaining that the *ad interim* General Calendar and *ad interim* particular calendars were to continue in use during the year 1971.

The conciliar principles for reforming the liturgical year and calendar are given specific expression in the *General Norms for the Liturgical Year and the Calendar.* Chapter 1 properly emphasizes the cycle of celebrations dealing with the mysteries of salvation. Sunday is restored to its preeminence as the original feast and thus "must be ranked as the first holyday of all" (GNLYC 4). The Easter Triduum is established as the high point of the liturgical year and begins with the evening Mass of the Lord's Supper and closes with evening prayer on Easter Sunday (GNLYC 18-21). The original focus of Lent as a preparation for the celebration of Easter is given added emphasis. The season is to dispose the catechumens and faithful to celebrate the paschal mystery: "catechumens through the several stages of Christian initiation; the faithful through reminders of their own baptism and through penitential practices" (GNLYC 27). Advent is seen as a period of devout and joyful preparation with a two-fold character: preparing for Christ's Second Coming (the first 2 1/2 weeks of the season) followed by preparing for Christmas, the commemoration of Christ's first coming (GNLYC 39). The Christmas season is given a more unified character and includes the celebration of "the memorial of Christ's birth and early manifestations" (GNLYC 32). The Septuagesima Season before Ash Wednesday is suppressed and the three Sundays of this period become Sundays of Ordinary Time. Thus the thirty-four Sundays outside a special season make up Ordinary Time; this time "throughout the year" (*tempus per annum*) occurs partly before Lent and mostly after Pentecost (GNLYC 43-44).

In an effort to assist the Church in placing the proper emphasis on the preeminent celebrations of the mysteries of salvation, the CSL required that many feasts of the saints "should be left to be celebrated by a particular Church or nation or religious family; those only should be extended to the universal Church that commemorate saints of truly universal significance" (CSL 111). The principles for revising the sanctoral cycle were based on this directive from the CSL. The number of devotional feasts were reduced, since many of these feasts reflected the piety of a particular age, religious order, or pious association, and consequently did not enjoy the same popularity everywhere. A critical examination of the historicity of the saints found in the 1960 calendar was undertaken. Saints were retained and added to the calendar based on their universal significance and the surety that they existed. The selection of saints includes representatives from the following categories: popes, non-Roman martyrs, and saints who were not martyrs. The days for the observance of the feasts were reexamined and, whenever possible, the celebrations of the saints were restored to their "birthday," that is, the date of their physical death. Finally, some saints were added to the calendar so that each of the continents would be represented. Along with these changes a new nomenclature was introduced in the calendar. The terms solemnity, feast, memorial, and optional memorial are used to indicate the rank of liturgical days.

In keeping with the norms and the spirit of these reforms, chapter 2 of the GNLYC directs that particular calendars be drawn up by competent authority and be approved by the Apostolic See which include "more specialized celebrations, arranged to harmonize with the general cycle" (GNLYC 49). In order to foster this development, the Congregation for Divine Worship issued on June 24, 1970, the instruction *Calendaria particularia,* on the revision of particular calendars and of the propers for Offices and Masses. The instruction states that its purpose is "to carry out the rest of the council's directive, namely, that appropriate celebrations of other saints should be observed only in those places where special reasons justify their being honored, that is, in the individual countries, dioceses, and religious institutes to which these saints more properly belong."

In accordance with *Calendaria particularia,* the National Conference of Catholic Bishops (NCCB), at its November 1971 plenary meeting, voted to include the following commemorations on the particular liturgical calendar for all dioceses of the United States of America: Blessed Elizabeth Ann Seton, memorial (January 4), Blessed John Neumann, memorial (January 5), Saint Isidore, optional memorial (May 15), Saint Peter Claver, memorial (September 9), Saints Isaac Jogues, John de Brebeuf and companions, memorial (October 19), and Our Lady of Guadalupe, memorial (December 12). This action was confirmed by the Congregation for Divine Worship on December 28, 1971. At their November 1971 meeting the bishops also determined that the General Roman Calendar, promulgated on February 14, 1969, would go into effect on January 1, 1972 in the dioceses of the United States. Since that time, several changes and additions have been made to the particular calendar for the United States of America (see *Newsletter,* Vol. XXVIII, December 1992, for a current listing).

For the most part the significant dimensions of the reform of the liturgical year and calendar have been successfully implemented in the United States. The centrality of Christ's paschal mystery has received greater prominence in the preparation and celebration of the liturgical year, and the primacy of Sunday has been restored to its preeminence in the lives of the faithful. The observance of the different liturgical seasons and various feasts and fasts remain an important dimension in the lives of the faithful.

Yet the study of the liturgical year and calendar continues to be an important focus for liturgical catechesis in the Church. The reforms inaugurated by the Second Vatican Council must be brought to bear on many of the contemporary issues that continue to challenge the Church in our present age. The revisions called for by the GNLYC need to be more deeply integrated into the lives of the faithful. And there still remain components of the GNLYC that need to be more fully developed.

Promoting the primacy and integrity of Sunday remains an important component of liturgical catechesis. The CSL restores the primacy of Sunday as the day the Church celebrates the paschal mystery, and "other celebrations, unless they be truly of greatest importance, shall not have precedence over the Sunday, the foundation and core of the whole liturgical year" (CSL 106). Yet the centrality of the paschal mystery is oftentimes obscured by various pastoral practices that have emerged in our country. The recent trend of preparing "theme" Masses is but one example in which the centrality of the paschal mystery is lost in an attempt to fabricate a particular focus for the Mass, usually without any regard to the orations and scriptural readings assigned for the day's celebration. Another problem arises with the increasing number of causes, collections, and observances scheduled on Sunday which, if given an improper emphasis, could violate the integrity of the Sunday liturgy or liturgical season. In response to cries raised against this danger, most, if not all, of the materials now being prepared for these national observances give proper regard to the liturgical readings and texts assigned for the day.

Even more important is the challenge to the primacy of Sunday by the increasing phenomenon of the scarcity of priests in many parts of the world, thereby rendering the complete liturgical celebration of Sunday an impossibility. In response to this growing concern the Congregation for Divine Worship issued the *Directory for Sunday Celebrations in the Absence of a Priest* on June 2, 1988 in an attempt "to ensure, in the best way possible and in every situation, the Christian celebration of Sunday." The first part of the *Directory* addresses the meaning of Sunday and its primacy of place in our tradition, and takes as its point of departure CSL 106. The *Directory* acknowledges the serious situation created by "priestless" Sundays, but notes that "what matters above all is ensuring that communities involved in the situation in question have the opportunity to gather together on Sunday, and in a way that coincides with the celebration of the liturgical year."

The CSL also emphasizes the dynamic reality of the mysteries of redemption that "are in some way made present in every age in order that the faithful may lay hold on them and be filled with saving grace" (CSL 102). Pope Paul VI reaffirmed this dynamic reality in *Mysterii paschalis,* recalling that the cycle of the liturgical year possesses a distinct sacramental power and efficacy to strengthen Christian life. Thus the CSL directed that the liturgical year be revised and the specific character of the sacred seasons be restored "so that they truly nourish the devotion of the faithful" (CSL 107). Yet the dynamic reality of the mysteries of redemption is oftentimes obscured by an overemphasis on liturgical reenactment of past events in the celebration of the liturgy. This is particularly true of liturgical celebrations during the Triduum and Christmas, when the liturgy is turned into an historical tableau, or when the unfolding of the liturgical year is perceived as a series of separate incidents. The *Circular Letter Concerning the Preparation and Celebration of the Easter Feasts,* issued by the Congregation for Divine Worship on January 16, 1988, states that the principal reason for this state of affairs "is the inadequate formation given to the clergy and the faithful regarding the paschal mystery as the center of the liturgical year and of Christian Life" (*Circular Letter* 3).

There are also elements of the conciliar reform of the liturgical year and calendar that have yet to be adequately addressed. For example, there has been little development of diocesan, regional, and religious calendars in the United States. In February 1974 the Congregation for Divine Worship issued a letter, *Novo Calendario Romano,* to bishops and general superiors of religious to speed up the preparation of particular calendars of dioceses and religious institutes. And in December 1977 the Congregation for the Sacraments and Divine Worship issued *Calendaria et Propria,* reminding these same groups that the revision of calendars and propers of both dioceses and religious institutes should have been completed five years from the date of publication of the new Roman Missal and of the Breviary, "yet six years after the *editio typica* of both the Roman Missal and *The Liturgy of the Hours,* the work of revising the calendars and propers of both dioceses and religious institutes is still not finished." Lack of development in this area, that is, diocesan, provincial, and regional calendars, results in many groups petitioning to have a particular saint or blessed included on the national calendar, even though the saint or blessed may not have particular significance for the entire nation, but only for various dioceses or regions of the nation.

Faced with an increasing number of requests to include saints and the blessed on the national particular calendar, the Bishops' Committee on the Liturgy prepared a policy statement *On the Inclusion of Saints and the Blessed in the Proper Calendar for the Dioceses of the United States of America.* The purpose of the statement is to provide clear guidelines for the Committee in determining which commemorations should be included on the national calendar, and which more properly belong on diocesan or religious calendars (see *Newsletter,* December XXVIII, 1992). This policy statement was approved by unanimous voice vote of the members of the NCCB on November 18, 1992 as an internal policy statement of its standing Committee on the Liturgy.

On the other hand the GNLYC encourages dioceses and religious institutes to show special honor to the saints belonging to them. The calendar of a diocese should include celebrations of its patrons, the anniversary of the dedication of the cathedral, and the saints and blessed who bear some special connection with that diocese (GNLYC 52a). Religious communities may also want to include the celebrations of their title, founder, or patron and those saints and blessed who were members of that religious family or had some special relationship to it (GNLYC 52b). Nevertheless the GNLYC 53 cautions that "care must be taken not to overload the calendar of the diocese or institute."

The GNLYC devotes a section to rogation and ember days, where "the practice of the Church is to offer prayers to the Lord for the needs of all people, especially for the productivity of the earth and for human labor, and to give them public thanks" (GNLYC 45). It directs that conferences of bishops should arrange the time and plan of their celebration and adapt the rogation and ember days to the various regions and different needs of the people (GNLYC 46). These are to be in harmony with the liturgical seasons and are to correspond to the purposes for which they were established.

In response to these directives the NCCB, at its November 1971 meeting, approved the following resolution: "That there be observed in the dioceses of the United States, at times to be designated by the local ordinary upon consultation with the diocesan liturgical commission, days or periods of prayer for the fruits of the earth, prayer for human rights and equality, prayer for world justice and peace, and penitential observance outside Lent." The resolution is included in the Appendix to the General Instruction for the Dioceses of the United States of America.

These days of prayer are in addition to the observances customary on certain civic occasions such as Independence Day, Labor Day, and Thanksgiving Day. The intent of the bishops' resolution was to provide a period of time during which new patterns for the observance of these days could emerge in a natural manner on the local level; this might eventually lead to a national consensus on the days' observance. Unfortunately the pastoral application of the 1971 NCCB resolution has, for the most part, gone unnoticed. Little has been done to date to foster critical reflection on and adaptation of these ember and rogation days so that they truly reflect the contemporary needs of our time and culture.

Finally, the revision of the liturgical year is an integral component of the liturgical renewal of the life of the Church. This renewal will not be effected by the mere revision of rubrics. The cycles of the liturgical year should shape our beliefs and transform our daily living. Thus, the implementation of the norms and the inculcation of the spirit of the Roman Calendar continues even more than twenty years after its promulgation. Since this time many issues remain unresolved and new concerns continue to surface. The designation of holy days of obligation has been a source of contention for many years in the United States. Abuses surrounding the celebration of the Triduum continue, despite the attempt of the Apostolic See to correct them through the publication of the *Circular Letter*. Tensions still arise over the celebration of the initiation sacraments during the season of Lent. And the controversy over televised Masses when, for example, because of production schedules, an Easter Sunday liturgy has to be taped in the studio during the first week of Lent, has yet to be resolved.

Solemnity of Mary, Mother of God

At their November 1991 plenary meeting, with follow-up mail balloting by those absent during the voting session, the members of the National Conference of Catholic Bishops approved two motions which affect the observance of holy days of obligation in the dioceses of the United States. The bishops decided that whenever January 1, the *solemnity of Mary, the Mother of God,* or August 15, the *solemnity of the Assumption,* or November 1, the *solemnity of All Saints,* falls on a Saturday or on a Monday, the precept to participate at the Eucharist is abrogated. This action was confirmed by the Congregation for Bishops on July 4, 1992 (see *Newsletter,* December 1992, vol. XXVIII).

This action will effect the celebration of the Solemnity of Mary, Mother of God, on January 1, 1994. In accordance with the decision of the NCCB, the precept to attend Mass on this day in 1994 (a Saturday) is abrogated. But, even though the obligation to participate in the celebration of the Eucharist has been removed, the celebration of the Solemnity of Mary, Mother of God, is still given priority in accordance with its nature as a solemnity in the liturgical calendar (see *Newsletter,* April 1993).

Dioceses and parishes should take note that the Solemnity of Christmas also falls on a Saturday, December 25, 1993. But, as noted above, the Solemnity of Christmas was *not* included among the three holy days which received special consideration in 1991. So Christmas remains a holy day of obligation, regardless of the day of the week on which it falls. The Vigil Mass of Christmas may be celebrated on the evening of December 24, 1993. And since Sunday, December 26, 1993, is the Feast of the Holy Family, careful consideration should be given to the schedule for Masses on this day.

In order to avoid confusion in the minds of the faithful, diocesan liturgical commissions and offices of worship should ensure that adequate catechesis is provided ahead of time. Also, all parishes should be reminded that they may use the alternate shorter reading of Colossians 3:12-17 in place of Colossians 3:12-21 on the Feast of the Holy Family (see *Newsletter,* November 1992).

Book of Common Worship

The Presbyterian Church (U.S.A.) and the Cumberland Presbyterian Church have recently issued a new service book, entitled *Book of Common Worship.* The book was prepared by the Theology and Worship Ministry Unit of the Presbyterian Church (U.S.A.) under the editorship of the Reverend Harold M. Daniels.

The last service book to bear this title was published in 1946. It was followed by the publication of the *Worshipbook* in 1970. The *Worshipbook* marked a significant stage in the liturgical renewal among American Presbyterians since it was the first service book to use contemporary English and to set forth the norm that Sunday worship should take the form of a service of Word *and* Sacrament (Eucharist). It was also the first Protestant service book to adopt a version of the Roman *Lectionary for Mass.* Unfortunately, that book quickly became outdated, since it appeared at the beginning of the liturgical reforms that were to take place in the following years among Roman Catholics, Episcopalians, Lutherans, and Protestants of various denominations.

The *Book of Common Worship* is an ecumenical book. It represents the work of liturgists from various Churches in addition to the Presbyterian Church. It attempts to be catholic by drawing upon many of the rites and texts of the Roman Catholic Church, the Episcopal Church, and the Lutheran Church. The Sunday celebration of the Word and the Eucharist is clearly normative, although provision is made for an alternative ending for the service which includes a prayer of thanksgiving when the eucharist is not celebrated. It is also a reformed book in its emphasis on the proclamation of the Word of God, preaching, and the provision of free prayer within an ordered structure. Finally, the new service book is evangelical in its concern that the good news of salvation is proclaimed to the world and that individuals are called to personal engagement in the gospel.

The *Book of Common Worship* contains an introduction which provides an historical overview of Presbyterian worship and the process for preparing the new book. Materials are provided for preparation before worship for use by individuals and leaders of worship. The Service for the Lord's Day takes the familiar ecumenical form so common in Catholic, Anglican, Lutheran, and Protestant Churches in recent years. Of particular note is the use of the recently published *Revised Common Lectionary* and twenty-four eucharistic prayers, thirteen of which are included in the resources for the liturgical year. Propers are provided for the full celebration of the liturgical year, including services for Ash Wednesday and the Easter Triduum.

Various services are given for Baptism and the Reaffirmation of the Baptismal Covenant. The Daily Prayer section provides Morning and Evening Prayer, Midday Prayer, a Saturday evening Vigil of the Resurrection, and Prayer at the Close of Day. A liturgical psalter is included in the book along with psalm prayers adapted from the Liturgy of the Hours. The remainder of the book provides services for Christian Marriage, Funerals, and a series of Pastoral Liturgies (including services with the sick that include anointing). This is the first American Presbyterian service book which includes a Service of Repentance and Forgiveness for Use with a Penitent Individual. The final section of the book contains the *Revised Common Lectionary,* the liturgical calendar, and a daily lectionary for use with the Daily Prayer section of the Book.

Heartfelt congratulations are due to Harold Daniels (who has recently retired from the Worship Staff of the Presbyterian Church) and to all the individuals who assisted in the preparation and publication of the *Book of Common Worship.* This new service book is sure to have a great influence on many other Protestant Churches in this country.

The *Book of Common Worship* is printed in two colors. And, as is the case with recent ICEL editions of the Roman liturgical books, each section is preceded by an outline of the service and care has been taken to make the book "user friendly." The *Book of Common Worship* (1108 pages) is available from the Presbyterian Publishing House, 100 Witherspoon Street, Louisville, KY 40202-1396, for $25.00 ($30.00 after January 1, 1994).

Form/Reform: The National Conference on Environment and Art for Catholic Worship

Form/Reform is the national conference on environment and art for Catholic worship sponsored by the Georgetown Center for Liturgy, Spirituality and the Arts. It is hosted this year by the offices of worship of the eleven Catholic dioceses of New England. Church professionals and all interested others are invited to attend this conference on August 22-25, 1993 at the Sheraton Tara Hotel and Resort in Danvers, MA. Major presentations include "Thirty Years of Renewal: Wandering in the Desert or Journeying Along the Pilgrim's Path" by John Buscemi, "Ancient Stories Told Anew: Faithful Guides in a Strange New Land" by Gertrud Mueller Nelson, and "Art and Craft in the Service of Vision: Nourishment on the Road; Comfort for Weary Travelers" by the Most Reverend Kenneth E. Untener. Twenty-six seminar sessions on a wide variety of environment and art topics are also scheduled. A special one-day workshop will be offered for participants who cannot attend the entire Form/Reform conference. For further information contact, Conference Services by Loretta Reif, P.O. Box 5084, Rockford, IL 61125. Telephone: 815-399-2140.

Resources

Order for the Solemn Exposition of the Holy Eucharist is a collection the rites and texts for use during the solemn exposition of the Holy Eucharist. The collection is arranged so that it may be used for a period of one or several days, according to local custom or pastoral need. In order to provide for liturgical prayer during the period of exposition three types of services are included: The Liturgy of the Hours during the Period of Exposition, Eucharistic Services of Prayer and Praise, and Celebration of the Eucharist during the Period of Exposition. Two forms for the Closing Celebration for the Solemn Exposition are also given, one taking place during Mass, and a second when Mass is not celebrated. A listing of suggested Scripture readings, some optional litanies, and music resources are given in the appendices. It is available in both a hardcover Minister's Edition (7 1/4 X 10 1/2, 176 pp., $34.95) and a People's Edition (5 3/8 X 8 1/4, 144 pp., $3.95) from: The Liturgical Press, Saint John's Abbey, Box 7500, Collegeville, MN 56321-7500. Telephone 1-800-858-5450. An organ accompaniment book with spiral binding is also available (7 X 10, 112 pp., $24.95). Prepublication prices are available before September 1, 1993.

A Ritual for Laypersons: Rites for Holy Communion and the Pastoral Care of the Sick contains those rites at which a layperson is able to preside in the absence of a priest or deacon. It gathers into one book rites excerpted from *Holy Communion and Worship of the Eucharist outside Mass, Pastoral Care of the Sick: Rites of Anointing and Viaticum,* and *Order of Christian Funerals.* Part I contains rites from Holy Communion Outside Mass. Included in this section are Holy Communion outside Mass (The Long Rite with the Celebration of the Word and The Short Rite with the Celebration of the Word) and Administration of Communion and Viaticum to the Sick (The Ordinary Rite of Communion to the Sick, The Short Rite of Communion to the Sick, and Viaticum Outside Mass). Part II contains Visits to the Sick and Visits to a Sick Child, excerpted from the *Pastoral Care of the Sick: Rites of Anointing and Viaticum.* Part III contains rites that pertain to the pastoral care of the dying: Commendation of the Dying (Chapter Five) and Prayers After Death (Chapter Six). Part IV presents a broad selection of scripture readings and psalms for use in the celebration of the various rites and Part V contains a collection of prayers for the dead and for mourners adapted to a variety of circumstances. The book is available in two-color printing (4 1/2 X 6 3/4, 200 pages), for $14.95 from The Liturgical Press, Saint John's Abbey, Box 7500, Collegeville, MN 56321-7500. Telephone: 1-800-858-5450.

Liturgy Digest is a new publication of the Notre Dame Center for Pastoral Liturgy. It is a resource designed for educators, liturgists, pastoral ministers, students and clergy who want to keep abreast of developments in the liturgical field but do not have the time or leisure to tackle the mountain of new material that appears every few months. Each issue of the Digest focuses on a single topic. The premier issue contains 148 pages on ritual studies, summarizing work done during the past decade by North American scholars. The Fall 1993 issue will highlight the work of women in worship studies, with special attention to language (vertical and horizontal) and to ritual as a means of negotiating power. The Digest is divided into four sections: 1) Reports summarizes books and articles, trends and movements that are presently shaping liturgical celebration and theology; 2) Lexicon zeroes in on key words and concepts that emerge from the material in "Reports"—especially ideas that are new to the field of liturgy, or that have been redefined by recent research; 3) Resources identifies recent books and articles on the topic and synopsizes their contents; and 4) Technology Review introduces innovative computing resources and examines their usefulness for liturgical studies. Subscription costs before September 1, 1993 are $32 per year or $60 for two years in the United States and Canada and after September 1, 1993 are $36 per year or $68 for two years in the United States and Canada. For more information, contact the Notre Dame Center for Pastoral Liturgy, P.O. Box 81, Notre Dame, IN 46556. Telephone: 219-631-5435.

Jubilee: A Time for Parish Renewal celebrates the fiftieth anniversary of The Liturgical Conference. The issue recalls the biblical imagery of Jubilee as described in Leviticus 25 and announced by Jesus in Luke 4:18-19 as the year of the Lord's favor, providing an intriguing image for renewed worship. The issue includes readings on renewing worship (Living as One Church, Doing Justice, Practicing the Presence, and Praising God, Honoring the Assembly), with each reading including discussion questions and suggestions for liturgy preparation and for relating religious education to liturgy, and additional suggestions concerning the intersection of life and prayer, possibilities for ecumenical celebrations, the question of where we go from here, and prayers for occasions. Finally, there is a listing of resources. For further information contact: The Liturgical Conference, 8750 Georgia Avenue, Suite 123, Silver Spring, MD 20910-3621. Telephone: 1-800-394-0885.

Becoming a Catholic Christian: A Pilgrim's Guide to the Rite of Christian Initiation of Adults by Julia Upton, RSM is an updated version of her previously published *Journey into Mystery*. In this book Upton leads catechumens and those seeking full communion with the Church upon a faith journey. Upton introduces the searchers on this journey to the rites that accompany the process and explores what happens to be catechumens, candidates, and the wider community during this time. The book is available from: The Pastoral Press, 225 Sheridan Street NW, Washington, DC 20011-1492. Telephone: 202-723-1254.

National Meeting of Diocesan Liturgical Commissions

The 1993 National Meeting of Diocesan Liturgical Commissions will be held from October 14-18 at the Stouffer Rochester Plaza in Rochester, NY. The meeting, cosponsored by the Federation of Diocesan Liturgical Commissions and the NCCB Committee on the Liturgy, will have as its theme "The Liturgy of the Hours: The Church at Prayer." It will feature as speakers: Dr. Paul Bradshaw ("The Psalms in Christian Prayer"); Sr. Janet Baxendale, SC ("The Liturgy of the Hours: Potential for Spiritual Growth"); Rev. Kevin Irwin ("Praying the Paschal Mystery: Theology of the Hours"); and Rev. Andrew C. Ciferni, O.Praem. ("Communal Celebration of the Hours"). Several special interest sessions will be offered on the Liturgy of the Hours.

For registration forms and additional information concerning the meeting call the FDLC National Office at 202-635-6990.

NATIONAL CONFERENCE OF CATHOLIC BISHOPS

COMMITTEE ON THE LITURGY

NEWSLETTER

1993
VOLUME XXIX
AUGUST/SEPTEMBER

Father Ronald F. Krisman on Sabbatical

Father Ronald F. Krisman, Executive Director of the NCCB Secretariat for the Liturgy since 1988, will be on sabbatical from September 1 through December 31, 1993. During this time he will remain the Executive Director of the Secretariat for the Liturgy and coordinate the work of the professional staff in Washington.

Father Krisman has served the Secretariat for the Liturgy for nearly twelve years, first as an Associate Director (1982-1988) and then as Executive Director. He will spend most of his sabbatical time in Hawaii, where he hopes to compose music, get some practical diocesan Marriage Tribunal experience, travel, and write.

Rereading the Constitution on the Liturgy (art. 112-121)

One of the most important components of the liturgy is its music. And perhaps no element of the liturgy was more affected by the post-conciliar liturgical reforms than was sacred music. Chapter VI of the *Constitution on the Liturgy* (CSL) presents a major shift in the Church's understanding of musical liturgy; it marks the movement from a purely technical consideration of sacred music to an emphasis on its pastoral-liturgical dimensions. It establishes the integral place of music in liturgical celebration, affirms its ministerial function, and fosters the active participation of the liturgical assembly through communal singing. But the change from Latin to the vernacular, the emphasis on the ministerial function of music in the liturgy, and the emphasis given to the participation of the assembly in song during liturgical celebrations sparked resistance on the part of some musicians and raised a number of liturgical and pastoral problems.

Consequently, the direction given by the CSL was supplemented by subsequent documentation issued during the period immediately following the Council in an effort to integrate more fully the distinctive role of music in Catholic worship and to promote the active participation of the assembly in song. The most noteworthy of these documents was the instruction *Musicam sacram* (MS), issued on March 5, 1967 by the Congregation of Rites, to address some "problems about music and its ministerial function" in the hope that the relevant principles of the CSL could be brought out more clearly. It is a seminal document, and its principles find their application in the role that music plays in all the revised liturgical books.

In the United States preparations were begun at once to implement the decrees found in articles 112-121 of the CSL. In January 1965 a Music Advisory Board made up of a subcommittee of priests and laity was established to prepare ministerial chants for use at sung celebrations of the eucharistic liturgy in the vernacular. At the request of the Bishops' Commission on the Liturgical Apostolate, the subcommittee also prepared a formal statement which addressed the need for music to be used in the vernacular liturgy. The statement, *Music in the Renewal of the Liturgy,* was issued on May 5, 1965. It urged the composition of good music suitable for the celebration of the liturgy that respects the different liturgical roles (including that of the community) and gives due regard to the liturgical action and the texts being used.

In 1966 the Bishops' Commission on the Liturgical Apostolate approved three additional statements on the role of music in the liturgy. The first, entitled the *Role of the Choir,* called for a reexamination of the role of the choir in the restored liturgy since "it is evident that the choir will have more varied roles than in the past." The second, *The Use of Music for Special Groups,* addressed the "need for musical compositions in idioms that can be sung by the congregation and thus further communal participation." And the third, *The Salaries of Church Musicians,* requested that parishes employ well trained and competent musicians to promote the sung liturgy and that these musicians be compensated with fair and just salaries.

3211 FOURTH STREET NE • WASHINGTON, DC 20017

The most significant statement on the role of music in the liturgy was issued by the Bishops' Committee on the Liturgy (BCL) in November 1967 and was entitled *The Place of Music in Eucharistic Celebrations*. After undergoing an extensive review several years later, the statement was reissued in 1972 as *Music in Catholic Worship* (MCW). It provides basic principles for understanding the role of music in the liturgy and highlights its ministerial function when it points out that "[music] must serve and never dominate" (MCW 23). It provides norms for evaluating the selection of music and, more importantly, sets priorities for leading every assembly in singing the acclamations, litanies, psalms, and songs of the liturgy in conformity with the norms set forth in the CSL. Perhaps its most significant contribution is its opening paragraphs, which set forth a theology of celebration, thereby providing an appropriate context for considering music in worship.

Ten years later the NCCB Liturgy Committee issued a supplementary statement to MCW, entitled *Liturgical Music Today* (LMT). It addresses some issues not covered in MCW while it also reflects on the growth and development which had occurred during the previous decade. It provides general principles that govern music in the liturgy, addresses the issue of progressive solemnity in liturgical celebrations, and provides norms for music in the celebration of other sacraments and rites (Christian initiation, reconciliation, marriage, burial, the Liturgy of the Hours, and the liturgical year).

Despite these attempts to promote the preeminence of music in the liturgy, indications abound that the Church still has a long way to go before the principles set forth in the conciliar and post-conciliar documents on music have been fully appropriated. The *Constitution on the Liturgy* gives preeminence to music in the liturgy because "as sacred song closely bound to the text, it forms a necessary or integral part of the solemn liturgy" (CSL 112). One of the hallmarks of the conciliar reform was the emphasis given to the relationship between music and ritual text. Music is not merely an adornment or an embellishment to the liturgy, and the CSL points out that sacred music "will be more holy the more closely it is joined to the liturgical rite" (CSL 112).

Thus the CSL stresses the importance of singing the Mass, and not merely singing during Mass. The distinction is an important one. Already in 1967 *Musicam sacram* gives first priority to singing the entrance rites (the priest's greeting and the congregation's response and the opening prayer); the liturgy of the word (the gospel acclamation); and the liturgy of the eucharist (the prayer over the gifts, the preface with its opening dialogue and the *Sanctus*, the Lord's Prayer with its invitation and embolism, the greeting *May the peace of the Lord*, the prayer after communion, and the final dismissal). *Music in Catholic Worship* reaffirms the principles of the CSL and states that music "should heighten the texts so that they speak more fully and more effectively" (MCW 23).

In spite of these efforts to promote the sung liturgy, preference continues to be given to singing *during* the Mass instead of singing the Mass. In fact many of the faithful interpret singing the liturgy to mean singing hymns or songs. Thus those involved in liturgical preparation oftentimes confine themselves to the selection of hymns as their first priority and neglect the singing of ritual texts. Likewise many composers give preference to the composition of hymns and other sacred songs rather than to the ritual texts of the liturgy.

MCW 52 provides some historical background to this development and points out that "two patterns formerly served as the basis for creating and planning liturgy. One was the 'High Mass' with its five movements, sung Ordinary and fourfold sung Proper. The other was the four-hymn 'Low Mass' format that grew out of the *Instruction of Sacred Music* of 1958. The four-hymn pattern developed in the context of a Latin Mass which could accommodate song in the vernacular only at certain points. It is now outdated, and the Mass has more than a dozen parts that may be sung, as well as numerous options for the celebrant."

In 1969 the Sacred Congregation of Rites responded to a inquiry on whether the instruction of September 3, 1958, which allowed for the singing of four vernacular hymns during a recited Mass still applied. The response, published in *Notitiae,* stated: "That rule has been superseded. What must be sung is the Mass, its Ordinary and Proper, not 'something,' no matter how consistent, that is imposed on the Mass. Because the liturgical service is one, it has only one countenance, one motif, one voice, the voice of the Church. To continue to *replace the texts of the Mass being celebrated* with motets that are reverent and devout, yet out of keeping with the Mass of the day amounts to continuing an unacceptable ambiguity: it is to cheat the people. Liturgical song involves not mere melody, but words, text, thought and the sentiments that the poetry and music contain. Thus texts must be those of the Mass, not others, and singing means singing the Mass not just singing during Mass" (*Notitiae* 5 [1969] 406).

The *General Instruction of the Roman Missal* (GIRM) also develops the principle that music is integral to the ritual action of the reformed liturgy and states that "in choosing the parts actually to be sung, however, preference should be given to those that are more significant and especially to those to be sung by the priest or ministers with the congregation responding or by the priest and people together" (GIRM 19). Some progress has been made in this area. Most understand the importance of the liturgical assembly's participation through the singing of the eucharistic acclamations. The responsorial song is often sung, and the gospel acclamation is rarely recited. Yet the GIRM cites other instances where music is a central component of the ritual action, i.e., music for the entrance and communion processions. Unlike song which accompanies the ritual movement of the presentation of the gifts or the recessional, music for the entrance and communion processions is constitutive of the ritual act itself. Thus these sung elements of the liturgy require more than a random selection of hymns familiar to the assembly.

CSL 114 guards against any misunderstanding that the musical tradition of the Church should be discarded. "The treasure of sacred music is to be preserved and fostered with great care" insofar as it is consonant with the spirit of the reformed liturgy (CSL 114). Church choirs are to be promoted, and the cathedral church is to be a model for liturgical celebration. Yet all of this is conditioned on the fact that "whenever a liturgical service is to be celebrated with song, the whole assembly of the faithful is enabled, in keeping with art. 28 and 30, to contribute the active participation that rightly belongs to it" (CSL 114).

Achieving a proper balance between the role of the choir and the right of the assembly to participate actively in song has sometimes been difficult. Immediately after the Council some persons resisted the principle that the faithful have an integral role in liturgical music. Others felt that the role of the choir needed to be denigrated. But the CSL promotes both the role of the choir and the active participation of the faithful in song based on the norm in CSL 28 that "in liturgical celebrations each one, minister or layperson, who has an office to perform, should do all of, but only, those parts which pertain to that office by the nature of the rite and the principles of liturgy."

Musicam sacram further clarifies the norms set forth in CSL 114. It explains that the active participation of the assembly is manifested by singing "especially the acclamations, responses to the greetings of the priest and the ministers and responses in litanies, the antiphons and psalms, the verses of the responsorial psalm, and other similar verses, hymns, and canticles" (MS 16a). Furthermore, it calls for catechesis that "should lead the people gradually to a more extensive and indeed complete participation in all the parts proper to them" (MS 16b), and directs that "the practice of assigning the singing of the entire Proper and Ordinary of the Mass to the choir alone without the rest of the congregation is not to be permitted" (MS 16c). In keeping with CSL 114 it also promotes the development of choirs, especially in cathedrals, other major churches, seminaries, and religious houses of study as well as in smaller churches (MS 19a-b), but advises that "choir directors and pastors or rectors of churches are to ensure that the congregation always joins in the singing of at least the more simple parts belonging to them" (MS 20).

The 1966 statement of the Bishops' Commission on the Liturgical Apostolate, *The Role of the Choir,* acknowledges the growing dissatisfaction on the part of some musicians and choirs with the introduction of the reformed liturgy in the vernacular. In accord with the directives of CSL 114, the statement carefully delineates the role of the choir in relationship to the entire worshiping community. A more fully developed exposition of the diversity of liturgical ministries, however, is found in *Music in Catholic Worship,* which promotes the musical roles of the congregation, the cantor, the choir, and the instrumentalists.

Finally the revised *Ceremonial of Bishops* (CB) integrates the principles and norms of CSL 114 in its second chapter, which treats the Offices and Ministries in the Liturgy of Bishops. CB 40 directs that musicians keep in mind those norms that especially "regard the participation of the people in singing." It promotes the diversity of liturgical ministries, stating that "all who have a special part in the singing and music for the liturgy—choir directors, cantors, organists, and others—should be careful to follow the provisions concerning their functions that are found in the liturgical books and other documents published by the Apostolic See" (CB 39). And it fosters the role of the psalmist or cantor of the psalm and encourages their participation at celebrations presided over by the bishop so that the faithful may be assisted "to join in the singing and to reflect on the meaning of the texts" (CB 33).

Since music plays an integral and normative role in the liturgy, it is not surprising that the CSL devotes a special article to "the teaching and practice of music in seminaries, in the novitiates and houses of study of religious of both sexes, and also in other Catholic institutions and schools" (CSL 115). This article goes hand and hand with CSL 16, which states that "the study of liturgy is to be ranked among the compulsory and major courses in seminaries and religious houses of studies; in theological faculties it is to rank among the principal courses." But the lack of musical formation in seminaries and houses of religious studies has long been a source of concern in the United States. Oftentimes formation in liturgical music is the first practicum to succumb to the effects of budget constraints. Yet MCW 21 points out that "no other single factor affects the liturgy as much as the attitude, style, and bearing of the celebrant" and thus "the style and pattern of song ought to increase the effectiveness of a good celebrant" (MCW 22). Priests, and indeed other ministers, need to be more aware of their responsibility to sing appropriate liturgical texts. For this reason music for ministerial chants is found in the *Sacramentary*.

The Foreword to the present U.S. edition to the Sacramentary explains that music is included for chants of all the prefaces of the eucharistic prayer; chants of the priest and people together (such as the *Sanctus* and the Lord's Prayer); alternate settings of the Lord's Prayer and additional chants proper to the priest, including the body of the four eucharistic prayers; and seasonal ministerial chants, such as the Easter proclamation of the deacon.

CSL 115 also calls for the genuine liturgical training of musicians and singers. Beyond basic musical skills, musicians should have an adequate grasp of the liturgy and know ritual thoroughly. LMT 65 states that "colleges and universities offering courses of studies in liturgical music, as well as a growing number of regional and diocesan centers for the formation of liturgical ministers, are encouraged to initiate or to continue programs which develop musical skills and impart a thorough understanding of the liturgy of the Church." The teaching and practice of music in Catholic schools devoted to the formation of children should not limit their repertoire to songs seldom heard outside liturgies especially prepared for children. Children need to be formed in liturgical music that is both traditional and consistent with what is sung in the Sunday assembly. This formation should incorporate them as singing members of the assembly and encourage them to assume other ministerial roles that pertain to music ministry, such as cantor or choir member. Lastly, more attention needs to be given to the musical formation of the assembly so that they come to believe that their song is essential to the liturgical celebration.

CSL 116 acknowledges the distinctive role of Gregorian chant in the Roman liturgy but adds that "other kinds of sacred music, especially polyphony, are by no means excluded from liturgical celebrations, provided they accord with the spirit of the liturgical service, in the way laid down in art. 30." In consonance with this principle, CSL 119 recognizes the importance of the musical traditions of people of different cultures in all parts of the world and directs that due importance "be attached to their music and a suitable place given to it, not only in forming their attitude towards religion, but also in adapting worship to their native genius." Thus the 1966 statement of the Bishops' Commission on the Liturgical Apostolate on The *Use of Music for Special Groups* states that "in modern times the Church has consistently recognized and freely admitted the use of various styles of music as an aid to liturgical worship."

The years following the promulgation of the CSL showed signs of extensive creativity in the area of liturgical music in the United States. But opinions remain divided as to the quality and value of much of this music. In addressing this deficiency MCW provides specific principles for determining "the value of a given musical element in a liturgical celebration" (MCW 25). In fact the core of *Music in Catholic Worship* is its explanation of the three-fold critical judgment to be used in determining the value of a given musical element in the liturgy: the musical-liturgical-pastoral judgment.

Inspite of this important criterion for judgment, the quality of contemporary liturgical music is still the subject of much debate. The Milwaukee Symposia for Church Composers addresses the issue in their ten-year report, which is an "observation, study, reflection and dialogue concerning the nature and quality of liturgical music in the United States, especially within the Roman Catholic tradition." The report identifies several areas where broader reflection is needed. These include "more collaboration among composers, liturgists and text writers; a better understanding of the role of art in the liturgy; the need to develop a solid repertoire of liturgical music; a fuller understanding of Christian ritual action; and an ongoing commitment to the active participation of every Christian in the liturgy."

CSL 117 calls for the completion of the typical edition of the books of Gregorian chant and expresses the desire that "an edition be prepared containing the simpler melodies for use in small churches." The *Graduale simplex in usum minorum ecclesiarum* (*Simple Gradual for the Use of Small Churches*) was published by decree of the Congregation of Rites on September 1, 1967. It is intended for those churches which find it difficult to perform the more ornate melodies of the *Roman Gradual* correctly in order to foster sacred song and the active participation of the faithful in sacred celebrations. The vernacular translation was prepared by the International Commission on English in the Liturgy (ICEL). But in order to provide a wider choice of music for congregational singing at Mass the National Conference of Catholic Bishops (NCCB) approved the use of other collections of psalms and antiphons in English "as supplements to the Simple Gradual, including psalms arranged in responsorial form, metrical and similar versions of psalms, provided they are used in accordance with the principles of the Simple Gradual and are selected in harmony with the liturgical season, feast or occasion." This action was confirmed by the Consilium for the Implementation of the Constitution on the Liturgy, December 17, 1968. And in 1969 the NCCB approved the use of other sacred songs chosen in accord with the criteria stated above for the entrance, offertory, and communion songs (see *Appendix to the General Instruction of the Roman Missal for the Dioceses of the United States,* nos. 26, 50, and 56i).

The decisions approved by the NCCB were made to foster the active participation of the assembly in song. Yet it is unfortunate that the fourth option, which permits "the use of other sacred songs," has developed as the normative practice in the United States to the neglect of the first three options provided in the Appendix. On the other hand composers of liturgical music need to bear in mind the directives of CSL 121, which counsel them that "the texts intended to be sung must always be consistent with Catholic teaching; indeed they should be drawn chiefly from holy Scripture and from liturgical sources."

CSL 120 decrees that the pipe organ is to be held in high esteem in the Latin Church but allows that "other instruments also may be admitted for use in divine worship, with the knowledge and consent of the competent territorial authority and in conformity with art. 22.2., art. 37, and art. 40. This applies, however, only on condition that the instruments are suitable, or can be made suitable, for sacred use, are in accord with the dignity of the place of worship, and truly contribute to the uplifting of the faithful." In November 1967 the NCCB approved the use of musical instruments other than the organ, provided they are played in a manner suitable to public worship (see *Appendix,* no. 275). The use of the organ and other instruments was affirmed in MCW 37, which also provides practical information on the proper placement of the organ and choir and encourages their placement near the front pews in order to facilitate congregational singing and so that the choir "appear(s) to be part of the worshipping community."

Since the promulgation of the CSL and the publication of MCW numerous issues have arisen that pertain to the role of instrumental music in the liturgy. LMT acknowledges that instrumental accompaniment is a great support to an assembly and can "assist the assembly in preparing for worship, in meditating on the mysteries, and in joyfully progressing in its passage from liturgy to life", but it should never replace song, times of silence in the liturgy, nor ever "degenerate into idle background music" (LMT 59). Furthermore, recorded music, as a general norm, should "never be used within the liturgy to replace the congregation, the choir, the organist or other instrumentalists" (LMT 60). Although LMT admits of some exceptions to this principle, it endeavors to preserve the integrity of the community's participation in song.

In many cases the advancements made in technology enhance the environment for worship. Proper sound reinforcement systems help to create a better auditory environment and can promote flexibility in worship. At times, however, technology threatens to replace both musicians and the assembly. Digital recording, for example, is now widely available; it makes it possible for musicians to prerecord music that can be played back during liturgical celebrations. For some persons this technological development appears to eliminate the need to provide for competent musicians at the liturgy. Yet removing the human element from worship violates the very principle articulated in LMT 60, i.e., that prerecorded music should never replace the congregation, the choir, the organist. When the human element is removed from worship the very nature of ritual is threatened and authentic worship is diminished. As advances in technology progress, new directives may need to be established which will preserve the integrity of the Church's celebrations.

As the liturgical renewal in the Church continues in the United States, the conciliar and post-conciliar norms dealing with music need to be more fully integrated into the revised liturgical books. For example, ICEL is already focusing on music for the revised Missal. In 1985 and 1986 a consultation took place on the current musical settings for the Order of Mass and the music subcommittee's proposed revisions of this music. The consultation involved one hundred musicians from English-speaking countries. In order to foster the active participation of the assembly in song, the style of music composed for the revised Missal is simple, unaccompanied chant. The revised corpus of chants contains a mixture of settings adapted from the chant formulas provided in the Latin *Missale Romanum* as well as newly composed chant settings. ICEL also is in the process of preparing new translations of the entrance and communion antiphons and, as in the case of the *Simple Gradual,* appropriate psalm verses will be indicated for each of the antiphons as an option.

The provision of ritual music in the celebration of the other sacraments and in the Liturgy of the Hours continues to challenge the Church. LMT states that what is treated in MCW "is applicable to all other liturgical celebrations which include a liturgy of the word" (LMT 7). We still have a long way to go before the assembly's responses in song become the normal pastoral practice in many of these celebrations. This is particularly true in celebrations of weddings and funerals. Liturgical formation is necessary to enable composers as well as the assembly to understand the structure of the rites and their need for music.

The development and appropriation of ritual music for all of the revised liturgical rites remains one of the most important tasks of the Church in the United States as the liturgical renewal progresses.

Ecumenical Directory

The *Directory for the Application of Principles and Norms on Ecumenism* was promulgated on March 25, 1993 by the Pontifical Council for Promoting Christian Unity. This long-anticipated document updates the previous *Ecumenical Directory*, which was issued in two parts, one in 1967, the second in 1970.

The Directory includes a treatment of two issues which have great importance for the liturgy. Numbers 183-186 of the Directory speak of common or inter-confessional translations of sacred Scripture. The Directory notes, "While the Catholic Church continues to produce editions of the Bible that meet her own specific standards and requirements, it also cooperates willingly with other Churches and communities in the making of translations and in the publication of common editions in accordance with what was foreseen by the Second Vatican Council and is provided for in the Code of Canon Law" (no. 183).

In the United States there has long been ecumenical cooperation in the preparation of new translations of Scripture. It is now the common practice for Catholic and Protestant Scripture scholars to work together to produce new biblical translations in English. The *New Revised Standard Version* of the National Council of Churches of Christ and the *Contemporary English Version* of the American Bible Society are but two recently published examples of ecumenical translations prepared in this country. Both have received the *imprimatur* of the National Conference of Catholic Bishops. The *New Revised Standard Version* will be used in one of the two American editions of the Lectionary for Mass, second edition, and the *Contemporary English Version* is now available in the *Lectionary for Masses with Children.*

The second point of interest for the liturgy which is treated in the Directory is its encouragement for the preparation of liturgical texts that can be used in common by the Christian Churches. "Churches and ecclesial communities whose members live within a culturally homogeneous area, should draw up together, where possible, a text of the most important Christian prayers (the Lord's Prayer, Apostles' Creed, Nicene-Constantinopolitan Creed, a Trinitarian doxology, the Glory to God in the Highest). These would be for regular use by all the Churches, and ecclesial Communities or at least for use when they pray together on ecumenical occasions." (no. 187).

This has in fact long existed in the English-speaking world. The International Consultation on English Texts (ICET) produced the ecumenical versions of these prayers that are presently used in the Mass. In 1988 a revision of these texts was published by the successor to ICET - the English Language Liturgical Consultation (ELLC). Some of these revised texts will be proposed to the National Conference of Catholic Bishops for inclusion in the new edition of the *Sacramentary*. It should be noted that the ICET contemporary version of the Lord's Prayer is being used by Catholics in several countries, e.g., the Philippines and New Zealand, but it has not been adopted for use in the United States. Contrary to press reports, no decision has yet been made as to whether the contemporary English version of the Lord's Prayer will be proposed to the Conference of Bishops of this country.

The Directory also states that "agreement on a version of the psalter for liturgical use, or at least of some of the more frequently used psalms would be desirable; a similar agreement for common scriptural readings for liturgical use should also be explored" (187). Since the publication of the *Lectionary for Mass* in 1970, a large number of Churches in the United States have been using some form of the Roman Lectionary, but adapted to their particular needs. In 1983 the North American Consultation on Common Texts (CCT), an ecumenical liturgical organization with representation from Catholic and Protestant Churches in the United States and Canada, produced its *Common Lectionary.* This is an attempt to provide a Lectionary that can be used by all the Churches in the United States. The *Revised Common Lectionary* of 1992 is a further revision of the earlier text based on the actual use of the *Common Lectionary* over a period of nearly ten years. Of all the liturgical reforms, that of the Lectionary has had the greatest ecumenical impact in this country. The use of common translations of Scripture and of the same pericopes has had a profound impact on those Churches that use them and has led to a renewal of biblically-based preaching.

Finally, the Directory recommends that common hymn books or a common repertoire of hymns to be included in the hymnals of the various Churches are to be encouraged. This is an area where there is still much to be done in the United States. Although many hymns are now commonly found in a number of hymnals, there still are no hymnals which are produced in common by several Churches.

Conferences

Southwest Liturgical Conference

The 1994 Southwest Liturgical Conference Study Week will be held from January 19-22, 1994 at the Sheraton Tyler Hotel in Tyler, TX. The theme of the thirty-second annual conference is "Come to the Table: Rites of Welcome and Initiation." The conference will explore the why and the how of the *Rite of Christian Initiation of Adults* and its special ramifications for unbaptized or uncatechized children who come seeking fellowship with the Lord and his Church. Major speakers include the Most Reverend Donald W. Trautman ("From the Storeroom—Both the Old and the New"); Rev. Domingo Rodriguez, ST ("Make Room at the Table"); Ms. Adele Gonzalez ("Come to the Table: Who Invites and Who Gets Invited"); Ms. Victoria M. Tufano ("RCIA: An Initiation into the Story"); Sr. Catherine Dooley, OP ("Liturgical Catechesis: Forming and Reforming the Story"); and the Most Reverend Ricardo Ramirez ("As One Family; the Multicultural Issues"). Six sets of workshops will be offered, including one in Spanish. For registration forms and additional information concerning the Study Week contact: SWLC 1994 Study Week, Diocese of Tyler, P. O. Box 130275, Tyler, TX 75713. Telephone: 903-534-1077.

Celebrating the Eucharist: Thirty Years Later

Celebrating the Eucharist: Thirty Years Later—Is the Whole Church Fully Alive? commemorates the 30th anniversary of the *Constitution on the Liturgy*. The Conference will be held on Thursday, November 11, 1993, at the Seminary of the Immaculate Conception, Huntington, NY. The keynote presentation is by the Reverend Peter Fink, SJ. For more information, contact the seminary at 516-423-0483.

Liturgy Conference '93

Liturgy Conference '93, sponsored by the Los Angeles Archdiocesan Office for Worship, will be held on November 12-13, 1993, at the Westin Bonaventure Hotel, Los Angeles. This annual conference will include nationally known speakers Nathan Mitchell and Reverend J-Glen Murray, SJ, with more than 20 presenters offering workshops focusing on the liturgy. In addition to the general sessions, three specialized tracks will be offered. These include Architecture and Building, featuring John Buscemi and Dr. Marchita Mauck; Music, featuring Robert Batastini, David Haas, and Bob Hurd; and Children's Liturgies, featuring Barbara O'Dea, DW, Paul Inwood, and Bob Piercy. A companion conference in Spanish will be held on Saturday, October 16, 1993, at the Cantwell Sacred Heart of Mary High School in Montebello, CA. For additional information, contact the Office for Worship, 1531 West Ninth Street, Los Angeles, CA 90015-1194. Telephone: 213-2513262.

Resources

History of the Mass, authored by Robert Cabie and translated by Lawrence J. Johnson, shows how the custom of Christians gathering on Sunday to celebrate the Eucharist has it origins in the early days of the Church. Cabie shows how this is a living tradition which through the centuries has been shaped by various cultures and languages, spiritualities and theologies. The book details the history of the Mass as it unfolds throughout five major periods: the Mass before the formation of liturgical books (Chapter 1); the creative period in which various structural elements of the celebration were expanded (Chapters 2-4); the changes that appeared during the Carolingian period concerning the priest's role in the Mass (Chapter 5); the changes that began in the twelfth century and had a large effect on eucharistic piety (Chapter 6); the Mass as it appeared in the missal published by Pius V after the Council of Trent (Chapter 7); the popular devotions and piety that accompanied the implementation of this missal (Chapter 8); the liturgical movement that began in the nineteenth century and culminated in the Second Vatican Council (Chapter 9), and the Mass as it was reformed in the missal of Paul VI in 1970 (Chapter 10). The book is available in paperback from: The Pastoral Press, 225 Sheridan Street NW, Washington, DC 20011. Telephone: 202-723-1254.

The *1994 Sourcebook for Sundays and Seasons* is a carefully organized, pastorally practical tool for those who preside at or who prepare for the liturgy in parishes. The book functions in the way that a liturgical ordo does, with a daily calendar of feasts and fasts, saints' days and commemorations, all with ideas for their observance in the life of the parish. The proper liturgical color and the lectionary number for each day is noted, and a brief summary of the day's readings is offered. The 1994 edition includes season-by-season and Sunday-by-Sunday pastoral notes dealing with the Order of Mass, music, worship environment,

Sacramentary, Lectionary and the Liturgy of the Hours for Year B; an expansive look at the weekdays of the whole year with seasonal introductions in place; supplementary seasonal materials, including optional prayer texts, and art work by Adam Redjinski of Boston that may be reproduced for parish use; many of ICEL's alternative prayers, and translations from European sacramentaries; the Christmas and Epiphany proclamations; reflections on the 25th anniversary of the promulgation of the *Rite of Baptism for Children;* and an extensive bibliography, including a list of music resources. The cost of the book is $10.00 (single copy) or $7.50 (2 or more copies). Order from: Liturgy Training Publications, 1800 North Hermitage Avenue, Chicago, IL 60622-1101. Telephone: 1-800-933-1800.

Children's Daily Prayer for the School Year: 1993-1994 is a book of prayer for the classroom designed to be used by the students themselves to lead prayer. It includes Morning Prayer for each school day, as well as Lunchtime and End-of-the-Day Prayers for each month. These reflect the spirit of the Church's seasons and feasts. For each day there is a format for daily prayer in the morning (or at another time), at lunchtime, and at the close of the school day. Some prayers may be reproduced as needed for students, and a special section incorporates prayers and blessings, and the rosary. Simple directions and preparation pages make this resource easy to use by the teacher. The cost of the book is $15.00 (single copy) or $10.00 (10 or more copies). Order from: Liturgy Training Publications, 1800 North Hermitage Avenue, Chicago, IL 60622-1101. Telephone: 1-800-933-1800.

The National Association of Pastoral Musicians has issued its 1993 *Organ Builders Directory.* The Directory lists 100 builders in 32 states in the United States and three provinces in Canada. It is available from: National Association of Pastoral Musicians, 225 Sheridan Street NW, Washington, DC 20011. Telephone: 202-723-5800.

Staff Change at the BCL Secretariat

On August 6, 1993 Mr. Scott Obernberger, who had served in the position of administrative secretary to the Liturgy Secretariat, resigned his position in order to begin graduate studies at Marquette University Law School. While administrative secretary, Mr. Obernberger had responsibility for all aspects of office management: telephone, receptionist, word processing, filing, processing *Newsletter* subscriptions, etc. His services to the Committee and its Secretariat have been greatly appreciated. Mr. Obernberger leaves the Secretariat with our deepest gratitude for all he has done and our hope that he will find his graduate studies both challenging and rewarding.

Ms. Ellen McLoughlin has replaced Mr. Obernberger as administrative secretary at the Liturgy Secretariat. Ms. McLoughlin had worked as administrative secretary in Pastoral Care for Migrants and Refugees in the Department of Migration and Refugee Services from 1989 to the present. Future communications to the Liturgy Secretariat regarding all aspects of *Newsletter* subscriptions and maintenance should be addressed to Ms. McLoughlin.

COMMITTEE ON THE LITURGY

NEWSLETTER

1993
VOLUME XXIX
OCTOBER

NATIONAL CONFERENCE OF CATHOLIC BISHOPS

NCCB Administrative Committee Meeting

The Administrative Committee of the National Conference of Catholic Bishops met on September 14-16, 1993 at the NCCB/USCC headquarters building in Washington, DC. In the course of the meeting Bishop Wilton D. Gregory, Chairman of the NCCB Liturgy Committee, requested that three action items of the Liturgy Committee be placed on the agenda of the November meeting of the NCCB. The Administrative Committee approved each of these motions.

The first action item requests that the NCCB approve the *NCCB Procedure for Approving the Revised Roman Missal.* The procedure was prepared by the Committee on the Liturgy in response to the desire of some members of the NCCB to have a greater sense of participation in the preparation and approval of liturgical texts of the revised *Roman Missal (Sacramentary).*

The second action item requests that the NCCB approve *The Grail Psalter (Inclusive Language Version)* for liturgical use in the dioceses of the United States of America. In September 1993 the *ad hoc* Committee for the Review of Scripture Translations recommended the granting of the *imprimatur* to *The Grail Psalter (Inclusive Language Version).*

The third action item requests that the NCCB approve the *Ritual de Exequias Cristianas,* the Spanish translation of the *Order of Christian Funerals,* for liturgical use in the dioceses of the United States of America.

FDLC Address of Bishop Wilton D. Gregory

On October 14, 1993 the Most Reverend Wilton D. Gregory, Auxiliary Bishop of Chicago and Chairman of the Bishops' Committee on the Liturgy, addressed the delegates to the 1993 National Meeting of Diocesan Liturgical Commissions in Rochester, NY. The text of that address follows.

I would like to depart from the typical order of my presentations of the last two years. On each one of those previous occasions, I concluded my remarks with a recognition of the work and the service of the staff of the Bishops' Committee on the Liturgy. This year, I would like to begin my comments with such an acknowledgment. I do so for several reasons. This will be my last opportunity to address the delegates to the National Meeting of Diocesan Liturgical Commissions in my capacity as Chairman of the Bishops' Committee on the Liturgy and I want to publicly acknowledge that my service has been made immeasurably easier and more effective because of the kindness and dedication of Ronald Krisman, Alan Detscher, and Linda Gaupin. On more than one occasion, bishops from our conference have commented to me that the sheer volume of work that the BCL undertakes for the Church in the United States would dissuade them from ever considering the chairmanship of this committee. It would be impossible were it not for people such as those who staff the committee. I have a second reason for wanting to begin my comments with this recognition. Often, public speakers put the things of lesser import last and I do not want our staff to ever feel that the work that they do for our conference is anything less than vital.

Thirty years ago, in 1963, fourteen thousand participants gathered in Philadelphia's spacious Convention Hall to attend the 24th North American Liturgical Week. In many respects this annual gathering of men and women, inspired with zeal for promoting the liturgical life of the Church, was no different than other Liturgical Weeks which had been a part of the American scene for twenty four years. What made this gathering so unique, however, was the expectation of the forthcoming approval and promulgation of the *Constitution on the Liturgy.*

3211 FOURTH STREET NE ● WASHINGTON, DC 20017

In his opening address to the participants Reverend Jospeh M. Connolly, a member of the Board of Directors of the Liturgical Conference, characterized this period as one of "exciting times, these years of preparation and actual celebration of the Second Vatican Council. They have been given a special name by Pope John the Good, who convoked the Council. He has called this an age of renewal within the Church."

At the same time Connolly cautioned that the dramatic decisions being made in liturgy, on issues such as adaptation and language, would not be realized instantly. He predicted: "It will take us, in the parishes and in the dioceses of the world, many years to reap the full harvest of what our fathers in Christ are giving us in the Second Vatican Council."

Connolly's words provide an appropriate context for the BCL report that I am honored to present to the delegates of the 1993 National Meeting of Diocesan Liturgical Commissions in Rochester, NY this evening. As we approach the thirtieth anniversary of the promulgation of the *Constitution on the Liturgy,* we find ourselves still deeply involved in the work of liturgical reform inaugurated by the Second Vatican Council. And thirty years later we realize that we still have a long way to go before we will "reap the full harvest of what our fathers in Christ were giving us in the Second Vatican Council."

During the past year the Bishops' Committee on the Liturgy has spent much of its time dealing with the same two issues identified by Connolly thirty years ago: those of adaptation and language. At your national meeting last year, you listened to presentations on the revised *Roman Missal (Sacramentary)* and in my BCL report I urged you to consider strategies for catechesis. This year I am pleased to report that the National Conference of Catholic Bishops (NCCB) received the first segment of liturgical texts from the proposed revision of the English-language *Roman Missal (Sacramentary)* from ICEL in early September 1993.

You will notice that the members of the NCCB will be receiving the proposed revisions of the English-language *Roman Missal* in segments. This is in accord with a recent decision made by the Episcopal Board of ICEL to present the revised English-language *Sacramentary* to the ICEL-member conference of Bishops in several segments over the course of the next two years.

The first segment of material contains proposed translations and newly composed prayers for the Sundays of Ordinary Time. This was sent to all Latin rite members of the NCCB on September 14, 1993. It is anticipated that the six remaining segments will be issued by ICEL approximately every four months until the complete *Sacramentary* is made available to the conferences of bishops by September 1995.

You may be aware that over the past two years some members of the NCCB have expressed the desire for a greater sense of participation in the preparation and approval of the liturgical texts proposed for the revision of the *Roman Missal (Sacramentary).* During this past year the Bishops' Committee on the Liturgy has worked on special procedures to be used for approving the revised *Roman Missal.* The procedures provide for each segment of the revised liturgical text of the *Sacramentary* to be sent to the members of the NCCB as soon as they are received from the ICEL secretariat. Every subsequent plenary meeting of the NCCB will consider all the segments of the *Sacramentary* which have been sent to the bishops since the time of the previous plenary meeting, provided that the members of the NCCB have had a minimum of two (2) months to study a particular segment of the text and all necessary consultation has taken place. The bishops will vote on these procedures at the November 1993 plenary meeting. If they are approved, you may expect that the NCCB will be considering these texts at least until their November 1995 plenary meeting.

I know that many bishops seek the advice of their Diocesan Liturgical Commission and/or Offices of Worship on liturgical documentation that they receive for their plenary meetings. In light of this I would encourage all of you to take time to seriously study the three progress reports issued by ICEL since 1988. They provide substantial background information on the process and research used by the various experts engaged by ICEL in their work on these proposed texts. Even more importantly I would ask you to review at length the Holy See's Instruction on the Translation of Liturgical Texts (*Comme le prevoit,* January 25, 1969) which provides "important theoretical and practical principles for the guidance of all who are called upon to prepare, to approve, or to confirm liturgical translations."

In January 1992 many of you participatcd in a survey that was sent to all the Latin rite bishops of our country and to all diocesan liturgical commissions/offices of worship. I am pleased to report that the Task Group on American Adaptation of the *Roman Missal* has carefully studied the results of the questionnaire and, in light of it, has reviewed all of the American material presently contained in the *Sacramentary.* A summary of their work can be found on pages seven and eight of the *Report of the NCCB Secretariat for the Liturgy* that is contained in the materials you received when you registered.

Last year the delegates to the 1992 National Meeting of Diocesan Liturgical Commissions adopted Position Statement 1992 A on Informational Materials for Revision of the *Roman Missal* which directs that the "FDLC and the BCL collaborate in producing informational materials, such as teleconference, video, and other media technology, which promote the proposed revisions and additions." The members of the Bishops' Committee on the Liturgy discussed this position statement at their meetings in March and June of this year. At the June meeting the Liturgy Committee voted to endorse this statement and to broaden the audience for these materials so that they will be an excellent catechetical tool to help *all* people understand the revised sacramentary both before and after its implementation. At this time Father Spillane is working in conjunction with ICEL and the BCL staff on the preparation of these materials.

Another concern that is being addressed by the Bishops' Committee on the Liturgy involves the issue of inclusive language in liturgical texts. As you are already aware, the National Conference of Catholic Bishops has carefully reviewed the use of inclusive language in liturgical texts and has approved such language since 1978; and gender-inclusive language has been used by ICEL in all the second-generation liturgical books.

At the November 1991 plenary meeting the NCCB approved the *New Revised Standard Version* of the Bible for liturgical use. This was confirmed by decree issued by the Congregation for Divine Worship and the Discipline of the Sacraments in May 1992. At their plenary meetings in June and November of 1992 the NCCB approved Volumes I and II of the revised second edition of the *Lectionary for Mass* which uses the *New American Bible with Revised New Testament and Book of Psalms*. The NCCB is still awaiting confirmation from the Apostolic See.

I am pleased to report that in September 1993 the *ad hoc* Committee for the Review of Scripture Translations recommended the granting of the *imprimatur* to *The Grail Psalter (Inclusive Language Version)*, 1993 edition. At the November 1993 plenary meeting of the NCCB the Committee on the Liturgy will request that the inclusive language version of *The Grail Psalter* be approved for liturgical use in the dioceses of the United States. Approval of this action item will require a 2/3 majority vote of the *de iure* Latin rite members of the NCCB and the subsequent confirmation of the Apostolic See.

The Committee on the Liturgy has also been asked to study the question of inclusive language in liturgical texts which are not scheduled to be revised for several years. This pertains specifically to texts on the *Sacramentary* and in the *Liturgy of the Hours*. This request came from a resolution concerning inclusive language approved by the members of the NCCB at their meeting in November 1992. The Committee on the Liturgy discussed this proposal at their March 1993 meeting and asked the staff of the Secretariat for the Liturgy to prepare a draft text of interim guidelines for discussion at the June 1993 meeting of the BCL. The Committee reviewed the *Interim Guidelines for Inclusive Language* at their June meeting and requested that the draft be sent to the Committees on Doctrine and on Pastoral Practices for their additional input. Once these have been finalized by the Committee for the Liturgy they will be presented to the NCCB for approval.

These are but a few of the major projects that the Committee and its secretariat have been working on during the past year. Many of our other projects are listed in the written report submitted for this meeting.

This will be my final opportunity to present the BCL address at the national meeting of the FDLC. My term as chairman of the Committee is completed with the November plenary meeting of the NCCB. But during the time that I have had the privilege to address this group, it has been my custom to provide you with more than just a progress report of the BCL and its secretariat. I have also been concerned to address areas that pose a particular challenge to your liturgical ministry on a diocesan level. And I have done this in order to urge all of you to continue to work so that the liturgical renewal may be more fully integrated into the life of the Church in the United States.

Consequently, it is my hope that you will not forget the challenges presented to you over the past two years. In 1991 and 1992 I spoke to you about the need to further liturgical catechesis in your dioceses so that the liturgical reform would not be limited to just the revision of our liturgical books, but would lead to the transformation of the lives of all the baptized as well. I urged you to seriously consider the obstacles we face in trying to implement a revised *Roman Missal* when a fair number of clergy and laity still do not understand the basic principles according to which these liturgical texts were revised. And I called for a reintroduction of a complete liturgical catechesis based upon a sound and renewed understanding of the Church, a theology that has been informed by the developments of the last thirty years and thoroughly grounded in the tradition of the Church.

I also encouraged you to confront the many issues associated with our worship with children. If our children belong in the assembly and have a right to the liturgy by virtue of their baptism, it is imperative that we begin to identify those attitudes and expressions that may be inhospitable to children and/or reduce their liturgical expression to childish activity or opportunities for religious education. I called for critical reflection on the theological and ecclesiological presumptions that we bring to our liturgical preparations for children, especially those that lead us to speak in terms of an "adult Mass" or to implement practices that counteract the fullest reality of the liturgical assembly—children and adults together (*Lectionary for Masses with Children,* no. 54).

I have challenged you to pursue new and creative ways to promote the *Liturgy of the Hours* as the communal prayer of the Church gathered in faith to praise God. I urged you to give serious study to the changes that need to be made to make parish celebrations of the *Liturgy of the Hours* more popular and to extend these celebrations beyond just seasonal occasions. I sincerely hope that this national meeting on The Liturgy of the Hours: The Church at Prayer will provide you with the opportunity to address these issues and promote a true restoration of the public celebration of the *Liturgy of the Hours* in the parish.

Finally, I have called your attention to one of the greatest concerns of our liturgical agenda for the days ahead: inculturation of the liturgy. The broader adaptation of the liturgy, as foreseen by the *Constitution on the Liturgy* 37-40, has yet to become a reality in the liturgical life of the Church in the United States. And thus I have reminded you of the enormous amount of work that needs to be done before we can really speak of fundamental adaptation of the liturgy to make it fully American while remaining truly faithful to the Roman rite.

As we approach the twenty first century we find ourselves entering into a new stage of liturgical awareness which will bring with it its own unique set of challenges. It is imperative that you continue to address these issues in your diocesan ministry as well as those new challenges that will emerge in the future.

At the conclusion of his opening address in Philadelphia, Father Connolly asked the 14,000 participants one final question, "What will this renewal cost each one of us?" Unlike those who were in attendance at this Liturgical Week thirty years ago, those of you present here are able to answer this question all too well. Throughout my three year term as chairman of the Bishops' Committee on the Liturgy, I have come to appreciate more than ever the work that all of you have done to promote the liturgical life of our Church. Most of you labor long hours behind the scenes to ensure that your dioceses have adequate liturgical formation and good liturgical celebrations. I am also aware that a number of diocesan offices of worship have been closed or merged with other offices in a number of locations throughout the country. This has caused considerable concern among you. Although regrettable, the sometimes extreme financial constraints faced by many dioceses has, at times, forced decisions of this nature to be made. On the other hand, perhaps even these apparently unfortunate events provide us with the opportunity to begin dialogue on new ways to make diocesan offices of worship more effective and to seek new models that address the changing liturgical needs of our times. This final challenge may be the most important of all if our offices of worship are to continue to exercise a major role in promoting the liturgical renewal of the Church.

Finally, speaking for the bishops of the United States of America, I want to thank you and your colleagues for all that you have done for the Church in helping us to worship God with beauty and grace. I would also like to thank the Federation of Diocesan Liturgical Commissions for the support they have given me, the Committee on the Liturgy and its Secretariat throughout the past three years. I am confident that you will continue to extend this same support and welcome to Bishop Donald Trautman when he begins his term as chairman of the Bishops' Committee on the Liturgy this November.

Resources

Documents of Christian Worship: Descriptive and Interpretive Sources by James F. White is a resource for students and scholars who are engaged in studying and teaching the forms and meaning of Christian worship. White utilizes original documents and classical statements related to worship, and examines historically the application of liturgical practice in parish life. The book includes photographs, charts, and maps. The book is available in paperback (257 pages) from: Westminster/John Knox Press, 100 Witherspoon Street, Louisville, KY 40202-1396.

COMMITTEE ON THE LITURGY

NEWSLETTER

**1993
VOLUME XXIX
NOVEMBER**

November 1993 Liturgy Committee Meeting

The NCCB Liturgy Committee met in Washington, DC, on November 14, 1993. The Committee studied the *Motions Requesting Further Consideration* submitted by the bishop members of the NCCB for *Segment One: Ordinary Time from the Proposed Revision of the Roman Missal (Sacramentary).* The Committee also reviewed the following liturgical items on the agenda of the NCCB plenary meeting: 1) *NCCB Procedure for Approving the Revised Roman Missal (Sacramentary); 2) The Grail Psalter (Inclusive Language Version);* and 3) the *Ritual de Exequias Cristianas,* the Spanish translation of the *Order of Christian Funerals.*

The Committee also discussed the following: 1) provisional liturgical texts for the commemoration of Mary, Star of the Sea; 2) provisional liturgical texts for Saint Marguerite Bourgeoys; 3) a proposal for a Four-Week Psalter using the Revised NAB psalms; and 4) the Pastoral Guidelines for the Celebration of the Sacraments with Persons with Disabilities.

NCCB Plenary Meeting

The National Conference of Catholic Bishops met in plenary assembly from November 15-18, 1993, at the Omni Shoreham Hotel, Washington, DC. During the course of their meeting the bishops approved two liturgical items presented by the Committee on the Liturgy.

The first action item was approved by majority vote of the *de iure* Latin Rite members. The action requested approval of the NCCB Procedure for Approving the *Revised Roman Missal (Sacramentary)* as requested by the NCCB Committee on the Liturgy. The procedure was prepared by the Committee on the Liturgy at its June 1993 meeting in New Orleans in response to the desire of some of the members of the NCCB to have a greater sense of participation in the preparation and approval of liturgical texts. This procedure will be used for all segments of the *Revised Roman Missal (Sacramentary)* presented for approval by the members of the NCCB.

The second action item was approved by two-thirds majority vote of the *de iure* Latin Rite members and now requires confirmation of the Apostolic See. This action requested approval of the *Ritual de Exequias Cristianas,* the Spanish translation of the *Order of Christian Funerals,* for liturgical use in the dioceses of the United States of America.

The membership of the NCCB voted to postpone their consideration of *Segment One: Ordinary Time from the Proposed Revision of the Roman Missal (Sacramentary)* until the November 1994 plenary meeting of the NCCB.

Balloting on the motion to approve for liturgical use in the dioceses of the United States of America *The Grail Psalter (Inclusive Language Version)* remains inconclusive pending the reception of the mail-in votes of *de iure* Latin Rite members of the NCCB who were not present at the time of the balloting during the meeting.

New Chairman to the Committee on the Liturgy

On November 18, 1993, the Most Reverend Donald W. Trautman, Bishop of Erie, assumed the chairmanship of the Liturgy Committee of the National Conference of Catholic Bishops. Having been elected to a three-year term by the members of the NCCB at their November 1992 Plenary Assembly,

Bishop Trautman replaces outgoing chairman, the Most Reverend Wilton D. Gregory, Auxiliary Bishop of Chicago, who served as chairman of the Committee since November 1990.

Grateful appreciation is expressed to Bishop Gregory, who has served the Committee these past three years and to the other members of the Liturgy Committee who have served under his chairmanship.

1993 National Meeting of Diocesan Liturgical Commissions

The annual national meeting of diocesan liturgical commissions and offices of worship was held in Rochester, NY, from October 14-18, 1993. Two hundred thirty-five delegates, representing over 120 dioceses, attended the meeting, which was jointly sponsored by the Federation of Diocesan Liturgical Commissions and the NCCB Committee on the Liturgy.

The general theme of the meeting was "The Liturgy of the Hours: The Church at Prayer." Major presentations were given by Dr. Paul Bradshaw ("The Psalms in Christian Prayer"); Sr. Janet Baxendale, SC ("Liturgy of the Hours: Potential for Spiritual Growth"); Dr. Kevin W. Irwin ("Praying the Paschal Mystery: Theology of the Hours"); and Dr. Andrew C. Ciferni, O.Praem. ("Communal Celebration of the Hours").

The delegates approved three position statements (see below) which had been formulated at regional meetings of the delegates during the spring of 1993 and one resolution of immediate concern drafted in the course of the national meeting.

During the business meeting of the FDLC Board of Directors, which was held on October 14, Reverend James P. Moroney (Worcester) was elected chairperson for the coming two years. Also elected as officers of the Board of Directors were: Reverend Daniel J. Vogelpohl (Covington), vice-chairperson; Ms. Mary Ann Wittgen (Evansville), treasurer; Reverend Joseph Fata (Youngstown) and Reverend Edward J. Hislop (Helena), delegates-at-large. Sister Anthony Peorio, IBVM (Phoenix) remains on the executive committee as the past chairperson.

Resolutions of the 1993 National Meeting of Diocesan Liturgical Commissions

The following position statements were adopted by the delegates to the 1993 National Meeting of Diocesan Liturgical Commissions, held in Rochester, NY, October 14-18, 1993. The degree of commitment to each statement is indicated in parentheses. The voting scale is graded from ×3 (highest degree of commitment) to -3 (complete opposition to the statement). A commitment of ×1.5 is required for acceptance.

Liturgical Renewal
PS 1993 A

It is the position of the delegates to the 1993 National Meeting of Diocesan Liturgical Commissions that the Federation of Diocesan Liturgical Commissions, in conjunction with the Bishops' Committee on the Liturgy, develop a strategy to promote and foster the formation and continued existence of Diocesan Liturgical Commissions and Diocesan Offices for Worship, as these are called for by the Constitution on the Sacred Liturgy and the Pastoral Directory for Bishops. This strategy should include the development of promotional materials for distribution to bishops, worship offices and commissions throughout the United States. (Passed + 1.73)

Availability of Spanish Language Resources
PS 1993 B

It is the position of the delegates to the 1993 National Meeting of Diocesan Liturgical Commissions that the Executive Committee of the Federation of Diocesan Liturgical Commissions provide for existing FDLC bulletin inserts to be translated into Spanish and be made available within three years and that the Executive Committee ensure that new FDLC resource materials prepared in English for parish use be issued in Spanish in a timely manner. We further direct the Board of Directors of the FDLC to communicate to the publishers of liturgical resource materials and to the Bishops' Committee on the Liturgy the urgent need for liturgical rites and other resources to be provided in Spanish as well as English. (Passed + 1.83)

Liaison with National Organizations that Deal with Liturgical, Sacramental, and Ritual Matters
PS 1993 C

It is the position of the delegates to the 1993 National Meeting of Diocesan Liturgical Commissions that the FDLC Board of Directors establish liaisons between the FDLC and national organizations that deal with liturgical, sacramental, and ritual matters. Such organizations would be determined by the FDLC Board of Directors. (Passed + 2.29)

Introduction of Perpetual Exposition in Parishes
RIC 1993 D

It is the position of the delegates to the 1993 National Meeting of Diocesan Liturgical Commissions that the movement fostering the practice of perpetual exposition of the Blessed Sacrament in parishes is a matter of significant and immediate concern; and the delegates further urge that the Board of Directors of the FDLC assist the BCL to encourage the Executive Committee of the NCCB to clarify with the appropriate Vatican Congregations or Secretariats the matter of Eucharistic adoration and Eucharistic exposition and communicate this clarification to the bishops of the United States as soon as possible and in an appropriate way. (Passed + 2.87)

Newsletter Subscription Renewals

All subscribers to the Bishops' Committee on the Liturgy *Newsletter* will be sent computerized renewal notices in December for the upcoming calendar year. To avoid interruption in service, the completed forms should be returned promptly. (Subscriptions which have not been renewed by the time the January 1994 *Newsletter* goes to press will be placed in an active file and reinstated once payment is received). Individual subscription rates are $10.00 domestic mail and $12.00 foreign airmail.

In order that subscribers' accounts may be properly credited, the instructions accompanying the renewal forms should be followed. The "renewal coupon" portion of the invoice must be included with payment. Coupon and payment should be returned in the self-mailer envelope which has been provided. This envelope is preaddressed for direct deposit to the bank. Payment should not be sent to the NCCB Secretariat for the Liturgy since this needlessly prolongs the renewal process.

Subscribers who have not received a renewal notice by the end of December 1993 should contact the Liturgy Secretariat so that a duplicate invoice can be sent. (*Newsletter* recipients whose subscription number is 205990, 205995, or 205999 are receiving *gratis* copies and will receive no renewal notice.)

The gratitude of the Liturgy Secretariat is extended to all subscribers for their cooperation in the *Newsletter* renewal process.

New Official Appointed for Vatican Congregation

On October 15, 1993 Pope John Paul II appointed Monsignor Carmelo Nicolosi as Undersecretary of the Congregation for Divine Worship and the Discipline of the Sacraments.

In Memoriam: Cardinal Francesco Carpino

Italian Cardinal Francesco Carpino, former head of the Congregation for the Sacraments and a longtime Vatican official, died in Rome on October 5, 1993 at the age of 88. A native of Sicily, he was called to Rome in 1929 to teach at the Lateran University. He collaborated on several important Vatican documents over the years, and he also gained renown for the aid he offered to refugees during World War II. In 1951 he was named Archbishop of Monreale, Sicily, and ten years later Pope John XXIII named him to the Vatican department that handled the appointment of bishops. He was named a cardinal by Pope Paul VI in 1967 and at the same time was appointed prefect of the Congregation for the Sacraments, a position which he held for only a few months before being named Archbishop of Palermo, Sicily.

Resources

BCL Newsletter: 1986-1990 includes all issues of the *Newsletter* from 1986-1990 along with a 19-page index that allows the user to go directly to any matter discussed in the volume. Published by the Bishops' Committee on the Liturgy, these pages cover a wide range of matters. This book is essential for diocesan offices, for university and seminary libraries, and for quick reference in the parish. It is available in paperback ($22.00) from: Liturgy Training Publications, 1800 North Hermitage Avenue, Chicago, IL 60622-1101. Telephone: 1-800-933-1800.

The Liturgy of the Hours by Andrew Ciferni, O. Praem. is a series of four bulletin inserts offered to parishes as an introduction to the Liturgy of the Hours. Starting with a basic understanding of the word "liturgy", Ciferni treats the place of praying the Hours in the life of the Church. These inserts are available in 8½" X 11" photo ready copy for reprinting or xeroxing locally. They are available from: FDLC, P.O. Box 29049, Washington, DC 20017. Telephone: 202-635-6990.

A paperback Study Edition of the *Lectionary for Masses with Children* is available (after January 1, 1994) from Liturgy Training Publications. The Study Edition will have the same design and pagination as the ritual book and is to be used for liturgical preparation, but not at Mass. The ritual edition is used for all liturgical celebrations. It is available from: Liturgy Training Publications, 1800 North Hermitage Avenue, Chicago, IL 60622-1101. Telephone: 1-800-933-1800.

Companion to the Calendar by Mary Ellen Hynes is a resource book that makes the saints accessible for today's children, young people, and adults. It includes the observances that are found in LTP's annual poster calendar called *The Year of Grace*. It answers a host of questions that pertain to the liturgical calendar. Why is Lent 40 days long? Who is Kateri Tekakwitha? It contains an amazing variety of information on how our saints and special days hold meaning in our life today. The *Companion to the Calendar* helps all to see how our lives mesh with the rhythms of life in the church around the world. A list of readings, a bibliography and a handy index are included. It is an excellent resource for parish and school libraries, religious education teachers, homilists, families and individuals who want to deepen their understanding of our Christian heritage. The lay-open binding and large print format make it easy for reading in the classroom. It is available from: Liturgy Training Publications, 1800 North Hermitage Avenue, Chicago, IL 60622-1101. Telephone: 1-800-933-1800.

A Baptism Sourcebook by J. Robert Baker, Larry J. Nyberg and Victoria M. Tufano contains texts taken from poetry, hymnody, scripture and liturgical and patristic texts for pondering the mystery of baptism. As with others in the *Sourcebook* series, this volume is designed to stay open for display, study and homily preparation. Section titles suggest the enormous richness of the symbols and gestures of christening: election, faith and creed, water, naming, light, festivity and mission. Book illustrations are by Southwest artist, G. E. Mullan. It is available from: Liturgy Training Publications, 1800 North Hermitage Avenue, Chicago, IL 60622-1101. Telephone: 1-800-933-1800.

Sing a New Song: The Psalms in the Sunday Lectionary by Irene Nowell, OSB addresses the riches of the responsorial psalm for every Sunday in the three-year cycle. It explains the psalm genre, offers exposition on the meaning and beauty of the psalm itself, and comments on the relationship of the responsorial psalm to the other readings. It is available in paperback ($17.95) from: The Liturgical Press, St. John's Abbey, Box 7500, Collegeville, MN 56321. Telephone: 1-612-363-2213.

Celebration of the Word by Lucien Deiss, CSSp addresses the richness and imperfections of the Lectionary (Chapter 1), considers the relationship between the celebration of the Word and the celebration of the Covenant (Chapter 2), and then comments on the role of the Responsorial Psalm (Chapter 3), the homily (Chapter 4), the Prayer of the Faithful (Chapter 5), the participant in the celebration of the Word (Chapter 6), and the objects, places and rites which make up the ritual environment (Chapter 7) of this celebration. It is available in paperback ($11.95) from: The Liturgical Press, St. John's Abbey, Box 7500, Collegeville, MN 56321. Telephone: 1-612-363-2213.

COMMITTEE ON THE LITURGY
NEWSLETTER

NATIONAL CONFERENCE OF CATHOLIC BISHOPS

1993
VOLUME XXIX
DECEMBER

Presentation of Bishop Wilton D. Gregory to the NCCB

At the November plenary meeting of the NCCB Bishop Wilton D. Gregory gave a special presentation that addressed some questions and misunderstandings about the preparation and translation of liturgical texts. The text of that address follows.

The Liturgy Committee wishes to present four (4) Action Items for the approval of the membership of the NCCB. They deal with 1) *Segment One: Ordinary Time of The Proposed Revision of the Sacramentary;* 2) the *Procedure for approving the revised Roman Missal* at future meetings; 3) the *Grail Psalter (Inclusive Language Version);* and 4) the Spanish translation of the *Order of Christian Funerals.*

Action Item One is concerned with the first segment of texts of the *Sacramentary,* but before I begin my summary of that Action Item, I wish to deal with some questions and misunderstandings about the preparation and translation of liturgical texts.

First of all I would like to point out that all liturgical texts in English must be approved by the Conference of Bishops and confirmed by Rome before they can be used in the celebration of the liturgy. For the most part, liturgical texts in English are prepared by the International Commission on English in the Liturgy (which is commonly referred to as ICEL) for the English-speaking conferences of bishops. ICEL is an international body established at the request of the Apostolic See by the English-speaking conferences of bishops. It is governed by a board of bishops composed of one bishop from each of the eleven member conferences of bishops.

ICEL has the responsibility of translating the official Latin texts of the reformed liturgical books into English, and it also prepares additional liturgical texts that its member conferences might desire. ICEL usually prepares an interim or provisional translation for comment by the episcopal conferences, and the conferences may request Rome for the approval and subsequent use of these provisional texts. Usually, after several years, a final translation is prepared based on the comments that have been received on the provisional translation. Each conference of bishops is free to approve or reject any ICEL translation, but before any English text can be used in the liturgy, it must first be confirmed by the Apostolic See. Thus all ICEL translations presently in use have been authorized by the Congregation for Divine Worship and the Discipline of the Sacraments in Rome, after they were approved by our own episcopal conference.

A few liturgical texts have NOT been prepared by ICEL, but by the English Language Liturgical Consultation, an ecumenical body representing the Catholic Church and the various English-speaking Christian Churches throughout the world. The Apostolic See had encouraged such cooperative ecumenical efforts, as is noted in the recently published Ecumenical Directory from Rome. These texts are the ecumenical versions of the Gloria, Creed, Sanctus, and Lord's Prayer. Each conference of bishops is free to use these texts or not. In the United States, we have used these ecumenical texts with the exception of the Lord's Prayer, since the late 1960's. In recent years some suggested revisions have been made in these prayers and the bishops will consider whether to adopt the revised versions of these ecumenical texts for use in the new translation of the *Sacramentary* in November of next year.

In addition to the *Sacramentary* a second book is needed for the celebration of Mass: the *Lectionary for Mass,* which contains the Scripture readings. The revision of the American edition of the *Lectionary for Mass* has NOT been an ICEL project, but rather has been a project of the National Conference of Catholic Bishops itself. Our second edition of the Lectionary is based on the Latin second edition and uses the revised New Testament and Psalms of the *New American Bible.* The Lectionary has already been approved by the NCCB and now awaits the confirmation of the Congregation for Divine Worship and the Discipline of the Sacraments. A second version of the *Lectionary for Mass* will also be published; it will use the *New Revised*

Standard Version of the Bible, Catholic Edition, which has been approved for liturgical use by our conference of bishops and confirmed by the Congregation for Divine Worship. In addition, the NCCB has approved a special *Lectionary for Masses with Children,* which has been authorized for use by the Apostolic See. This special *Lectionary for Masses with Children* is the only one approved for use in the United States.

I would also like to note that bishops, of course, are sensitive to the legitimate expressions of concern by the faithful in matters liturgical, however, we must evaluate these concerns in the light of the Church's official teaching and the requirements of the liturgy as reformed by the Second Vatican Council and mandated by Pope Paul VI and Pope John Paul II.

In our Action Item One today the members of the NCCB are asked to approve the first portion of the revised English text of the *Roman Missal* or *Sacramentary,* as it is called in the United States and Canada. Rome has already issued two editions of the Latin Missal and intends to prepare a third Latin edition sometime in the future. We have used our English texts for over twenty years and, like other language groups—for example, the French, German, and Italian speaking conferences of bishops, whose revised Sacramentaries have already been approved and issued or are under preparation—we are now revising our translation of the Mass prayers in the light of our experience of celebrating the liturgy in English. These new translations are both faithful to the meaning of the Latin and reflect a higher and more worthy English style.

Since 1978 all ICEL translations have used gender-inclusive language in reference to persons. Every liturgical book approved by the NCCB and confirmed by the Apostolic See has employed a gender-inclusive language since that time, for example, the Rite for the Dedication of a Church, Pastoral Care of the Sick, the Rite of Christian Initiation of Adults, the Order of Christian Funerals, and the Collection of Masses of the Blessed Virgin Mary. Our own conference of bishops has used inclusive language regarding persons in its official documents for many years. On November 15, 1990, during the plenary assembly of the NCCB, the bishop members approved the *Criteria for the Evaluation of Inclusive Language Translations of Scriptural Texts Proposed for Liturgical Use.* These guidelines were prepared to insure that all Scriptural texts destined for liturgical use are doctrinally sound. It should be noted that language regarding God has NOT been changed in the Sacramentary texts or the *Lectionary for Mass.*

This rather long preface to our action items is to remind all of the lengthy process leading to the revised translations, and that this process has already involved the bishops through preliminary consultations and study books. The proposed ICEL revision of the Missal is not a new liturgy, rather it is a new and improved translation of the one we already have, supplemented at times by alternative texts, for example, the new optional opening prayers that correspond to the three year cycle of the Lectionary.

New Liturgical Texts

The Secretariat for the Liturgy has received numerous requests for information on the status of new liturgical texts. The following information provides an update on the current status of these texts.

Sunday Celebrations in the Absence of a Priest: Leader's Edition

Editorial work has finally been completed on *Sunday Celebrations in the Absence of a Priest: Leader's Edition.* The text has been submitted to The Catholic Book Publishing Company and should be available in the first quarter of 1994.

Revised edition of the *Lectionary for Mass*

At the June 1992 plenary meeting the National Conference of Catholic Bishops (NCCB) approved Volume I (Sundays, Solemnities, and Feasts of the Lord) of the revised *Lectionary for Mass* using the *New American Bible with Revised New Testament and Psalms.* Volume II (Weekdays, Saints, Commons, Ritual Masses, and Masses for Various Needs and Occasions) was approved by the NCCB at the November 1992 plenary meeting. Both volumes were sent to Rome following their approval by the NCCB for the required confirmation by the Apostolic See. To date the Conference has not received any official notification on the status of the *Lectionary for Mass* using the *New American Bible.*

The *New Revised Standard Version* (NRSV) of the Bible was approved for liturgical use by the NCCB at their November 1991 plenary meeting. This action was confirmed by decree of the Congregation of Divine

Worship and the Discipline of the Sacraments dated April 6, 1992 (Prot. N. CD 1261/91). The translation of the NRSV edition of the *Lectionary for Mass* may be used once the date for the publication of the revised lectionary has been determined by the NCCB.

Provisional Liturgical Texts for Saint Marguerite Bourgeoys

On Thursday April 1, 1993 the bishops of the Province of Chicago voted to include Saint Marguerite Bourgeoys as an optional memorial (January 12) on the calendar of the dioceses of the Province of Chicago in conformity with the guidelines *On the Inclusion of Saints and Blessed in the Proper Calendar for the Dioceses of the United States of America* adopted by the NCCB in November 1992. The Bishops' Committee on the Liturgy is in the process of preparing provisional liturgical texts in English and Spanish for those dioceses that have included Saint Marguerite Bourgeoys on their calendars. The Liturgy Committee will discuss these texts at the March 1994 meeting.

Provisional Liturgical Texts for Mary, Star of the Sea

On March 1, 1991 the Congregation for Divine Worship and the Discipline of the Sacraments confirmed the Latin text of the Mass of the Blessed Virgin Mary, Star of the Sea. This was done at the request of the Pontifical Council for the Pastoral Care of Migrants and Itinerant People. It is intended for use in oratories dedicated to the Apostleship of the Sea. The USCC Migration and Refugee Services Office for the Apostleship of the Sea has asked for an English translation of this Mass for use by port chaplains and others in this ministry. ICEL has prepared a draft translation of these texts which have been approved by the Episcopal Board of ICEL. The conferences of bishops are free to employ this draft of Green Book translation for interim use, with the necessary approbation and confirmation. The Liturgy Committee will examine these texts at the March 1994 meeting.

The Grail Psalter (Inclusive Language Version)

At the November 1993 plenary meeting of the National Conference of Catholic Bishops (NCCB), the bishops were asked to approve for liturgical use in the dioceses of the United States of America *The Grail Psalter (Inclusive Language Version)* as requested by the NCCB Committee on the Liturgy. The ballot was inconclusive pending the reception of the mail-in votes of *de iure* Latin rite members of the NCCB who were not present at the time of the balloting during the meeting. After a tally of the mail-in votes, *The Grail Psalter (Inclusive Language Version)* failed to receive the required two-thirds vote of the *de iure* Latin rite members of the NCCB. To pass, the motion needed 173 votes. The final vote was 150 for the action and 98 against. Approval for liturgical use, as with all liturgical texts, requires a vote of the whole Conference and confirmation by the Holy See.

In September 1993 *The Grail Psalter (Inclusive Language Version)* was granted an *imprimatur* by the President of the NCCB at the recommendation of the Conference's *Ad Hoc* Committee for the Review of Scripture Translations. *Imprimaturs* granted to Scripture translations permit their publication in Catholic editions for general use (e.g. study, reading, private, devotional prayer).

1994 Great Lakes Pastoral Ministry Gathering

The 1994 Great Lakes Pastoral Ministry Gathering will be held March 4-6, 1994, at the Holiday Inn O'Hare/Kennedy in Chicago, Illinois. The theme for the 18th annual conference is *Releasing the Fire Within*. Goals are: to journey through unknown and unexplored territory of the spirit; to confront the violence and uncertainty in our Church and society in light of the dying and rising of Jesus Christ; to gather and nurture all who breathe hope in the Church; and to re-ignite for service the diverse gifts of the gathered. Vincent Donovan, CSSP, Dr. Diana Hayes, and Christopher Walker will present the general sessions. Over 25 different seminar sessions will also be presented on a variety of topics including spirituality of lay people, women in the 90's, the Christian response to cultural propaganda, building healthy stepfamilies, new life in pastoral ministry, the liturgy of weddings, and Lenten reconciliation. Features for the 1994 Gathering will be an artistic presentation of song, story, dance, and prayer; entertainment by Greg Risberg; exhibits and showcases; and numerous liturgical events. For more information and registrations forms contact: Conference Services by Loretta Reif, P.O. Box 5084, Rockford, IL. Telephone: 815-399-2150.

Johannes Hofinger Catechetical Conference

The 16th annual Johannes Hofinger Catechetical Conference will be held January 7-8, 1994, at the Hyatt Regency in New Orleans, Louisiana. The conference is sponsored by the Religious Education Office of the Archdiocese of New Orleans. The theme is *Bridging the Gaps: Church and Family Together.* The keynote address will be given by the Most Reverend Edward T. Hughes. Andrew and Terri Lyke will present Friday afternoon's address and Dr. David M. Thomas will give Saturday morning's presentation. Over 30 breakout sessions will be presented by a variety of speakers. Topics for the breakout sessions include aging, single lifestyle, abuse, family faith development, multicultural family lifestyles, family rituals, communication, and marriage relationships. In addition there will be two professional track series to be given by Maureen Gallagher, Ph.D. and Michael Downey, Ph.D. These special four-part sessions will focus on finding holiness in family life and interpersonal communion. For more information and registration forms contact: Conference Services by Loretta Reif, P.O. Box 5084, Rockford, IL 61125. Telephone: 815-399-2150.

Resources

To Do Justice and Right Upon the Earth is a collection of papers delivered at the Virgil Michel Symposium on Liturgy and Social Justice at St. John's University, Collegeville, Minnesota in July 1991. The symposium honored the centenary of *Rerum Novarum.* In the spirit of this encyclical the papers bring the insights of noted scholars to bear on the question of how Christians can become truly social in prayer and in life through participation in the liturgy. Authors include Rosemary Haughton (The Spirituality of Social Justice); Eugene La Verdiere, SSS (Worship and the Persian Gulf War); R. Kevin Seasoltz, OSB (Liturgy and Social Consciousness); Stanley M. Hauerwas (In Praise of *Centesimus Annus*); Regina Wentzel Wolfe (The Ethical Imperative of the Eucharist: Responding in the Workplace); Daniel Rush Finn (Poverty and Prosperity in Global Economics: Making Sense of Conflicting Claims); and Bernard F. Evans (God's Creation and the Christian Response). It is available in paperback ($9.95) from: The Liturgical Press, St. John's Abbey, Box 7500, Collegeville, MN 56321. Telephone: 1-612-363-2213.

A Brief History of Christian Worship by James F. White is written from the perspectives of the 1990's in North America. This book is a revisionist work, attempting to give new directions to liturgical history by treating the experience of worship of the people of the pews as the primary liturgical document. Relishing the liturgical diversity of recent centuries as firm evidence of Christianity's ability to adapt to a wide variety of peoples and places, White shows that this tendency has been apparent in Christian worship since its inception in the New Testament churches. Instead of imposing one tradition's criteria on worship, he tries to give a balanced and comprehensive approach to the development of the dozen or more traditions surviving in the modern world. It is available in paperback from: Abingdon Press, 201 Eighth Avenue, South, Nashville, TN 37203.

The Liturgical Dictionary of Eastern Christianity edited by Peter D. Day is a guide to the multitude of Eastern Christian Liturgical terms. The readership of this book is likely to be drawn from those who are looking for a simple explanation of a term rather than a definitive, lengthy, and scholarly explanation. Eastern terms have been anglicized to facilitate easy use of the book. A Quick Reference Guide at the end of the book further assists users by listing Western terms with their Eastern equivalents. It is available in hardcover ($39.50) from: The Liturgical Press, St. John's Abbey, Box 7500, Collegeville, MN 56321. Telephone: 1-612-363-2213.

Scepter Publishing, Inc. and the Midwest Theological Forum, an educational organization assisting the pastoral ministry of bishops, diocesan priests, catechists, and lay people, have recently published the *Daily Roman Missal* and the *Handbook of Prayers.* The *Daily Roman Missal* includes the Latin Order of Mass and all the scriptural readings and psalm texts for the liturgical year. It also includes tables of the principal celebrations of the year and the readings of weekdays and Sundays in Ordinary Time; a wide selection of Common Masses, Ritual Masses, Votive Masses, Masses for Various Occasions and Needs and Masses of the Dead; and a brief biography of each of the lives of the saints. It is available in leather cover (1993 Edition, 2,144 pages, 6 3/4 X 4 1/4 X 1 1/2, gilded pages, two colors, Latin-English) from: Midwest Theological Forum, 1410 W. Lexington Street, Chicago, IL 60607 or Scepter Publishing (1-800-322-8773). The cost is $59.95.

COMMITTEE ON THE LITURGY

NEWSLETTER

NATIONAL CONFERENCE OF CATHOLIC BISHOPS

1994
VOLUME XXX
JANUARY

Instruction *Comme le prèvoit* (January 25, 1969)

At the November 1993 plenary meeting of the NCCB, Bishop Wilton D. Gregory, Chairman of the Bishops' Committee on the Liturgy, reported to the bishops that the English version of Comme le prèvoit was not ICEL's own translation from the French but one of six official versions in different languages prepared and issued simultaneously, with papal approval, by the Consilium for the Implementation of the Constitution on the Sacred Liturgy, the official Vatican agency established to oversee liturgical reform around the world after the council. During his report Bishop Gregory read aloud a letter from the secretary of the Consilium confirming the source of the English translation. Subsequently the staff at the Secretariat for the Liturgy has received several requests for copies of the letter read by Bishop Gregory from the secretary of the Consilium, Father Annibale Bugnini, C.M. The text of the letter follows.

Consilium Ad Exsequendam Constitutionem
De Sacra Liturgia

Prot. N. 21/69   January 8, 1969

Dear Father McManus,

I am sending you the final text of the Instruction on translations of liturgical texts. You have already given us an English translation of this document, but, as you can see, some changes have been made in the beginning and at the end new things have been added.

Right now an English translation is being prepared here at the Secretariat, using the one you gave us as a basis. This is being done so that, as soon as possible, it can be sent to the various English-speaking episcopal conferences.

Thank you for your continual co-operation. I hope that the New Year brings you much success in your work.

Sincerely yours in Christ,

(A. Bugnini, C.M.)
Secretary

Father Krisman Completes Term as Executive Director

Reverend Ronald F. Krisman, Executive Director of the Secretariat of the Bishops' Committee on the Liturgy for the past five years, completed his term as Executive Director on December 31, 1993. Father Krisman joined the staff of the Secretariat of the Bishops' Committee on the Liturgy in 1982 as Associate Director and was appointed Executive Director of the Secretariat effective December 1, 1988. Father Krisman, a priest of the Diocese of Lubbock, was ordained to the priesthood in 1973. He received the S.T.M. in theology from Woodstock College and the bachelor's degree in music, with specialization in organ performance, composition, and church music, from Manhattanville College in Purchase, NY. During his time at the Secretariat Father Krisman pursued further studies in Canon Law and completed his dissertation for the degree of licentiate in Canon Law.

3211 FOURTH STREET NE • WASHINGTON, DC 20017

Father Krisman served as a member of the board of directors of the Federation of Diocesan Liturgical Commissions (FDLC), as treasurer of the FDLC, and as the chairman of its Music Committee. He is a member of the Music Subcommittee of the International Commission on English in the Liturgy (ICEL) and was appointed a member of the Advisory Committee of ICEL in January 1992. He is currently a member of the North American Academy of Liturgy, the Societas Liturgia, and The Canon Law Society of America. Father Krisman has also been a participant in the Milwaukee Symposia for Church Composers since its inception in 1982.

While Father Krisman served as Executive Director of the Secretariat for the Liturgy he wrote many publications for the Bishops' Committee on the Liturgy and oversaw the preparation of numerous liturgical books and documents for use in the United States. Father Krisman promoted the publication of liturgical books in Spanish and served as the staff person to the Hispanic Liturgy Subcommittee of the BCL. He also participated in international activities and recently attended the Eucharistic Congress in Seville, Spain (June 1993) and the International Symposium on the Catechumenate in Lyons, France (July 1993).

Monsignor Robert N. Lynch, General Secretary of the NCCB, announced that "Father Ron Krisman's thirteen years of service to the NCCB, the last five of which as Director of the Bishops' Committee on the Liturgy, have been marked by great dedication and skill. Father Krisman's tenure has witnessed the publication of many significant liturgical books, study guides, and other helpful material. His own gifts as a musician enhanced the prayer and worship of the conference and added to his contributions to the life of prayer of the Church in our country."

Father Krisman's energetic and dedicated service to promote the postconciliar liturgical reforms in the United States is an inspiration for many. Those who have worked side by side with him know, that whatever the project or the challenge, he constantly strives to serve the Church and not make the Church serve him. The faith, understanding and perseverance that he brought to his work in the Secretariat for the Liturgy will undoubtedly be a source of inspiration for the faithful in the Diocese of Lubbock, TX where Father Krisman will continue his priestly ministry.

> Take heart from realizing what service your work renders to the cause of christian belief, which has its public and solemn expression in divine worship and from the same source receives a strength that assists both individuals and society. The service we refer to as coming from your work is a service to Christ's epiphany, his manifestation, which the liturgy in word, sacrament, and priesthood makes so intense that it can be experienced, even felt, by the hearts of the faithful and there become alive.... We speak, too, of the service whereby you aid the people of these times through the attractiveness of the humble yet sublime beauty of the liturgy; you invite them to rediscover the lost world proper to the spirit where the divine mystery is present in an inexpressible and incomparable way.
>
> (Address to the members and *periti* of the
> Consilium by Pope Paul VI, October 13, 1966).

Lectionaries for Masses with Children

The Secretariat for the Liturgy has received numerous requests for clarification on the official status of other lectionaries published for use at Masses with children. The *Lectionary for Masses with Children,* approved by the National Conference of Catholic Bishops on November 13, 1991 and confirmed by decree of the Congregation for Divine Worship and the Discipline of the Sacraments on May 27, 1992 (Prot. N. 1259/91), is the ONLY lectionary approved for liturgical use at Masses with children in the United States. Archbishop William H. Keeler's decree promulgating the new *Lectionary for Masses with Children* states: "As of 1 September 1993 the *Lectionary for Masses with Children* may be published and used in the Liturgy. The First Sunday of Advent, 28 November 1993, is hereby established as the effective date for the use of the *Lectionary for Masses with Children* in the dioceses of the United States of America. From that day forward no other English lectionary for Masses with Children may be used."

Prior to the publication of the *Lectionary for Masses with Children,* the *Lectionary for Children's Mass: For Sundays and Solemnities of Years A, B, and C,* published by Pueblo Publishing Company, was approved for use in the United States until that time when the NCCB approved their own lectionary for Masses with children. The *Lectionary for Children's Mass: For Sundays and Solemnities of Years A, B, and C,* contains a selection of biblical readings for liturgies with children prepared in conformity with nos. 41-47 of the *Directory for Masses with Children* (DMC) for use on occasions when, because the appointed readings seem less suited to the comprehension of children, it is permissible to choose other passages either from the *Lectionary for Mass* or directly from the Bible. This Lectionary was for use only at Masses with children in which only a few adults participate. It was not to be used at Masses with adults in which children also participate, that is, with a large number of adults and a smaller number of children, unless the bishop permitted such an adaptation (see DMC 19).

Many have asked if the Lectionary approved by the Canadian Conference of Catholic Bishops may be used in Masses with children in the United States of America. The Canadian Conference of Catholic Bishops has NOT approved a lectionary for Masses with children for liturgical use in Canada. Father John Hibbard, Director of the National Liturgical Office in Canada, states that *Sunday: Book of Readings Adapted for Children* is published by Treehaus Communications, Inc. "It is not the work of the National Liturgical Office of the Canadian Conference of Catholic Bishops (CCCB) nor of the 'Canadian Bishops' as suggested in various advertisements. This work was not requested nor commissioned by the National Liturgical Office or the CCCB. After its publication **SUNDAY** was submitted to the National Liturgical Office and the Episcopal Commission for Liturgy for approval for liturgical use. The Commission officially endorsed **SUNDAY** for liturgical use in Canada *for liturgies of the word with children.* The endorsement does not come from the Canadian Conference of Catholic Bishops, but from the Episcopal Commission for Liturgy. **SUNDAY** is not a children's lectionary per se, but an adaptation of the readings for children. The position of the Episcopal Commission for Liturgy is that there is one Lectionary—the Roman Lectionary." In other words the National Liturgical Office and the Episcopal Commission for Liturgy gave permission for *Sunday: Book of Readings Adapted for Children* to be used in Canada only for Service of the Word liturgies and not for use during the Mass even when this includes a separate Liturgy of the Word with children.

The *Directory for Masses with Children* (DMC 43) makes it very clear that the conferences of bishops oversee the production of lectionaries for Masses with children. Also, the numerous additional liturgical norms regarding lectionaries state that only the conferences of bishops have the authority to approve lectionaries. The *Sunday: Book of Readings Adapted for Children (Years A, B, and C)* published by Treehaus Communications was submitted to the NCCB *Ad Hoc* Committee for the Review of Scripture Translations. Upon the recommendation of this Ad Hoc Committee the National Conference of Catholic Bishops, in keeping with the authority granted to it by canon 825.1 of the Code of Canon Law, did NOT grant the *imprimatur* to the three-volume publication, *Sunday: Book of Readings Adapted for Children (Years A, B, and C).* Thus *Sunday: Book of Readings Adapted for Children* is not approved for liturgical use in the dioceses of the United States of America. Although a particular liturgical book may be approved for liturgical use in one country, it may be used in another country in the liturgy only when the episcopal conference of the second country has canonically authorized its use in the liturgy.

It should be noted that the meaning of "mandatory effective date" for the *Lectionary for Masses with Children* differs from the usual one for a liturgical book. The *Lectionary for Masses with Children* is used *ad libitum* in the liturgy. (It *need not* be used at all; but if a lectionary for Masses with children is used, it must be the approved version (i.e. the *Lectionary for Masses with Children*). One may still use the *Lectionary for Mass* at Masses with children. The advantage of using the *Lectionary for Masses with Children* is that it employs a translation of Scripture that uses a vocabulary and sentence structure geared for a third-grade reading level. Older elementary school children should be led to appreciate the more standard translations used in the *Lectionary for Mass.* In view of this it is important not to refer to the *Lectionary for Mass* as the "adult" lectionary. No such distinction exists.

Time for the Celebration of the Easter Vigil and Easter Sunday Masses

Each year the Secretariat for the Liturgy receives letters expressing concern regarding the erosion of the liturgical spirit and intent of the Paschal Triduum. One area of particular concern has been the celebration of the Easter Vigil late Saturday afternoon or early Saturday evening before nightfall.

The *Roman Missal* states that "the entire celebration of the Easter Vigil takes place at night. It should not begin before nightfall; it should end before daybreak on Sunday." Lack of adherence to this norm prompted the 1988 *Circular Letter Concerning the Preparation and Celebration of the Easter Feasts* to repeat this rubric from the *Sacramentary* and to add that "This rule is to be taken according to its strictest sense. Reprehensible are those abuses and practices which have crept in many places in violation of this ruling, whereby the Easter Vigil is celebrated at the time of day that is customary to celebrate anticipated Masses."

Many of the abuses associated with the untimely scheduling of the Easter Vigil are due to a general lack of understanding regarding the nature of the celebration of the annual Pasch. It is incumbent upon diocesan liturgical commissions/offices of worship to provide catechesis on the Easter Vigil. This is best done far in advance of the celebration.

This year celebrations for the Easter Vigil will occur on Saturday, April 2, 1994 **before** the clocks will have moved ahead one hour for daylight savings time. Pastoral planners should contact a local weather station for the time sunset will occur on April 2, 1994. To that time another 45 minutes or one hour should be added to determine the approximate time of nightfall. For example, if sunset occurs at 6:32 p.m. EST in a given location, the celebration of the Easter Vigil should not begin before 7:30 p.m.

Please be aware that this year we will move clocks ahead one hour for daylight savings time at 2:00 a.m. **Sunday, April 3, 1994**. This will occur **after** the celebration of the Easter Vigil but **before** the celebrations of Mass on Easter Sunday morning. Given the confusion that often results when clocks are moved ahead, offices of worship/diocesan liturgical commissions should ensure that parishes are made aware of this fact ahead of time.

In Memoriam: Father Michael Joseph Marx, OSB

Father Michael Joseph Marx, OSB, a monk of Saint John's Abbey and former managing editor of *Worship,* died on May 5, 1993 and was buried in the abbey cemetery in Collegeville, MN. Father Marx spent his youth in the pioneer Catholic German-American community of Saint Michael, Minnesota, which provided nine vocations in its history. He had eleven sisters and two brothers. Four members of his family followed him into the monastic life. Father Marx did his preparatory and college program at Saint John's and his theology studies at the Collegio di' Sant' Anselmo, in Rome, Italy, where he was ordained in 1941 and was the recipient of a doctorate in theology in 1943 and an S.S.L. degree from the Pontifical Biblical Institute in 1945. His dissertation was entitled, "Incessant Prayer in Ancient Monastic Literature." He returned to Saint John's in 1946 and began a long and notable career as professor of Systematic Theology at the seminary and graduate school until his retirement from teaching in 1982. He had a lengthy and dedicated career as managing editor of *Worship* from 1963-1983. With Father Tegels he was jointly awarded the prestigious Berakah Award from the North American Academy of Liturgy.

> God of blessings,
> source of all holiness,
> the voice of your Spirit has drawn countless men and women
> to follow Jesus Christ
> and to bind themselves to you
> with ready will and loving heart.
>
> Look with mercy on Michael
> who sought to fulfill his vows to you,
> and grant him the reward promised to all good and
> faithful servants.
>
> May he rejoice in the company of the saints
> and with them praise you for ever.
>
> (Order of Christian Funerals, 398.24)

Institute for Music and Liturgy

The St. Lawrence Catholic Campus Center is sponsoring an Institute for Music and Liturgy to be held June 19-23, 1994 in Lawrence, Kansas. Presenters include Dr. Fred Moleck, Theresa Koernke, IHM, John Romeri, Wendy Zaro-Fisher, Rev. James Telthorst, Dr. Patrick Malloy and Mr. Lynn Trapp. For more information contact: Sally Hudnall, St. Lawrence Center, 1631 Crescent Road, Lawrence, KS 66044, Telephone: 913-843-0357.

COMMITTEE ON THE LITURGY

NEWSLETTER

NATIONAL CONFERENCE OF CATHOLIC BISHOPS

1994
VOLUME XXX
FEBRUARY

New Members, Consultants, and Advisors to the BCL

Bishop Donald W. Trautman, Chairman of the Bishops' Committee on the Liturgy, has appointed the following bishops as members of the Committee for a three year term: Most Reverend Anthony G. Bosco, Bishop of Greensburg; Most Reverend Edward M. Grosz, Auxiliary Bishop of Buffalo; Most Reverend Jerome Hanus, OSB, Bishop of Saint Cloud; His Eminence Roger Cardinal Mahony, Archbishop of Los Angeles; Most Reverend Frank J. Rodimer, Bishop of Paterson; and Most Reverend Emil A. Wcela, Auxiliary Bishop of Rockville Centre.

His Eminence Joseph Cardinal Bernardin, Archbishop of Chicago, continues to serve as a consultant to the Committee in his capacity as a member of the Congregation for Divine Worship and the Discipline of the Sacraments. The Most Reverend Daniel E. Pilarczyk, Archbishop of Cincinnati, also continues as consultant to the Committee in his capacity as NCCB representative to the Episcopal Board of the International Commission on English in the Liturgy. Bishop Trautman has also appointed the following as consultants to the Committee for a three year term: His Eminence James Cardinal Hickey, Archbishop of Washington; Most Reverend Patrick G. Cooney, Bishop of Gaylord; Most Reverend Roberto O. Gonzalez, OFM, Auxiliary Bishop of Boston.

Three new advisors have recently been appointed by Bishop Trautman to replace outgoing advisors Dr. Marchita B. Mauck, Sister Barbara O'Dea, DW, and Reverend Michael Witczak. Appointed to three year terms are Sister Janet Baxendale, SC, Director, Office of Worship, Archdiocese of New York; Sister Kathleen Hughes, RCSJ, Dean, Catholic Theological Union; and the Right Reverend Marcel Rooney, OSB, Abbot of Conception Abbey, Conception, MO. Reverend James P. Moroney, the new chairman of the FDLC Board of Directors, has replaced Sister Anthony Poerio, IBVM as an advisor to the Committee. Other advisors to the Committee are: Reverend Samuel J. Aquila, Reverend Jeremy Driscoll, OSB, Sister Rosa Maria Icaza, CCVI, Reverend Kevin W. Irwin, Reverend Joseph Levesque, CM, and Reverend Michael Spillane.

The position of Executive Director remains vacant at this time. Reverend Monsignor Alan F. Detscher and Sister Linda L. Gaupin, CDP, continue to serve as Associate Directors of the Secretariat for the Liturgy. Monsignor Frederick McManus is consultant to the staff. Ms. Ellen McLoughlin serves as the administrative secretary to the Liturgy Secretariat.

NCCB Procedure for Approving the Revised *Roman Missal (Sacramentary)*

At the November 1993 meeting of the NCCB, the agenda was modified so that the proposed *NCCB Procedure for Approving the Revised Roman Missal* might be treated before the first segment of the *Sacramentary*. After a prolonged discussion two amendments were made to the proposed procedure. The first amendment, proposed by the Liturgy Committee, requests that *Motions Requesting Further Consideration* must be submitted to the Office of the General Secretary no more than five months after a segment has been mailed to the members of the NCCB and at least two weeks prior to the start of the plenary meeting at which the texts will be considered for approval. This was approved by the NCCB and inserted into number 6 of the Procedures.

The second amendment was proposed by Bishop Donald W. Trautman in response to concerns expressed during the debate on the Procedure that the Doctrine Committee had not examined the texts. His proposed amendment, approved by the NCCB, delineates the responsibilities of the Liturgy and Doctrine Committees in regard to the review of the Missal texts and establishes a Joint Committee composed of the

Chairman of the Liturgy Committee and the Chairman of the Doctrine Committee and the Executive Director of the Liturgy Secretariat and the Executive Director of the Secretariat for Doctrine. This amendment was inserted into number 4 of the Procedure.

In light of the amendments, it was decided not to examine the first segment of the Roman Missal until it has gone through the process set out in the amended Procedure approved at that meeting.

The final text of the Procedure follows:

NCCB Procedure for Approving the Revised Roman Missal
(Approved by the NCCB, November 1993)

1. Each segment of the revised liturgical text of the *Sacramentary* will be copied and sent to the members of the National Conference of Catholic Bishops as soon as the NCCB has received it from the ICEL Secretariat. (In other words, no segment will be held until the time of a usual mailing of documentation before a forthcoming plenary meeting.) This will provide more time than is usually given for the study of plenary meeting documentation.

2. Once the segments of the *Sacramentary* begin arriving from the ICEL Secretariat, every subsequent plenary meeting of the NCCB will deal with all of the segments of the *Sacramentary* which have been sent to the bishops since the time of the previous plenary meeting, provided that the members of the NCCB have had a minimum of two (2) months to study a particular segment of the text.

3. The liturgical texts of the revised *Sacramentary* have been individually approved by the ICEL Episcopal Board and are presented as the definitive unified text for the approval of all the ICEL-member conferences of bishops. In accordance with the instruction *Comme le Prevoit,* no. 42.3, these texts may only be APPROVED or NOT APPROVED by the individual conferences. For texts failing to receive the requisite approval of the NCCB, requested changes or substitutions are to be communicated to the ICEL Secretariat. After the appropriate consultation with the other ICEL-member conferences, ICEL may propose a substitute text for the approval of all the conferences. In the event that the other ICEL-member conferences do not wish to join the NCCB in approving a modified text, the NCCB may again be asked by its Committee on the Liturgy to approve the ICEL text as originally proposed. If that originally proposed text fails to receive the 2/3 majority vote necessary for approval, or if the Committee on the Liturgy has decided not to resubmit the original text for a second scrutiny of the NCCB, the Committee will then prepare its own substitute text for the approval of the NCCB membership.

4. The NCCB Committee on the Liturgy will be responsible for reviewing each segment of the revised *Sacramentary* prior to its being submitted for the approval of the NCCB at an upcoming plenary meeting. This process will include a review by the Committee of all texts contained in the segment as well as a detailed review of all materials found objectionable by individual members of the Committee or the NCCB (see no. 5 below). Consultation with the NCCB Committee on Doctrine and with other NCCB committees is to be included in this review. The Chairman of the Liturgy Committee and the Chairman of the Doctrine Committee, together with the Executive Director of the Liturgy Secretariat and the Executive Director of the Secretariat for Doctrine, will review the ICEL texts in the particular segment being submitted to the body of bishops, surface those texts which appear to raise doctrinal concerns, and submit those texts to the Doctrine Committee for study and recommendations. The conclusions of the Doctrine Committee will be forwarded to the Liturgy Committee. Where there is need for dialogue or clarification over these conclusions, the Chairmen will seek to facilitate joint discussions between committee members and committee consultants. The Liturgy Committee will report to the body of Bishops the recommendations received from the Doctrine Committee, when the Liturgy Committee presents the action item for approval of the proposed liturgical texts.

5. Ordinarily all texts contained in a segment of the revised *Sacramentary* will be moved for approval *en bloc* at a plenary meeting of the NCCB. If any *de iure* member of the NCCB wishes to register an objection to a particular text, he must identify the text on a "Motion Requesting Further Consideration" form, copies of which will be provided with each segment of material sent to the bishops, and give a rationale for why he believes the text is not adequate and, if he so chooses, illustrate this alleged inadequacy by offering an alternate wording for consideration of the NCCB Liturgy Committee.

6. All "Motions Requesting Further Consideration" must be submitted to the NCCB Office of the General Secretary no more than five months after a segment has been mailed to the members of the NCCB and at least two weeks prior to the start of a plenary meeting at which the texts in question will be considered for approval. No additional motions requesting further consideration can be made after that time. This time line is important in order to allow the members of the NCCB Liturgy Committee to carefully study all materials that have been submitted by the bishops. The Liturgy Committee will also consult with other NCCB committees, when necessary.

7. If the Liturgy Committee determines that in certain cases it wishes to retain the ICEL-approved text and to recommend that one or more "Motions Requesting Further Consideration" NOT be approved by the members of the NCCB, it is to include a rationale for each rejected "Motion Requesting Further Consideration" in a supplementary document entitled "Reject *en bloc.*" On the other hand, if the Liturgy Committee determines that it wishes to accept one or more "Motions Requesting Further Consideration," thereby recommending to the members of the NCCB that they NOT APPROVE certain ICEL-approved texts, these are to be included in a supplementary document entitled "Remand to ICEL for Further Consideration." Each of the items in this second document will be voted on separately by the members of the NCCB.

8. Individual bishops will be able to have their "Motions Requesting Further Consideration" which have been placed by the Liturgy Committee in the first supplementary document ("Reject *en bloc*") considered by the full membership of the NCCB if they request this on the floor of the assembly.

9. To approve a "Motion Requesting Further Consideration" and thereby remand a particular text back to ICEL for further action, a simple majority vote of the *de iure* Latin-rite voting members of the NCCB is necessary.

Biblical Translations Approved For Liturgical Use

The Liturgy Secretariat has received a large number of inquiries concerning which biblical translations are approved for liturgical use, as well as about several lectionaries that do not currently enjoy official authorization. In a letter addressed to the members of the NCCB, Bishop Donald W. Trautman, Chairman of the Committee on the Liturgy, communicated the following information.

At the present time the following biblical translations have been approved by the National Conference of Catholic Bishops for use in the liturgy and have received the confirmation of the Apostolic See:

New American Bible [NAB] (1970 edition);
Revised Standard Version [RSV] (1966 edition);
Jerusalem Bible [JB] (1966 edition).

All three of these translations were also published as editions of the *Lectionary for Mass* in 1970. The RSV and JB versions of the *Lectionary for Mass* are out of print.

The NCCB has also approved the *New Revised Standard Version [NRSV]* for liturgical use and this has been confirmed by the Apostolic See. It has not yet been published as a Lectionary, but may now be used in liturgical celebrations.

The NCCB has also approved for liturgical use an adaptation of the *Revised New Testament of the New American Bible,* and the *Revised Psalms of the New American Bible.* Both these biblical translations use inclusive language in regard to persons. The Psalms have received Roman confirmation, however, we are awaiting the confirmation of the rest of the NAB text since it is contained in the second edition of the *Lectionary for Mass,* which was approved by the NCCB two years ago. Once the NAB version of the Lectionary is approved, it will be published as quickly as possible. At the same time, an NRSV version of the Lectionary will also be published. Until these two second English editions of the Latin *Ordo Lectionum Missae* (1981) are published, the first edition of the *Lectionary for Mass* remains in effect.

An additional translation of the Bible, the *Contemporary English Version* of the American Bible Society, was approved by the NCCB for liturgical use and has received the necessary permission from the Congregation for Divine Worship for it to be used in the *Lectionary for Masses with Children* that was published last year.

Specific questions have been raised about two lectionaries: the lectionary published by the Priests for Equality and *Sunday,* published by Treehaus Communications, Inc. Information on lectionaries for Masses with Children was published in the January 1994 Newsletter (Vol. XXX). The Priests for Equality lectionary for Sundays and Weekdays is advertised as an inclusive language lectionary. *It has neither been approved by the National Conference of Catholic Bishops nor confirmed by the Apostolic See for liturgical use.*

International Liturgical Update

Irish Episcopal Conference

In October 1992 the Irish Bishops' Conference approved the *New Jerusalem Bible* and the *New Revised Standard Version* (NRSV) for use in worship.

At the request of the Irish Bishops' Conference, a presentation on the work of the revised *Roman Missal (Sacramentary)* was given at their October 1992 meeting. It was organized by the National Secretariat for Liturgy and involved Fr. Chris Walsh, the new chair of the Advisory Committee of ICEL, Fr. Sean Collins and Ms. Margaret Daly, both members of the Advisory Committee, and Fr. Patrick McGoldrick, a member of the sub-committee on translations and revision. The session was chaired by Bishop Diarmaid O Suilleabhain, the Irish member of the Episcopal Board of ICEL.

England, Wales, and Scotland

The national secretariat in England and Wales has produced a major revision of the *Rite of Marriage.* It also has produced a directory on televising the Mass. *Televising the Mass: Guidelines for Broadcast Worship* was prepared by the Broadcast Worship Subcommittee of the Pastoral Liturgy Committee of the Catholic Bishops' Conference of England and Wales. Sections are provided for the priest and ministers in the parish, for television directors, for musicians, and for religious advisers.

The Bishops' Conference of England and Wales has established a process for the approval of the revised *Sacramentary.* This process provides for each segment to be sent to the voting bishops at the latest two months before the voting meeting. Any bishop who intends to enter a *non placet* vote (this does not indicate a preferred or different rendering of a text, but means that the text is totally unacceptable) should notify Bishop McMahon of the text and his reasons, at the latest one month before the voting meeting. (This will allow for clarification or explanation to be sought from ICEL if necessary). Any bishop still intending to vote *non placet* on any text should submit his reasons in writing to Archbishop Bowen before the voting meeting. At the voting meeting all or any proposed deletions should be voted on first and must have 33% of competent votes to be carried. The full segment of the Sacramentary, incorporating any such deletions as have attracted 33%, should then be voted on, and must attract 66% of competent votes to be carried. The bishops will vote on segment one of the Sacramentary during their voting meeting scheduled after the second Sunday of Easter.

Resources

Christian Liturgy: An Annotated Bibliography for Jesuits by John F. Baldovin, SJ is the topic of the November 1993 issue of *Studies in the Spirituality of Jesuits.* Although this bibliographical essay is offered to Jesuits in particular, it is an excellent resource for all those interested in liturgical and apostolic renewal in the Church. It is divided into four sections. The first section on Resources lists information under the categories of Dictionaries, Periodicals, and Collections of Texts (Post-Conciliar and Historical). The second section focuses on General Studies and provides bibliographical information under the headings of General Introductions and Handbooks, Comparative Liturgy, Liturgy and Culture, Liturgical Theology, Ritual Studies, Essay Collections, and Liturgical History. The third section contains information on specific areas including Eucharist, Initiation, Liturgical Year, Liturgy of the Hours, Penance/Reconciliation, Anointing of the Sick, Weddings/Marriage, Ordination/Ministry, Liturgy of Christian Burial, Music and the Liturgy, Liturgical Art and Architecture, Liturgical Language and Feminism, and Liturgy, Justice and Peace. Section four is directed to Jesuits and the Liturgy. It is available from: The Seminar on Jesuit Spirituality, 3700 West Pine Boulevard, St. Louis, Missouri 63108.

COMMITTEE ON THE LITURGY

NEWSLETTER

**1994
VOLUME XXX
MARCH**

NATIONAL CONFERENCE OF CATHOLIC BISHOPS

March Meeting of the Liturgy Committee

The bishop members and bishop consultants of the NCCB Committee on the Liturgy met in Washington, DC, on March 18, 1994. Bishop Trautman welcomed the new members and consultants and especially thanked those members who agreed to serve another term on the BCL. Bishop Trautman began the meeting with reports on the following topics: 1) the proposed ICEL translations of the *Sacramentary* and contact with the Doctrine Committee; 2) the June 1994 Study Day on Translations; 3) the request to compose two new Eucharistic Prayers; 4) the response to the survey on the *Revised Common Lectionary,* the use of the term *presbyter* in the intercessory section of Eucharistic Prayers III and IV, and lines 13-16 of the Nicene Creed; and 5) the "We Believe" statement.

The principal agenda item of the meeting was the Committee's plans and programs for 1995, which will be submitted for approval at the November 1994 plenary meeting of the National Conference of Catholic Bishops. The ongoing work of the Secretariat in 1995 will include the publication of the *Newsletter,* preparation of liturgical books for approval and publication, response to liturgical inquiries, preparation of the liturgical calendar, and review of participation aids and other liturgical materials. The Secretariat will also work on the following: preparation of the revised edition of the *Sacramentary* in collaboration with the International Commission on English in the Liturgy (ICEL); preparation of American variations in the revised English translation of the *Sacramentary;* preparation of the English translation of the *Order for Celebrating Marriage* in collaboration with ICEL and the preparation of American Adaptations of the revised *Order;* the development of guidelines for Televised Masses in collaboration with the NCCB Communications Committee; collaboration with the Federation of Diocesan Liturgical Commissions on position statements approved at national meetings; participation in ecumenical liturgical consultations, such as the North American Consultation on Common Texts (CCT), the English Language Liturgical Consultation (ELLC), the North American Academy of Liturgy (NAAL), and the Commission on Worship and the Arts of the National Council of Churches of Christ (NCC).

The Secretariat will engage in the preparation, publication, implementation and/or promotion of the following in 1995: *Lectionary for Mass* (second typical edition), the *Rites of Ordination of Bishops, Presbyters, and Deacons,* the *Sacramentario* (the Spanish-language Sacramentary), *Guidelines for Cremation and Other Funeral Practices,* and additions to the *Study Texts* and *Liturgy Documentary Series.* It will also pursue several issues pertaining to the Christian initiation of children.

The Committee also discussed the following action items: 1) Interim Inclusive Language Guidelines; 2) Provisional Liturgical Texts for Saint Marguerite Bourgeoys; 3) Provisional Liturgical Texts for *Mass of the Blessed Virgin Mary, Star of the Sea;* 4) the request to place Damien of Molokai on the Particular Calendar of the Dioceses of the U.S.A.; 5) the request to place Blessed Mary of Jesus the Good Shepherd on the Particular Calendar of the Dioceses of the U.S.A.; 6) the Provisional Translation of the *Rites of Ordination of Bishops, Presbyters, and Deacons;* and 7) the request to have the BCL rescind its decision that the NAB translation and the NRSV translation be made available at the same time.

30th Anniversary of the Bishops' Committee on the Liturgy *Newsletter*

September 1995 marks the thirtieth anniversary of the first Bishops' Committee on the Liturgy (BCL) Newsletter *which was published in September 1965. The* Newsletter *was originally intended for bishops of the United States and their diocesan liturgical commission, but its circulation was soon widened to include a much broader circulation than was first envisioned. The* Newsletter *was initiated by Archbishop Dearden and contains a record of the activities of the BCL and its Secretariat. In order to commemorate the 30th anniversary of the BCL Newsletter a series of articles will be published that chronicle some of the more memorable liturgical achievements during the past thirty years. This first article details the origin of the Bishops' Committee on the Liturgy.*

Thirty years ago the Congregation of Rites (Consilium) issued the Instruction (first), *Inter Oecumenici* (IO), on the orderly carrying out of the Constitution on the Liturgy, on September 26, 1964. Chapter XII entitled "Liturgical Commission of the Assembly of Bishops" called for the establishment of a liturgical commission by each territorial authority composed of "bishops themselves or at least include one of them, along with priests expert in liturgical and pastoral matters and designated by name for this office" (IO, 44). This liturgical commission was to be entrusted with the following duties:

"a. to carry out studies and experiments in keeping with the norms of the Constitution art. 40.1-2;

b. to further practical initiatives for the whole region that will foster liturgical life and the application of the Constitution on the Liturgy;

c. to prepare studies and the resources required as a result of decrees of the plenary assembly of bishops;

d. to control pastoral liturgy in the whole nation, to see to the application of decrees of the plenary assembly, and to report on these matters to the assembly;

e. to further frequent consultation and promote collaboration with regional associations involved with Scripture, catechetics, pastoral care, music, and art, as well as with every kind of lay religious association" (OI, 45).

The instruction also encouraged members of the institute of pastoral liturgy, as well as experts called to assist the liturgical commission, to be generous in aiding individual bishops to promote pastoral-liturgical activity more effectively in their territory.

In effect the instruction further refined the mandate of the Constitution on the Liturgy (CSL) which called for the establishment of "a liturgical commission, to be assisted by experts in liturgical science, music, art, and pastoral practice. As far as possible the commission should be aided by some kind of institute for pastoral liturgy, consisting of persons eminent in these matters and including the laity as circumstances suggest" (CSL 44).

At this time the conference had already established the Episcopal Commission for the Liturgical Apostolate. The bishops had discussed the establishment of this liturgical commission at their Thirty-Ninth annual meeting. On November 14, 1957 Bishop Leo Dworshak (Auxiliary Bishop of Fargo) moved "that a committee be appointed to study the competence of a liturgical commission should one be appointed by the bishops and a report of this committee be made at next year's meeting." The motion was approved by the bishops. On November 13, 1958 the bishops approved the establishment of an Episcopal Committee for the Liturgical Apostolate comprised of five archbishops and bishops with rotating membership. Archbishop Joseph Ritter of St. Louis was appointed as the first chairman of the committee.

In light of article 44 in the Constitution on the Liturgy and article 45 of *Inter Oecumenici* the Commission redefined its competence. Both documents made reference to a pastoral-liturgical institute of specialists and scholars working with the national liturgical commission. Several countries had already established a national institute such as Germany, Canada, and France. It was decided that instead of sponsoring or creating an institute in the United States, the Commission would turn to advisors and individual specialists drawn from the following categories: academic programs at the University of Notre Dame and The Catholic University of America; diocesan commissions and offices of worship; private resources of voluntary associations and publishing houses; and other independent centers.

The composition of the Commission was exclusively episcopal, unlike the possibility envisioned in *Inter Oecumenici* which permitted nonbishop members. Originally the conference of bishops designated the bishop membership on the Commission with the members then choosing the chairman of the Commission. In 1966 this was changed so that the chairman was elected by the conference for a three year term. He in turn had the authority to choose other members (with a limit of six) for a three year term. Consultant bishops were also permitted to be added to the Commission and this included the NCCB representative on the episcopal board of ICEL.

During 1965 several important advances were made under the leadership of Archbishop Dearden, Chairman of the Episcopal Commission of the Liturgical Apostolate. In January 1965 he created a Secretariat to assist the Commission and Reverend Frederick R. McManus was named the Director of the new Secretariat for the Bishops' Commission on the Liturgical Apostolate. The purpose of the new Secretariat was to function as an instrument of the Bishops' Commission in its service of the American bishops for liturgical matters. The duties of the Secretariat included the following: the preparation of materials and documents for the Commission to be sent to the bishops of the United States, to serve as a channel for documents and official responses from the postconciliar commission or "Consilium" for the implementation of the CSL, to handle official inquiries to the Commission from the bishops and diocesan liturgical commissions, and to function as a liaison for the Commission and various organizations concerned with liturgical renewal. Because the Secretariat was created to directly serve the Bishops' Commission, it did not engage in promotional or education activities. The Secretariat for the Liturgy was housed at the NCWC in Washington, DC. Archbishop Dearden also initiated a monthly *Newsletter* intended for bishops and diocesan commissions to chronicle the work of the Commission. And in May 1965 subcommittees of the Commission were established. The first was the Music Advisory Board which paved the way and established the structure for other subcommittees such as the Hispanic Liturgy Subcommittee.

In 1967 it was decided that the National Commission on the Liturgical Apostolate, structured in response to CSL 44 and OI 45, would now be called the Bishops' Committee on the Liturgy (BCL). Although both conciliar documents used the term "commission," the change to Bishops' Committee on the Liturgy was done to be more in accord with the general pattern of designating both standing and *ad hoc* bodies of the National Conference of Catholic Bishops as "committees."

Finally in October 1968 the Bishops' Committee on the Liturgy convoked a meeting of Diocesan Liturgical Commission personnel in Chicago to prepare for the implementation of the *Ordo Missae*. At this time a resolution was passed which called for the creation of an Advisory Committee to the BCL. The advisory Committee was to be made up of members elected from the twelve episcopal regions of the United States. During 1969, the Advisory Committee became a Federation of Commissions. In January 1970 the Federation of Diocesan Liturgical Commissions (FDLC) was formally established and a Constitution and Bylaws were adopted. The BCL then began to cosponsor meetings of the diocesan commission members together with the new FDCL. The Executive Director and the Chairperson of the FDLC serve as *ex officio* advisors to the BCL.

International

Italian Episcopal Conference

The Italian Episcopal Conference recently published "The Permanent Deacon in the Church in Italy: Guidelines and Norms." The document was drawn up by the Episcopal Commission for the Clergy in collaboration with the Episcopal Commission for juridical problems. It was examined and approved during the 36th General Assembly of the Italian bishops, October 26-29, 1992. After receiving the required *recognitio* of the Holy See, it was published on June 1, 1993. The document focuses on the fact that the diaconate, as a proper and permanent part of the hierarchy and not just a period of transition towards the priesthood, as proposed by the Second Vatican Council for the latin Church, has become a reality in the Church in Italy.

Irish Episcopal Conference

At its October 1993 meeting the Episcopal Conference approved the use of shorter versions of two readings. The readings in the Lectionary—feast of the Holy family, year A: Colossians 3:12-21, and Twenty-First Sunday of year B: Ephesians 5:21-32—have presented pastoral difficulties and the Episcopal Commission for Liturgy, with the Irish Commission for Liturgy, had requested the use of shorter versions as alternative readings. The shorter versions are Colossians 3:12-17 and Ephesians 5:25-32. The approval of the Conference is subject to the *confirmatio* of the Congregation for Divine Worship and the Discipline of the Sacraments. These readings are the same as those approved by the NCCB for use in the United States and confirmed by the Apostolic See in June 1992.

Philippines

At the meeting of the Catholic Bishops' Conference of the Philippines last July 1993 Archbishop Onesimo Gordoncillo, DD, of the Archdiocese of Capiz was re-elected Chairman of the Episcopal Commission on

Liturgy for another term of three years. Archbishop Gordoncillo reappointed Father Anscar Chupungco, OSB, Executive Secretary of the Episcopal Commission for another term of three years.

The Episcopal Conference of the Philippines recently approved Segment I: Ordinary Time of the proposed revision of the *Sacramentary*.

Resources

Spanish translations of *Seek the Living God Bulletin Inserts* by J. Michael McMahon. These are a series of six bulletin inserts translated in to Spanish which provide an overview of the *Rite of Christian Initiation of Adults* (RCIA). Meant to be used at various times during the liturgical year, these inserts will help parishioners understand the rites of initiation was well as their own role in the process. The series includes: Insert 1: Initiating Adult Members, An Overview; Insert 2: The Ministries of Adult Initiation; Insert 3: Welcoming, Evangelization and Pre-Catechumenate; Insert 4: Following Christ, Living the Gospel: The Catechumenate; Insert 5: The Lenten Journey: Rite of Election and Period of Purification and Enlightenment; and Insert 6: Easter Mysteries: Joined to the Risen Lord sacraments of Initiation and Period of Mystagogy. They are available from: FDLC, P.O. Box 29049, Washington, D.C. 20017. Telephone: 202-635-6990.

The Sacristy Manual by G. Thomas Ryan contains everything you always wanted to know about the building and the materials used in liturgy. Based on the premise that "correct attention by sacristans to liturgical details is fundamental to healthy liturgy," the book provides an excellent source of information not only for sacristans but for parish liturgy committees, master of ceremonies etc. The book is divided into four parts. Part I, Preparing for the Sacred Mysteries, contains four chapters which form an introduction to the rest of the book, setting the later details into this framework of church and liturgy. It addresses topics on The Church (Chapter 1), History of the Sacristy (Chapter 2), The Sacristan (Chapter 3), and the Sacred Mysteries and Liturgical Art (Chapter 4). Part II, Equipping the Church Complex, is an excursion through liturgical space providing information on A Place for the Eucharistic Assembly (Chapter 5), The Presider's Chair (Chapter 6), The Altar (Chapter 7), the Ambo (Chapter 8), The Sanctuary (Chapter 9), the Baptistry (Chapter 11), Chapel of Reconciliation (Chapter 13), Shrines and Other Areas for Private Devotions (Chapter 15), and the Chapel for the Reservation of the Eucharist (Chapter 14). There is even a section on the gathering place for catechesis and prayer (Chapter 12). Part II, Equipping the Sacristy, has twelve chapters which describe the sacristy's holdings and functions and deals with topics that include Sacristy Furnishings (Chapter 19), Liturgical Books (Chapter 20), Liturgical Vessels (Chapter 21), Incense and its Implements (Chapter 25), and Flowers (Chapter 26). Part IV, Checklists, provides a series of checklists for major feasts and rites that encompasses the Basic Checklist for Celebration of the Eucharist (Chapter 32), Checklists for Liturgical Seasons and Feasts (Chapter 33), Checklists for Other Rites (Chapter 34), and Checklists for Rites at Which a Bishop Presides (Chapter 35). It is available in paperback ($15.00) from: Liturgy Training Publications, 1800 North Hermitage Avenue, Chicago, IL 60622-1101. Telephone 1-800-933-1800.

A Baptism Sourcebook compiled by Victoria Tufano, J. Robert Baker, and the late Larry Nyberg, is the eighth in the series of anthologies on specific aspects of liturgy. It continues the tradition of bringing together texts from various sources to be used for prayer, meditation and homily preparation. It is available in paperback ($12.95, wirebound) from: Liturgy Training Publications, 1800 North Hermitage Avenue, Chicago, IL 60622-1101. Telephone 1-800-933-1800.

The Godparent Book by Elaine Ramshaw offers over a hundred suggestions for building a relationship with your godchild through sharing memories, thoughts, values, prayers, and the ordinary and extraordinary times and seasons of Christian life. This book offers an abundance of ideas for things to do with your godchild from before his or her baptism into adulthood. It is available in paperback ($8.95) and hard cover ($15.95) from: Liturgy Training Publications, 1800 North Hermitage Avenue, Chicago, IL 60622-1101. Telephone: 1-800-933-1800.

COMMITTEE ON THE LITURGY

NEWSLETTER

NATIONAL CONFERENCE OF CATHOLIC BISHOPS

1994
VOLUME XXX
APRIL

Altar Servers

The following letter was received by Archbishop Keeler, President of the NCCB/USCC from Cardinal Antonio Maria Javierre Ortas, the Prefect of the Congregation for Divine Worship and the Discipline of the Sacraments, on the authentic interpretation of Canon 230.2 of the Code of Canon Law. The Committee on the Liturgy will consider the implications of this document at their June 1994 meeting.

Congregation for Divine Worship
and the Discipline of the Sacraments

Prot. 2482/93

Rome, 15 March 1994

Excellence,

It is my duty to communicate to the Presidents of the Episcopal Conferences that an authentic interpretation of Canon 230.2 of the Code of Canon Law will soon be published in *Acta Apostolicae Sedis.*

> As you know, canon 230.2 lays down that:
> "Laici ex temporanea deputatione in actionibus liturgicis munus lectoris implere possunt; item omnes laici muneribus commentatoris, cantoris aliisve ad normam iuris fungi possunt."

The Pontifical Council for the interpretation of Legislative Texts was recently asked if the liturgical functions which, according to the above canon, can be entrusted to the lay faithful, may be carried out equally by men and women, and if serving at the altar may be included among those functions, on a par with the others indicated by the canon.

At its meeting of 30 June 1992, the members of the Pontifical Council for the interpretation of Legislative Texts examined the following *dubium* which had been proposed to them:

> "Utrum inter munera liturgica quibus laici, sive viri sive mulieres, iuxta C.I.C. Can.2302, fungi possunt, adnumerari etiam possit servitium ad altare."

The following response was given: "Affirmative et iuxta instructiones a Sede Apostolica dandas."

Subsequently, at an Audience granted on 11 July 1992 to the Most Reverend Vincenzo Fagiolo, Archbishop Emeritus of Chieti-Vasto and President of the Pontifical Council for the Interpretation of Legislative Texts, Pope John Paul II confirmed this decision and ordered its promulgation. This will be done in the near future.

In communicating the above information to your Episcopal Conference, I feel obliged to clarify certain aspects of Canon 230.2 and of its authentic interpretation:

1) Canon 230.2 has a permissive and not a preceptive character: "Laici . . . *possunt.*" Hence the permission given in this regard by some Bishops can in no way be considered as binding on other Bishops. In fact, it is the competence of each Bishop, in his diocese, after hearing the opinion of the Episcopal Conference, to make a prudential judgment on what to do, with a view to the ordered development of liturgical life in his own diocese.

2) The Holy See respects the decision adopted by certain Bishops for specific local reasons on the basis of the provisions of Canon 230.2. At the same time, however, the Holy See wishes to recall that it will always be very appropriate to follow the noble tradition of having boys serve at the altar. As is well

known, this has also led to a reassuring development of priestly vocations. Thus the obligation to support such groups of altar boys will always continue.

3) If in some diocese, on the basis of Canon 230.2, the Bishop permits that, for particular reasons, women may also serve at the altar, this decision must be clearly explicated to the faithful, in the light of the above-mentioned norm. It shall also be made clear that the norm is already being widely applied, by the fact that women frequently serve as lectors in the Liturgy and can also be called upon to distribute Holy Communion as Extraordinary Ministers of the Eucharist and to carry out other functions, according to the provisions of the same Canon 230.3.

4) It must also be clearly understood that the liturgical services mentioned above are carried out by lay people "ex temporanea deputatione," according to the judgment of the Bishop, without lay people, be they men or women, having any right to exercise them.

In communicating the above, the Congregation for Divine Worship and the Discipline of the Sacraments has sought to carry out the mandate received from the Supreme Pontiff to provide directives to illustrate what is laid down in Canon 230.2 of the Code of Canon Law and its authentic interpretation, which will shortly be published.

In this way, the Bishops will be better able to carry out their mission to be moderators and promoters of the liturgical life in their own dioceses, within the framework of the norms in force in the Universal Church.

In deep communion with all the members of your Episcopal Conference, I remain

Yours sincerely in Christ

Cardinal Antonio Martia Javierre Ortas
Prefect

+Geraldo M. Agnello
Secretary

Monsignor Alan F. Detscher Appointed Executive Director

On April 7, 1994 Reverend Monsignor Robert N. Lynch, General Secretary of the NCCB/USCC, announced that Reverend Monsignor Alan F. Detscher, Associate Director of the Secretariat of the Bishops' Committee on the Liturgy, has been appointed as the new Executive Director of the Liturgy Secretariat, effective immediately. Monsignor Detscher was named as Staff Consultant to the Secretariat of the Bishops' Committee on the Liturgy in May 1986 and was named an Associate Director of the Secretariat by Reverend Monsignor Daniel F. Hoye, General Secretary of the NCCB/USCC on February 9, 1987.

Monsignor Detscher holds a licentiate and a doctorate in liturgy from the Pontifical Liturgical Institute of Saint Anselm in Rome. He has served in advisory and consulting roles with the Bishops' Committee on the Liturgy, the International Commission on English in the Liturgy serving as a member of the Subcommittee on the Presentations of Texts, and with the Liturgical Office of the Diocese of Saint Maron (Maronite Rite). A priest of the Diocese of Bridgeport, Connecticut, he has served as the Director of the Office of Liturgy and as secretary to Bishop Walter W. Curtis.

Monsignor Detscher has been a member of the Board of Directors of the Federation of Diocesan Liturgical Commissions and is presently a member of the North American Academy of Liturgy and the Societas Liturgica.

The members, advisors, consultants and staff of the Bishops' Committee on the Liturgy extend their congratulations to Monsignor Detscher and look forward to his new role as Executive Director of the Liturgy Secretariat.

Instruction on The Roman Liturgy and Inculturation

On March 18, 1994, His Eminence Antonio Maria Cardinal Javierre, Prefect of the Congregation for Divine Worship and the Discipline of the Sacraments (CDWDS), sent the presidents of episcopal conferences a copy of the text of the Instruction prepared by that dicastery, on the Roman Liturgy and Inculturation (Prot. 160/94/L). This instruction is "designated the fourth in order of time ad exsecutionem

Constituionis de sacra Liturgia recte ordinandam, *and specific reference is made to the interpretation and right application of articles 37-40 of the conciliar Constitution* Sacrosanctum Concilium." *A copy of the text is published in* Origins *(April 14, 1994). The English translation of the Instruction was prepared by the CDWDS. The following is a statement of Bishop Donald W. Trautman, Chairman of the Bishops' Committee on the Liturgy, on* The Roman Liturgy and Inculturation IVth Instruction for the Right Application of the Conciliar Constitution on the Liturgy (nos. 37-40).

The recently released instruction on inculturation and the liturgy of the Congregation for Divine Worship and the Discipline of the Sacraments stands as a significant stage in the continuing application of the Second Vatican Council's *Constitution on the Liturgy.*

The instruction provides norms for the adaptation of the liturgy to the temperament and conditions of different peoples in keeping with numbers 37-40 of the *Constitution on the Liturgy.* These norms have been given to assist bishops and episcopal conferences in putting into effect the adaptations provided in the revised liturgical books and, according to the needs of particular cultures, to make more profound adaptations.

The document clearly reaffirms the importance of letting the gospel take flesh in the particular cultures while, at the same time, introducing elements of these cultures that are not inimical to the faith of the Church into its life (see no. 4). By assimilating these cultural elements into the liturgy, the Christian message is deepened and more effectively expressed.

The instruction notes that in most Western countries the adaptations already provided in the liturgical books will be sufficient, but in particular cases even further adaptations may need to be made. In countries where the gospel does not have a long tradition, a more profound adaptation of the liturgy may need to be made.

Episcopal conferences and the Apostolic See have the responsibility to see that the faith of the Church is maintained whenever the liturgy is inculturated in a particular country. In order to insure this, the instruction provides several general principles that must be kept in mind. The rites and texts of the liturgy should more clearly express the holy things they signify so that the people may fully and actively participate in them. In doing this, the substantial unity of the Roman rite must be preserved, and any adaptations that are made in the liturgy must be approved by both the conference of bishops and the Apostolic See. Liturgical adaptations should be made only for the good of the people and should be done with great care. In particular, adaptation may be made in the language of the liturgy, in music and song, in posture and gesture, and in art.

The instruction concludes by pointing out the general areas where the revised Roman liturgical books provide for adaptations that can be made by the celebrant or by the conference of bishops, and it encourages them to take full advantage of these provisions. It also points out that priests or other ministers may make only those adaptations in the rites for which specific provision is made. All other adaptations require the express approval of the conference of bishops and the confirmation of the Apostolic See.

Finally, the instruction explains that in certain circumstances and places an even more radical adaptation of the liturgy may be necessary, as is foreseen in number 40 of the *Constitution on the Liturgy.* These more extensive adaptations need not be restricted to missionary countries. They presume that the adaptations provided in the liturgical books have been made and are not sufficient for the pastoral needs of the people. Such adaptations may involve liturgical language, song, gesture, art, etc. The instruction also indicates the procedures to be used by conferences of bishops when they wish to make these more extensive adaptations.

The *Fourth Instruction for the Right Application of the Conciliar Constitution on the Liturgy* of the Congregation for Divine Worship and the Discipline of the Sacraments clearly shows that the Apostolic See has not abandoned the liturgical reform and renewal of the Church, but wishes to encourage it by promoting liturgical inculturation and the full use of the adaptations already provided in the liturgical books as well as more extensive adaptations when necessary and appropriate.

The Roman revision and restoration of the liturgical books was the first stage of the liturgical reform mandated by the Second Vatican Ecumenical Council and implemented by Pope Paul VI and Pope John Paul II. The second stage now lies before us—the inculturation of the liturgy. This stage may well prove to be far more difficult and take much longer than the renewal of the liturgical books. Just as the ancient Roman liturgy was inculturated as it spread throughout Europe, so it must now once again take flesh in the many cultures of the world as it exists today. The Committee on the Liturgy recognizes the challenge that lies before it, and will do all that is necessary to make the Church's liturgy a living and prayerful experience for Catholics in this country.

NCCB Administrative Committee Meeting

The Administrative Committee of the National Conference of Catholic Bishops (NCCB) met on March 22-24, 1994 at the NCCB/USCC headquarters building in Washington, DC. In the course of the meeting Bishop Donald W. Trautman, Chairman of the NCCB Liturgy Committee, presented the Information Report of the Bishops' Committee on the Liturgy (BCL) and gave oral reports of the following: 1) the results of the joint meeting of the bishop chairmen and secretarial staffs of the Committees on Doctrine and Liturgy for review of Segment One of the proposed of the *Sacramentary;* 2) an update on the June 1994 Study Day on the Translation of Liturgical Texts; 3) the status of the revised NAB version of the *Lectionary for Mass* approved by the NCCB two years ago; and 4) the response of the Congregation for Divine Worship and the Discipline of the Sacraments to the NCCB request to prepare two new Eucharistic Prayers. Bishop Trautman also presented one action item for approval of the Administrative Committee (see below).

Four-Week Psalter of the New American Bible

During the March 22-24, 1994 meeting of the Administrative Committee Bishop Trautman presented one action item seeking approval to use the revised psalms of the *New American Bible* in a printed booklet containing the four-week psalter as an alternative to the *Grail Psalms* when the *psalms are sung.* The revised NAB psalms were approved for use in the liturgy by the National Conference of Catholic Bishops (NCCB) in November 1991 and this action was confirmed by the Apostolic See on May 27, 1992. In 1983 the NCCB approved using the psalms of *New American Bible, Revised Standard Version,* and *Jerusalem Bible* when the office is sung. The intent of this decision was to allow all the versions of the psalms that had been approved for liturgical use to also be used for the *Liturgy of the Hours.* Since the revised psalms of the *New American Bible* have now been approved for liturgical use, they would also come under the 1983 decision. This action was approved by all the members of the Administrative Committee in a voice vote at the March 1994 meeting.

NAB and NRSV translations of the *Lectionary for Mass*

On March 18, 1994 the Bishops' Committee on the Liturgy discussed a proposal to reconsider its decision not to publish the *New Revised Standard Version* edition of the *Lectionary for Mass* until the *New American Bible* edition is ready for publication. After considerable discussion, the BCL decided that it still wished to wait for the NAB confirmation by the Congregation for Divine Worship and the Discipline of the Sacraments before publishing the NRSV Lectionary.

Report of the Committee on Doctrine

The NCCB Committee on Doctrine met on Monday, March 21, 1994. At this meeting the Committee examined Segment One: Ordinary Time of the proposed revision of the *Sacramentary.* In a letter addressed to Bishop Trautman dated March 22, 1994, Bishop Alfred C. Hughes, Chairman of the Committee on Doctrine, reported that "the Committee is happy to report that we find no doctrinal error in the proposed texts. In fact, the new translations represent a significant improvement over the texts currently in use." The Doctrine Committee also engaged in extended discussion over the principles of translations and the way these have been interpreted by ICEL. Bishop Hughes noted that "although the Committee was divided, some expressed concern that a preoccupation with philological and euchological issues has become more important than precision and fullness of meaning in the decisions on translation." These and other issues of liturgical translation will be addressed at the June Study Day for the Translation of Liturgical Texts.

COMMITTEE ON THE LITURGY
NEWSLETTER

**1994
VOLUME XXX
MAY**

Age for Confirmation

On April 29, 1994, Monsignor Robert N. Lynch, General Secretary of the NCCB/USCC, notified the members of the National Conference of Catholic Bishops (NCCB) that the Congregation for Bishops has confirmed the Conference's action approving the norm for the age of confirmation in the Latin rite dioceses of the United States. The norm was approved by the Latin rite members of the NCCB at their June 1993 plenary meeting in New Orleans, LA. It does not apply to the Eastern Catholic Churches who have their own legislation regarding confirmation (chrismation).

The decree from the Congregation for Bishops, dated February 8, 1994, states that "in consideration of the vote of the bishops, the above-mentioned norm is approved for five years, in order that the bishops, with the lapse of time and the addition of new perspectives, may again raise this question and bring a norm once again to the Holy See for review." In a decree issued May 1, 1994 Archbishop Keeler, President of the NCCB, states that the general decree will become effective July 1, 1994 and continue to be effective through July 1, 1999. The text of Archbishop Keeler's decree follows.

NATIONAL CONFERENCE OF CATHOLIC BISHOPS
UNITED STATES OF AMERICA

DECREE OF PROMULGATION

In June 1993, the members of the National Conference of Catholic Bishops of the United States of America approved the following action:

> "The National Conference of Catholic Bishops hereby decrees that the sacrament of Confirmation in the Latin rite shall be conferred between the age of discretion, which is about the age of 7, and 18 years of age, within the limits determined by the diocesan bishop and with regard for the legitimate exceptions given in canon 891, namely, when there is danger of death or, where in the judgment of the minister grave cause urges otherwise."

The Congregation for Bishops has given the formal *recognitio* for this action of the National Conference of Bishops, made in accord with canon 891 of the Code of Canon Law, for five years, in a general decree (Prot. No. 296/84), signed by Bernardin Cardinal Gantin, Prefect of the Congregation, and dated February 8, 1994.

By the authority given to me by the Conference, I hereby declare that this general decree will become effective July 1, 1994 and continue to be effective through July 1, 1999.

Given at the offices of the National Conference of Catholic Bishops in Washington, DC, May 1, 1994.

+ Most Reverend William H. Keeler
Archbishop of Baltimore
President, National Conference of Catholic Bishops

Monsignor Robert N. Lynch
General Secretary
NCCB/USCC

3211 FOURTH STREET NE • WASHINGTON, DC 20017

Special Assembly for Africa: Inculturation

During the Special Assembly for Africa of the Synod of Bishops, Cardinal Hyacinthe Thiandoum, Archbishop of Dakar, Senegal, and General Rapporteur, gave the Relatio ante disceptationem. *The following is an excerpt from his talk which concerns inculturation.*

Although inculturation is a relatively new word, the reality it connotes has always been part and parcel of the evangelizing mission of the Church down the ages. It has to do with rooting the Gospel message in the culture of a people. It has become a major concern of the Church in Africa and Madagascar because of the relative newness of Christianity among our peoples, and the foreign origin of its heralds in most places. Many have therefore a strong feeling of having received a faith not yet fully at home in our life and culture.

The synod documents treat inculturation within the framework of a theology of the Incarnation. That is to say that inculturation is more than a simple adaptation to cultural modes of expression—what has been called the theology of "adaptation". It goes deeper, into ways of understanding the faith and living it out in practical experience. It is an all-embracing process which in the last analysis is the work of the Holy Spirit leading the believer into the full knowledge of the truth.

Inculturation is an ecclesial task, involving all levels of the Church, each at its own place and according to its own role. It is not only a question of theological speculation by experts, but involves the Christian life of the people at the grassroots. However, Bishops have a special responsibility to promote, guide and supervise the process of inculturation in communion with the universal Church, while theologians play an indispensable role in study, documentation and research in communion with the hierarchy and at the service of the People of God. The Church in Africa ought not to fear inculturation; the contrary should be the case, for the origins of inculturation go back to the very beginnings of Christianity. That is to say that inculturation has indissoluble links with the Good News of salvation in Jesus Christ.

In the concrete application of the general principles of inculturation, we are faced with the great diversity of cultures and pastoral situations in Africa. The general concerns of inculturation are valid not only for Africa and the so-called "mission-lands". Every nation and culture must constantly face the challenge of finding a relevant and living expression of the Christian message. The efforts of each culture in this regard enrich the universal Church.

Inculturation touches every aspect of life. In the African context, the following areas come to mind as necessary and urgent.

In the matter of theological expression, the project of an *African Theology* must continue with all vigor and commitment, respecting the principles of compatibility with the Gospel and communion with the universal Church. New grounds are likely to be broken if more effort were made to do theology in the local languages, despite the difficulties which such an effort would entail.

Worship and liturgy are specially privileged fields for inculturation. The ancient rites of the Church, including those of Africa, in Egypt and in Ethiopia, are fruits of liturgical inculturation. More attention should be paid to these ancient African rites as we try to evolve new ones in other parts of Africa. In this regard, the experience of Zaire, approved by the Holy See, is a step in the right direction. The emergence of such rites is as *of right* not as concession.

Marriage and family need to be looked at more closely, in order to recover and promote the precious values of the traditional African family. This could be a great contribution to finding an effective response to the crisis of the family in many modern societies. We need greater appreciation for our various customary laws of marriage and serious effort to harmonize them with Church laws on marriage.

Initiation rites common in many African cultures can enrich and offer powerful symbolism for the Christian rites of initiation, the sacraments and even the religious life.

Inculturation presupposes a positive attitude to our cultures, especially the religious aspects of these cultures. Conversion to the Christian faith is always in the line of continuity with faith in God and acceptance of his sovereign will. We need to distinguish clearly in our minds between true inculturation and inadmissible syncretism. The *Instrumentum laboris* (cf. Synod of Bishops, Special Assembly for Africa, *Instrumentum laboris,* nn. 105-106) indicates useful lines of discernment in its long list of positive and negative aspects of the African Traditional Religion. Finally, we need to acknowledge the limits of inculturation. Its aim is not to remove all difficulties from the Christian life but to facilitate a more authentic, convinced and convincing way *of living the Gospel.*

Liturgical Calendar 1996

The NCCB Liturgy Secretariat recently prepared its 1996 edition of the liturgical calendar for the dioceses of the United States of America. The calendar lists each day's celebration, rank, liturgical color(s), and lectionary citations.

For many years the information in the annual calendar prepared by the Liturgy Secretariat was made available only to commercial publishers of other calendars, *ordines,* etc. in the United States. For the past two years it has been published in an inexpensive format and made available to anyone desiring a copy.

Liturgy Calendar 1996 (8 1/2 X 11 in.) may be purchased from: Bishops' Committee on the Liturgy, 3211 Fourth Street NE, Washington, DC 20017-1194. Att: Ms. Ellen McLoughlin. All orders must be accompanied by a check made out to "Bishops' Committee on the Liturgy" in the amount of $6.00 to cover printing, postage, and handling.

International

Canada

The National Liturgical Office reports that the ritual, *Sunday Celebrations of the Word,* is currently being piloted across Canada. Evaluation forms have been provided for those parishes who are participating in the pilot project. An editorial committee is involved with the preparation of pastoral notes which will accompany the ritual.

England and Wales

Martin Foster has been appointed Assistant Secretary at the Liturgy Office in London. He is a member of the Church Music Committee of the Bishops' Conference of England and Wales. The Bishops' Conference Liturgy Office recently lost both its General Secretary, Father Ernest Sands, and its Assistant Secretary, Jennifer Demolder, in the space of one month over the new year. Father Sands is returning to the United States to resume his doctoral studies. Mrs. Demolder recently resigned as assistant secretary to take a position in a school in Essex.

The Episcopal Conference of England and Wales recently approved Segment I: Ordinary Time of the proposed revision of the *Roman Missal (Sacramentary)* during their April 1994 plenary meeting.

Ireland

The Advisory Committee on Sacred Art and Architecture for the Irish Episcopal Commission for Liturgy has published *The Place of Worship: Pastoral Directory on the Building and Reordering of Churches.* It will be available in late April 1994.

In Memoriam

Jan Vermulst

Jan Vermulst was born on October 30, 1925 in Stiphout, the Netherlands, and was educated at the Conservatory of Tilburg. He died on February 4, 1994. He was organist and choirmaster at the Church of Our Lady in Helmond. Omer Westendorf first experienced his music in the churches of Holland after World War II, and shortly after the 1958 Liturgical Conference held in Cincinnati, began writing to Vermulst requesting music for the Church in the United States. This resulted in the "Mass for Christian Unity." The revision of the Mass texts in 1970 produced another commission, the "People's Mass." In the years following the liturgical reforms of the Second Vatican Council, his music was well known in almost every Roman Catholic Church in the United States.

> Into your hands, O Lord,
> we humbly entrust our brother Jan.
> In this life you embraced him with your tender love;
> deliver him now from every evil
> and bid him enter eternal rest.

The old order has passed away:
welcome him then into paradise,
where there will be no sorrow, no weeping nor pain,
but the fullness of peace and joy
with your son and the Holy Spirit
for ever and ever.
(*Order of Christian Funerals*, 398.4)

Father Carroll Stuhlmueller, CP

Father Carroll Stuhlmueller, CP, professor of Old Testament studies at Catholic Theological Union in Chicago, died on February 21, 1994. A prominent figure in the field of Scripture scholarship, Stuhlmueller was respected in both Roman Catholic and ecumenical circles. He played a key role in improving the stature of Roman Catholic biblical scholarship following the Second Vatican Council. He was editor of *The Bible Today* and the 23 volume commentary *Old Testament Message*. He served on the editorial boards of the *Journal of Biblical Literature* and the *Catholic Biblical Quarterly*.

Faithful God,
we humbly ask your mercy for your servant Carroll,
who worked so generously to spread the Good News:
grant him the reward of his labors
and bring him safely to your promised land.
(*Order of Christian Funerals*, 398.24)

Resources

Dining in the Kingdom of God by Eugene La Verdiere is about the origins of the eucharist according to Luke. The work makes connections between the eucharist, the gospel and the worshiping assembly. It can help all of those involved in the liturgical life of the Church to celebrate the eucharistic memorial of Christ and to identify and work with the issues that arise from a eucharist that in fact makes a memory of the entire gospel. It is available in paperback ($11.95) from: Liturgy Training Publications, 1800 North Hermitage Avenue, Chicago, IL 60622-1101. Telephone: 1-800-933-1800. (Note: Liturgy Training Publications offers a 40% discount to all diocesan worship or liturgy offices and commissions on any purchase of their materials.)

The *Eucharist as Sacrament of Initiation* by Nathan Mitchell is the second in the Forum Essay Series on adult initiation published by Liturgy Training Publications. In this book Mitchell argues that the Rite of Christian Initiation of Adults presupposes and requires a commitment to the vision of Jesus, whose distinctive ministry of eating anything with anyone redefined the religious and cultural meaning of dining. It is available in paperback ($6.00) from: Liturgy Training Publications, 1800 North Hermitage Avenue, Chicago, IL 60622-1101. Telephone: 1-800-933-1800.

Infant Baptism: A Parish Celebration by Timothy Fitzgerald applies the standards of the liturgical reform—the full, conscious and active participation of the assembly; the word proclaimed and preached; the integration of music and ritual; the abundant use of symbols, gestures and movements—to the *Rite of Baptism for Children*. The book emphasizes infant baptism as a parish celebration that is an action of the community that begets new believers and nurtures the faith of all. It is available in paperback ($8.95) from: Liturgy Training Publications, 1800 North Hermitage Avenue, Chicago, IL 60622-1101. Telephone: 1-800-933-1800.

The Mystery of Easter by Raniero Cantalamessa details how one might explore the liturgy and scripture to appreciate the depth and richness of the Paschal Mystery. The book provides an in-depth reflection on the Easter Vigil and shows how such reflection continues in a regular pattern through one's life toward an understanding of the Paschal Mystery as recorded in scripture and as expressed in the liturgy. It is available in paperback ($9.95) from: The Liturgical Press, Saint John's Abbey, Box 7500, Collegeville, MN 56321-7500. Telephone: 1-800-858-5450.

COMMITTEE ON THE LITURGY

NEWSLETTER

1994
VOLUME XXX
JUNE/JULY

Suggested Guidelines Regarding Altar Servers

The following guidelines were prepared by the Bishops' Committee on the Liturgy and presented to the National Conference of Catholic Bishops for discussion at the June 1994 Special Assembly on Thursday, June 16, 1994. The suggested guidelines may be used as a basis for developing diocesan guidelines.

1) Although institution into the ministry of acolyte is reserved to lay men, the diocesan bishop may permit the liturgical functions of the instituted acolyte to be carried out by altar servers, men and women, boys and girls. Such persons may carry out all the functions listed in no. 68, para. 2 and nos. 142-147 of the *General Instruction of the Roman Missal.*[1]

   The determination that women and girls may function as servers in the liturgy should be made by the bishop on the diocesan level so that there might be a uniform diocesan policy.

2) No distinction should be made between the functions carried out in the sanctuary by men and boys and those carried out by women and girls. The term "altar boys" should be replaced by "servers". The term "server" should be used for those who carry out the functions of the instituted acolyte.

3) Servers should be mature enough to understand their responsibilities and to carry them out well and with appropriate reverence. They should have already received holy communion for the first time and normally receive the eucharist whenever they participate in the liturgy.

4) Servers should receive proper formation before they begin to function. The formation should include instruction on the Mass and its parts and their meaning, the various objects used in the liturgy (their names and use), and the various functions of the server during the Mass and other liturgical celebrations. Servers should also receive appropriate guidance on maintaining proper decorum and attire when serving Mass and other functions.

5) Since the role of server is integral to the normal celebration of the Mass, at least one server should assist the priest. On Sundays and other more important occasions, two or more servers should be employed to carry out the various functions normally entrusted to these ministers.

6) Servers should normally be vested. This is within the tradition of the Church and prevents difficulties regarding appropriate dress for these ministers. All servers should wear the same liturgical vesture.[2]

7) Servers carry the cross, the processional candles, hold the book for the priest celebrant when he is not at the altar, carry the incense and censer, present the bread, wine, and water to the priest during the preparation of the gifts or assist him when he receives the gifts from the people, wash the hands of the priest, assist the priest celebrant and deacon as necessary.

8) Servers respond to the prayers and dialogues of the priest along with the congregation. They also join in singing the hymns and other chants of the liturgy.

9) Servers should be seated in a place where they can easily assist the priest celebrant and deacon. The place next to the priest is normally reserved for the deacon.

---

[1]Number 70, para. 1, the second sentence no longer applies (this restricted the liturgical functions in the sanctuary only to men).

[2]The alb is the preferred vestment for servers (see *General Instruction of the Roman Missal,* no. 298).

3211 FOURTH STREET NE • WASHINGTON, DC 20017

10) Servers may not distribute holy communion unless they have been mandated for this function by the bishop.

11) The *Order for the Blessing of Altar Servers, Sacristans, Musicians, and Ushers* (*Book of Blessings*, nos. 1847-1870) may be used before servers first begin to function in this ministry.

Keynote Address: Study Day on Liturgical Translations

On June 23, 1994 Mr. Dennis McManus gave the following keynote address entitled "Principles of Translation: Issues in the Application of the Hermeneutics of Comme le prévoit" at the study day on liturgical translations following the June 1994 Special Assembly of the NCCB in La Jolla, CA. The text of that address follows.

Introductory Remarks

Thank you, Your Excellency, for your kind welcome. I am fully appreciative of the important concerns of the Conference in the area of liturgy and its competent translation. Addressing this very significant issue has been made easy, however, by the gracious reception I have been afforded from the very beginning in the kind letter of invitation I received from Archbishop Keeler, President of the Conference. Though I am not a member of ICEL, it is in my role as General Editor of The Ancient Christian Writers Series at Paulist Press, that I was happy to examine with you the principles of translation of liturgical texts. As well, the solicitousness of Bishop Trautman as chairman of the Bishops' Committee on the Liturgy and of Archbishop Pilarczyk, as head of ICEL have been complete in every way. It goes without saying that so much of what the Conference enjoys in the preparation of its liturgical materials—and of any documents I requested as background for these remarks—is due to the dedication and hard work of Monsignor Alan Detscher and Sister Linda Gaupin of the Secretariat for the Liturgy. Monsignor Detscher has provided me with insight and direction at every turn. Sister Gaupin has inspired me and offered the practical wisdom so vital to a project such as this one. I am grateful to both of them.

As well, I was impressed and enthused by all who gave me their time so generously in the many interviews which formed the backbone of my appraoch to the issues at hand. To the numerous members of the Conference who allowed me easy access to their schedules for thorough discussions on all that lies before us, I am very grateful. In particular, I am thankful for the very generous extension of time and the high quality of reflection which I enjoyed from all members of the ICEL staff with whom I met in Washington or Chicago. Dr. John Page, the Executive Director of ICEL, was of special assistance in many ways. I would be remiss in my responsibilities if I did not acknowledge his expertise in every area of concern to me and how completely he presented himself and his resources at the disposal of the Conference to assist in addressing pertinent issues. In particular, Dr. Page's extraordinary openness to the exploration of all aspects of translation theory and its application to the liturgy promoted an important creativity in our conversations which was supportive and practical. Indeed, his insights were of the greatest help in eventually developing the approaches to liturgical hermeneutics suggested in this paper.

Additionally, I am grateful to Fr. O'Brien of CREDO and to Fr. Fessio of Ignatius Press, who both spoke to me on different occasions regarding their positions on the translation issues which face the Conference. It was a pleasure to explore with them the bases of important hermeneutical concerns. Their contributions to this project are deeply appreciated.

It would not be an exaggeration for me to say that my experience of interviewing and meeting with so many concerned parties was a model of communication in the respect accorded me in the name of the Conference. I was deeply impressed by the evident sincerity, deep faith and specific competence of all who spoke with me. It was a grace to see the diverse gifts of the Church made clear and ready for the service of the Conference.

These remarks will be approximately thirty minutes in length. Three important points will be discussed: (1) that the use of a "sacred language" system in the Roman Rite must be explored for two very important consequences; (2) that hermeneutic questions are in need of special attention in vernacularization; and (3) that a distinct forum for dealing with such issues may be a desirable concept for the Conference to consider.

The Acts of the Apostles presents the wonderful events of Pentecost with a simplicity which startles. "Suddenly," the text tells us, "a sound came from heaven like the rush of a mighty wind and it filled all the house where they were sitting (Acts 2.2)." As the mystery unfolds, we see a singular event—not only in the life of the Church but in the history of language as well—taking shape. For the Holy Spirit descends upon the apostles, moving them to speech which is at once universal and yet completely local and personal. We are told how "the multitude became bewildered, because each one heard them speaking in his own language (Acts 2.6)." What is more, each hears the same message: that Christ has died and risen, calling us by faith to enter into his new life with the Father. The effects of this and Peter's sermon which follows are completely personal, for the Acts describe the reaction of the listeners: "But when they heard this they were cut to the heart, and said to Peter and the rest of the apostles, 'Brethren, what shall we do?'" From the wondrous and universal proclamation of the good news, to its hearing in each local tongue, to its final rest in the heart of everyone who heard it, God's Word is transformed and made to bear much fruit. I would like to propose that as we begin an examination of the issues of translation, that the Pentecost account from the Acts of the Apostles be our guide in understanding that all good liturgical translation must reflect these three characteristics found in the transformation of language at Pentecost: (1) that the content of the Church's prayer is universal, embracing the faith of all believers; (2) that the expression of the Church's prayer is thoroughly local, adopting an idiom and sound which is intelligible and accessible to the believer while (3) having for its goal the personal conversion of each heart, ever deepening its conversion to the following of Christ. With these solid guides, some of the issues before us may be seen in new perspectives, helpful to a resolution of certain conflicts to the task of vernacularization.

No adequate discussion of the principles of translation of liturgical texts as found in *Comme le prévoit* can be made without first identifying the presuppositions of that important document. And it is here that much of our discussion will be centered, for the most essential of *Comme le prévoit*'s assumptions is that the post-conciliar Church would retain what was previously referred to as a "sacred language" system.

This important term—"sacred language"—needs careful presentation. In the Roman west, traditionally, "sacred language" has, in the first order, referred to Scriptural languages, but most especially to Hebrew and Greek. By extension, Latin has been referred to as a "sacred language" since for so long it carried not only the enormous responsibilities of worship, but also because the more original Scriptural languages were not studied, leaving the Vulgate as the principal Biblical text for ecclesiastical and academic use. It is in this more extended sense that I will refer to Latin within these remarks as a "sacred" language.

In any case, it is important to understand that the choice to retain an ancient language for worship, law, doctrine, scripture and patristics is filled with serious consequences for ecclesial communication. "Sacred language" systems are, by nature, differently structured and used than are contemporary vernaculars. Some brief reflection on their unique characteristics may be in order.

Whether by consensual usage, hierarchical decision or any process of institutionalization, a language can change its status from "secular" to "sacred" in predictable fashion. What is most important to note is that such languages, once designated as "sacred," are seen as servicing primarily the faith community which has chosen them. Christianity is not alone in the development of sacred languages. The Lubbavitch movement, in its high maintenance of Talmudic Hebrew, is a contemporary example of the development of a kind of sacred language. Koranic studies, as well, reveal the presence of more "sacred" Arabic found in the earlier texts of the Koran as well as in discussion of their traditions. In all cases, these languages serve a special purpose: the preservation of the experience of the faith community in select areas of its life and thought through fixed language forms.

Typically, sacred languages cease to develop in the same ways in which vernaculars do. A "living" or popular language welcomes outside experiences in order to master its ever-changing associations in the world-at-large. A sacred language is "closed" by comparison, developing primarily from within, i.e., using elements such as vocabulary and syntax already found within it but in subtly different patterns often centered around questions shaped by worship and belief systems of the host community. When compared with vernaculars, sacred languages appear "dead" or unresponsive to the usual stimuli of language development. Their genius, however, is in the preservation of privileged vocabulary, syntax and rhetorical forms which can often remain accessible to a given community of readers and speakers long after vernaculars have lost any power to communicate.

For all intents and purposes, Latin is the chosen "sacred" or "closed" language of Roman Catholic ecclesial life. It is the first and principal presupposition of *Comme le prévoit* that Latin would retain this privileged role. A corollary of this is that adequate translations of Latin texts into vernaculars would be manageable under most circumstances. But is this still true?

A sacred language system works well for a given Church only when two conditions are present. First, translators of the sacred language must be adequately aware of the special claims which the sacred language makes upon the areas of Church life it services. For example, as a sacred language in the Roman Rite, Latin claims to be the language of the entire Church at prayer. Such a phenomenal claim is filled with consequences, both theological and pastoral, which the language of private prayer does not carry. Throughout the Church's life and daily business, its sacred language in the Roman Rite makes special claims in law, worship, dogmatics, patristics, scripture and in ecumenism. Only when translators are fully aware of these special claims, can they begin to develop a comprehensive approach to the use of a chosen vernacular.

This also directly affects the development of principles of translation. No effective hermeneutic guidelines can be formulated until the special claims referred to above have been identified and understood. Only then do comprehensive principles emerge for the variety of translation projects needed in Church life. The claims of a sacred language in a legal code will be substantially different from those made in worship. While certain common claims and hermeneutics may emerge between areas, careful attention must be given to the particular way in which hermeneutics are developed and applied within a given area of Church life.

This first great assumption of *Comme le prévoit*—that a sacred language system would remain in place for the Roman rite—prompted a rush of translation efforts unparalleled in translation history. The intent of the Council—to provide Catholics everywhere with the rites of the Church in a vernacular tongue—was and remains an enormous undertaking. It is also important to note how this kind of translating differs from all other similar efforts.

Nowadays, any qualified scholar may presume to translate an ancient text by use of any desirable literary critical method. Indeed, bookstores are full of new approaches to Homer, Ovid and Catullus, each making use of some new insight of sociolinguistic or literary theory. The resulting translations are then judged by a wide readership of scholars and others who hold similar interests.

The translation of sacred language texts, however, is completely distinct from this. The translator approaches the sacred language text with a special task in mind, viz., to render a sacred language into a vernacular one, while preserving the special claims of the sacred in the vernacular. This is a very unique process indeed, since the sacred language can claim legitimately to hold within itself a kind of "language memory" of belief, doctrine, identity and prayer which, if mistranslated, is effectively lost to the community of believers. It is then obvious that this very specialized translation of sacred language texts can only be done by those profoundly familiar with the claims, structure and content of the sacred language. For the balance of these remarks, I will refer to this privileged kind of translation as "vernacularization."

Vernacularization must be understood as a uniquely late twentieth century language phenomenon. This is not to imply that vernacularized texts were not previously produced; but they were done for private use and were rarely intended to represent authoritatively the Roman Catholic tradition. Vernacularization as directed by the Council, on the other hand, is intended to touch every text of significance in the renewal of the Church's life. To date, this process has barely received any attention from scholars for its distinctive problems and unique purposes. But because it is so new a movement—there having elapsed only twenty years since its intense post-conciliar beginnings—it is not surprising that the special claims and particular hermeneutics it carries have not been fully developed. Neither the Concilium, nor the Conference, nor ICEL can be expected to have fully developed the hermeneutics issues only now being framed. As well, the Conference should not be alarmed at the relative novelty of many of the issues encountered and the approaches developed over the last twenty years. A single generation of texts represents only the beginning of the development of important new skills in this aspect of the renewal of the liturgy.

Nor can *Comme le prévoit,* as an early document in the reform of the liturgy, carry the full weight of responsibility for establishing the principles of vernacularization for all sacred Latin texts. *Comme le prévoit* is insightful, indeed brilliant, but shows its limitations when confronted with the issues in vernacularization which translators now face. It is a further complicating factor, for example, that just as the Council decided to make appropriate use of the vernacular, English in the United States was at the start of one of its most productive cycles of development. New discoveries in the hard and behavorial sciences—especially in psychology—as well as influences from the major cultural movements of the sixties and seventies created wave after wave of important vocabulary and syntactical changes in English which *Comme le prévoit* could not possibly have foreseen. As the nineties have begun, a new cycle of linguistic change—which come almost predictably in periods of twenty five to thirty years—has commenced with important new expressions in gender, human disability, victimization and violence making contributions to English frequently. The challenge to vernacularization is correspondingly immense.

Some reflection on a central issue raised by many in my interviews may be appropriate here. Liturgical vernacularization is, by nature, a complex matter. For not only must scholars be aware of the unique claims of a sacred language and be ready to transfer them into a vernacular, they must also fashion a vernacular language fit for worship—itself a demanding task. This double burden has been widely appreciated by Conference members, but a serious question has been raised about one aspect of the vernacularization process.

Specifically, it has been widely asked how liturgical vernacularization best preserves the special claims which its Latin originals make in the area of doctrine. This is a very legitimate and indeed, a very central question. While there is no simple answer theoretically, it can be said that great care must be given to preserving the tradition of Catholic belief in and through every vernacularization. In sacred language systems, the beliefs and identities of the faith communities which use them are often "encoded" as it were in the vocabulary and special structures which are found in important texts. A failure to know and accurately vernacularize the tradition preserved in key texts can unwittingly lose valuable components of that very tradition. This is also why there is no absolute answer to the question of "literal" versus "liberal" translation styles. If the goal of the vernacularization is to faithfully present a tradition of Christian life, then each passage must be judged individually for its ability to be rendered best. On some occasions, a literal translation will prove most powerful and faithful in presenting the sense of the Latin original; on other occasions, a literal translation will obscure or even destroy the message offered in the sacred language. The development of hermeneutics which carefully guide the vernacularization process generally is a task of the highest importance.

The main interviews I conducted with ICEL and CREDO leadership have shown that both groups are concerned about the very delicate balance between two aspects of vernacularization: (1) the exploration of received Latin texts for their important meanings and special claims in the liturgy and (2) the development of English vernacular which fully respects the needs of the proclaimer and the hearer in the context of worship. Important concerns regarding euchology, scansion, pastoral suitability, aesthetics and theology are of intense interest to members of both groups. In all conversations, I found that diverse scholars were convinced of the Pentecost qualities of good translations mentioned at the start of these remarks: that the content of the Church's prayer is universal, embracing the faith of all believers; that the expression of prayer must adopt an idiom and sound which is intelligible and accessible to the believer while having for its goal the personal conversion of all who use it.

In neither organization did I find any reluctance to examine the obvious need for hermeneutics and their application to liturgical texts. Consequently, there seems to have emerged significant common ground for discussion between scholars ready to present positions in an effort to clarify and improve the worship language of the Church.

Having briefly examined the first of *Comme le prévoit*'s two principal assumptions—that a sacred language system with vernacularizations was the goal of the Council—we now turn our attention to its second: that Latin as a sacred language will be maintained in such a fashion as to remain the base language for communication within the Church. This too is an assumption whose consequences need testing in some brief reflections here.

It is a general observation of many in diverse areas of Church life—including universities, seminaries, tribunals, chanceries and the like—that the maintenance of reading and compositional skills in Latin has declined drastically since 1970. With the onrush of vernacularization processes, an abandonment of Latin competency as a requirement for ordination, doctoral degrees, etc. has contributed to two important changes in the use of Latin as a sacred language in the Roman Rite.

First, a lack of curricular support for Latin has left many without the ability to read original texts which can best carry the weight and meaning of the Catholic tradition in the Roman west. The growing tendency of degree and ministerial preparation programs to substitute vernacularized texts completely in place of original sacred language texts has helped to shape an entire generation of students whose familiarity with their own tradition may be less certain than it once was.

Second, the general modernization in style and accuracy of the Latin composition used for correspondence, study documents and, on occasion, liturgical or dogmatic texts has helped to generate a series of texts which may risk unwittingly destroying the very language structures, vocabulary and syntax which must be preserved in a sacred language system.

This has enormous consequences for the process of vernacularization. When a text of this quality is received, a translator in any project can only render it in another language to the extent that the substance of the composition enables this to happen. Poor vernacularizations—often in English which is flat, without the richness of theological reflection and unaesthetic—are occasionally mirroring their Latin original. The blending of Latin texts or their adaptation or retranslation must be done with the utmost care in order to produce coherent compositions of clarity and beauty.

A last caution must also be noted. If Latin is to be used as the final language of a document whose original drafts were prepared in modern languages, great care must be taken in the composition of the Latin, that it remain stylistically, syntactically and conceptually within the best Latin tradition of the Roman Rite. This will often mean a "rethinking" of the modern language original into a complex, indeed, at times difficult, Latin idiom consistent with the intellectual and theological tradition about which we are speaking. But it is fair to say that only such a Latin style can then serve as the inspiration for a single, unifying text for the universal Church, allowing in turn each vernacular to draw equally from the original message and to express it fully in its own genius. Allowance must also be made for translation styles which need to vary from genre to genre within each major area of vernacular usage. A failure to address these issues in the maintenance of Latin composition in particular risks transforming a sacred language into merely an administrative one.

Both of these assumptions in *Comme le prevoit* are together the most fundamental underpinnings of the issues before the Conference. Until some address is made to the deeper problems surrounding the processes of vernacularization—as described above—English texts will be at risk of an imbalance or a kind of pastoral ineffectiveness; likewise, Latin texts may not be able to serve fully the tradition entrusted to them, which, like the speech of the Apostles at Pentecost, must inspire the highest quality vernacularizations.

The appropriate forum for the pursuit of hermeneutic issues in vernacularization is not easy to identify within existing NCCB/USCC structures. Would the present design and assignments of ICEL make it a likely place for the examination of these questions? Other existing agencies do not seem to provide the scope or background of personnel in which these specialized and critical questions can be dealt with. Could it be time for the Conference to consider the creation of a forum which can help to address the host of issues surrounding vernacularization in those areas of Church life continually affected by them?

Such a forum—to which I will refer, for lack of a better term, as the "Forum on the Vernacular"—would have three important tasks:

1. To identify the special claims which Latin as a sacred language makes on each area of vernacularization;
2. To develop appropriate hermeneutics for each area of vernacularization;
3. To assist in the incorporation of such hermeneutics into existing vernacularization projects, where appropriate.

Various decisions on the stucture and the all-important issue of accountability would deserve Conference attention and creativity.

Allow me, Bishops, to succinctly summarize my most important points to you:

1. The most fundamental problems you face with *Comme le prevoit* are not so much in its contents as in its assumptions;
2. Two important problems with the assumptions of *Comme le prevoit* are evident:

   a. that vernacularization is in need of a detailed hermeneutical philosophy to guide its application in liturgical texts in particular;
   b. that the maintenance of ecclesiastical Latin needs attention if a sacred language system is to function with vitality in the Roman Rite;

3. The Conciliar decision to use the vernacular in worship is one whose long-term consequences are only now being sensed;
4. A special forum for the full development of vernacularization issues may be an option for the Conference to consider;
5. There is a wide agreement amongst many concerned parties outside the Conference that such a forum would be a welcome way in which to jointly investigate the issues at hand.

I thank the members of the Conference for their kind attention and return the podium to Archbishop Keeler, President of the Conference, for the opening question and answer session.

Sunday Celebrations in the Absence of a Priest: Leader's Edition

Sunday Celebrations in the Absence of a Priest: Leader's Edition is now available at local religious supply houses and bookstores and is published by The Catholic Book Publishing Company. It is available in a hardbound bilingual edition (English and Spanish), 7 1/4 by 10 1/2 inches, printed in two colors with stained edges and costs $24.95.

In Memoriam: Reverend Edward J. Kilmartin, SJ

Reverend Edward J. Kilmartin, SJ, professor at the Pontifical Oriental Institute in Rome, died of cancer Thursday, June 16, 1994 at Brigham and Women's Hospital. He was 71. A native of Maine, Father Kilmartin entered the Society of Jesus in 1941 and was ordained a priest at Weston in 1954. After earning a doctorate in theology at the Gregorian University in Rome, he served as a professor of theology at Weston College for the next seventeen years. During this period he served as Dean of the theology faculty, assistant editor of New Testament Abstracts, and as a member of the Boston College Theology Department.

From 1975-1984 he was a professor of theology at Notre Dame University. For the last ten years he had been associated with the faculty of the Pontifical Oriental Institute specializing in the field of liturgy. During this period he spent several years on the Boston College faculty and when his illness was detected he spent many months each year as a resident of the Jesuit Community at Boston College while he received treatment in Boston.

Father Kilmartin was a prolific writer of scholarly articles and books devoted to understanding Christian worship in the East and the West through the study of prayers and rites. He was a fellow of the American Theological Schools and a member of the Catholic Biblical Association, the Catholic Theological Society of America, Societas Liturgica, the North American Academy of Liturgy, and Instituto Paulo VI. In 1978 he received the John Courtney Murray award from the Catholic Theological Society of America and this past January the North American Academy of Liturgy gave him its Berakah Award for a distinguished lifetime contribution to the field of liturgical theology.

> Lord God,
> you chose our brother Edward to serve your people as a priest
> and to share the joys and burdens of their lives.
>
> Look with mercy on him
> and give him the reward of his labors,
> the fullness of life promised to those who preach your
>   holy Gospel.
>
> We ask this through Christ our Lord.
> *(Order of Christian Funerals,* no. 398.19)

Reverend Cuthbert Johnson, OSB

The Holy Father appointed Fr. Cuthbert Johnson, OSB as a Bureau Chief in the Congregation for Divine Worship and the Discipline of the Sacraments (May 3, 1994).

Resources

Renewing the City of God: The Reform of Catholic Architecture in the United States by Michael E. DeSanctis is number five in the series of Meeting House Essays. The essay grew out of a paper delivered by the author at the Society of Architectural Historians. The essay provides a synthesis of history, analysis and interpretation of Catholic architecture in hopes that readers might better understand the impact of Vatican Council II on Catholic life and art. It is available in paperback ($6.00) from: Liturgy Training Publications, 1800 North Hermitage Avenue, Chicago, IL 60622-1101. Telephone: 1-800-933-1800.

The *Liturgy Appointment Calendar for 1995* contains necessary liturgical information and plenty of space for notes and appointments. A quote for each weekly spread adds a point of reflection to this calendar.

It is available ($12.95) from: Liturgy Training Publications, 1800 North Hermitage Avenue, Chicago, IL 60622-1101. Telephone: 1-800-933-1800. Also available from Liturgy Training Publications is the *Year of Grace Liturgical Calendar* wall poster and notebook sized version. The art is by Judy Jarrett and the saints depicted around the edges are explained on the back of the smaller version. Cost: $7.00 (less in larger quantities) and the pack of notebook calendars is $10.00 for a pack of 25.

The 1994-1995 edition of *Children's Daily Prayer* by Elizabeth McMahon Jeep is in its fifth year of publication. It has been widely hailed for its ease of use by teachers and students in daily prayer. It will be ready in late 1994 from: Liturgy Training Publications, 1800 North Hermitage Avenue, Chicago, IL 60622-1101. Telephone: 1-800-933-1800.

Journey with the Fathers: Commentaries on the Sunday Gospel (Year A, Year B, and Year C - available in September 1994) edited by Edith Barnecut, OSB, provides meditations on the Sunday gospels by the Fathers of the Church. The books aim to make accessible to the general reader many treasures hidden in the Fathers' writings, and to present them in such a way as to bring out the message which the revised cursus of Scripture readings intends to convey. The books are available in paperback from: New City Press, 86 Mayflower Avenue, New Rochelle, NY 10801.

Worship and Culture in Dialogue is an ecumenical examination of the contemporary as well as historical relationships between culture and Christian liturgy, church music, and church architecture. Chapters on Baptism and Eucharist in the cultural contexts of the New Testament, the Lutheran Reformation, and the present day are authored by Gordon W. Lathrop, a New Testament scholar and professor of liturgy at the Lutheran Theological Seminary in Philadelphia. Chapters on Baptism, Eucharist, and music in the cultural contexts of the early Church as well as today are authored by Anscar J. Chupungco, OSB, who heads a liturgical institute in Manila, the Philippines. Chapters on the cultural contexts of architecture in both the early Church and today are written by S. Anita Staffer, LWF Study Secretary for Worship and Congregational Life, Geneva. A chapter on culture and church music is written by Mark P. Bangert, an ethnomusicologist at the Lutheran School of Theology at Chicago. A report of seven case studies from around the world is provided by Marcus Felde, professor of theology at the Martin Luther Seminary, Lac, New Guinea. An extensive multilingual bibliography is also included.

The issues regarding worship and culture are shared across ecumenical lines and the book is global in perspective and in authorship. It provides not only pioneering biblical and historical background, but also an analytical framework for considering today's issues. It is available in paperback ($10.00 - surface mail or $20.00 - air mail) from: Lutheran World Federation, Publications Office, P.O. Box 2100, CH-1211 Geneva 2, Switzerland.

1994 National Meeting of Diocesan Liturgical Commissions

The annual national meeting of diocesan liturgical commissions and offices of worship will be held at the Adam's Mark Hotel in Saint Louis, MO, from October 7-11, 1994. The meeting is jointly sponsored by the Federation of Diocesan Liturgical Commissions and the NCCB Committee on the Liturgy.

The general theme of the meeting is "Marriage: A Communion of Life and Love." Major presentations will be given by Reverend Joseph M. Champlin ("The Challenge of Pastoral Adaptation"); Mister Paul Covino ("The Theology of Marriage"); Reverend Ronald F. Krisman ("The Rite of Marriage"); and Sister Barbara Markey, ND ("Who is Getting Married").

Special interest sessions include Marriage as Process (Markey), Marriage in Church Law (Quinn), Interfaith Marriage, Multicultural Marriage, Music for Weddings (Romeri and Soboleski), Environment and Art (Woeger), and The Diocesan Office/Commission: Mission and Purpose in Today's Church (McLaughin and Fitzgerald). Optional Tours will be available.

The meeting is open to FDLC members and non-FDLC members. For more information call: Federation of Diocesan Liturgical Commissions at 202-635-6990.

COMMITTEE ON THE LITURGY

NEWSLETTER

**1994
VOLUME XXX
AUGUST/SEPTEMBER**

NATIONAL CONFERENCE OF CATHOLIC BISHOPS

June Special Assembly of the NCCB

The National Conference of Catholic Bishops (NCCB) met in Special Assembly from June 17-21, 1994, at the Sheraton Grande Torrey Pines Resort, San Diego, CA. The theme of the Special Assembly was "Shepherding a Future of Hope." Speakers included Br. Louis DeThomasis, FSC, Dr. Susan Muto, and Rev. James Gill, SJ ("Prophetic Imagination: Threshold to the Future"); Rev. Michael Himes, Ms. Margaret Steinfels, and Mr. George Weigel ("Challenges and Opportunities to Hope in Church and Society"); Rev. Anscar Chupungco, OSB ("Experiencing Hope in the Paschal Mystery"); Sr. Linda Gaupin, CDP ("Sunday Celebrations in the Absence of a Priest: Pastoral and Liturgical Implications"); Rev. Walter Burghardt ("Preaching of Hope"); Rev. Joseph Champlin ("Sacramental Inclusion"); Rev. Virgil Elizondo ("Rooting Hope in the Local Community" and "Evangelization and Hope"); Ms. Molly Kelly ("Youth and Hope"); and Rev. Philip Murnion ("Parish Ministry and Hope").

On Thursday, June 16, 1994 the NCCB met in executive session. During this time the bishops discussed the *Suggested Guidelines for Altar Servers* prepared by the Bishops' Committee on the Liturgy (see *Newsletter,* June/July 1994). The NCCB also expressed overwhelming support for the decision of the Holy See to allow service at the altar by women and girls and approved the following motion:

> It is the opinion of the National Conference of Catholic Bishops (NCCB) that the option of having women and girls serve at the altar is a welcome one, subject always to the guidance of the diocesan Bishop. The NCCB expresses its gratitude to the Holy Father and his collaborators for their pastoral concern on this matter.

On Wednesday, June 23, 1994 the NCCB held a study day on liturgical translations. Mr. Dennis McManus gave the keynote address entitled "Principles of Translation: Issues in the Application of the Hermeneutics of *Comme le prevoit*" (see *Newsletter,* June/July 1994). Archbishop William H. Keeler facilitated the meeting which included the keynote address and time for discussion and interaction with a panel. The panelists included: Most Reverend Donald W. Trautman (USA), Chairman of the NCCB Committee on the Liturgy; Reverend Anscar J. Chupungco, OSB (Philippines), President of the Pontifical Liturgical Institute of St. Anselm, Rome, Italy; Reverend Augustine DiNoia, OP (USA), the Director for the Secretariat for Doctrine and Pastoral Practices at the National Conference of Catholic Bishops in Washington, D.C.; Monsignor Alan F. Detscher (USA), the Executive Director of the Secretariat for the Liturgy of the National Conference of Catholic Bishops in Washington, D.C.; Most Reverend Raymond J. Lahey (Canada), Bishop of Saint George's, Canada and chairman of the Episcopal Commission for Liturgy from 1989-1993; Mr. Dennis McManus, Acquisitions Editor at Paulist Press and the General Editor of the *Ancient Christian Writers* series; Prof. Dr. Heinrich Rennings (Germany), the Executive Secretary of the Liturgiekommission der Deutschen Bischofskonferenze and Director of the German Liturgical Institute; and Right Reverend Abbot Marcel Rooney, OSB (USA), the Abbot of Conception Abbey and Chancellor of Conception Seminary College. A tape of the keynote address was distributed to all the bishops of the Conference courtesy of the Federation of Diocesan Liturgical Commissions (FDLC).

June Meeting of the Committee on the Liturgy

The Liturgy Committee (members, consultants, and advisors) met on Monday-Tuesday, June 13-14, 1994, at Saint Francis Seminary, San Diego, California. The Committee discussed and took action on several items, including: 1) American Adaptations of the Roman Missal; 2) a request to revise the American edition of the *Liturgy of the Hours* for inclusive language purposes; 3) Suggested Guidelines for Altar

Servers; 4) national workshops for the implementation of *Sunday Celebrations in the Absence of a Priest: Leader's Edition;* 5) requests for authorization to publish computer programs for participation materials and for a computer version of the *Lectionary for Masses with Children;* and 6) the Swiss Synod Eucharistic Prayer (ICEL).

The Committee also discussed the following: 1) the program and schedule for the June 22, 1994 Study Day on Liturgical Translations; 2) the status of the proposed Interim Inclusive Language Guidelines; 3) the reservation of the Holy Oils; 4) the use of non-alcoholic wine in the liturgy; 5) the appropriate liturgical role of the Deacon in the Good Friday service; and 6) the reception of the large volume of letters and signatures of those supporting the We Believe Statement.

The Committee also heard status reports on the following: 1) indults for the transfer of the Solemnity of the Ascension to Sunday; 2) Priests for Equality Lectionary and the lectionary published by Treehaus; 3) *Sunday Celebrations in the Absence of a Priest: Leader's Edition;* 4) American Sign Language as a liturgical language; and 5) the March 1994 joint committee meeting (chairman and staff of the Liturgy and Doctrine Committees) on Segment I of the proposed revision of the *Roman Missal (Sacramentary).*

The Committee also heard several subcommittee and Task Group reports. These included the Task Group on American Adaptation of the Roman Missal, Hispanic Liturgy Subcommittee, Committee for Televised Masses, and the Task Group on Cremation.

Archbishop Pilarczyk reported on the work of ICEL, noting that the *Sacramentary* is currently the main project that ICEL is working on in the present. Reporting on the work of the Federation of Diocesan Liturgical Commissions (FDLC), Father Michael Spillane announced that the national meeting of the FDLC will be held in Saint Louis, October 7-11, 1994. The theme is "Marriage: A Communion of Life and Love." The FDLC will also make available to every bishop in the United States a tape of the main address given at the Study Day on Liturgical Translations by Mr. Dennis McManus. Because of time constraints the presentation of the Position Statements of the FDLC was postponed until the October meeting of the BCL. Sister Rosa Maria Icaza reported on the work of the Instituto de Liturgia Hispana and informed the Committee that the newly elected president of the Instituto is Father Raul Gomez.

Future meetings of the Committee were set for: Baltimore, MD, on October 24, 1994 and Washington, DC on November 13, 1994.

NCCB Administrative Committee Meeting

The Administrative Committee of the National Conference of Catholic Bishops met on September 13-15, 1994 at the NCCB/USCC headquarters building in Washington, DC. In the course of the meeting Bishop Donald W. Trautman, STD, SSL, Chairman of the NCCB Liturgy Committee, requested that the Administrative Committee approve three action items of the Liturgy Committee. The members of the Committee approved the following action items which require the confirmation of the Congregation for Divine Worship and the Discipline of the Sacraments: 1) provisional (interim) translation of the *Mass of the Blessed Virgin Mary, Star of the Sea;* 2) the provisional translations of English and Spanish texts for the optional memorial of Saint Marguerite Bourgeoys for use in those dioceses or religious communities that have included her on their calendars; and 3) the provisional (interim) English translation of the *Eucharistic Prayer for Masses for Various Needs and Occasions.*

At the request of Bishop Trautman the Administrative Committee also approved the following action items for placement on the agenda of the November 1994 Plenary Meeting of the NCCB.

The first action item requests that the NCCB approve Segment I: Ordinary Time, Segment II: Proper of Seasons, and Segment III: Order of Mass I of the proposed revision of the *Roman Missal (Sacramentary)* for placement on the agenda of the November 1994 Plenary Meeting of the NCCB. During the November 1993 Plenary Meeting of the NCCB, a motion was made to defer the consideration of Segment One: Ordinary Time of *The Proposed Revision of the Sacramentary* until after it had been reviewed by the Committee on Doctrine. Following the procedure approved by the NCCB, the chairmen of the Liturgy and Doctrine Committees with the assistance of their staffs reviewed the texts that were indicated in November as being problematic. The Liturgy Committee provided extensive documentation to the Doctrine Committee in response to the questions raised. This documentation was sent to all the bishops in June of this year. The Doctrine Committee concluded that the texts contained no doctrinal errors and that they were superior to the translations in the present edition of the *Sacramentary*. They differed, however, as to the completeness of meaning regarding some terms such as *mereamur*.

According to the procedure approved by the members of the NCCB, Segment One: Ordinary Time will be subject to vote by the bishops during the November 1994 meeting. The "Motions Requesting Further Consideration" submitted for the November 1993 NCCB plenary meeting for Segment I will be voted upon at the November 1994 meeting. Segment II: Proper of Seasons was sent to all bishops in the Spring of this year and bishops have until September 22, 1994 to send in their "Motions Requesting Further Consideration." Segment III: Order of Mass I was sent to all bishops on August 19, 1994. Bishops have until October 31, 1994 to send in their "Motions Requesting Further Consideration."

The Administrative Committee approved placing all three segments on the agenda of the November 1994 Plenary Meeting of the National Conference of Catholic Bishops. The Administrative Committee also approved placing on the agenda for the November 1994 plenary meeting the American adaptations for the Order of Mass for use in the dioceses of the United States of America which have been prepared by the Committee on the Liturgy.

Segment III: Order of Mass I contains all the texts of the Order of Mass and Eucharistic Prayers with the exception of the prefaces, solemn blessings, and prayers over the people. The book is divided into three sections and two appendices: Section 1: Liturgical Texts for the Order of Mass; Section 2: Variations and Pastoral Introduction; Section 3: The Order of Mass (comprehensive layout); Appendix 1: Introductory Documents for the Sacramentary; and Appendix 2: The Apostolic See's Introduction on the Translation of Liturgical Texts.

Approval of all the texts contained in the three segments of the proposed revision of the *Roman Missal (Sacramentary)* requires a two-thirds affirmative vote of the *de iure* Latin rite members of the NCCB and the subsequent confirmation of the NCCB. ICEL has asked that requests for the confirmation of the segments not be made until all the segments constituting the first volume of the *Sacramentary* are approved by an episcopal conference. All the pastoral introductions prepared by ICEL are subject to amendment by the NCCB by a simple majority vote, as are any adaptations that are proposed by ICEL or the Committee on the Liturgy.

Proposed American Adaptations of the Roman Missal

The Task Group on American Adaptation of the Roman Missal was established in light of the forthcoming ICEL revision of the *Sacramentary*. The purpose of the Task Group is to determine what, if any, variations in the English-language *Sacramentary* for the Dioceses of the United States of America should be proposed for the consideration of the Committee on the Liturgy and, eventually, the entire membership of the NCCB. The Task Group, under the chairmanship of Bishop Jerome Hanus, OSB, met in June 1991, August 1992, March 1993, August 1993, and February 1994. The Task Group has carefully studied the results of the questionnaire sent in January 1992 to all the Latin rite bishops of the country as well as to diocesan liturgical commissions/offices of worship and, in light of it, has reviewed all of the American material presently contained in the *Sacramentary*.

The Task Group has completed the following work which has been submitted to the Committee on the Liturgy:

1) The *Proper Calendar for the Dioceses of the United States of America* has been prepared. This calendar integrates the Roman Calendar and the Particular Calendar for the United States into a single calendar.

2) Biographical notes have been prepared for each of the American saints and those who have been given the title "blessed" in the same style used by ICEL. ICEL is proposing that a brief biographical note precede each Mass formulary in the Proper of Saints of the *Sacramentary*. These biographical notes are already found in French, German, and Italian editions of the *Roman Missal*.

3) The *Appendix to the General Instruction of the Roman Missal for the Dioceses of the United States of America* has been revised. Much of the material that followed the statement of each decision by the NCCB has been removed, since it is now given in the pastoral introductions to the various parts of the *Sacramentary*. No. 21 (on the posture of the people) has been revised to indicate that a gesture, i.e., bow, is to be made by the people after each set of the words of institution when kneeling during the eucharistic prayer is

"prevented by the lack of space, number of people present, or some other good reason," as a sign of reverence. Provision has been made for the option of kneeling when the penitential rite is used during the season of Lent. A proposal will be made to provide for the sign of peace at the beginning of the liturgy of the eucharist before the preparation of the gifts and altar. The directives on communion under both kinds have been updated. All of these items will be voted on in November.

4) The *Pastoral Introduction to the Order of Mass* has been reviewed and some additional material has been inserted which reflects the needs of our country.

5) The *Order of Mass* has been examined by the Task Group and a series of proposed changes have been accepted by the Liturgy Committee, which will be proposed to the NCCB: an alternate greeting for use during the season of Easter; the ICEL proposal to divide the introductory rites into a series of individual opening rites, only one of which is to be chosen for each Mass; the people may kneel for the penitential rite during the season of Lent; an alternative to the Gloria is proposed for use during the season of Easter; moving the sign of peace to its ancient position after the general intercessions; the people may extend their hands during the Lord's Prayer. Several minor rubrics have also been highly rephrased.

6) Alternative texts have been provided for the Chrism Mass for use when the renewal of commitment to priestly service takes place on a day other than Holy Thursday. In response to suggestions made by many bishops, a rite of renewal of commitment for bishops, presbyters, and deacons has been provided for use on occasions other than the Chrism Mass.

7) An alternative form for the *Reproaches* has been proposed that is sensitive to concerns about anti-semitism. A version of the *Exsultet* with optional acclamations has been discussed. The Task Group has requested ICEL to provide translations of texts intended for use when the Vigil of Pentecost is celebrated in an extended manner (as at the Easter Vigil).

8) Revised forms for *The Proclamation of the Birth of Christ, The Proclamation of the Date of Easter on Epiphany,* and *The Reception of the Holy Oils Blessed at the Chrism Mass* have been prepared.

The Task Group has formed an editorial subcommittee to revise the propers for the United States in accord with the style of the second edition of the *Sacramentary*. The Task Group hopes to complete its work on these texts in February of 1995.

Clarification Concerning the Holy Oils

The NCCB Secretariat for the Liturgy has received requests for clarification on the practice of diluting the Holy Oils. Many parishes have begun the laudable practice of displaying the oils in larger and more dignified containers. The problem exists where parishes receive only a small amount of each oil blessed by the bishop at the Chrism Mass. To fill the containers some pastors are using unblessed oil, unconsecrated chrism, or oil left over from the preceding year. Concerns have also been raised about the practice of diluting the Chrism, for whatever reason, to such a degree that the validity of the sacrament is affected.

Some of the ambiguity regarding the dilution of the holy oils arises from the practice permitted in the 1917 Code of Canon Law. Canon 734.2 of the 1917 Code stated that when the holy oils are about to give out, other olive oil that has not been blessed may be added, even repeatedly, but always in smaller quantity than the holy oils. Canon 847 of the 1983 Code of Canon Law, by not repeating the provisions of Canon 734.2 of the 1917 Code, suppresses the practice of adding unblessed oil to the blessed oils when the supply runs low. On April 18, 1994 the Congregation for Divine Worship and the Discipline of the Sacraments issued the following response to these questions: 1) Is canon 734.2 of the 1917 Code suppressed?; and 2) If the practice is lawful, what are the conditions when unblessed oil may be added to blessed oil?:

> While canon 734.2 of the 1917 Code of Canon Law is indeed suppressed, the spirit of the law is not suppressed. Therefore, *in case of true necessity only,* a priest may increase the volume of the blessed oils by adding unblessed oil to them. It would be an abuse however, if this practice became routine for the sake of expedience or convenience (Prot. N. 589/94/L).

The Congregation's response clearly permits adding unblessed oil only in cases of true necessity. This would exclude diluting the oils merely in order to fill the oil stocks that will be displayed.

One pastoral response to this situation is to ensure that parishes receive sufficient amounts of oil at the Chrism Mass to meet the liturgical, catechetical, and pastoral needs of their parish. Some dioceses have their parishes send in forms at the beginning of Lent and prior to the Chrism Mass to indicate the amount of each oil they require for use over the coming year. In some places the small vials used to transport the oils to the parish have been replaced with larger containers (e.g., glass jars with screw top lids) which are placed in attractively built carrying cases for transport to the parish. The oils are then placed in appropriate vessels.

Status of Interim Guidelines for Inclusive Language Liturgical Texts

During the November 1992 meeting of the National Conference of Catholic Bishops (NCCB), the bishops questioned whether the NCCB might be able to provide some pastoral remedy for the use of inclusive language in liturgical texts which are not scheduled to be revised for several years (such as texts from the *Liturgy of the Hours*). Following some discussion the NCCB approved the following resolution: "the full body of bishops instruct the Liturgy Committee to give study to the question of incorporating inclusive language into older liturgical texts, and to come back to this body with its findings." This motion was seconded and approved without debate.

The Bishops' Committee on the Liturgy discussed the matter at its March 1993 meeting in Washington, DC, and instructed the Secretariat staff to prepare a draft of "Interim Guidelines for Inclusive Language" for presentation to the Committee at their June 1993 meeting in New Orleans. The Committee first discussed the proposed guidelines in June of 1993. In March of 1994 a revised version of the *Interim Inclusive Language Guidelines* was presented to the members of the Liturgy Committee. The proposed document spelled out quite clearly the parameters of what could be changed in liturgical texts. The Committee discussed at length the following issues: 1) to whom would these guidelines be addressed; 2) the possibility that these would open the door to further changes in inclusive language that would not be acceptable; 3) the concern that the guidelines would be giving formal approval to a new way of adapting liturgical texts; 4) the fact that the NCCB is already working on a formal way of changing these texts; and 5) the fear of giving the perception that people can go ahead and change these texts as they wish.

After much discussion the Committee on the Liturgy decided that it is not in the Conference's best interests at this time to come up with interim guidelines. The Committee ultimately agreed to permanently table the *Interim Inclusive Language Guidelines* and this decision was reported to the Administrative Committee at its September 1994 meeting.

Ecumenical

Anglican/Roman Catholic Dialogue Affirmations on the Eucharist as Sacrifice

On March 11, 1994 Edward Idris Cardinal Cassidy, president of the Pontifical Council for promoting Christian Unity, wrote to the co-chairman of the Anglican/Roman Catholic International Commission (ARCIC) acknowledging the receipt of clarifications recently issued on the various aspects of the ARCIC document on the Eucharist and Ministry. Cardinal Cassidy stated that "the agreement reached on Eucharist and Ministry by ARCIC-I is thus greatly strengthened and no further study would seem to be required at this stage" (Prot. N. 1278/94/e). In the USA the Anglican/Roman Catholic Dialogue has published a statement on the sacrificial nature of the Eucharist. The text of the statement follows.

At the forty-first meeting of the Anglican/Roman Catholic Dialogue of the United States of America (ARC/USA), on January 6, 1994, having in mind the significant agreement on the Eucharist represented by *The Final Report* of the Anglican/Roman Catholic International Commission and responding to the request in the *Vatican Response to the Arcic-I Final Report* for clarification, we wish as the official representatives of our two Churches in the United States to make together the following affirmations:

1. *We Affirm* that in the Eucharist the Church, doing what Christ commanded his apostles to do at the Last Supper, makes present the sacrifice of Calvary. We understand this to mean that when the Church is gathered in worship, it is empowered by the Holy Spirit to make Christ present and to receive all the benefits of his sacrifice.

2. *We Affirm* that God has given the Eucharist to the Church as a means through which all the atoning work of Christ on the Cross is proclaimed and made present with all its effects in the life of the Church. His work includes "that perfect redemption, propitiation, and satisfaction, for all the sins of the whole

world" (Cf. Art. 31 BCP, p. 874). Thus the propitiatory effect of Christ's one sacrifice applies in the Eucharistic celebration to both the living and the dead, including a particular dead person.

3. *We Affirm* that Christ in the Eucharist makes himself present sacramentally and truly when under the species of bread and wine these earthly realities are changed into the reality of his body and blood. In English the terms *substance, substantial* and *substantially* have such physical and material overtones that we, adhering to *The Final Report,* have substituted the word *truly* for the word *substantially* in the clarification requested by the Vatican Response. However, we affirm the reality of the change by consecration as being independent of the subjective disposition of the worshippers.

4. *Both our Churches affirm* that after the Eucharistic celebration the body and blood of Christ may be reserved for the communion of the sick, "or of others who for weighty cause could not be present at the celebration" (BCP, p. 408-409). Although the American Book of Common Prayer directs that any consecrated bread and wine not reserved for this purpose should be consumed at the end of the service, American Episcopalians recognize that many of their own Church members practice the adoration of Christ in the reserved sacrament. We acknowledge this practice as an extension of the worship of Jesus Christ present at the Eucharistic Celebration.

5. *We Affirm* that only a validly ordained priest can be the minister who, in the person of Christ, brings into being the sacrament of the Eucharist and offers sacramentally the redemptive sacrifice of Christ which God offers us.

As the Vatican Response has already recorded the notable progress toward consensus represented by *The Final Report* in respect of Eucharistic doctrine, in the light of these five affirmations ARC/USA records its conclusions that the Eucharist as sacrifice is not an issue that divides our two Churches.

+ Frank T. Griswold, Bishop of Chicago
Episcopal Co-Chair of ARC/USA

+ John J. Snyder, Bishop of Saint Augustine,
Roman Catholic Co-Chair of ARC/USA

Subscribed unanimously by all ARC/USA members
present at the forty-first meeting

January 6-7, 1994
Delray Beach, Florida

Episcopal Roman Catholic Bishop Pilgrimage

The following prayer on the *Ecumenical Formation in Service of the Gospel* is for the November 3-10, 1994 pilgrimage to Rome and Canterbury of the Bishops of the Roman Catholic and Episcopal churches in the United States of America.

ECUMENICAL FORMATION IN SERVICE OF THE GOSPEL

O Lord Jesus Christ,
who prayed that all may be one as you
and the Father are one,
bless and guide this pilgrimage of bishops,
that by prayers, study and witness,
we may promote the visible unity
of Anglicans and Roman Catholics
in your Church on earth as we strive
in the service of your Kingdom.
We ask this through the power
of the Holy Spirit, who with you,
O Christ, and your Father
reigns world without end.

Amen

1995 Week of Prayer for Christian Unity

The 1995 Week of Prayer for Christian Unity will be observed on January 18-25, 1995. Resource materials containing an ecumenical celebration of the word of God, an exegetical reflection on the scriptural theme, daily scripture and prayer guide, homily notes, music suggestions, sample pulpit and bulletin announcements and press release suggestions are available for purchase from: Graymoor Ecumenical & Interreligious Institute, Route 9, P.O. Box 300, Garrison, NY 10524-0300. Telephone: 914-424-3458.

Los Angeles Liturgy Conference

Liturgy Conference '94, a two-day event sponsored by the Los Angeles Archdiocesan Office for Worship, will be held Friday and Saturday, November 11-12, 1994 at the Los Angeles Hilton and Towers, Los Angeles. This annual conference will include nationally known keynote speakers Reverend Anscar Chupungco, OSB and Sister Kathleen Hughes, RSCJ with more than 20 other presenters. Along with the general theme of liturgical enculturation, four specialized tracks will be offered: *music* with Bobby Fisher, David Haas, Chris Walker and Grayson Brown; a *clergy* track featuring Reverend John Baldovin and Reverend Kenneth Martin; *initiation* with Richelle Pearl Koller and Doris Donnelly; and a track on *liturgies for children* with Bob Percy and Joan Patano-Vos. Other well-known speakers include Gabe Huck, Reverend Virgil Funk, David Philippart and Sister Rosa Maria Icaza. Along with a choice of workshops, participants will be able to attend special eucharistic and prayer experiences, music showcases, a Friday night concert featuring Grayson Brown and shop at exhibitors' booths. Participants can also take advantage of the Hilton's special room rates for the convention and come early for the Thursday night Art Festival where 30 plus artisans will have displays and samples of their work appropriate for liturgical spaces. A companion conference in Spanish will be held Saturday, October 22, 1994, at Cantwell Sacred Heart of Mary High School in Montebello. For more information, contact the Office of Worship, 1531 W. Ninth Street, Los Angeles, CA 90015 or call (213) 251-3262.

Resources

Ceremonial of Bishops: A Reader contains the major presentations of the national workshop on the *Ceremonial of Bishops* held from November 30 to December 3, 1989 at Saint Mary's Cathedral in San Francisco, CA. Chapters include: Episcopal Liturgy as a Theological *Locus* for Ecclesiology (Jerome P. Theisen, OSB); An Overview of the *Caeremoniale Episcoporum:* History and General Norms (Piero Marini); The Sacraments: The Paschal Presence of the Bishop (John F. Baldovin, SJ); The Cathedral (Daniel P. Coughlin); The Stational Mass: From Refinements to Renewal (Alan F. Detscher); Offices and Ministries in Episcopal Liturgy (Ronald F. Krisman); The Cathedral Musician (Michael Connolly); and The Church at Prayer: Going Beyond Rubrics to the Heart of the Church's Worship (Frederick R. McManus). It is available in paperback ($9.95, no. 819-3) from: USCC Publishing Services: 1-800-235-USCC.

Journeysongs is Oregon Catholic Press's newest worship program which is a permanent hymnal combined with an annual supplement. It contains over 750 songs and acclamations which include traditional hymnody, contemporary songs, seasonal music, Spanish/bilingual music, spirituals/gospel music, psalmody, music for the rites, and service music. The easy-to-use format also contains the Order of Mass and special rites (RCIA, Reconciliation, Funeral Mass, and Morning and Evening Prayer). The Assembly edition (hardbound, large print, 6 1/2 X 9 3/8) comes with a special packet in the back cover to accommodate annually updated supplements. A Keyboard Accompaniment Edition, Guitar Accompaniment Edition, Solo Instrument Edition, and Annual Supplement Accompaniment Edition are also available. *Journeysongs* does not contain scripture readings or presidential prayers. For more information call: 1-800-LITURGY (548-8749).

The *Companion Missal* is Oregon Catholic Press's newest missal program designed as a companion to *Journeysongs*. It is an annual edition and includes readings and prayers for every Sunday and Holy Day, music for proper responses (Eucharistic acclamations, responsorial psalms, gospel acclamations, etc.), ritual and votive Masses, special rites and prayers, basic selection of traditional hymnody (text only), and an optional music insert. Subscriptions of 50 or more receive free 1 accompaniment book, 2 copies of *Respond and Acclaim* every year, 1 subscription to *Today's Liturgy*, and 2 copies of *Prayers of the Faithful* every year. For more information call: 1-800-LITURGY (548-8749).

Sourcebook for Sundays and Seasons: 1995 is a carefully organized, pastorally practical tool for presiders and all who prepare parish liturgy. There are introductions to the seasons, suggestions for music and the worship environment, prayer texts and challenges for the liturgy team. Each Sunday and feast is dated and comes with a full set of notes; options for every day of the year are noted. The cost of the book is $10.00 (single copy) or $7.50 (2 or more copies). Order from: Liturgy Training Publications, 1800 North Hermitage Avenue, Chicago, IL 60622-1101. Telephone: 1-800-933-1800.

Children's Daily Prayer for the School Year: 1994-1995 is a book of prayer for the classroom designed to be used by the students themselves to lead prayer. It includes Morning Prayer for each school day, as well as Lunchtime and End-of-the-Day Prayers for each month. These reflect the spirit of the Church's seasons and feasts. For each day there is a format for daily prayer in the morning (or at another time), at lunchtime, and at the close of the school day. Some prayers may be reproduced as needed for students, and a special section incorporates prayers and blessings, and the rosary. Simple directions and preparation pages make this resource easy to use by the teacher. The cost of the book is $15.00 (single copy), $13.00 (2-9 copies), or $10 (10 or more copies). Order from: Liturgy Training Publications, 1800 North Hermitage Avenue, Chicago, IL 60622-1101. Telephone: 1-800-933-1800.

Postures of the Assembly during the Eucharist Prayer by Nathan Mitchell and John Leonard is a project of the Notre Dame Center for Pastoral Liturgy. It makes a unique contribution to the debate of the postures assumed by the assembly during the eucharistic prayer. Here is a wealth of historical source material. Use this book to gain an understanding of the historical and theological significance to posture in the Graeco-Roman world; the religious values of standing, kneeling and prostration; posture during ritual meals during the time of Jesus and the early church; and the evolution of posture in the liturgy from the patristic era to the present. Copious endnotes and an index will guide further study. The cost is $11.95. Order from: Liturgy Training Publications, 1800 North Hermitage Avenue, Chicago, IL 60622-1101. Telephone: 1-800-933-1800.

On the Rite of Election by Rita Ferrone is the third in the Forum Essay Series on adult initiation published by Liturgy Training Publications. This book examines the history, shape and theology of the rite with great insight and analysis of the questions. It is available in paperback ($6.00) from: Liturgy Training Publications, 1800 North Hermitage Avenue, Chicago, IL 60622-1101. Telephone: 1-800-933-1800.

Gather: Second Edition contains almost twice as many selections as the original *Gather* and is ideal for the parish that primarily uses contemporary music but wants the best-known traditional hymns. It includes new music by the most widely sung contemporary composers of our day; Hispanic, African-American music; Taize-like chants and other proven selections from various cultures in English and native languages; and 112 settings of the most frequently sung psalms in the Church today. It is available in a hardback edition ($9.75) from: GIA Publications, 7404 S. Mason Avenue, Chicago, IL 60638. Telephone: 1-800-GIA-1358.

No East or West: Discovering the Gifts of Diversity asks what it means for the church in North America to be hospitable. It will help users discover, implement and celebrate the rich feast of cultural diversity in the Christian church. The resource is developed from an ecumenical perspective and it includes articles by Gail Ramshaw, James Notebaart, Blair Gilmer Meeks, Robert Bela Wilhelm and others. It is available in paper back (60 pages, $10.95, 8 1/2 X 11) from: The Liturgical Conference, 8750 Georgia Avenue, Suite 123, Silver Spring, MD 20910. Telephone: 301-495-0885.

COMMITTEE ON THE LITURGY

NEWSLETTER

1994
VOLUME XXX
OCTOBER

Sister Gaupin Resigns as Associate Director

Sister Linda L. Gaupin, CDP, Associate Director of the Secretariat of the Bishops' Committee on the Liturgy for the past three years, resigned her position effective December 1, 1994. Sister Gaupin joined the staff of the Secretariat for the Liturgy on September 3, 1991.

Sister Gaupin, a Sister of Divine Providence from Pittsburgh, Pennsylvania, served as Director of Worship for the Diocese of Wilmington, where she had charge of directing liturgy, music and the implementation of the *Rite of Christian Initiation of Adults* for the diocese. From 1986 to 1991 Sister Gaupin served as an adjunct professor in the Graduate Religion Department of La Salle University, Philadelphia. Previously she served as chairperson of the Religious Studies Department of La Roche College in Pittsburgh and as an instructor in the Department of Religion and Religious Education at The Catholic University of America, Washington, DC.

Sister Gaupin holds a B.A. in Theology and History from La Roche College, an M.A. in Systematic Theology from Loyola University of Chicago, and an M.A. and a Ph.D. from The Catholic University of America. Her doctoral dissertation was entitled "First Eucharist and the Shape of Catechesis in the Twentieth Century since *Quam Singulari.*"

Sister Gaupin will assume her new position in Orlando, Florida on December 1, 1994 as Diocesan Director of Religious Education.

1994 National Meeting of Diocesan Liturgical Commissions

The annual national meeting of diocesan liturgical commissions and offices of worship was held in Saint Louis, MO, from October 7-11, 1994. The national meeting is jointly sponsored by the Federation of Diocesan Liturgical Commissions and the NCCB Committee on the Liturgy.

The general theme of the meeting was "Marriage: A Communion of Life and Love." Major presentations were given by Mister Paul Covino ("The Theology of Marriage"); Reverend Ronald F. Krisman ("The Rite of Marriage"); Sister Barbara Markey, ND, ("Who is Getting Married"); and Reverend Joseph M. Champlin ("The Challenge of Pastoral Adaptation"). Special interest sessions included Marriage as a Process (Markey), Marriage in Church Law (Quinn), Interfaith Marriage, Multicultural Marriage, Music for Weddings (Romeri and Soboleski), Environment and Art (Woeger), and The Diocesan Office/Commission: Mission and Purpose in Today's Church (McLaughin and Fitzgerald).

The delegates approved six position statements (see below) which had been formulated at regional meetings of the delegates during the spring of 1994 and two resolutions of immediate concern drafted in the course of the national meeting.

Resolutions of the 1994 National Meeting of Diocesan Liturgical Commissions

The following position statements were adopted by the delegates to the 1994 National Meeting of Diocesan Liturgical Commissions held in Saint Louis, MO, October 7-11, 1994. The degree of commitment to each statement is indicated in parentheses. The voting scale is graded from +3 (highest degree

3211 FOURTH STREET NE • WASHINGTON, DC 20017

of commitment) to -3 (complete opposition to the statement). A commitment of +1.5 is required for acceptance.

PS 1994 A
Recognition for Liturgical Renewal

It is the position of the delegates to the 1994 National Meeting of Diocesan Liturgical Commissions that the Executive Committee of the Federation of Diocesan Liturgical Commissions establish a means of recognizing significant contributions to furthering liturgical renewal in the United States. Be it further resolved that the Chair of the FDLC Board annually appoint an ad hoc committee to determine a suitable candidate to receive this FDLC recognition. Such recipients shall have made a significant contribution to the liturgical renewal in the United States. (Passed + 1.96)

PS 1994 B
Rites for Engagement, Wedding, Anniversaries, Family Reconciliation, and Renewal

It is the position of the delegates to the 1994 National Meeting of Diocesan Liturgical Commissions that the Board of Directors of the FDLC request that the BCL prepare an American adaptation of the *Order of Celebrating Marriage* which includes, but is not limited to, rites for engagement, wedding, anniversaries, family reconciliation, and renewal of commitment. (Passed + 2.14)

PS 1994 C
Consultation on the Revised Rite of Marriage

It is the position of the delegates to the 1994 National Meeting of Diocesan Liturgical Commissions that in order better to meet the diversity of pastoral needs of the church in the United States, the Federation of Diocesan Liturgical Commissions' Board of Directors, in collaboration with the Bishops' Committee on the Liturgy, coordinate a general consultation process with diocesan liturgical commissions, offices of worship, offices for marriage and family life, local clergy, and the married faithful, conveying the results to the task force established by the Bishops' Committee on the Liturgy to adapt the *editio typica altera* of the *Order of Celebrating Marriage*. (Passed + 2.29)

PS 1994 D
National Leadership for Televised Liturgies

It is the position of the delegates to the 1994 National Meeting of Diocesan Liturgical Commissions that the FDLC Board of Directors request the Bishops' Committee on the Liturgy provide a means for the establishment of liturgical leadership and direction for the televising of the liturgies of the Church, especially the Mass, in accord with number 20 of the *Constitution on the Liturgy*:

> Radio and television broadcasts of the sacred rites must be marked by discretion and dignity under the leadership and direction of a competent person appointed for this purpose by the bishops. This is especially important when the service to be broadcast is the Mass;

and that preparations for and the televising of all liturgical celebrations would be in accord with paragraph 22 of *Eucharisticum Mysterium*:

> the celebration should be marked with such care and dignity that it is a model of celebrating the sacred mysteries according to the laws of the liturgical reform. (Passed + 2.64)

PS 1994 E
Ministries in the *Order of Celebrating Marriage*

It is the position of the delegates to the 1994 National Meeting of Diocesan Liturgical Commissions that the Federation of Diocesan Liturgical Commissions' Board of Directors request the Bishops' Committee on the Liturgy to prepare additional pastoral notes that clearly articulate the role of the bride and groom, the presiding ministers, the assembly and other ministers in the *Order of Celebrating Marriage*. Such notes should include but not be limited to the role of the various ministers in the order of procession and opening rites, posture and position at the exchange of consent, and reception of the nuptial blessing. (Passed + 2.385)

PS 1994 F
Updating the *Guidelines for Multilingual Masses*

It is the position of the delegates to the 1994 National Meeting of Diocesan Liturgical Commissions that the Board of Directors of the Federation of Diocesan Liturgical Commissions refashion the *Guidelines for Multilingual Masses* as Guidelines for Multicultural Liturgical Celebrations, giving greater emphasis to the liturgical year, environment and the visual arts, music, gesture and movement, ministries, and liturgical preparation, including preaching, all of which are elements of the multicultural experience of the church in the United States. (Passed + 2.48)

RIC 1994 G

Approval of Segments I, II, and III of the revised *Sacramentary* as well as approval of the proposed American adaptations for the Order of Mass.

WHEREAS in November, 1993, the National Conference of Catholic Bishops (NCCB) voted to delay the vote on Segment I of the proposed revision of the *Sacramentary* until November, 1994;

WHEREAS the NCCB approved a procedure for the review of the segments by a joint committee composed of the chairmen and staffs of the Committees on Liturgy and Doctrine;

WHEREAS the Doctrine Committee determined that there was no heterodoxy in Segment I of the proposed revision of the *Sacramentary*;

WHEREAS the June 23, 1994 Study Day on Translations of the NCCB discussed the concept of a forum on vernacularization, which has subsequently been used by some to delay the process of approval of the segments of the *Sacramentary*;

WHEREAS the proposed revision of the *Sacramentary* has been done by competent and faithful scholars and in accord with the principles outlined in the 1969 *Instruction on the Translation of Liturgical Tests (Comme le prévoit)*;

The delegates to the 1994 National Meeting of Diocesan Liturgical Commissions are resolved that the approval of Segments I, II, and III of the proposed revised *Sacramentary* as well as the approval of the proposed American adaptations for the Order of Mass is a matter of significant and immediate concern, and they urge the bishops to vote for approval of these texts at the November, 1994 plenary meeting of the NCCB. (Passed + 2.95)

RIC 1994 H
Confirmation of the revised *Lectionary for Mass*

The delegates to the 1994 National Meeting of Diocesan Liturgical Commissions are resolved that the delay of confirmation by the Apostolic See of the *Lectionary for Mass* using the New American Bible with the revised New Testament and Psalter is a matter of significant and immediate concern. Furthermore, because of the value of the new RSV as a translation of the Scriptures based on sound biblical scholarship and approved by the NCCB in 1991 and confirmed by the Apostolic See, they urge its continued liturgical use. (Passed + 2.89)

International

Philippines

At their January and July meetings this year the bishops of the Philippines approved the submission of the following requests to the Vatican Congregation for Divine Worship and the Discipline of the Sacraments for confirmation:

1. The *ad interim* use of the English translation of the Rites of Ordination prepared by the International Commission on English in the Liturgy (ICEL). The translation is based on the second Latin typical edition which was issued in 1989.

2. The *ad interim* use of the English translation of Eucharistic Prayers for Masses for Various Needs and Occasions (formerly "Eucharistic Prayer for Swiss Synod") also prepared by ICEL. The

Latin typical edition was published by the Congregation for Divine Worship and the Discipline of the Sacraments in 1991 for universal use. This eucharistic prayer will be used in one of the Masses during the papal visit in Manila in January 1995.

3. The *ad interim* use of the ICEL translation of the Mass of the Blessed Virgin Mary, Star of the Sea. The Episcopal Commission on Liturgy recommends that the formulary be used for Filipino migrant workers.

4. The inclusion in the Philippine Liturgical Calendar of St. Peter Julian Eymard, known for eucharistic devotion, as optional memorial on August 2, and of St. Ezechiel Moreno, OAR, as optional memorial on August 19. St. Ezechiel worked as a missionary in the Philippines before he was named bishop in Colombia in 1906. Pope John Paul II canonized him in 1992 on the occasion of the fifth centenary of the evangelization of the Americas.

Johannes Hofinger Catechetical Conference

The 17th annual Johannes Hofinger Catechetical Conference will be held January 6-7, 1995, at the Hyatt Regency in New Orleans, Louisiana. The conference is sponsored by the Religious Education Office of the Archdiocese of New Orleans. The theme for the 1995 Hofinger Conference is *Being Catholic in a Changing World*. The Conference goals include: to name and personally claim fears about our changing world; to revitalize our passion for the gospel as it is proclaimed by our Catholic heritage; to deal with life issues in order to open doors of communication among diverse groups;

There will be a keynote address given by Dr. Elinor R. Ford. Dr. Diana L. Hayes, Ph.D., STD, will present a major address on Friday afternoon and Rev. Frank J. McNulty will give a major address on Saturday morning. Over 30 breakout sessions will be presented by a variety of speakers including Marian Davis Fussey, Rev. Russell J. Harrington, Kim Eyler-Duty, Margaret McGuirk, OP, Patricia Martens Miller, Frances Trampiets, SC, Mary McEntee McGill, Rev. Thomas J. Caroluzza, Graziano Marcheschi, Nancy Seitz Marcheschi, Rev. John Kavanaugh, SJ, Ph.D, and Sr. Cora Marie Billings. Breakout session topics include liturgical celebrations for children, conscience formation, ministering to diversity, prayer, value formation for students, the African American faith experience, youth ministry, and nurturing faith. In addition there will be two Professional Track series to be given by Dr. Oralisa Martin and Thomas P. Sweetser, SJ. These special four-part sessions are for persons who wish to explore a particular topic in greater depth.

The 1995 Hofinger Conference will feature a large number of exhibitors from various publishing companies, bookstores, and organizations. For more information and registration forms contact: Conference Services by Loretta Reif, P.O. Box 5084, Rockford, IL 61125. Telephone: 815-399-2150.

Resources

Liturgies of Lament by J. Frank Henderson provides five kinds of liturgy that are powerful responses to tragedy: the Liturgy of the Word, Evening Prayer, a liturgy based on the structure of the lament psalms, penitential services and processions. Also included are models for liturgies lamenting the Holocaust, the bombing of Hiroshima and Nagasaki, violence against creation, and violence against individuals or groups. Lists of scripture, prayers and other texts are included, and an appendix examines the opportunities and challenges of interchurch and interfaith prayer. This book is for parish leaders, liturgy committees, and most especially, for social justice committees and for all those who help people call upon God in their distress and stand ready to be part of God's answer to their prayers. J. Frank Henderson is the editor of the National Bulletin on Liturgy published by the Canadian Conference of Catholic Bishops. The cost is $11.95. Order from: Liturgy Training Publications, 1800 North Hermitage Avenue, Chicago, IL 60622-1101. Telephone: 1-800-933-1800.

COMMITTEE ON THE LITURGY

NEWSLETTER

NATIONAL CONFERENCE OF CATHOLIC BISHOPS

1994
VOLUME XXX
NOVEMBER

Including Saints or the Blessed in Diocesan Calendars

The NCCB Secretariat for the Liturgy has received requests for clarification about a number of issues pertaining to the preparation of particular calendars for a diocese or province. The first of these concerns the procedures for the inclusion of a saint or blessed in a diocesan calendar.

A number of dioceses have received requests from religious communities to place a saint or blessed of their community on the particular calendar of a diocese. In some cases, these requests originate in response to the policy statement *On the Inclusion of Saints and the Blessed in the Proper Calendar for the Dioceses of the United States of America* which was approved by the NCCB on November 18, 1992 as an internal policy statement of its standing Committee on the Liturgy (see *BCL Newsletter*, Vol. XXVIII, December 1992). This statement requires that before a saint or blessed may be considered for inclusion on the national calendar for the United States of America, the following guidelines are to be applied:

1) As a general practice, before being considered for inclusion on the national calendar, saints or the blessed of a religious community must first be included on diocesan calendars for a significant period of time (usually 5 to 10 years) in order to insure that they have a genuine *cultus* in the United States;

2) The *cultus* of the saint or blessed must exist in a significant number of dioceses throughout the country before the saint or blessed may be proposed for inclusion on the national calendar. This *cultus* must be broader than in a particular area or region of the country in order to demonstrate that the saint or blessed is of significance to the entire country;

3) Normally the saint or blessed must have served in the United States of America;

4) Such commemorations of saints or the blessed will ordinarily be given the rank of optional memorial.

Requests to place a saint or blessed on a diocesan calendar are to be submitted to the local ordinary of the diocese. In the case of diocesan calendars, the inclusion of a saint or blessed requires the approval of the local ordinary. If the local ordinary approves this request, it **must then be submitted to the Congregation for Divine Worship and the Discipline of the Sacraments for confirmation**.

Requests for clarification have also been received for guidelines that enable dioceses to determine which saints or blessed belong on a diocesan calendar. The policy statement *On the Inclusion of Saints and the Blessed in the Proper Calendar for the Dioceses of the United States of America* states the following:

In order to determine which saints or blessed belong on the particular calendar of a nation or region, or on diocesan or religious calendars, some general norms are to be observed:

1) Care must be taken not to overload the national calendar or that of a diocese or religious institute (see GNLYC 53).

2) Saints and the blessed should be included on a particular calendar only if they have particular significance for the entire nation, diocese, or religious family (see GNLYC 53b).

3) Other saints and blessed are to be celebrated only in those places with which they have closer ties (see GNLYC 53c).

FDLC Address of Bishop Donald W. Trautman, S.T.D., S.S.L.

On October 7, 1994 the Most Reverend Donald W. Trautman, Bishop of Erie and Chairman of the Bishops' Committee on the Liturgy, addressed the delegates to the 1994 National Meeting of Diocesan Liturgical Commissions in Saint Louise, MO. The text of that address follows.

Friends and co-workers of the Lord:

3211 FOURTH STREET NE • WASHINGTON, DC 20017

I would like to preface my report with a word of gratitude to all of you who are engaged in the liturgical ministry of the Church. With God's grace, you make good liturgy happen. I think of Diocesan Liturgical Commissions and Offices of Worship and Church musicians and parish liturgical coordinators and liturgists in classrooms, religious and priests — liturgists at every level. In the name of the bishops and in the name of all God's people, I want to affirm you and thank you for your work and witness in furthering the liturgical movement of the Second Vatican Council.

You have promoted the liturgical reforms of Vatican II against great odds. You have struggled to produce full, conscious, active participation by all the people in a culture that scorns community celebration — in a culture that promotes individualism, a Lone Ranger mentality — in a culture indifferent to transcendence and mystery — in a culture that seeks entertainment models of participation, with the assembly as audience and ministers as performers. Against this backdrop, you have taken the renewal and reforms of Vatican II to the people and with great success. However, you know from you experience, that liturgical renewal is far from complete and still wanting in many parishes.

Despite all the ritual reform of the past thirty years, we are still missing at times the spiritual renewal — the transformation of attitudes — the deeper understanding of the sacred mysteries intended by those ritual reforms.

In the September 10th edition of *America*, Father Lawrence Madden argues for a new liturgical movement — a second liturgical movement. He calls for a grassroots infusion of energy and commitment to make good liturgy happen. The Church needs this desperately.

What has the Bishop's Committee on the Liturgy done this year to help bring this about? During the past year I've had the opportunity to visit many of your regional FDLC meetings and I've come to know firsthand your successes and challenges; I've come to know the grounds for hope as well as your problems and frustrations and concerns. There is a need for solidarity among liturgists when it comes to responding to those voices in the Church that would repeal the liturgical momentum of Vatican II. With charity and patience, we must give better instruction. We must dialogue with those blinded to liturgical renewal. We must become more pro-active, writing articles on liturgical reforms for our diocesan newspapers. We must teach, teach, teach, so that we can persuade all to understand that when a faith community celebrates liturgy well, transformation can take place. That parish becomes a powerful sacrament of Christ, a leaven in our midst.

I thank Fr. Jim Moroney and Fr. Mickey Spillane for their work on the Bishops' Committee on the Liturgy. I personally appreciate their support and cooperation. They have represented the FDLC in an outstanding way.

The last twelve months have seen many changes in the Committee on the Liturgy: I succeeded Bishop Wilton D. Gregory as the chairman of the Committee on the Liturgy after the November meeting of the NCCB; Father Ronald F. Krisman returned at the end of December to the Diocese of Lubbock where he now serves as the moderator of the curia; shortly after Easter, Monsignor Alan F. Detscher was appointed as the Executive Director of the Liturgy Secretariat. With a sense of sorrow, I must announce that Sister Linda L. Gaupin has accepted an appointment as the Diocesan Director of Religious Education for the Diocese of Orlando effective at the end of November. Sister Linda has been a great asset to the Liturgy Secretariat and will be greatly missed by Msgr. Detscher and myself. I thank Sister Linda on behalf of the Committee on the Liturgy and the members of the NCCB for her dedication, expertise, and penetrating insights which often challenged us. On a personal note, I commend and thank Msgr. Detscher and Sister Linda for their cooperation, help, and support to me. I speak with them almost every day and some days several times. The volume of the BCL work has been intense and overwhelming with all the ICEL translations plus the regular responsibilities.

The departure of Sister Linda means that there are two staff positions for associate director open to the Secretariat. Efforts are being made at the present time to fill these positions. As you might suspect, it is difficult to find persons with necessary qualifications and the willingness to work in the Secretariat in Washington. Msgr. Detscher and I would be happy to receive the names of individuals you might feel are qualified and willing to serve in the Secretariat. This is a critical time for liturgy in the United States. The BCL is keenly aware of this and we are trying to give liturgical leadership in sensitive circumstances.

During the past year liturgy has been a topic of much public discussion and debate. At the center of it all has been the proposed ICEL revision of the *Roman Missal (Sacramentary)*. ICEL has spent over ten years in revising the English translation of the prayers of the Missal and in providing original prayers, pastoral introductions, and other materials. When the first segment of the proposed revision was presented to the bishops last November several constituencies emerged which voiced opposition. Consideration of the texts was delayed. A procedure was approved by the NCCB for the consideration of the various segments of the *Sacramentary* which involves the review of the text by the chairmen of the Liturgy and Doctrine Committees and their staffs and when agreed upon, the referral of the problematic texts to the Doctrine Committee. The Doctrine Committee has not found any doctrinal error in the texts they have examined so far, although some members of that committee and others are concerned that some terms are not translated to their satisfaction. Some would say that the full Latin meaning is not conveyed by the English translation. The BCL in cooperation with ICEL prepared a booklet responding to these concerns. I am flying tomorrow to a Doctrine Committee meeting on the topic of the liturgy and will be rejoining you on Sunday evening.

In June a study day on translation was held at the end of the NCCB assembly in San Diego. I chaired the Committee that planned this special day. Our keynoter, Mr. Dennis McManus, gave a scholarly, balanced, and provocative presentation. Our panel of liturgical experts helped focus the issues. The study day did much to clear the air and bring proper perspective. Bishops' concerns were clarified and the complexity of translating was better understood.

At the heart of the controversy is an attempt to reinterpret the principles of translation contained in a 1969 Roman document, entitled: *Comme le prévoit*, dealing with the principles of translation. Some individuals and groups are pressing for a revision of this document in the direction of a more literal style of translation. I believe the majority of bishops do not find the proposed ICEL translations radical, but rather very similar to those of the French, Italian, German, and Spanish.

"This is a critical time for liturgical language, it is a time of transition, of new challenges and new opportunities. It is a time for reflection, serious study, analysis, critique, prayer and debate. It is a time to cherish the best language of our long tradition, experiment with new approaches to liturgical language and look ahead to the needs of the 21st century" (National Bulletin on Liturgy, Summer 1994).

There are several languages of liturgy: musical languages, non-verbal languages including symbol and space, art and environment ministry. There are verbal languages including the Sacred Scriptures, preaching, liturgical texts and there is the language of silence. In all of this there must be noble simplicity. All of these languages must be within the people's power of comprehension and faithful to our own Catholic tradition.

Addressing women using male language denies women their own identity. When women are not named specifically, they're excluded from full participation. This diminishes Church. It is a problem for the whole Church, for men and women alike. The BCL is grateful to the signers of We Believe statements which urge continuing liturgical renewal and inclusive language. The statements give encouragement to all liturgists.

In November, Segments I, II and III will go before the body of Bishops for a vote. I would hope that many of you would be able to advise your bishops on these texts and help them to see the merits of the proposed liturgical translations.

The BCL has completed the preparation of a series of adaptations of the *Sacramentary* for the USA and these will be considered by the bishops in November. Please study the document that has been sent to your bishop and help him understand the rationale for the proposals.

The bishops will also be asked to approve the "Eucharistic Prayer for Various Needs and Occasions." This is a revision of the so-called "Swiss Synod" eucharistic prayer, and although it cannot be used with prefaces of the Missal, it does provide four thematic prayers that can be used on a variety of special occasions. It is intended for only weekdays. You can provide a valuable service to your bishop by carefully going over all the liturgical documentation for the November meeting with him.

The *Lectionary for Mass* is still under review by the Congregation for Divine Worship and the Discipline of the Sacraments. You should not be surprised to learn that the difficulties encountered with the approval of the English translation of the Catechism have had their effect on the NAB Lectionary. The biblical scholars who were involved in the preparation of the Lectionary are in the process of responding to the concerns that have been raised. The longer the confirmation is delayed the greater difficulty we will have in preventing people from changing biblical texts on the basis of their own personal likes and dislikes. I fear that great havoc is being done to the inspired word by people not trained in Scripture. The NCCB a few years ago put out *Criteria for the Evaluation of Inclusive*

Language Translations of Scriptural Texts proposed for Liturgical Use. I served on that committee which drafted these norms. The Bishops' Committee on the Liturgy and the Doctrine Committee cooperated in writing these norms. In accord with this document the BCL has responded to concerns relative to inclusive language.

Later this month the Liturgy Committee will complete the examination of the ICEL translation of the Ordination rites and the American adaptations to them. They will probably not go to the bishops until June. The Committee will also discuss the concerns that have been raised about perpetual exposition of the Blessed Sacrament in parishes, a practice about which many of you have expressed serious pastoral concerns. There is confusion between perpetual adoration and perpetual exposition. Are liturgical directives being followed in this regard?

The past year has continued to see the closing of worship offices, but there may be signs of hope, since some dioceses that have previously closed offices are in the process of re-establishing them.

And hope brings me to my final point. In spite of all the negative things we have experienced this past year, there still is hope. Liturgical reform and renewal have been well established. Those who wish to turn back the clock are few, but vocal. There may be some setbacks but there can never be an undoing of the work of the Second Vatican Council. Many who reject the liturgical reforms, do so because of our past failure to provide an adequate catechesis. A renewed catechesis on the nature of the liturgy is essential for producing hope.

Liturgists can lose hope. Liturgists can become tired from the infighting and tensions of your ministry. You can become bruised and battered and broken. There will be suffering and scars from your service. There will be the pain of rejection, the pain of being misunderstood, the pain of being criticized, the pain of frustration, the pain of discouragement. If we incur these crosses for the Gospel, if we lift them up to the Lord, we shall share in the triumph of Christ who had the last word — and it was a word of Alleluia — a word of victory — a word of resurrection and new life.

Christian hope is not putting on rose-colored glasses and pretending things will get better. Christian hope refuses us melancholy. Christian hope is realistic and built on the certainty of Jesus' resurrection. What is hope? Christian hope is the courage to be in the circumstances where you find yourself. Christian hope is the art of perseverance.

Listen to the words of Pope John Paul: "Do not fear to take up your role in the Church. It has need of you. You are the Church. Place your talents at its service and help to create vibrant Communities." Let us do this with hearts full of hope and courage.

In Memoriam: Father Heinrich Rennings

Father Heinrich Rennings, Executive Secretary of the Liturgiekommission der Deutschen Bischofskonferenz, died on October 3, 1994 in Lampaden, Germany. Father Rennings was born on July 9, 1926 in Moers and was ordained a priest on December 17, 1955. He had doctorates in Philosophy and Theology and was a prominent international figure in the field of liturgy. He served as the Director of the German Liturgical Institute; honorary professor of the Theological Faculty at the University of Trier; Business Director of the Standing Commission for the publication of common German language liturgical books; and Secretary of the Internationalen Arbeitsgemeinschaft der Liturgischen Kommissionen im deutschen Sprachgebiet (IAG). Most recently Father Rennings graciously accepted the invitation to come to the United States and participate on the panel for the Study Day on Liturgical Translations for the National Conference of Catholic Bishops.

DURCH CHRISTUS
UND MIT IHM UND IN IHM
IST DIR, GOTT, ALLMÄCHTIGER VATER,
IN DER EINHEIT DES HEILIGEN GEISTES
ALLE HERRLICHKEIT UND EHRE
JETZT UND IN EWIGKEIT.
AMEN

NATIONAL CONFERENCE OF CATHOLIC BISHOPS

COMMITTEE ON THE LITURGY

NEWSLETTER

1994
VOLUME XXX
DECEMBER

Altar Servers

The text of the response to the question presented to the Pontifical Council for the Interpretation of Legislative Texts regarding the interpretation of canon 230 § 2 of the Code of Canon Law *was recently published in the* Acta Apostolica Sedis *(vol. 86, pages 541-542). The response mentions the "instructions given by the Apostolic See," a reference to the circular letter sent to presidents of Conferences of Bishops by Cardinal Antonio Maria Javierre Ortas, Prefect of the Congregation for Divine Worship and the Discipline of the Sacraments, dated March 15, 1994. Cardinal Javierre's letter was printed in the April 1994 issue of the* Newsletter *(volume XXX, pages 13-14). The following is an unofficial translation of the response.*

The Fathers of the Pontifical Council for the Interpretation of Legislative Texts, gave the following response at a regular meeting on June 30, 1992 to the question indicated below:

Question: Whether among the liturgical offices which laity, male or female, are able to carry out according to the *Code of Canon Law*, canon 230 § 2, may be included also service at the altar.

Response: Affirmative, according to the instructions given by the Apostolic See.

The Supreme Pontiff, John Paul II, in an audience on July 11, 1992 with those indicated below, was informed of the above decision, confirmed it, and ordered it to be promulgated.

+ Vincenzo Fagiolo
Archbishop Emeritus of Chieti-Vasto
President

+ Julian Herranz Casado
Titular Bishop of Vertarensis
Secretary

October and November Meetings of the BCL

The bishop members and consultants of the Committee on the Liturgy met in Washington, D.C. on October 22-23, 1994. Bishop Trautman informed the Committee that Sister Linda Gaupin had submitted her resignation as Associate Director of the Secretariat for the Liturgy and that she would be leaving the office after the November meeting of the NCCB. He expressed the thanks of the Liturgy Committee to her for her fine work on behalf of the Committee over the past three years. Bishop Trautman then reported that the Administrative Committee of the NCCB agreed in September to place the first three segments of the *Sacramentary*, the adaptations of the Order of Mass for the dioceses of the United States, and the *Eucharistic Prayer for Masses for Various Needs and Occasions* on the agenda of the November NCCB meeting. He noted in his report to the Committee that two dioceses in the United States had received indults to allow the presence of cremated human remains in the church during the funeral Mass. He explained that the Committee was still working on guidelines for cremation and other burial practices and expressed the hope that individual dioceses would wait until these are completed before taking any action.

3211 FOURTH STREET NE • WASHINGTON, DC 20017

The Liturgy Committee discussed the status of the *Lectionary for Mass*, the *New Revised Standard Version* of the Bible, and the *Revised Psalms of the New American Bible*. Bishop Trautman explained that efforts are being made to resolve these issues with the Congregation for Divine Worship and the Discipline of the Sacraments and the Congregation for the Doctrine of the Faith in Rome.

The Committee discussed concerns that have been raised by the Federation of Diocesan Liturgical Commissions and individual bishops over the practice of Perpetual Exposition of the Blessed Sacrament. The Committee decided to bring some of the matters discussed to the attention of the Congregation for Divine Worship through Cardinal Keeler when he visits the Congregation in November. A request was received from a bishop that the Liturgy Committee re-evaluate and, if necessary, revise *Environment and Art in Catholic Worship*. The legal status of this document has been frequently questioned and clarifications are apparently necessary. The Committee agreed to review *Environment and Art in Catholic Worship* as a part of its future Plans and Programs. The Committee also discussed the National Plan for the *Rite of Christian Initiation of Adults* (RCIA) that was approved at the same time as the RCIA. The National Plan called for several studies to evaluate the implementation of the rite and also the American adaptations of the RCIA. Major funding is required to carry out the proposed evaluation and such funding is not presently available to the Committee. The possibility of a grant to fund the study will be investigated.

The Federation of Diocesan Liturgical Commissions (FDLC) has expressed its concern over the closing of diocesan offices for worship and the disbanding of diocesan liturgical commissions. The Committee agreed that this was a serious concern and recognized that in some cases the closing of offices has been dictated by lack of proper funding. An *ad hoc* group was established to prepare a position paper on the issues involved for the Committee. The Committee also discussed a second motion approved by the FDLC regarding the availability of Spanish translations of liturgical resources. The Committee acknowledged the concerns of the FDLC, but noted that the Hispanic Liturgy Subcommittee is attempting to make the necessary Spanish liturgical texts available as soon as it is able. The Spanish translation of the *Order of Christian Funerals* is awaiting confirmation by the Congregation for Divine Worship. The Hispanic Liturgy Subcommittee is still working on a Spanish edition of the missal for the USA. The Hispanic Liturgy Subcommittee is nearing completion of a Spanish translation of the blessings proper to the United States contained in the *Book of Blessings*.

The remainder of the meeting was devoted to an examination of the "motions for further consideration" that had been received on the first three segments of the proposed ICEL revision of the *Sacramentary*, as well as the amendments that had been submitted on the American adaptations of the Order of Mass.

The bishop members and consultants of the Committee on the Liturgy met again in Washington, D.C. on November 13, 1994. The Committee received an additional request for the review of *Environment and Art in Catholic Worship*. Because it had already agreed in October to re-examine the document, the Committee agreed to notify the bishops who had made the request that a review of *Environment and Art in Catholic Worship* would be done. The remainder of the meeting was spent in reviewing the action items of the Liturgy Committee that would be on the agenda of the November NCCB meeting and formulating responses to the motions and amendments that had been received. The next meeting of the Committee on the Liturgy will take place on March 13, 1995 in Washington, D.C.

November Meeting of the NCCB

The Plenary Meeting of the National Conference of Catholic Bishops took place in Washington, DC, from November 13-16, 1994. A large portion of the meeting was dedicated to discussion and voting upon several liturgical items.

The members of the NCCB voted to request approval from the Congregation for Divine Worship and the Discipline of the Sacraments of the liturgical use of the *Eucharistic Prayer for Masses for Various Needs and Occasions*. The bishops also approved the English translation of this prayer prepared by the International Commission on English in the Liturgy.

The major action taken by the NCCB was the approval of Segments One and Two of the proposed ICEL revision of the *Sacramentary*. Approval of each segment required a two-thirds affirmative vote of the all the *de iure* Latin rite bishops, that is, at least 175 bishops. Segment One was approved by a vote of 224 affirmative votes and 14 negative votes. Segment Two was approved by 185 affirmative votes and 17 negative votes. The bishops asked ICEL to give further consideration to 23 prayers in Segment One and 33 prayers in Segment Two. These prayers were sent back to ICEL, not because they lack orthodox doctrine, but so that particular words or phrases might be revised. These texts will ultimately have to come back to the bishops for approval after all the conferences of bishops have voted on all the segments of volume one of the *Sacramentary*. The strong positive vote to approve the first two segments is a positive sign that the bishops approve the work of ICEL and that the process for the approval of the *Sacramentary* that was established by the NCCB in November of 1993 is working.

The Pastoral Introductions to Ordinary Time in Segment One and the Pastoral Introductions to the other seasons, as contained in Segment Two, were also approved by the required two-thirds majority vote. Because the Committee on Doctrine was unable to review Segment Three: Order of Mass I, the voting on the third segment and the corresponding American adaptations was delayed until the June meeting of the NCCB. Two additional segments will be sent to the bishops in the first half of 1995: Segment Four: Prefaces, Solemn Blessings, and Prayers over the People; Segment Five: Easter Triduum and Appendixes. It is hoped that the bishops will be able to vote on these remaining segments of volume one of the *Sacramentary* by the end of 1995.

Eucharistic Prayer for Masses for Various Needs and Occasions

As indicated above, this new eucharistic prayer was approved the members of the NCCB for use in the United States as was its provisional (interim) English translation. This eucharistic prayer was originally prepared on the occasion of the Swiss Synod (1972-1975) and approved by Sacred Congregation for Divine Worship in August of 1974. The prayer was composed in German and then translated into French and Italian, since these are the languages used in Switzerland. By 1987 the prayer had been translated into twelve languages and was in use throughout the world. The Swiss Synod Eucharistic Prayer was included in the common Spanish translation of the Order of Mass and the Eucharistic Prayers (*Ordinario del la Misa*) which was published in this country in 1989. However, the prayer was not available for use in English in the United States.

In 1991, the Congregation for Divine Worship and the Discipline of the Sacraments published a revised Latin version the Swiss Synod eucharistic prayer under the title: *Eucharistic Prayer for Masses for Various Needs and Occasions*. The Congregation noted that, "Since from the very beginning different editions of the text of this eucharistic prayer have been available in German, French, and Italian, it seems necessary to issue a Latin text of this prayer to serve as the *editio typica* for all languages." The Congregation also indicated that previously approved versions of this prayer must conform to the new typical edition when new editions of the *Roman Missal* are published.

The new eucharistic prayer has corresponding sets of prefaces and intercessions based on four themes: "The Church on the Way to Unity," "God Guides the Church on the Way of Salvation," "Jesus, Way to the Father," and "Jesus, the Compassion of God." Although printed as one eucharistic prayer, the new eucharistic prayer is, in reality, four different prayers, each with its own theme. As its title indicates, the prayer is intended for use at Masses for various needs and occasions. Because the prefaces are integral to the prayer, the prayer may not be used with the variable prefaces of the *Sacramentary* or on occasions when there is a proper preface. The introductory notes printed with the eucharistic prayer indicate which theme is appropriate to each of the Masses for various needs and occasions contained in the *Sacramentary*.

The *Eucharistic Prayer for Masses for Various Needs and Occasions* was approved by the NCCB at its November 1994 Plenary Meeting and the Congregation for Divine Worship and the Discipline of the Sacraments has been asked to confirm the decision of the NCCB. Once the requisite confirmation has been received, Cardinal William Keeler, President of the NCCB, will establish the effective date for the use of this new eucharistic prayer.

Appointment of New Advisors

Bishop Donald W. Trautman has appointed the Reverend Dr. Michael Walsh as an advisor to the Committee on the Liturgy. Father Walsh, a priest of the Diocese of Brooklyn, did his seminary studies at the Canisianum in Innsbruck, Austria. After ordination to the priesthood in 1970 he studied spirituality at the Pontifical Gregorian University in Rome and was awarded a doctorate in sacred theology. His dissertation was on the heart of Christ in the writings of Karl Rahner. Father Walsh served as the Associate Director the Secretariat for Doctrine and Pastoral Practices from 1988 to 1989 and as its Executive Director from 1989 to 1992 and as a result is familiar with the work of the Committee on the Liturgy and its Secretariat. He is presently the pastor of Saint Stanislaus Kostka Church in Maspeth, NY.

Bishop Trautman has also appointed Father Raúl Gómez, SDS as an *ex officio* advisor to the Committee on the Liturgy. Father Gómez succeeds Sister Rosa Maria Icaza as the president of the Instituto de Liturgia Hispana. Father Gómez is a member of the Society of the Divine Savior (Salvatorian Fathers) and is presently engaged in liturgical studies at the Catholic University of America.

North American Summit on the Future of Christian Worship

The first North American Summit on the Future of Christian Worship was held from December 9-11, 1994 in Nashville, TN. The purpose of the Summit was to act as a place of conversation between the various traditions of worship. Over one hundred and twenty individuals represented thirty-eight different denominations. A large number of the participants came from the Free Church and Evangelical traditions. This first Summit addressed the issue of the relationship between worship and evangelism. Dr. James White of Notre Dame gave an historical overview of evangelism in the United States with a special emphasis on camp meetings and revivals. Dr. Gilbert Bilezikian spoke of the new evangelical "seeker" church movement. He described the reasons behind the establishment of churches which have as their primary service on Sunday one which focuses on the unchurched. These "seeker" services include music, drama, and preaching which may not be overtly Christian, but which is intended to draw people into a relationship with believers and lead them to making a Christian commitment. Monsignor Alan Detscher presented the renewal of the catechumenate in the Roman Catholic Church and the *Rite of Christian Initiation of Adults*. A "seeker" service was celebrated as was the Rite of Acceptance into the Order of Catechumens. Small groups reflected on the presentations and the services that were celebrated. The Summit sought to take the work of scholars and build bridges of understanding and practice to the local churches. It was evident that those of the Free Church tradition are interested in worship and many were especially interested in the RCIA and how it could be adapted to the needs of their communities.

NATIONAL CONFERENCE OF CATHOLIC BISHOPS

COMMITTEE ON THE LITURGY

NEWSLETTER

1995
VOLUME XXXI
JANUARY / FEBRUARY

Time for the Celebration of the Easter Vigil

Over the past several years the Liturgy Secretariat has provided information about the time of sunset on the evening of Holy Saturday in order that the time for the celebration of the Easter Vigil may be properly planned. There is no provision on Holy Saturday for the usual Sunday vigil Mass that ordinarily takes place late on Saturday afternoon. According to the *Sacramentary*, "the entire celebration of the Easter Vigil takes place at *night*. It should not begin before nightfall; it should end before daybreak on Sunday."

The Congregation for Divine Worship, in the *Circular Letter Concerning the Preparation and Celebration of the Easter Feasts* (January 16, 1988) expressed its concern that in some places the Easter Vigil "is celebrated as if it were an evening Mass, in the same way and at the same time as the Mass celebrated on Saturday evening in anticipation of Sunday." The *Circular Letter* goes on to quote the rubric from the *Sacramentary* as given above, and states that, "This rule is to be taken according to its strictest sense. Reprehensible are those abuses and practices that have crept into many places in violation of this ruling, whereby the Easter Vigil is celebrated at the time of day that is customary to celebrate anticipated Sunday Masses."

The liturgies of the Easter Triduum reflect some of the most ancient practices of the Church. It is important that parishes be given adequate instruction on the nature of these services and why they take place at times different from the usual Sunday liturgies. Appropriate material for catechesis is provided in the Congregation for Divine Worship's *Circular Letter Concerning the Preparation and Celebration of the Easter Feasts* (Publication No. 219-5, Office of Publishing and Promotion Services, United States Catholic Conference, Telephone: 1-800-235-8722).

The celebration of the Easter Vigil will take place this year on Saturday, April 15, 1995. Sunset will occur on this day in Washington, D.C. at 6:45 p.m. EST. Total darkness will follow 45 minutes to one hour after sunset. Accordingly, the Easter Vigil should not begin, at the earliest, before 7:30 p.m. To find the time of sunset in different regions of the country, the National Weather Service should be contacted.

Christmas 1995

Questions have been received regarding whether Christmas is to be observed as a holy day of obligation in 1995, since it occurs on a Monday. The members of the National Conference of Catholic Bishops decided at their November 1991 plenary meeting that whenever January 1, the solemnity of Mary, Mother of God, or August 15, the solemnity of the Assumption, or November 1, the solemnity of All Saints, falls on a Saturday or a Monday, the precept to attend Mass is abrogated. This decision was confirmed by the Congregation for Bishops on July 4, 1992 (Prot. N. 296/84). The decree of the Congregation of Bishops was published in the *Newsletter* (Vol. XXVII, December 1992). Because Christmas is not one of the solemnities of precept that are included in the bishops' decision, it remains a day of precept whether or not it occurs on a Saturday or a Monday.

3211 FOURTH STREET NE • WASHINGTON, DC 20017

New Associate Director for Liturgy Secretariat

Sister Ann F. Rehrauer, O.S.F., a member of the Sisters of Saint Francis of the Holy Cross has accepted an appointment as an Associate Director of the Liturgy Secretariat. Sister Rehrauer received an M.A. in liturgical studies from Saint John's University in Collegeville, MN in 1982 and a J.C.L. degree from The Catholic University of America in 1985. She is presently Chancellor of the Diocese of Green Bay and a judge on the diocesan Marriage Tribunal. Sister Rehrauer has served on the Board of Governors of the Canon Law Society of America and has been a member of the Society's Committee on Convention Liturgies. Due to her expertise in liturgical and sacramental law she has given workshops on liturgical law for the National Association of Pastoral Musicians and the Canon Law Society of America. She has served on the Green Bay Diocesan Liturgical Commission and on worship committees in parishes and of her own religious community. The Committee on the Liturgy is pleased to welcome Sister Rehrauer as the new Associate Director of the Liturgy Secretariat. Sister Rehrauer will begin her term of service in July. A search is still being conducted for a priest who will also serve as an Associate Director of the Liturgy Secretariat.

Proposed Revision of the Sacramentary

The members of the National Conference of Catholic Bishops will be considering *Segment III: Order of Mass I* of the proposed International Commission on English in the Liturgy (ICEL) revision of the *Sacramentary* at their June meeting in Chicago. This segment is divided into three sections: Section 1: Liturgical Texts for the Order of Mass; Section II: Variations and Pastoral Introduction; Section 3: The Order of Mass (Comprehensive Layout).

Contents of Section 1: Three sets of texts are provided in this section. Each set is preceded by a general introduction or, as in the case of the eucharistic prayers, specific introductions that explain the approach to the translation. A number of texts are also provided with brief notes. The first set of texts contains the texts for the Order of Mass, the second set, the eucharistic prayers, and the third set, the ecumenical texts prepared by the English Language Liturgical Consultation (ELLC), the successor group to the International Consultation on English Texts (ICET) which produced the ecumenical translations now in use. The liturgical texts in Section 1 are given as individual texts outside their normal context of the Order of Mass. In order that these texts may be seen in relationship to one another, the complete Order of Mass, properly formatted and rubricated, is provided in Section 3.

The four principal guidelines which guided the revision of the Order of Mass texts were:

1. Ritual responses and other short prayers memorized by the people should be left unchanged if possible. Revisions required for serious reasons should be made in such a way that they do not create undue pastoral problems for the assembly.
2. Short texts which are publicly proclaimed by the priest or other liturgical ministers and which invite a congregational response (for example, greetings and invitations) should not be changed unless the current translation is inaccurate.
3. Longer occasional prayers (for example, the blessing of water), which are often not memorized, may be more readily changed for style and accuracy of translation.
4. Inaudible prayers of the priest should be examined for difficulties and may be changed.

Eucharistic Prayers I-IV have been carefully revised. Because these prayers were issued before the publication of the whole *Roman Missal* there was more time devoted to their study and the preparation of their translation. One consequence of this is that they have worn well with use and have generally been favorably received over the past two decades. The revised translations have changed only that which was necessary for greater fidelity to the Latin text or for the sake of proclamation. The Eucharistic Prayers for Masses of Reconciliation and for Masses with Children have not been used as frequently as the four Roman Eucharistic Prayers and were originally issued only in a provisional form. Hence, these prayers have been subject to greater revisions than the four Roman prayers. The prayers for Masses with Children were given over to a special team of revisers more expert in dealing with children and more knowledgeable about the effectiveness of the language of the texts for children. This is in keeping with no. 10 of the Roman introduction to these prayers which says:

> It is strongly recommended that this work of translation be given to a group of men and women with competencies not only in the area of liturgy, but also of pedagogy, catechetics, language, and music.

The introduction to the Eucharistic Prayers for Masses with Children, no. 11, also indicates that:

> The committee of translators should always remember that in this case the Latin text is not intended for liturgical use. Therefore, it is not to be merely translated.

Accordingly, although the Latin text determines the purpose, substance, and general form of these prayers, "the style of the vernacular text is in every aspect to be adapted to the spirit of the respective language as well as to the manner of speaking with children in each language concerning matters of great importance."

The translation of several of the texts in the Order of Mass approved for use in the English-speaking conferences of bishops were prepared by the International Consultation on English Texts (ICET), founded in 1969 to provide ecumenically acceptable translations of the liturgical texts used in common by the Churches. ICEL participated in this consultation as the representative of the English-speaking Roman Catholic Churches. The ICET texts went through several editions from 1970 through 1975 and were published under the title *Prayers We Have in Common*. Although we are using the first version of these prayers, other conferences of bishops are using the 1975 version of these texts. These ecumenical texts have been in use for twenty years. In 1985 the English Language Liturgical Consultation (ELLC) was formed as the successor body to ICET. ELLC represents a total of forty Churches throughout the English-speaking world, and once again ICEL represented the Roman Catholic Churches on this body. After a decade of use it became clear that the original ICET texts needed to be revised. The texts were revised and published in 1990 under the title *Praying Together*. As with the texts published in *Prayers We Have in Common*, the texts in *Praying Together* have extensive notes which are repeated in Segment III. Four principles guided the revision of these ecumenical texts:

1. In order to avoid pastoral disruption, only necessary changes should be made.
2. Sensitivity should be shown to the need for inclusive language.
3. The revision should be made bearing in mind that these texts are for use in the liturgical assembly. The ease with which they can be said, heard, and sung is an essential element of the revision.
4. The revision should use language that is contemporary and suited to the present version of the ICET texts.

In addition to the translated liturgical texts of the Order of Mass, at the request of a number of episcopal conferences, ICEL has also provided a number of original texts to supplement those of the Order of Mass:
1. Four new greetings based on 1 Timothy 2:1 and 2 Peter 1:2; Exodus 34:6 and Sirach 2:11; Ephesians 2:19; and 2 Thessalonians 3:18;

2. An additional invitation (B) and prayer of blessing (C) for the Rite of Blessing and Sprinkling of Water;
3. New invitations (3) for use with the Litany of Praise;
4. New invitations (3) for use with the Kyrie;
5. New invitations (3) for use with the Gloria;
6. New invitations to the memorial acclamations;
7. New invitations (3) for use with the Lord's Prayer;
8. New invitations (2) for use with the Sign of Peace;
9. New invitations (2) to Communion,
10. An additional form for the Blessing.

It should be noted that the vast majority of these texts are based on the Scriptures.

Section II of Segment III provides ICEL's proposed variations in the Order of Mass and also its Pastoral Introduction to the Order of Mass. The materials in this section are different from the texts in Section I in that they are supplementary materials offered by ICEL to the individual conferences of bishops. A conference is free to use them or not and may modify them as it sees fit.

The Variations in the Order of Mass are thirteen in number. They were developed as a result of a consultation with the conferences of bishops in 1986 and refined by the Advisory Committee and Episcopal Board of ICEL in the following years. The variations are ritual or rubrical adaptations that reflect either the developing or desired pastoral practice in English-speaking countries or the approved rubrics in the Sacramentaries of other language groups that seem applicable to this revised edition of the *Sacramentary* for English-speaking Catholics.

Variation 1: Introductory Rites

This variation proposes a simpler form for the celebration of the introductory rites of the Mass. It is based on the *Roman Missal*, but takes into account what has been approved in the French, German, and Italian editions. The proposal was developed as the result of the 1986 ICEL consultation with the episcopal conferences and was first proposed in the *Second Progress Report on the Roman Missal* (1990). The conferences were asked to respond to this report and a number requested that this modest rearrangement of the introductory rites be included in the *Sacramentary*. The Committee on the Liturgy, which has the responsibility for proposing liturgical rites and texts to the members of the NCCB, examined the proposal and indicated to ICEL that it would like to present the proposed revision of the introductory rites to the NCCB for approval. In essence the proposed introductory rites would take the following form: Entrance Procession (accompanied by Entrance Song), Greeting (Sign of the Cross and Greeting), Opening Rite, Opening Prayer. The Opening Rite may take one of six forms: 1) the Blessing and Sprinkling of Water; 2) Penitential Rite (present first two forms of the Penitential Rite); 3) Litany of Praise (present third form of the Penitential Rite, but without the absolution); 4) Sung Kyrie; 5) Sung Gloria; 6) Other Opening Rite as provided in the *Sacramentary*, *Liturgy of the Hours*, or the other liturgical books (Baptism, Marriage, Funerals). Only one of these Opening Rites is to be used on any given occasion. The Committee on the Liturgy is proposing that, by way of exception, the Gloria might be added to another Opening Rite on occasions of special solemnity. The Committee on the Liturgy surveyed the members of the NCCB on the acceptability of the ICEL proposal and the majority of those who responded were in favor of the proposed simplification of the introductory rites.

Variation 2: Response to Greeting C

The alternative response to the third form of the greeting, "Blessed be God, the Father of our Lord Jesus Christ" is rarely if ever used. It seems to be better to simply eliminate it as a response to the greeting.

Variation 3: Rubric at the Rite of Blessing and Sprinkling of Water

The present rubric indicates that this rite may be used at Sunday Masses (this also includes Sunday Vigil Masses). A revised rubric indicates that the rite may take place on Sundays or "on other suitable occasions." This is an acknowledgment of common pastoral practice. The rite is often used in connection with confirmation or other occasions when it is appropriate to recall Christian initiation even when there is no renewal of the baptismal promises.

Variation 4: Concluding Prayer of the Blessing and Sprinkling of Water

The concluding formula of the Rite of Blessing and Sprinkling Water has been transferred to the end of the Penitential Rite as an alternative formula of absolution. This prayer does not work well in its present position and seems to serve more appropriately as a formula of absolution.

Variation 5: Rubric at Form B of the Penitential Rite

The possibility of the invocations being spoken by another "suitable minister" has been added. This brings Form B in conformity with the already existing provision of the present third form of the Penitential Rite (called the Litany of Praise in the revised Order of Mass) where the priest or another minister may make the invocations.

Variation 6: Rubric at the Acclamation after the Gospel

The possibility of "Praise to you, Lord Jesus Christ," or "another suitable acclamation" is mentioned. The practice of repeating "Alleluia" or some other acclamation after the gospel is followed in some places and is provided for in the German *Meßbuch*.

Variation 7: Rubric at the Profession of Faith

Provision has been made for the omission of the Nicene Creed when the rite for the renewal of baptismal promise and sprinkling with holy water takes place after the homily (as in the Easter Sunday liturgy), since the renewal serves as a profession of faith and the use of the Nicene Creed is a duplication.

Variation 8: Rubric at the Profession of Faith

The Apostles' Creed has been added as an alternative form for the profession of faith when permitted by a conference of bishops. A similar provision is found in the Sacramentaries of most other countries. In addition to the usual form of the Apostles' Creed, an alternative question form is provided which is similar to that used for the renewal of baptismal promises.

Variation 9: Invitation to the Prayer over the Gifts

In addition to the *Orate, fratres*, an alternative form is provided: "Let us pray," followed by silence. This variation is already found in the German *Meßbuch*. It allows the prayer over the gifts to follow the same pattern as the opening prayer and the prayer after communion, that is, "Let us pray," followed by silence and the prayer.

Variation 10: Rubric at the Invitation to the Memorial Acclamation

The possibility of the deacon giving the invitation to the memorial acclamation has been added: "Then the priest or the deacon sings or says." This serves to clarify further the role of the deacon as the one who guides the assembly in its participation, as at the sign of peace and dismissal. It is also in keeping with the role of the deacon in the various liturgies of the Eastern Churches. The possibility of the deacon giving this invitation is already found in the German *Meßbuch*.

Variation 11: Last Rubric under the Sign of Peace

The proposed rubric indicates that the priest gives the sign of peace to "the deacon and the ministers" rather than "the deacon or the minister." This slight revision reflects usual practice. It is anomalous that the priest should exchange the sign of peace with only a single person when the members of the assembly properly exchange it with at least those on either side of them.

Variation 12: Rubric at the Breaking of the Bread and Invitation to Communion

Provision has been made in these rubrics for the possibility of the preparation of additional cups at the breaking of the bread and for the holding up of both the consecrated bread and the cup at the invitation to communion. The possible need for preparing additional cups is indicated by the phrase "as necessary." This slight change in these two rubrics is needed because of the number of cases of the assembly receiving communion under both kinds has increased. The holding up of both the consecrated bread and the cup of consecrated wine is the uniform practice of the Eastern Churches. It is appropriate even when communion is not to be distributed under both kinds. It helps to call attention to the Church's teaching that communion under both kinds is the more complete liturgical sign (see *Eucharisticum mysterium,* no. 32; General Instruction of the Roman Missal, no. 56:b).

Variation 13: Sprinkling and the Entrance Procession

If the greeting and blessing of water take place at the Church door, provision is made for the possibility of the sprinkling being done during the entrance procession (see Pastoral Introduction, no. 72).

Pastoral Introduction to the Order of Mass

In keeping with what has been done with other liturgical books (*Pastoral Care of the Sick, Rite of Christian Initiation of Adults,* and *Order of Christian Funerals*), ICEL has proposed to the Conferences of Bishops a Pastoral Introduction to the Order of Mass. This introduction is offered as a supplement to the General Instruction of the Roman Missal (GIRM). It presumes the GIRM and is in no way intended to replace it. This introduction will follow the GIRM at the front of the *Sacramentary.* The proposed pastoral introduction rests on a dual assumption of, first, common cultural elements arising from the use of the English language, and, second, a range of shared pastoral experiences among English-speaking Catholics. This introduction is intended to assist those involved in the preparation, celebration, and catechesis of the liturgy in the English-speaking conferences. Since different countries and regions within the English-speaking world enjoy particular cultures and traditions, the conferences are invited to adapt the introduction to local needs. The Committee on the Liturgy will propose specific adaptations of the introduction for the dioceses of the United States of America. The introduction helps to clarify and systematize the somewhat scattered material of the GIRM and supplements it with material taken from other liturgical documents on the Mass. The introduction helps to reinforce the rubrics and directives of the GIRM and gives further explanatory material on them. It provides explanations for minor variations that are within the competence of the conferences of bishops. It augments the GIRM's treatment of the roles of the ordained, instituted, and non-instituted ministers, and of the assembly itself. The Pastoral Introduction has the following outline:

I. THE CELEBRATION OF MASS
> The Assembly and Its Ministers
>> Assembly
>> Liturgical Ministers
> The Eucharistic Celebration and Its Symbols
>> Gesture and Posture
>> Words
>> Music
>> Silence
>> Materials and Objects
> Adapting the Celebration to Particular Circumstances

II. INTRODUCTORY RITES
> Entrance Procession
> Greeting

Opening Rite
Opening Prayer

III. LITURGY OF THE WORD
Biblical Readings
Responsorial Psalm
Gospel Acclamation
Gospel Reading
Homily
Profession of Faith
General Intercessions

III. LITURGY OF THE EUCHARIST
Preparation of the Gifts
    Preparation of the Altar
    Presentation of the Gifts
    Prayer over the Gifts
Eucharistic Prayer
Communion Rite
    Lord's Prayer
    Sign of Peace
    Breaking of the Bread
    Communion
    Period of Silence or Song of Praise
    Prayer after Communion
Concluding Rite
    Announcements
    Greeting
    Blessing
    Dismissal

Liturgical Resources for the Visually Impaired

The Liturgy Secretariat periodically receives inquiries concerning LARGE TYPE PRINT editions of the *Sacramentary* and *Lectionary for Mass* for use by priests with visual impairment. These texts are available for Sunday and Weekday Masses. Font sizes range from 20 to 44 points in regular or bold print. Also available are the *Sacramentary* and Gospels in Spanish as well as the *Sacramentary* and *Lectionary for Mass* in Braille. For more information contact: Mrs. Susan T. Woodward, 4704 Chevy Chase Boulevard, Chevy Chase, MD 20815-5342 or call (301) 652-9099.

Workshops and Conferences

Proclaiming the Eternal Word in a Changing Church
The Notre Dame Center for Pastoral Liturgy will sponsor a workshop for those whose ministries are centered around the proclamation of the Word on March 19-22, 1995. How can the lost art of storytelling and the forgotten art of liturgical preaching be recovered? The workshop will also explore current biblical interpretation, the skills of proclaiming and preaching, bring the Word to flesh in a changing society and Church. For additional information contact: Notre Dame Center for Pastoral Liturgy, Box 81, Notre Dame, IN 46556 or call (219) 631-5435 or Fax (219) 631-6968.

Pastoral Liturgy Conference 1994

"Behold, I Am Making All Things New" will be the theme of the June 19-22, 1995 Pastoral Liturgy Conference sponsored by the Notre Dame Center for Pastoral Liturgy. The Conference marks the twenty-fifth anniversary of the Center for Pastoral Liturgy and considers the reform of the liturgy and the Church a generation after Vatican II. Has the Vatican Council's reform of the liturgy and Church been realized? How has the reform succeeded and how has it failed? What are the new issues and questions the renewal has raised? What reforms of the Church and of the liturgy have yet to be realized? For additional information contact: Notre Dame Center for Pastoral Liturgy, Box 81, Notre Dame, IN 46556 or call (219) 631-5435 or Fax (219) 631-6968.

National Conference on Preaching

The Catholic Coalition on Preaching will sponsor a conference on preaching from September 24-27, 1995 at the Holiday Inn O'Hare in Rosemont, IL (Northwest Suburb of Chicago). The conference will have the theme: WORD for a Hungering World. It will focus on identifying the hungers that are present both in the hearers of preaching and in the preachers themselves. It will be sensitive to the complexities of life of the parish preacher. There will be large and small group discussions as well as fourteen special interest sessions on such issues as Preaching and Violence, Hungers of Children, Hungers of the African American Community, Hungers of the Hispanic Community, Preaching and the New Catechism, Imagination and the Poetic Spirit, and Retreat and Renewal Preaching. Further information can be obtained from: Conference Services by Loretta Reif, P.O. Box 5084, Rockford, IL 61125 or call (815) 399-2150.

Resources

From Ashes to Fire - C: Planning for the Paschal Season

The Liturgical Conference has announced the publication of the final volume of its series: From Ashes to Fire. The book provides commentaries the Sunday Scripture readings, hints for readers, suggestions for music, art, and environment. In addition, the book has a model for using the three-volume series, celebration ideas for children, household prayers, an article on Lent and the catechumenal process, introductions to the seasons, and a service of word and prayer for Ascension Day. The book sells for $10.95 and is available from The Liturgical Conference, 8750 Georgia Avenue, Suite 123, Silver Spring, MD 20910-3621 or call 1-800-394-0885.

A Rereading of the Renewed Liturgy - Adrian Nocent, O.S.B.

In this book Father Nocent assesses what has been accomplished by the liturgical reform set into motion by the Second Vatican Council. Examining the liturgical reforms, he raises questions and makes suggestions for further reforms in the light of thirty years of liturgical renewal. The price is $11.95 and it is available from The Liturgical Press, Saint John's Abbey, Collegeville, MN or call 1-800-858-5450.

COMMITTEE ON THE LITURGY

NEWSLETTER

1995
VOLUME XXXI
MARCH

NATIONAL CONFERENCE OF CATHOLIC BISHOPS

March Meeting of the Committee on the Liturgy

The bishop members and bishop consultants of the Liturgy Committee met on March 13, 1995 at the headquarters of the National Conference of Catholic Bishops in Washington, D.C. The members of the Committee approved the Liturgy Committee's "1996 Plans and Programs" at the beginning of the meeting.

Bishop Donald W. Trautman, chairman of the Liturgy Committee, spoke about a number of matters in his report to the Committee. He noted that a small group of bishops and Scripture scholars went to Rome in January to discuss issues related to the approval of the *Lectionary for Mass*. As press reports indicated at the time, he felt that the meeting achieved its goals and expressed his confidence that the Lectionary would be approved in due course. While in Rome, Bishop Trautman and Monsignor Alan F. Detscher, Executive Director of the Secretariat for the Liturgy, visited the Congregation for Divine Worship and the Discipline of the Sacraments and met with the Prefect and Secretary of the Congregation. Bishop Trautman told the members of the Liturgy Committee that he thanked the Congregation and its staff for the resolution of the issue of female altar servers. He reported to the Congregation that the implementation has gone smoothly and that nearly all the dioceses of the United States are permitting women and girls to serve at Mass. At the request of the Liturgy Committee he raised a number of questions about perpetual adoration and exposition. An inquiry was made about the delay in the confirmation of the Spanish version of the funeral rites and also about the *Leccionario Hispanoamerica*. A process was agreed upon that would lead to the confirmation and publication of these two books.

Bishop Edward Grosz reported on his meeting with representatives of the Federation of Diocesan Liturgical Commissions. The main concern of the Federation is with the closing of diocesan offices of worship. Bishop Grosz will work with the Federation to determine ways that the Committee on the Liturgy can encourage and support the continuation and establishment of offices of worship in dioceses. Bishop Patrick Cooney, who had chaired the Task Group on Cremation and Other Burial Practices explained to the Committee that the work of his task group has been finished and that the statement that it had prepared is undergoing revision so that it can be submitted to the Liturgy Committee. He expressed hope that it would come to the Committee in June for discussion and approval. Archbishop Jerome Hanus informed the members of the Liturgy Committee that the work of the Task Group on American Adaptations of the *Sacramentary* had completed its work. Bishop Roberto Gonzalez told the Committee that the Hispanic Liturgy Subcommittee was continuing its work on the preparation of the Spanish translation of the *Sacramentary*. It is also working on the revised marriage rite and a Spanish translation of the American blessings contained in the *Book of Blessings*. The last report was given by Monsignor Detscher on behalf of the Task Group for Televised Masses (see below).

The remainder of the meeting was spent going through the various amendments and motions submitted by bishops on *Segment III: Order of Mass I* of the proposed revision of the *Sacramentary* and on the proposed adaptations of the Order of Mass for use in the dioceses of the United States of America. The Committee was unable to finish its review of the amendments and motions submitted by the members of the National Conference of Catholic Bishops and decided to schedule another meeting for April 7, 1995.

3211 FOURTH STREET NE • WASHINGTON, DC 20017

March Administrative Committee Meeting

The Administrative Committee of the National Conference of Catholic Bishops met March 14-16, 1995 at the headquarters of the NCCB/USCC in Washington, D.C. The Committee on the Liturgy had two action items on the agenda. The Liturgy Committee asked the Administrative Committee to place *Segment III: Order of Mass I* of the proposed ICEL revision of the *Sacramentary* on the agenda of the June plenary meetingof the NCCB for approval by the Latin rite members of the NCCB. This request of the Liturgy Committee was unanimously approved by the members of the Administrative Committee. The Liturgy Committee requested that the adaptations of the Order of Mass prepared by the Committee on the Liturgy also be placed on the agenda of the same meeting for approval by the bishops. This second action was approved by all the members of the Administrative Committee. Both these actions were originally scheduled to be voted upon last November, but the Doctrine Committee was unable to review Segment III in time for the NCCB plenary meeting.

In keeping with the procedure approved by the bishops in 1993, the chairmen of the Liturgy and Doctrine Committees and the Executive Directors of the Liturgy and Doctrine Secretariats met to surface texts that might have doctrinal implications. As a result of that meeting and a subsequent meeting of the Doctrine Committee, Archbishop John R. Quinn, chairman of the Committee on Doctrine, was able to affirm that all the texts were theologically orthodox and any other concerns that may have been raised have been satisfactorily addressed by the Liturgy Committee.

Bishop Trautman explained to the Administrative Committee that the approval of Segment III of the *Sacramentary* will be accomplished by a series of votes. The bishops will first be asked to approve the liturgical texts of the *Sacramentary*. Next they will be asked to approve the ecumenical texts for the *Kyrie*, *Gloria*, Apostles' and Nicene Creeds, *Sanctus*, and *Agnus Dei*, which were prepared by the English Language Liturgical Consultation (ELLC). Then the bishops will be asked to approve the variations in the Order of Mass proposed by ICEL (see *Newsletter*, vol. XXXI, January/February 1995, pages 4-6). The series of adaptations prepared by the Liturgy Committee for the dioceses of the United States of America will then be voted upon by the bishops. Finally, the bishops will vote on the Pastoral Introduction to the Order of Mass as adapted for use in the dioceses of the United States.

Task Group on Televised Masses

On March 8, 1995, the Task Group on Televised Masses held its first meeting under the chairmanship of the Most Reverend Anthony Bosco, Bishop of Greensburg. The task group consists of two bishops from the Liturgy Committee, a bishop representative of the Communications Committee, a representative of the Federation of Diocesan Liturgical Commissions and several individuals with expertise in liturgy, communications, and television. This task group was established as the result of a request from the Federation of Diocesan Liturgical Commissions. The FDLC has been concerned with the quality of televised Masses and with the apparent lack of involvement of liturgical offices in the preparation and broadcast of Masses on television. The task group discussed the various concerns that have been raised by liturgists, as well as the concerns of those who are involved in the production of televised Masses. There was general agreement on the importance of TV Masses and the need for positive guidelines that would be of assistance to the bishops of dioceses that regularly broadcast the Mass on television. An initial draft of a document is being prepared for discussion by the task group.

New Advisor to the Committee on the Liturgy

Sister Joyce Ann Zimmerman, C.PP.S. has been appointed as an advisor to the Committee on the Liturgy by Bishop Donald W. Trautman. Sister Zimmerman, a professed member of the Sisters of the Precious Blood of Dayton, Ohio, will represent the Leadership Conference of Women Religious (LCWR). She replaces Father Joseph Levesque who had represented the Conference of Major Superiors of Men

(CMSM). These two organizations alternate in providing an advisor for the Liturgy Committee. Dr. Zimmerman has an M.A. in liturgical studies from Saint John's University (Collegeville, MN), a Ph.D. from the University of Ottawa, and a S.T.D. from Saint Paul's University in Ottawa. She is a member of the North American Academy of Liturgy. Sister Zimmerman is the author of a number of books and articles on liturgy and religious education. She presently serves as Professor of Liturgy and Director of Seminary Liturgy at Conception Seminary College in Missouri and as the founding Director of the Institute for Liturgical Ministry at the Maria Stein Center. The Committee on the Liturgy looks forward to the participation of Sister Joyce Zimmerman in the work of the Committee.

Lectionary Numbers in the Ordo

The Secretariat for the Liturgy has received a number of calls concerning the Lectionary numbers in the various publications of the *Ordo* for 1995. The liturgical calendar upon which the *Ordo* is based is prepared annually by the Secretariat. Because the publishers of the calendar and *Ordo* often work several years in advance, the liturgical calendar is prepared two years in advance of its publication. When the *Ordo* was prepared for 1995, it was our hope that the *Lectionary for Mass* would already be in print. For that reason, the Lectionary numbers of the *Ordo* correspond to the second edition of the *Ordo Lectionum Missae* which is the basis for the second edition of the Lectionary for Mass, presently awaiting confirmation from the Congregation for Divine Worship and the Discipline of the Sacraments. The second edition of the Lectionary changes the position of the Chrism Mass and as a result the readings are off by one from the Chrism Mass (in the Sunday portion of the Lectionary) until Thursday of Holy Week (in the weekday portion of the Lectionary). The following chart will help you to determine the proper numbers for the readings.

1995 Ordo numbers	Numbers in the present Lectionary
1-38	1-38
260	39
39-259	40-260
261-749	261-749

December 9, 1996, the Solemnity of the Immaculate Conception

The Liturgy Secretariat has received several telephone calls requesting clarification of the status of the Solemnity of the Immaculate Conception in 1996. Because many parishes schedule Masses more than a year in advance, questioners have asked whether the Solemnity of the Immaculate Conception will be observed as a holyday of obligation in 1996. The solemnity will fall on the Second Sunday of Advent and, according to the "Table of Liturgical Days (according to their precedence)" contained in the *Sacramentary,* the Sundays of Advent may not be replaced by a solemnity of the Blessed Virgin Mary. The liturgical celebration of the Immaculate Conception must, therefore, be transferred to the first free day: December 9, 1996. Although the liturgical celebration is transferred, the obligation to attend Mass is not transferred. The Immaculate Conception is to be celebrated on Monday, December 9th, but the faithful are not obligated to participate in Mass on that day. Because of the devotion of the people to this feast of the Mother of God, it may be appropriate to schedule additional Masses on that day even though it will not be observed as a holyday of obligation in 1996.

American Adaptations for the *Sacramentary*

The January/February 1995 issue of the *Newsletter* (vol. XXXI, pages 2-7) contained a summary of the contents of *Segment III: Order of Mass I* of the ICEL proposed revision of the *Sacramentary*. As that summary indicates, the International Commission on English in the Liturgy has proposed a series of thirteen variations or adaptations of the *Roman Missal* as a result of the requests of a number of episcopal conferences. The Liturgy Committee of the NCCB, in addition, is proposing additional variations or adaptations for use in the dioceses of the United States.

Some people have asked by what authority these adaptations are being made. The *General Instruction of the Roman Missal* states: "In accord with the Constitution on the Liturgy, each conference of bishops has the power to lay down norms for its own territory that are suited to the traditions and character of peoples, regions, and various communities" (no. 6). This reference to the Constitution on the Liturgy is to numbers 37-40 of that document. This section of the Constitution comes under the title: "Norms for Adapting the Liturgy to the Culture and Traditions of Peoples." The Constitution notes that:

> Even in the liturgy the Church has no wish to impose a rigid uniformity in matters that do not affect the faith or the good of the whole community; rather the Church respects and fosters the genius and talents of the various races and peoples. The Church considers with sympathy and, if possible, preserves intact the elements in these peoples' way of life that are not indissolubly bound up with superstition and error. Sometimes in fact the Church admits such elements into the liturgy itself, provided they are in keeping with the true and authentic spirit of the liturgy (no. 37).

The Constitution then goes on to apply this general principle to the revision of the liturgical books:

> Provisions shall be made, even in the revision of liturgical books, *for legitimate variations and adaptations* to different groups, regions, and peoples, especially in mission lands, provided the substantial unity of the Roman Rite is preserved; this should be borne in mind when rites are drawn up and rubrics devised (no. 38, emphasis added).

To see that these provisions have been taken seriously by the Apostolic See, one only has to look at the already published missals in French, German, Spanish, and Italian. In each of these missals, there are a large number of variations and adaptations which have been introduced by the conferences of bishops and which were approved by the Apostolic See. The substantial unity of the Roman rite has been maintained by the use of the *editio typica* of the *Missale Romanum* as the basic source and structure for these missals. Even when more profound adaptations have been introduced, as in Zaire, the resulting liturgy is still considered to be the Roman rite, but as adapted for the dioceses of Zaire. The variations and adaptations introduced by conferences of bishops usually are of two types. The first are those foreseen in the General Instruction of the Roman Missal. The Constitution on the Liturgy speaks of this type of variation in the following manner:

> Within the limits set by the *editio typica* of the liturgical books, it shall be for the competent, territorial ecclesiastical authority mentioned in art. 22, § 2 to specify adaptations, especially in the case of the administration of the sacraments, the sacramentals, processions, liturgical language, sacred music, and the arts. This is to be done in accord with the fundamental norms laid down in this Constitution.

The second type of variations are those not specifically mentioned in the General Instruction, but which are of a similar type, that is, pastoral adaptations of texts or rites similar to those already provided by the Apostolic See. The variations proposed by the International Commission on English in the Liturgy and the variations and adaptations proposed by the Committee on the Liturgy are of these two types.

The next issue of the *Newsletter* will continue this discussion of variations and adaptations.

COMMITTEE ON THE LITURGY
NEWSLETTER

NATIONAL CONFERENCE OF CATHOLIC BISHOPS

1995
VOLUME XXXI
APRIL

Liturgical Psalter

The International Committee on English in the Liturgy (ICEL) has published for study and comment a new translation of the psalter based on the original texts. This new English translation of the psalms was prepared with communal song and recitation in mind. The project of preparing a psalter suitable for liturgical use was part of the original mandate of ICEL in 1964, but due to the great demands of preparing translations of the revised liturgical books ICEL was not immediately able to start the liturgical psalter project. In 1967 ICEL listed the principles that would guide its later work on the psalter:

1) The best existing versions both critical and literary should be consulted.
2) Greater freedom should be allowed in translating psalms than most of the books of the Bible because they are poetry and must be such in English and because they are meant for the frequent and inspiring use of the people, choirs, and cantors in the liturgy.
3) Rhythm suited to the English language should be used in the translation.

The actual work on the psalter did not begin until 1978 when the Episcopal Board of ICEL authorized the establishment of a subcommittee on the liturgical psalter. The subcommittee consisted of specialists in Hebrew language and poetry, liturgical history and theology, music, English poetry, and literary and language theory. In 1984 twenty-two psalms were prepared and subjected to extensive consultation. In 1987 twenty-three psalms were published along with musical settings under the title *Psalms for All Seasons: From the ICEL Liturgical Psalter Project*. Four working groups were then established to complete work on the remaining psalms and the biblical canticles that are used in the liturgy and their work was revised by an editorial committee. The completed psalter was approved as a publication for study and comment by the ICEL Episcopal Board. The Liturgical Psalter was then submitted to the *Ad Hoc* Committee for the Review of Scripture Translations of the National Conference of Catholic Bishops. At the recommendation of this committee Cardinal William Keeler, president of the National Conference of Catholic Bishops, granted an *imprimatur* to the Liturgical Psalter on January 5, 1995.

The ICEL subcommittee on the Liturgical Psalter has attempted to create a translation 1) that would faithfully render into English the best critical Hebrew and Greek texts available; 2) that would be guided by the liturgical use of the psalms and canticles, and be fitting for musical settings; 3) that would be received by the reader or listener as idiomatic English in contemporary poetic style; and 4) that would be sensitive to evolving gender usage in English, for example, as described in the "Criteria for the Evaluation of Inclusive Language Translations of Scriptural Texts Proposed for Liturgical Use" of the National Conference of Catholic Bishops of the United States.

By virtue of the *imprimatur* granted to the Psalter by the National Conference of Catholic Bishops, it may be used for private prayer and study, but it should be noted that the Liturgical Psalter in any form is not authorized for liturgical use in this country, i.e., in the Liturgy of the Hours. After several years of study and comment, ICEL will review the project in the light of the comments it has received, revise the texts of the psalms, and decide whether to propose the Liturgical Psalter to the conferences of bishops for liturgical use. Comments on the Liturgical Psalter should be sent to the International Commission on English in the Liturgy, 1522 "K" Street, NW, Suite 1000, Washington, DC 20005-1202 (this is ICEL's new address as of February 1995).

An edition of the ICEL Liturgical Psalter has been published by Liturgy Training Publications (LTP) under the title *The Psalter*. Hardbound and paperback editions are available for $18.00 and $12.00 respectively.

Veiling Statues

This year a number of inquiries have been received in the Liturgy Secretariat regarding the practice of covering crosses and statues at the end of the season of Lent. Previous to the publication of the revised edition of the *Roman Missal* (*Sacramentary*) in 1970, crosses and images were covered with veils during passiontide (the last two weeks of Lent). A rubric appeared in the 1962 edition of the Missal at the end of the Mass for Saturday of the Fourth Week of Lent. It stated that "After Mass, crosses and images in the church are covered. Crosses remain covered until the adoration of the cross on Good Friday and images remain covered until the intonation of the Gloria during the Easter Vigil."

When the revised Missal was published in 1970, a similar rubric was printed at the end of the Mass for the Saturday of the Fourth Week of Lent:

> "The practice of covering crosses and images in the church may be observed, if the episcopal conference decides. The crosses are to be covered until the end of the celebration of the Lord's passion on Good Friday. Images are to remain covered until the beginning of the Easter Vigil."

There are several significant differences in the two rubrics, the most significant of which is the statement in the second rubric that the practice "may be observed, if the episcopal conference decides." This statement is noted in the *Circular Letter Concerning the Preparation and Celebration of the Easter Feasts* published by the Congregation for Divine Worship on January 16, 1988. Number 26 of that document reaffirms that: "The practice of covering crosses and images in the church may be observed, *if the episcopal conference should so decide.*" The normal procedure in liturgical law requires the bishops to vote to abolish a practice or make it optional (e.g., they voted to make the anointing of infants with the oil of catechumens optional), but in this case the wording requires that they must vote to continue the practice, otherwise the practice ceases.

The National Conference of Catholic Bishops has never voted to continue the practice of covering crosses and images and so the practice, in accord with the rubric of the *Sacramentary,* has not been permissible for the past twenty-five years. Individual parishes are not free to reinstate the practice on their own.

American Adaptations for the *Sacramentary* (continued)

The March 1995 issue of the Newsletter *(vol. XXXI, pages 11-12) began a presentation on the proposed American Adaptations for the* Sacramentary. *This article is a continuation of that presentation.*

Pope John Paul II, in his apostolic letter *On the Anniversary of the Constitution on the Sacred Liturgy* (December 4, 1988), spoke of the work facing the future of the liturgical renewal. He singled out the adaptation of the liturgy to different cultures as an important task. The Holy Father states:

> The Constitution [on the Liturgy] set forth the principle [of adaptation], indicating the procedure to be followed by the Episcopal Conferences. The adaptation of languages has been rapidly accomplished, even if on occasion with some difficulties. It has been followed by the

adaptation of rites, which is a more delicate matter but equally necessary (no. 16).

As the Holy Father notes, the liturgy has been translated into the major languages of the world in the past thirty years. Translation itself is a form of adaptation since it is the attempt to make the transition from one cultural mode of expression (the Latin language) to other cultural forms of expression (the various vernacular languages). Most of the language groups have revised or are in the process of revising their initial translations of the liturgical texts. The proposed ICEL revision of the *Sacramentary* represents this second generation of vernacular liturgical texts. The majority of the other language groups have, as the Pope explains, also proposed particular adaptations and variations for the Missal. These adaptations have, for the most part, been lesser pastoral adaptations of the rubrics and the introduction of alternative liturgical texts. In the dioceses of Zaire, a significant cultural adaptation of the *Roman Missal* has been undertaken. The adapted Missal contains major adaptations of rites and texts that manifest the elements of the local African culture that are in harmony with the Christian faith.

Cultural adaptation must take into consideration that there are parts of the liturgy that cannot be changed because they are of divine institution and there are other parts that are open to change.

The notion of liturgical adaptation was again taken up by the Congregation for Divine Worship and the Discipline of the Sacraments in 1994 in *The Roman Liturgy and Inculturation: Fourth Instruction for the Right Application of the Conciliar Constitution on the Liturgy (nn. 37-40)*. This document explains the nature of adaptation and the parts of the liturgy that can be adapted.

It is in the light of this encouragement by the Apostolic See of responsible liturgical adaptation that the Committee on the Liturgy has prepared the adaptations of the Order of Mass which are now being proposed to the members of the National Conference of Catholic Bishops for their approval and ultimately for the confirmation of the Apostolic See.

In 1991, the Committee on the Liturgy established a task group on the adaptation of the *Sacramentary* for the dioceses of the United States of America. The task group was chaired by Archbishop Jerome Hanus, OSB, Coadjutor Archbishop of Dubuque. The members of the task group were former Executive Directors of the Liturgy Secretariat and others who have served as advisors to the Committee on the Liturgy.

The first action taken by the task group was to prepare a survey on a variety of issues related to the *Sacramentary*. The survey instrument was revised by the Liturgy Committee and then sent to all bishops and diocesan liturgical commissions and offices of worship. The responses of the bishops and commissions to the survey were used to give direction to the work of the task group. One hundred and forty-two of the bishops and most of the commissions and offices of worship responded to the survey. The results of the survey were communicated to the bishops, liturgical commissions, and offices of worship in 1992.

Among the items discussed in the survey were the following:

1) Rearrangement of the Introductory Rites — The Liturgy Committee requested ICEL to make a proposal to the Conferences of Bishops in this regard. The bishops and commissions seemed to be strongly in favor of the rearrangement of the introductory rites.
2) Presentation of the Gifts -- There seemed to be some misunderstanding as to the purpose of these rites, but the task group and the Liturgy Committee made no specific proposal for change. The rites of the revised Missal of 1970 no longer speak of an "offertory" rite, but of the preparation of the altar and the gifts. The reform in these rites is based on the notion of their preparatory character and that the true offering of the Mass takes place in the eucharistic prayer.

3) New Eucharistic Prayers — There was support for requesting permission from Rome to prepare additional eucharistic prayers. The members of the NCCB in June of 1993 approved a request for two additional eucharistic prayers, but there has been no formal response to this request from the Congregation for Divine Worship and the Discipline of the Sacraments. The prefect of the Congregation, Cardinal Javierre, has indicated that the matter of new eucharistic prayers will have to be discussed at a plenary meeting of the Congregation. In November of 1994, the members of the NCCB approved the ICEL English translation of the *Eucharistic Prayer for Masses for Various Needs and Occasions* (originally known as the "Swiss Synod" eucharistic prayer).

4) Posture during the Eucharistic Prayer -- The survey gave no clear mandate to change the present norms for the USA on kneeling during the eucharistic prayer from after the Sanctus through the final Amen. The Liturgy Committee is proposing a slightly modified text which clarifies the existing USA norms regarding posture.

The task group began its work by examining the Foreword to the *Sacramentary* and the *Appendix to the General Instruction of the Roman Missal for the Diocese of the United States of America*. It decided to remove from the Foreword much of the material that was no longer necessary or that repeated material contained in the new ICEL *Pastoral Introduction to the Order of Mass*. The *Appendix to the General Instruction* was revised to remove most of the commentary which was no longer needed so that the norms themselves would be more evident.

Next the task group proposed a series of additions to the ICEL *Pastoral Introduction to the Order of Mass* to cover topics that were felt to be appropriate for this country and were not contained in the ICEL material. The task group then studied the Order of Mass itself and prepared a series of proposals for specific adaptations for use in the dioceses of the USA. It then examined all the other material contained in the Sacramentary and proposed adaptations for some of the seasonal material, especially for the Easter Triduum. Lastly, the propers for the USA saints, the blessed, and national holidays were examined and a subcommittee was entrusted with the task of revising these proper texts to conform to the style used in the revised ICEL prayers.

Over the past two years, the Liturgy Committee has reviewed the proposals of the task group. It has accepted some of the proposals, revised others, and even rejected those proposals that it felt would not be acceptable to the members of the NCCB. The proposals have been further refined as a part of the NCCB amendment process.

CUA Liturgy Program Anniversary

The Catholic University of America will commemorate the twenty-fifth anniversary of its Liturgical Studies Program with a symposium at the University, Friday evening and Saturday, September 22-23, 1995, on "The Eucharist: Towards the Third Millennium." There will be presentations and discussion with David Power on "A Prophetic Eucharist in a Prophetic Church;" Margaret Mary Kelleher on "Ritual Studies and the Eucharist;" Kevin Irwin on "The Critical Task of Liturgical Theology;" Gerard Austin on "*In Persona Christi* at the Eucharist;" Frederick McManus on "A Common Lectionary for the Eucharist;" and Mary Collins on "Eucharistic Preaching: Connecting the Body." Alumni/ae will offer sessions on topics including Priestless Sundays, Women in the Eucharistic Assembly, Space and Environment for the Eucharist, and Eucharistic Devotions. For more information write: Reverend Kevin Irwin, The Catholic University of America, 125 Caldwell Hall, Washington, D.C. 20064 or call (202) 319-5481.

NATIONAL CONFERENCE OF CATHOLIC BISHOPS

COMMITTEE ON THE LITURGY
NEWSLETTER

1995
VOLUME XXXI
MAY

Eucharistic Prayer for Various Needs and Occasions

On May 24, 1995, Cardinal William Keeler, President of the National Conference of Catholic Bishops, received a letter from Antonio Cardinal Javierre, Prefect of the Congregation for Divine Worship and the Discipline of the Sacraments, which permits the interim use of the *Eucharistic Prayer for Various Needs and Occasions* which was approved by the members of the NCCB during their November 1994 meeting in Washington, D.C. (see the December 1994 issue of the *Newsletter*, vol. XXX, pages 47-48). The Congregation has asked that several modifications be made in the text, most of which are stylistic in nature. The eucharistic prayer is now being prepared for publication and once it is ready, Cardinal Keeler will set the effective date for its use. The text of Cardinal Javierre's letter follows.

Prot. N. 92/95/L

9 May 1995

Your Eminence,

This Congregation has received and examined the request of the National Conference of Catholic Bishops for the confirmation for the interim use of the ICEL translation of the **Eucharistic Prayers for Various Needs and Occasions**.

It has been decided that with this present letter permission is given to use this text only after the enclosed modifications have been made and may continue in use until such time as the new translation of the Roman Missal is presented for confirmation.

With every prayerful good wish, I remain,

Yours sincerely in Christ,

Antonio M. Card. Javierre
Prefect

+ Geraldo M. Agnelo
Archbishop Secretary

American Adaptations for the Sacramentary (continued)

This article is a continuation of the presentation on the proposed American adaptations for the Sacramentary which began in the March 1995 issue of the Newsletter (vol. XXXI, pages 11-12) and continued in the April 1995 issue (vol. XXXI, pages 14-16).

The members of the NCCB were sent the proposals of the Liturgy Committee for the adaptations of the Order of Mass in 1994. The proposals were contained in a document entitled: *The Sacramentary –Order of Mass: Adaptations for the Dioceses of the United States of America.* The document is divided into four sections: Section I: Liturgical Texts for the Order of Mass: Ecumenical Texts; Section II: Variations and Pastoral Introduction; Section III: The Order of Mass (Comprehensive Layout including the Adaptations for the Dioceses of the United States of America); Section IV: Introductory Documents: *Appendix to the General Instruction of the Roman Missal for the Dioceses of the United States of America* and *Appendix to the General Norms for the Liturgical Year and the Calendar for the Dioceses of the United States of America.*

The first section of the document contains comments on the ecumenical translation of the Nicene Creed prepared by the English Language Liturgical Consultation (ELLC). When the revised version of the translation of the Nicene Creed was first published several years ago, there was a general reaction against the manner in which the words referring to the incarnation had been translated. As a consequence, ICEL circulated a number of alternative wordings of this section of the Creed, on behalf of the English-speaking Roman Catholic Churches. The text being proposed to the bishops now says:

> "For us and for our salvation
> > he came down from heaven,
> > was incarnate of the Holy Spirit and the Virgin Mary
> > and was made man."

The variations in the Order of Mass contained in the second section of the document include the following: 1) an optional greeting for the season of Easter; 2) a rubric indicating that the Blessing and Sprinkling of Water is not used during the Season of Lent; 3) a change in the title of the "Litany of Praise" to "Litany of Praise for God's Mercy"; 4) a change in the title of "Gloria" to "Song of Praise" and a rubric to indicate that it is not used in Advent and Lent; 5) provision of a prayer of thanksgiving for water that has been previously blessed and corresponding rubrics; 6) optional provision for the people to kneel for the penitential rite during Lent, if appropriate; 7) an additional invitation to the penitential rite; 8) an optional canticle for use during the season of Easter; 9) optional provision for the sign of peace to take place at the beginning of the liturgy of the eucharist; 10) optional provision for the people to extend their hands during the Lord's Prayer; 11) slight modification of the rubrics for the breaking of the bread and the private preparation of the priest before communion to indicate that he does not wait for the Lamb of God to conclude; 12) an indication of when ministers of communion are to receive the eucharist; 13) rubrics to indicate that the people stand for the prayer over the gifts and the prayer after communion.

Several of these provisions deserve some comment: 1)The Easter Canticle is a composed text based on the hymnic material found in the Book of Revelation; it is a paraphrase rather than a direct translation. The canticle is proposed for optional use; the Gloria may <u>always</u> be used, if desired. The canticle is intended only for sung use. It should also be noted that the Liturgy Committee has made provision for the Song of Praise (Gloria or Easter Canticle) to be used on special occasions in addition to one of the other opening rites. 2) The Committee has decided to return to the ICEL terminology for the penitential rite (i.e., "confession of sin," "absolution," etc.) and to return to the ICEL texts for the absolution rather than the "Prayers for Mercy" originally proposed by the Liturgy Committee. 3) After reviewing the amendments regarding the Sign of Peace, the Committee has decided to restore the original proposal of its Task Group on Adaptation and now wishes to propose that the sign of peace be retained in its present position before communion and that it may optionally be celebrated at the beginning of the liturgy of the eucharist. Accordingly, the celebrant may choose either position for the sign of peace, depending on where it is more appropriate in a particular celebration.

The Liturgy Committee is also proposing that a number of additions be made to the ICEL *Pastoral Introduction to the Order of Mass* (see *Newsletter*, vol. XXXI, pages 6-7). Material has been proposed for inclusion which deals with matters such as: 1) the needs of children present along with adults; 2) the meaning of concelebration; 3) the decision of the bishops that male and female readers are to use the ambo for the readings; 4) mention that servers at the altar may be men or women, boys or girls, depending on the decision of the local bishop; 5) reference to the use of a flagon when communion is given under both kinds; 6) mention of the books containing the readings and books for use by the people; 7) a note on the use of the chasuble-alb; 8) color of vestments for funerals and Masses for the dead; 9) an indication that the priest may use his own words in place of the words given for the invitation to each of the forms of the opening rite; 10) clarifications regarding the blessing and sprinkling of water; 11) a note that indicates that the people may be invited to kneel for the penitential rite during Lent; 12) notes on the Song of Praise (Gloria or Easter Canticle); 13) notes explaining that the sign of peace may take place at the beginning of the liturgy of the eucharist or in its customary place before communion; 14) an explanation of who is to be named in the eucharistic prayer; 15) an indication that the people may extend their hands in the "orans" gesture during the Lord's Prayer; 16) notes explaining the decision of the bishops to permit communion in the hand.

Since a number of modifications have been made in the original proposals as a result of the amendments submitted to the Committee, and in order to assist the bishops in seeing just what is being proposed, a revised version of the comprehensive layout of the Order of Mass will be distributed to the bishops at the beginning of the June meeting of the NCCB.

The *Appendix to the General Instruction of the Roman Missal for the Dioceses of the United States of America* contains the liturgical norms approved by the NCCB in accord with the requirements of the *General Instruction of the Roman Missal* and is a revision of the document found in the present *Sacramentary*. Most of the norms contained in this section remain unchanged. Much of the explanatory material that was previously included has been removed, since it is no longer necessary or is found elsewhere in the *Sacramentary*. Of special note is the revision of no. 21 on actions and postures of the congregation. The Liturgy Committee is proposing that when circumstances suggest, the people may be invited to kneel for the penitential rite during the season of Lent. This is proposed only as an option. The Committee is also proposing that where appropriate, the people may extend their hands during the Lord's Prayer. This too is being proposed as an option and is not required. Finally, the Committee has reworded the material on the posture during the eucharistic prayer. The survey conducted by the Liturgy Committee several years ago did not indicate that there was a sufficient majority for changing the present norm of kneeling from after the Sanctus until the end of the final doxology. However, the Committee felt that it was necessary to indicate that no. 21 does already provide for particular cases when kneeling is not possible and that this exception clause also applies to the American norm (i.e., "unless prevented by the lack of space, the number of people present, or for some other good reason" [GIRM, 21]). The Committee also wishes to indicate that in these exceptional circumstances there should be some form of reverence and has therefore recommended that the norm indicate that the people bow when the priest genuflects after the consecration of the bread and the wine.

In this section, the Liturgy Committee is also proposing that the Apostles' Creed be permitted as an alternative to the Nicene Creed. Because this baptismal profession of faith is so rarely used, many of the faithful are forgetting it. The use of both professions of faith at Mass will allow Catholics to remain familiar with both symbols of our faith. The alternative use of the Apostles' Creed is permitted in Canada, Mexico, throughout Central and Latin America, and throughout Europe.

The *Appendix to the General Norms for the Liturgical Year and the Calendar for the Dioceses of the United States of America* contains the liturgical norms approved by the NCCB in accord with the requirements of the *General Norms for the Liturgical Year and the Calendar*.

The only new material in this section that has not already been approved by the members of the NCCB is the proposal that the name of María de la Cabeza, the wife of Isidore the Farmer, be added in the calendar to that of Isidore whose optional memorial is celebrated on May 15. Both Maria and Isidore are canonized saints. Although they were canonized at different times, they represent a husband and wife who were noted for holiness. Their commemoration provides the calendar with lay persons who are also a married couple, a category which is presently lacking in the calendar.

Liturgical Calendar 1997

The NCCB Liturgy Secretartiat recently prepared the 1997 edition of the liturgical calendar for the dioceses of the United States of America. The calendar lists each day's celebration, rank, liturgical color(s), and lectionary citations.

For many years the information in the annual calendar prepared by the Liturgy Secretariat was made available only to commercial publishers of other calendars, *ordines,* etc. in the United States. For the past several years it has been published in an inexpensive format and made available to anyone desiring a copy.

Liturgical Calendar 1997 (8½ x 11in.) may be purchased from: Secretariat for the Liturgy, 3211 Fourth Street, N.E., Washington, D.C. 20017-1194. All orders must be accompanied by a check made out to "Committee on the Liturgy" in the amount of $6.00 to cover printing, postage, and handling.

International

A number of countries have now voted on various segments of the proposed revision of the English translation of the *Sacramentary (Roman Missal)* prepared by the International Commission on English in the Liturgy:

> Australia - Segments 1 - 4 have been approved
> England and Wales - Segments 1 - 4 have been approved
> Scotland - Segments 1 - 3 have been approved
> Ireland - Segments 1 - 2 have been approved
> India - Segments 1 - 3 have been approved
> The Philippines - Segments 1 - 2 have been approved
> United States of America - Segments 1 - 2 have been approved
> Canada and New Zealand have delayed voting until they receive all of volume I
> Interterritorial Conference (Gambia, Liberia, Sierra Leone) - Segments 1 - 3 have been approved

The members of the National Conference of Catholic Bishops will vote on Segment III: Order of Mass I during their June 1995 meeting in Chicago. The remaining segments of volume I of the *Sacramentary* (Prefaces, Solemn Blessings, and Prayers over the People [Segment 4] and Holy Week and the Easter Triduum [Segment 6]) will be presented by the Committee on the Liturgy to the members of the NCCB in November.

Conferences

The National Association of Pastoral Musicians will have its eighteenth annual convention from July 24-28, 1995 in Cincinnati, Ohio. The theme of this year's conference will be: As a Story Handed Down. Speakers will include Rev. Michael Sparough, Mr. Graziano Marcheschi, Sr. Lorna Zemke, Rev. Lucian Deiss, Dr. Michael McMahon, Ms. Mary Beth Kunde-Anderson, and Sr. Joan Chittister. The program includes numerous workshops, performances, and showcases of new music. For registration information contact: NPM Conventions, 225 Sheridan Street, N.W., Washington, D.C. 20011-1492 or Telephone (202) 723-5800 or Fax (202) 723-2262.

The National Association of Pastoral Musicians is also offering a series of Summer Schools and Institutes on music during June, July, and August. Schools are provided for cantors, organists, guitarists, and pianists. Institutes are offered on liturgy, composition, Gregorian chant, and for choir directors. For further information write to NPM Schools and Institutes, 225 Sheridan Street, N.W., Washington, D.C. 20011-1492 or Telephone (202) 723-5800 or Fax (202) 723-2262.

COMMITTEE ON THE LITURGY

NEWSLETTER

1995
VOLUME XXXI
JUNE

Perpetual Exposition of the Blessed Sacrament

Over the past several years a number of questions have been raised regarding the practice of perpetual exposition of the Blessed Sacrament. The Liturgy Committee discussed the issues raised several times and decided to submit a series of questions regarding perpetual exposition to the Congregation for Divine Worship and the Discipline of the Sacraments. The following responses were received from the Congregation at the beginning of July. As these responses indicate, those who are responsible for perpetual exposition should carefully review the norms contained in nos. 82-100 of Holy Communion and Worship of the Eucharist outside Mass.

Should perpetual adoration or exposition of the Blessed Sacrament take place in parishes?

RESPONSE: The Roman Ritual: *Holy Communion and Worship of the Eucharist outside Mass* (HCWEOM), no. 90, states that, according to their constitutions and regulations, some religious communities and other pious groups have the practice of perpetual eucharistic adoration or adoration over extended periods of time. If by "perpetual eucharistic adoration" is meant prayer before the Blessed Sacrament in the tabernacle, this involves no special permission. However, if by "perpetual eucharistic adoration" is meant adoration of the Blessed Sacrament exposed in the ciborium or monstrance, the permission of the local Ordinary is required.

Perpetual exposition of the Blessed Sacrament is a devotion and practice which is permitted to those religious communities that have it as an integral part of their communal life and to pious associations of the laity which have received official recognition.

If a pious association of the laity, which has perpetual exposition as a part of its constitution, is established within a parish, the activity of that association should be seen as separate from that of the parish, although all members of the parish are free to participate in it.

May perpetual exposition take place in the parish church?

RESPONSE: Because perpetual exposition is a devotional practice of a religious community or a pious association, it should normally take place in a chapel of that religious community or association. If for some good reason perpetual exposition must take place in a parish church, it should be in a chapel distinct from the body of the church so as not to interfere with the normal activities of the parish or its daily liturgical celebrations.

When Mass is celebrated in a chapel where the Blessed Sacrament is exposed, the eucharist must be replaced in the tabernacle before the celebration of Mass begins.

May perpetual exposition take place twenty-four hours a day, 365 days a year?

RESPONSE: Groups authorized to have perpetual exposition are bound to follow all the liturgical norms given in *Holy Communion and Worship of the Eucharist outside Mass*, nos. 82-100. Under no circumstances may perpetual exposition take place during the Easter Triduum. There

3211 FOURTH STREET NE ● WASHINGTON, DC 20017

should always be a sufficient number of people present for eucharistic adoration before the Blessed Sacrament exposed (see HCWEOM, no. 88). Every effort should be made to ensure that there should be at least two people present. There must absolutely never be periods when the Blessed Sacrament is exposed and there is no one present for adoration. It may prove necessary to expose the Blessed Sacrament for adoration only at stated times when members of the faithful are present.

Who is responsible for overseeing perpetual exposition?

RESPONSE: The local Ordinary has the responsibility for the regulation of perpetual exposition. He determines when it is permissible and establishes the regulations to be followed in regard to perpetual exposition of the Blessed Sacrament. He normally entrusts the superior or chaplain of religious communities or the local pastor or chaplain, in the case of pious associations, with the responsibility of seeing that the liturgical norms and his regulations are followed.

Must the local bishop permit perpetual exposition?

RESPONSE: The bishop is responsible for all matters pertaining to the right ordering of the celebration of the Eucharist and adoration and devotion to the Eucharist outside Mass. It is his duty to promote and guide the liturgical life of the diocese. Consequently, he alone determines the pastoral appropriateness of perpetual exposition in his diocese and accordingly may permit it or not and may limit the number of places where it takes place.

Encyclical Letter - *Ut Unum Sint*

On May 25, 1995, the Apostolic See released the latest encyclical letter of Pope John Paul II, Ut Unum Sint (That they May Be One), *on commitment to ecumenism. In paragraphs 44-46 the Holy Father specifically speaks of Christians approaching one another through the Word of God and through divine worship. The text of these portions of the encyclical is given below.*

44. Significant progress in ecumenical cooperation has also been made in another area, that of the Word of God. I am thinking above all of the importance for the different language groups of ecumenical translations of the Bible. Following the promulgation by the Second Vatican Council of the Constitution *Dei Verbum*, the Catholic Church could not fail to welcome this development. These translations prepared by experts, generally offer a solid basis for the prayer and pastoral activity of all Christ's followers. Anyone who recalls how heavily debates about Scripture influenced divisions, especially in the West, can appreciate the significant step forward which these common translations represent.

45. Corresponding to the liturgical renewal carried out by the Catholic Church, certain other Ecclesial Communities have made efforts to renew their worship. Some, on the basis of a recommendation expressed at the ecumenical level, have abandoned the custom of celebrating their liturgy of the Lord's Supper only infrequently and have opted for a celebration each Sunday. Again, when the cycles of liturgical readings used by the various Christian Communities in the West are compared, they appear to be essentially the same. Still on the ecumenical level, very special prominence has been given to the liturgy and liturgical signs (images, icons, vestments, light, incense, gestures). Moreover, in schools of theology where future ministers are trained, courses in the history and significance of the liturgy are beginning to be part of the curriculum in response to a newly discovered need.

These are signs of convergence which regard various aspects of the sacramental life. Certainly, due to disagreements in matters of faith, it is not yet possible to celebrate together the same Eucharistic Liturgy. And yet we do have a burning desire to join in celebrating the one Eucharist of the Lord, and this desire itself is already a common prayer of praise, a single supplication. Together we speak to the Father and increasingly we do so "with one heart". At times it seems that we are closer to being able finally to seal this "real although not yet full" communion. A century ago who could even have imagined such a thing?

46. In this context, it is a source of joy to note that Catholic ministers are able, in certain particular cases, to administer the Sacraments of the Eucharist, Penance and Anointing of the Sick to Christians who are not in full communion with the Catholic Church but who greatly desire to receive these sacraments, freely request them and manifest the faith which the Catholic Church professes with regard to these sacraments. Conversely, in specific cases and in particular circumstances, Catholics too can request these same sacraments from ministers of Churches in which these sacraments are valid. The conditions for such reciprocal reception have been laid down in specific norms; for the sake of furthering ecumenism these norms must be respected.

Sister Ann Rehrauer, OSF, New Associate Director

Sister Rehrauer, who was appointed as Associate Director of the Secretariat for the Liturgy (see January/ February 1995 issue of the *Newsletter*) has now begun working in the Secretariat. We welcome her to the Secretariat staff.

Father Lawrence Heiman, C.PP.S.

Father Lawrence Heiman, C.PP.S., director of the Rensselaer Program of Church Music and Liturgy at Saint Joseph's College has stepped down after thirty-five years of directorship of the program he founded in 1960. In its thirty-five years as a summer school program, the Rensselaer Program of Church Music and Liturgy has provided musical and liturgical training to more than 1000 graduate and undergraduate students, including many participants in five annual workshops in Afro-American church music.

Father Heiman earned a doctorate, *summa cum laude*, in sacred music from the Pontifical Institute of Sacred Music in Rome, in 1970 and was awarded a gold medal by Pope Paul VI. Father Heiman has been active at all levels of Catholic church music. He has served as president of both diocesan and state units of the National Catholic Music Educators Association. He has been a member of its National Board of Directors and head of its Liturgical Department. He also participated in the early days of the Church Music Association, the Composers' Forum for Church Music, and the National Association of Pastoral Musicians.

Father James Challancin, liturgist, seminary professor, and former head of the Marquette, Michigan, Diocesan Office of Worship, has assumed the directorship of the Rensselaer Program of Church Music and Liturgy.

Today the program offers a three-summer sequence leading to the Diploma in Pastoral Liturgy as well as graduate and undergraduate degrees. The six-week summer program offers choices of emphasis in organ, voice, composition, conducting, and music education. For further information, contact Father James Challancin at Saint Joseph College, Renssalaer, Indiana.

Marian Hymn Competition

A Marian hymn competition is being sponsored by the Mariological Society of America. The Mariological Society is seeking new hymn texts, but not new melodies. With the release in 1992 of the English translation of the *Collection of Masses of the Blessed Virgin Mary* for general use, the Mariological Society sees a strong need for new Marian hymns that fit the liturgy. Accordingly, the Mariological Society has initiated a Marian hymn-writing contest in its search for good poetic texts that are scripturally based, doctrinally sound, and which will fit our present liturgy. Contest guidelines ask participants to use images of Mary found in recent church documents, prepare their compositions in hymnic form and meter, and develop the hymn for use in the context of the Mass. The texts should not be set to music. The deadline for submission is March 31, 1996.

For details about the contest, contact: Father Thomas Thompson, S.M., Mariological Society of America, University of Dayton, Dayton, OH 45469-1390, or telephone him at (513) 229-4252.

Instituto de Liturgia Hispana

The Seventh National Conference of the *Instituto de Liturgia Hispana* will take place in Houston, Texas from September 22-24, 1995. The theme of the conference will be *Quince Años: Juventud, Promesa, y Esperanza* (Fifteen Years: Youth, Promise, and Hope). The keynote speaker will be the Most Reverend Ricardo Ramírez, CSB, Bishop of Las Cruces, New Mexico, who will speak on worship and youth. Other major talks will be given by Dr. Carmen M. Cervantes, who will speak on Young People Celebrating the Faith, Father Virgilio Elizondo who will talk about Bringing Young People into the Liturgy, and Sister Angela Erevia, MCDP, who will speak about the Celebration of the *Quinceañera*. Six workshops on various subjects will be offered. All conferences will be given in Spanish, but translation facilities will be available. For further information on the conference write to: *Instituto de Liturgia Hispana*, Coordinator VII Conference, 625 Notingham Oaks Trail, Houston, TX 77079.

Resources

Sacred Mysteries: Sacramental Principles and Liturgical Practice by Dennis C. Smolarski, S.J. Father Smolarski, whose previous publications include, *Eucharistia: A Study of the Eucharistic Prayer*, *Liturgical Literacy,* and *How Not to Say Mass*, teaches at Santa Clara University in California and serves on the Presentation of Texts Subcommittee of the International Commission on English in the Liturgy (ICEL). Father Smolarski, in *Sacred Mysteries*, reflects on the liturgical renewal of the past quarter century and the success of its implementation on the parish level. After discussing the foundational principles for liturgical action, he moves to each of the sacraments and the way they are celebrated in the worshiping assembly. The final chapter addresses practices that are detrimental to the proper celebration of the rites. Priests, deacons and others who are involved in the celebration of the rites would do well to read this book and reflect on how faithfully they have carried out the implementation of the revised rites in their own parishes. The book is available from Paulist Press for $12.95.

Low Gluten Altar Bread and the Use of *Mustum*

On June 19, 1995, Cardinal William Keeler, President of the National Conference of Catholic Bishops, received a letter from Joseph Cardinal Ratzinger, Prefect of the Congregation for the Doctrine of the Faith. The letter was addressed to the Presidents of Episcopal Conferences and sets forth the norms of the Congregation permitting the use of low-gluten altar breads for people affected by celiac disease and revised procedures for permitting the use of mustum *for priests affected by alcoholism. The text of Cardinal Ratzinger's letter follows.*

Prot. N. 89/78   June 19, 1995

Your Eminence/Excellency:

In recent years, this Dicastery has followed closely the development of the question of the use of low-gluten altar breads and *mustum* as matter for the celebration of the Eucharist.

After careful study, conducted in collaboration with a number of concerned Episcopal Conferences, this Congregation in its ordinary session of June 22, 1994 has approved the following norms, which I am pleased to communicate:

I.   *Concerning permission to use low-gluten altar breads:*

A.   This may be granted by Ordinaries to priests and laypersons affected by celiac disease, after presentation of a medical certificate.

B.   Conditions for the validity of the matter:

1)   Special hosts *quibus glutinum ablatum est* are invalid matter for the celebration of the Eucharist;

2)   Low-gluten hosts are valid matter, provided that they contain the amount of gluten sufficient to obtain the confection of bread, that there is no addition of foreign materials, and that the procedure for making such hosts is not such as to alter the nature of the substance of the bread.

II.   *Concerning permission to use* mustum:

A.   The preferred solution continues to be Communion **per intinctionem**, or in concelebration under the species of bread alone.

B.   Nevertheless, the permission to use *mustum* can be granted by Ordinaries to priests affected by

3211 FOURTH STREET NE ● WASHINGTON, DC 20017

alcoholism or other conditions which prevent the ingestion of even the smallest quantity of alcohol, after presentation of a medical certificate.

C.   By *mustum* is understood fresh juice from grapes, or juice preserved by suspending its fermentation (by means of freezing or other methods which do not alter its nature).

D.   In general, those who have received permission to use *mustum* are prohibited from presiding at concelebrated Masses. There may be some exceptions however: in the case of a Bishop or Superior General; or, with prior approval of the Ordinary, at the celebration of the anniversary of priestly ordination or other similar occasions. In these cases, the one who presides is to communicate under both the species of bread and that of *mustum*, while for the other concelebrants a chalice shall be provided in which normal wine is to be consecrated.

E.   In the very rare instances of laypersons requesting this permission, recourse must be made to the Holy See.

III.   *Common Norms*:

A.   The Ordinary must ascertain that the matter used conforms to the above requirements.

B.   Permissions are to be given only for as long as the situation continues which motivated the request.

C.   Scandal is to be avoided.

D.   Given the centrality of the celebration of the Eucharist in the life of the priest, candidates for the priesthood who are affected by celiac disease or suffer from alcoholism or similar conditions may not be admitted to Holy Orders.

E.   Since the doctrinal questions have now been decided, disciplinary competence is entrusted to the Congregation for Divine Worship and the Discipline of the Sacraments.

F.   Concerned Episcopal Conferences shall report to the Congregation for Divine Worship and the Discipline of the Sacraments every two years regarding the application of these norms.

With warm regards and best wishes, I am

Sincerely yours in Christ,

Joseph Cardinal Ratzinger
Prefect

June Meeting of the Committee on the Liturgy

The Liturgy Committee (members, consultants, and advisors) met on Monday-Tuesday, June 12-13, 1995 at the Cenacle Retreat Center in Chicago, Illinois. The Committee discussed and took action on the texts and the amendments submitted for the *American Adaptations of the Roman Missal* and the *Pastoral*

Introduction to the Order of the Mass. Both sets of texts were then presented to the National Conference of Catholic Bishops for discussion and approval at the June plenary meeting. Proposed changes included a simplification of the Introductory Rites, the Apostles' Creed as an alternative to the Nicene Creed, new introductions for the Memorial Acclamation, and options for the placement of the sign of peace.

The Committee completed its discussion of the proposed texts for the ordination of bishops, presbyters, and deacons begun at last June's meeting and discussed the first draft of the document *Cremation and Other Burial Practices*. A second draft of the document will be prepared to take into account the comments of the Committee.

A proposal regarding the celebration of Divine Mercy Sunday (Second Sunday of Easter) had been received by the Committee. The members felt that this was not the appropriate time to request such a celebration for the United States. The Committee also received a report from the Task Group on Televised Masses which is preparing a draft of guidelines which will be submitted to the Committee in the near future.

The Committee also heard several information reports. Father Michael Spillane and Father James Moroney reported on the work of the Federation of Diocesan Liturgical Commissions and highlighted plans for the upcoming national meeting in Providence. They shared the results of the survey on offices of worship and liturgical commissions and presented the position statements and resolutions of immediate concern passed at the national meeting in St. Louis. The FDLC is currently working on the revision of the *Guidelines for Multilingual Masses* and has offered its assistance to the Committee on the Liturgy in its preparation of American adaptations for the revised *Order for Celebrating Marriage*.

Monsignor Alan Detscher reported on the work of the Hispanic Liturgy Subcommittee. The Subcommittee is continuing its work on the translation of the *Sacramentario* and has begun to work on the Spanish translation of the marriage rite and the *Book of Blessings*.

Father Raúl Gómez, SDS, president of the Instituto de Liturgia Hispana informed the Committee that the Instituto has a new director, Sister Doris Mary Turek, SSND and new office space at the Catholic University of America. The Instituto will host its seventh annual conference in Houston this September with the theme "Quince Años: juventud, promesa, y esperanza" (Fifteen Years: youth, promise, and hope). The theme celebrates the fifteenth anniversary of the Instituto and directs the attention of the participants to the quinceañera celebration.

June Plenary Assembly of the NCCB

The National Conference of Catholic Bishops (NCCB) met in plenary assembly from June 15-17, 1995 at the Hyatt Regency Hotel in Chicago, Illinois.

The bishops considered Segment III: *Order of the Mass I* of the proposed ICEL revision of the *Sacramentary* and the United States *Adaptations of the Order of Mass* prepared by the Committee on the Liturgy. The original agenda had also included action on the *Pastoral Introduction to the Order of Mass* but there was insufficient time for discussion of the text. The *Pastoral Introduction* and the USA adaptations of it, along with Segment IV: *Order of Mass II* which includes the Prefaces, Solemn Blessings, Prayers over the People, and Sample General Intercessions, will be discussed and voted upon at the November meeting.

Approval of liturgical texts requires a two-thirds affirmative vote of the *de jure* Latin rite members of the NCCB. At the time of the meeting, the required number of affirmative votes was 176. The balloting at the meeting was inconclusive and members who were not present received mail ballots subsequent to the meeting. After the mail ballots were counted, all of the items proposed by the Committee on the Liturgy were approved. The approved items include the liturgical texts for the Order of Mass with 183 affirmative, 72 negative votes; the ecumenical texts for the Order of Mass (with the exception of the Lord's Prayer) with 189 affirmative, 65 negative votes; ICEL variations for the Order of Mass with 179 affirmative, 75 negative votes; the USA adaptations of the *Order of Mass* with 189 affirmative, 54 negative votes; the *Appendix to the General Instruction of the Roman Missal for Dioceses of the United States* with 186 affirmative , 59 negative votes; and the *Appendix to the General Norms for the Liturgical Year and the Calendar for the Dioceses of the United States* with 221 affirmative and 25 negative votes.

Other documents approved by the bishops included *Guidelines for Celebration of Sacraments with Persons with Disabilities* presented by the Committee on Pastoral Practices. The bishops also approved the design for a Forum on Principles of Translation presented by the *ad hoc* Committee chaired by Archbishop Jerome Hanus.

New Advisors to the Committee on the Liturgy

Father Thomas A. Krosnicki, S.V.D., Mission Director of the Divine Word Missionaries in Techny, Illinois, has been appointed as an advisor to the Committee on the Liturgy by Bishop Donald W. Trautman. Father Krosnicki received a doctorate in Sacred Theology with a specialization in liturgy from the Pontifical Liturgical Institute in Rome. He served as an Associate Director of the Liturgy Secretariat from 1972-1978 and as Executive Director from 1978-1981. In 1981 Father Krosnicki accepted a mission assignment from his community to serve in Papua, New Guinea. Father Krosnicki recently served as a member of the Liturgy Committee's task group on American adaptations of the Roman Missal. The Liturgy Committee is pleased to welcome Father Krosnicki as one of its advisors.

Father Michael Driscoll, a presbyter of the diocese of Helena, Montana, has also been appointed as an advisor to the Committee on the Liturgy by Bishop Donald W. Trautman. Father Driscoll studied Sacramental Theology at the Pontifical Athenaeum of Saint Anselm in Rome and received a doctorate in Liturgy at the Institut Supérieur de Liturgie in Paris. Dr. Driscoll taught for many years at Carroll College in Helena and recently was appointed to the faculty for Liturgical Studies at the University of Notre Dame. The Liturgy Committee is happy to welcome Father Driscoll as an advisor.

Advisors Completing Their Terms

At the close of the June meeting, Reverend Kevin W. Irwin and Reverend Jeremy Driscoll, OSB completed their terms as advisors to the Committee. The Bishops' Committee on the Liturgy and the staff of the Secretariat wish to express their appreciation for the assistance and advice given by Father Irwin and Father Driscoll during their three years as advisors.

Kansas Letter on Sunday Celebrations of the Eucharist

The bishops of Kansas have written a pastoral statement reaffirming the importance of Sunday celebrations of eucharist and presenting their position on distribution of communion outside Mass on Sundays. In commenting on the reasons for the pastoral statement, Archbishop Keleher noted that the bishops are concerned about the apparent lack of understanding about the nature of the eucharist. The statement was written to heighten the distinction between the sacrifice of the Mass and a "communion service" and to reiterate the bishops' position that such communion services are not a substitute for Sunday Mass in the province of Kansas City, Kansas. The text of the pastoral statement follows:

SUNDAY EUCHARIST
Do This in Memory of Me

The Holy Eucharist is a priceless gift, essential to our identity as Catholics, and central to our life as Church.

Of all the gifts God has given to us, there is none so filled with grace as this one gift of the Eucharist celebrated at each Holy Mass.

The Eucharist holds within itself the Church's entire spiritual wealth: the fullness of Christ himself. The other Sacraments, like every other ministry of the Church and every other work of the apostolate, are irrevocably tied to the holy Eucharist and have it as their beginning and their end.

This clear and yet mysterious faith of the Church in the Eucharist makes us all that we are, and hope yet to be.

****

What, then, are we? What do we Catholics believe about this priceless, essential, and central gift? What is the Eucharist for us?

We believe that the Eucharist is Who is on the altar. But the Eucharist is also who is around the altar and beyond the altar.

We believe that the bread and wine, through the words of Christ and the power of the Holy Spirit, become Christ's body and blood.

We believe that the Lord, knowing his hour had come to leave this world, instituted the Eucharist as the memorial of his death and resurrection. We believe he commanded his apostles to celebrate it until his return, thereby constituting them as priests of the New Testament.

We believe that this awesome mystery stretches even to our place and our time when the priest takes bread in his hands, takes a cup of wine in his hands, and says the words of consecration. We believe that, while ordinary elements remain, an extraordinary difference has taken place through the invocation of the Holy Spirit. The ordinary elements of bread and wine have been totally and absolutely transformed into the very body and blood of Christ.

****

While the single voice of the priest proclaims the words of consecration, the whole Eucharistic Prayer also has a larger meaning. It is the prayer of the whole assembly. It expresses praise, reconciliation, remembrance, and intercession. It is the prayer through which the Holy Spirit transforms people as well as gifts.

The meaning of the Eucharistic Prayer is even larger still. It reaches those who are beyond the altar by means of those who are around the altar. It gives rise to ecumenism, evangelization, missionary activity, and stewardship.

The parish is the usual place where all the faithful gather for the Sunday celebration of the Eucharist. "The parish initiates the Christian people into the ordinary expression of the liturgical life: it gathers them together in this celebration; it teaches Christ's saving doctrine; it practices the charity of the Lord in good works and brotherly love . . . " [1]

"Participation in the communal celebration of the Sunday Eucharist is a testimony of belonging and being faithful to Christ and to his Church. The faithful give witness by this to their communion in faith and charity. Together they testify to God's holiness and their hope of salvation. They strengthen one another under the guidance of the Holy Spirit." [2]

The priest will always remain essential to the Eucharist, therefore, and will always be an important gift to the Church. In our day, many dioceses have begun to study the different look of this gift in the Church. Conditions have changed, as is evidenced by the declining number of priests, as is evidenced by the growing and shifting of our populations. Many dioceses have given sustained thought to these changed conditions, so that the celebration of the Sunday Eucharist may be made as widely available as possible.

These studies have resulted in more focussed pastoral actions such as the following:

• promotion and recruitment of vocations to the priesthood;

• systematic development of stewardship;

• continuing formation of lay ministers;

• amalgamation of parishes;

• reduction in Masses of convenience;

• distribution of Holy Communion and the worship of the Eucharist outside Mass.

We, the bishops of Kansas, have come to judge that Holy Communion regularly received outside of Mass is a short-term solution that has all the makings of becoming a long-term problem. It has implications that are disturbing:

---

[1] *Catechism of the Catholic Church*, 1994, #2179.

[2] Ibid, #2182.

• a blurring of the difference between the celebration of the Eucharist and the reception of Communion;

• a blurring of the distinction between a priest and a deacon or a non-ordained minister presiding over Communion Service;

• a blurring of the relationship between pastoral and sacramental ministry;

• a blurring of the connection between the Eucharist and the works of charity and justice;

• a blurring of the need for priests and therefore a blurring of the continual need for vocations;

• a blurring of the linkage between the local Church and the diocesan and universal Church that is embodied in the person of the parish priest.

These implications give us pause in approving the distribution of Holy Communion outside Mass on Sundays. Such practice could well contribute to the erosion of our many-sided belief in the Eucharist. IT IS FOR THIS REASON THAT WE RESTRICT SUCH SERVICES TO EMERGENCIES ONLY. And by that, we mean unforeseen circumstances when a priest is not available. We recognize that this policy calls some of the faithful to sacrifices and hardships that match those of our ancestors in the faith.

Where great distances impose unreasonable sacrifices and hardships, an exception to this policy may be made by the local bishop. Such an exception is rooted in the universal law of the Church.

"If because of lack of a sacred minister or for other grave cause participation in the celebration of the Eucharist is impossible, it is specially recommended that the faithful take part in the Liturgy of the Word if it is celebrated in the parish church or in another sacred place according to the prescriptions of the diocesan bishop, or engage in prayer for an appropriate amount of time personally or in a family, or, as occasion offers, in groups of families."[3]

In this context it may be helpful to recall the role of the priest beyond Word and Sacrament. The priest is not just a functionary who consecrates the Eucharist, pours water, anoints with oil, or absolves the penitent, important as these functions are. He is not just a circuit rider who offers Mass and celebrates the Sacraments.

He is also a builder of the communion of the faithful, a co-worker with the bishop in building up the diocesan Church, and a symbol of the universal Church in that particular parish. He is not only one who sanctifies, he is also one who proclaims the gospel. He is not only an administrator, he is also a shepherd who serves the cause of human dignity. He is none of these things alone, of course. Nor is he any of these first, of course. He comes to these, as we all come to these, by way of the family, and often by way of a parish family in which the seeds of his calling were first sown by a small band of lay persons or religious men and women.

To know the history of the faith in Kansas is to give thanks to God for the generosity of the

---

[3] *Code of Canon Law*, Can. 1248, par. 2. Holy Communion may be given outside of Mass with the Celebration of the Word (see Sacred Congregation for Divine Worship, *Holy Communion Outside of Mass*, June 21, 1973, no. 16 and *Directory for Sunday Celebrations in the Absence of a Priest*, June 2, 1988). The faithful should be instructed carefully that even when they receive communion outside Mass, they are closely united with the sacrifice which perpetuates the sacrifice of the cross (*Holy Communion Outside of Mass*, June 21, 1973, no. 15).

priests, lay women and men, and dedicated religious of our dioceses. An awareness of this history gives us a profound appreciation for the working of the Holy Spirit who inspires all the baptized to a more conscious placing of their gifts, talents, and charisms at the service of their brothers and sisters. There is nothing better than a gift carefully acknowledged and freely given for others. The result is a source of untold blessings and an immeasurable enrichment for the Church and for the entire human family.

We now call ourselves and all the faithful to preserve and to promote the prime place of the Sunday Eucharist in our lives as Catholics. We echo the Second Vatican Council in calling all Catholics to a full, active, and conscious participation in the Eucharistic worship.

May the Lord who has begun this good work in us bring it to fulfillment, making us one body in the Body of Christ.

Given on 18 June, the Solemnity of Corpus Christi, 1995.

Most Reverend James P. Keleher
Archbishop of Kansas City, KS

Most Reverend Stanley G. Schlarman
Bishop of Dodge City

Most Reverend George K. Fitzsimons
Bishop of Salina

Most Reverend Eugene J. Gerber
Bishop of Wichita

1995 National Meeting of Diocesan Liturgical Commissions

The annual meeting of diocesan liturgical commissions and offices of worship will be held in Providence, Rhode Island from October 5-9, 1995. The meeting, cosponsored by the Federation of Diocesan Liturgical Commissions and the NCCB Committee on Liturgy, will have as its theme "Mystery and Metanoia: Building Bridges Between Liturgy and Life." Major addresses include: "Vision: Voices from the Past" by Reverend Monsignor Frederick R. McManus; "Conversion: Metanoia of the Present" by Reverend Robert Duggan; "Passion: Heart of the Mystery" by Reverend Regis A. Duffy, OFM; and "Mission: Shaping the Future" by Sister Theresa F. Koernke, IHM. Several workshops developing particular aspects of the theme will also be offered.

During the course of the meeting Monsignor Frederick R. McManus, who served as the first Executive Director of the Liturgy Secretariat and was instrumental in the founding of the Federation of Diocesan Liturgical Commissions, will receive an award. In 1994 the National Meeting of Liturgical Commissions in Saint Louis voted to establish an award to recognize significant contributions to the liturgical renewal in the United States. In 1995 the Board of Directors of the FDLC voted to name this award in honor of Monsignor McManus, its first recipient.

For registration forms and additional information call the FDLC National Office at 202-635-6990.

COMMITTEE ON THE LITURGY
NEWSLETTER

NATIONAL CONFERENCE OF CATHOLIC BISHOPS

**1995
VOLUME XXXI
SEPTEMBER**

Confirmation of the Proper Text for the Mass of the Blessed Virgin Mary, Star of the Sea

On August 29, 1995, the National Conference of Catholic Bishops received the decree of the Congregation for Divine Worship and the Discipline of the Sacraments, dated August 2, 1995, confirming the proper English text for the Mass of the Blessed Virgin Mary, Star of the Sea. This Mass is intended for use by those engaged in the Apostolate of the Sea. The following is an unofficial translation of that decree:

Prot. 93/95/L

United States of America

At the request of His Excellency William Cardinal Keeler, Archbishop of Baltimore, President of the Conference of Bishops in the United States of America, contained in a letter dated 28 December 1994, and in virtue of the faculty granted to this Congregation by the Supreme Pontiff, John Paul II, we gladly confirm, *ad interim* and for a period of three years, the English text of the Mass of the Blessed Virgin Mary, Star of the Sea, for use by priests associated with the Apostolate of the Sea, as given in the attached example.

When the text is printed, this entire decree, by which the request to the Apostolic See has been confirmed, is to be included. Two copies of the printed text should be sent to this Congregation.

From the offices of the Congregation for Divine Worship and the Discipline of the Sacraments, 2 August 1995.

Archbishop Gerardo M. Agnelo
Secretary

Mario Lessi-Ariosto, S.J.

MASS OF THE BLESSED VIRGIN MARY, STAR OF THE SEA

This Mass may be celebrated on weekdays in Ordinary Time and on optional memorials in oratories dedicated to the Apostleship of the Sea.

ENTRANCE ANTIPHON — You have been blessed, O Virgin Mary, above all other women on earth by the Lord, the Most High God, for God has so exalted your name that human lips will never cease to praise you. *See Judith 13:23, 25*

3211 FOURTH STREET NE ● WASHINGTON, DC 20017

OPENING PRAYER

Lord God,
you willed that the Blessed Virgin Mary, Star of the Sea,
should shine for us
upon the storm-tossed voyage of life.
You chose the Mother of your Son to be our stronghold.
Free us from all perils of soul and body
through her guiding assistance
and steer our course at last
to the harbor of eternal peace.

We ask this through our Lord Jesus Christ, your Son
who lives and reigns with you in the unity of the Holy Spirit,
God for ever and ever.

R. Amen.

PRAYER OVER THE GIFTS

Be pleased, O Lord,
to accept the gifts of your Church,
so that, through the intercession of the loving Mother of your Son,
we may find mercy
and know the help of your grace in time of need.

We ask this through Jesus Christ our Lord.

R. Amen.

PREFACE OF THE BLESSED VIRGIN MARY I OR II

COMMUNION ANTIPHON

To you they cried, and they were saved; they trusted
and were not shamed.   *Psalm 22:6*

PRAYER AFTER COMMUNION

You have made us sharers, O Lord,
in eternal redemption.
As we honor the Mother of your Son,
give us joy in the fullness of your grace
and in the constant growth within us
of your saving power.

Grant this through Christ our Lord.

R. Amen.

READING I   Wis 14: 2b-7 or Is 43:1-3a, 4-7

RESPONSORIAL PSALM   Ps 107: 21-24,25-26,27-30
                                 R/. Give thanks to the Lord, his love is everlasting

ALLELUIA   R/. Alleluia
                                 A star shall advance from Jacob,
                                 and a staff shall rise from Israel.
                                 O Lord, our God, how wonderful your name in all the earth!
                                                       (Nm 24:17; Ps 8:2)

GOSPEL   Lk 1:26-38

Administrative Committee of the National Conference of Catholic Bishops

On September 12-14, 1995 the Administrative Committee of the NCCB met in Washington, D.C. At that meeting the Committee approved two liturgical action items for presentation and vote at the NCCB Meeting this November: the *Pastoral Introduction to the Order of Mass* and Segment IV of the *Sacramentary* which includes the Prefaces, Solemn Blesssings, Prayers Over the People, and Sample General Intercessions.

Scripture Translation

Recently the Oxford University Press released a translation of the *New Testament and Psalms: an Inclusive Version*, edited by Victor Roland Gold, et al. In response to this publication, Bishop Donald W. Trautman, chairman of the Bishops' Committee on the Liturgy wrote to the bishops of the United States. A copy of his memo follows:

"I wish to bring to your attention that within the next few weeks a new biblical translation of the New Testament will be published by Oxford University Press. It is called "The New Testament and Psalms: an Inclusive Version." It is a most irresponsible translation that offends the doctrine of the Church and revealed truth of Father, Son and Holy Spirit. This new English translation eliminates all references to God the Father. The Lord's Prayer begins "Our Father-Mother in heaven". The editors of this volume have done a real disservice to biblical scholarship and the need for a balanced use of inclusive language. In some instances the translation is not based on the inspired text and even adds words not found in the original. In my opinion it is not so much a translation as a rewrite based on contemporary political and social ideologies. This new version represents a radical and extreme reaction to the need for a balanced use of inclusive language. Without question it is a distortion of the inspired Word of God."

Papal Visit

Over the past two years the Liturgy Secretariat has been involved in the preparations for the pastoral visit of Pope John Paul II to the Archdioceses of Newark, New York, and Baltimore, and the Diocese of

Brooklyn. Monsignor Detscher, Executive Director of the Liturgy Secretariat, has served as the coordinator for the liturgical celebrations. Those responsible for the liturgical celebrations in each of the dioceses met several times over the past two years to discuss their plans and share their concerns. Each diocese made proposals for the liturgies to be celebrated in that diocese which were then brought to Monsignor Piero Marini, Master of Liturgical Celebrations of the Supreme Pontiff. Each of the liturgies was discussed in detail with Monsignor Marini and the results of the discussions were communicated to the local coordinators: Sister Janet Baxendale (New York), Monsignor Richard Gronki (Newark), Father John Tosi (Brooklyn), Father Michael White (Baltimore). The approved celebrations consisted of Evening Prayer at the Cathedral of the Sacred Heart (Newark), Celebration of the Eucharist at Giants Stadium (Newark), Celebration of the Eucharist at Aqueduct Racetrack (Brooklyn), Evening Prayer at Saint Joseph's Seminary (New York), Celebration of the Eucharist in Central Park (New York), Recitation of the Rosary in Saint Patrick's Cathedral (New York), Celebration of the Eucharist at Oriole Park (Baltimore), Reception of the Holy Father at Mary our Queen Cathedral (Baltimore).

Once the texts of the liturgies were approved, preparations were made in the Secretariat for the Liturgy for the publication of a sacramentary containing all the liturgies that the Holy Father would celebrate. The Catholic Book Publishing Company kindly offered to print the papal *Sacramentary*. A small number of copies of the book were printed and distributed to the respective dioceses. Additional copies of the book are not available.

The most vexing problem faced in each of the sites was the difficulty of distributing holy communion to huge numbers of people in a brief period of time. Various solutions were implemented at the different sites. In stadiums the coordinators had to face the problem of getting the ministers of communion to their stations quickly and with due reverence for the eucharist. This difficulty was compounded by the lack of access from the field level to the other levels of the stadium. In most of the sites it was necessary to have priests, deacons, and lay persons distribute the sacrament. The local coordinators and those who assisted them are to be congratulated for the fine celebrations which took place in each of their dioceses.

In Memoriam
Abbot Jerome Theisen, OSB

Abbot Jerome Theisen, OSB, Abbot Primate of the Benedictine Order and former abbot of Saint John's Abbey, Collegeville, MN died of a heart attack in Rome, Italy on September 11, 1995. Abbot Theisen was born in Loyal, Wisconsin and entered Saint John's Abbey in 1952. He received a doctorate in theology from Saint Anselm's in Rome and later taught theology and served as chancellor at Saint John's University in Collegeville. He had been abbot of Saint John's Abbey for thirteen years when he was elected to a six year term as abbot primate of the Benedictine Confederation in 1992. He was only the second U.S. Benedictine to hold that international position. Abbot Theisen was a major presenter at the workshops on the *Ceremonial of Bishops* and later played a leading role in the 1994 Synod of Bishops on religious life.

> All-powerful God,
> we pray for our brother Jerome,
> who responded to the call of Christ
> and pursued wholeheartedly the ways of perfect love.
> Grant that he may rejoice
> on that day when your glory will be revealed
> and in company with all his brothers and sisters
> share for ever the happiness of your kingdom.
> (*Order of Christian Funerals*, 398.22)

COMMITTEE ON THE LITURGY

NEWSLETTER

1995
VOLUME XXXI
OCTOBER

1995 National Meeting of Diocesan Liturgical Commissions

The annual national meeting of diocesan liturgical commissions and offices of worship was held in Providence, RI, October 5-8, 1995. The national meeting is jointly sponsored by the Federation of Diocesan Liturgical Commissions and the NCCB Committee on the Liturgy.

The general theme of the meeting was "Mystery and Metanoia: Building Bridges Between Liturgy and Life." Major addresses were given by Reverend Monsignor Frederick R. McManus ("Vision: Voices from the Past"); Reverend Robert Duggan ("Conversion: Metanoia of the Present"); Reverend Regis A. Duffy, OFM ("Passion: Heart of the Mystery"); and Sister Theresa F. Koernke, IHM ("Mission: Shaping the Future").

The delegates approved five position statements which had been formulated at regional meetings of the delegates during the spring of 1995 and two resolutions of immediate concern drafted in the course of the national meeting (see page 40).

FDLC Address of Bishop Donald Trautman

On October 5, 1995, the Most Reverend Donald B. Trautman, Bishop of Erie and Chairman of the Bishops' Committee on the Liturgy, addressed the delegates to the 1995 National Meeting of Diocesan Liturgical Commissions in Providence, RI. The text of his address follows:

In the name of the Bishops and in the name of all God's people, I would like to express gratitude for your ministry to the Church. You continue to promote the liturgical reforms of Vatican II with great commitment and competence. You have struggled against great odds to produce full, conscious, and active participation by all in the assembly.

The great liturgist, Josef Jungmann, had you in mind when he wrote: "For centuries, the liturgy, actively celebrated, has been the most important form of pastoral care." Through your deep involvement in Diocesan Liturgical Commissions and Offices of Worship and Music Ministry, and as parish liturgical coordinators and liturgists in classrooms, you have made these words real and concrete; you have put "flesh on these dry bones." Time and time again, you have demonstrated and proven that liturgy, actively celebrated, is the most important form of pastoral care. And so, I affirm you and thank you for your work and witness.

It has been a long, and at times, a difficult year since we last met in St. Louis. At the same time, it has been a year filled with hope and confidence, a year when we have seen the end results of more than ten years of work on the translation of liturgical texts. ICEL has completed its task of translating nearly 2,000 texts in the Roman Missal and deserves the thanks of the Church for its scholarly work. Three segments of the proposed ICEL revision of the *Sacramentary* have already been approved by the National Conference of Catholic Bishops. All the action items pertaining to the revision of the *Sacramentary*, so far presented to the American Catholic Bishops by its Liturgical Committee, have been approved by a two-thirds vote. This is good news for all liturgists, and I thank you for your support and help in interpreting these liturgical items to your bishop. Biblical scholars are presently at work revising the New American Bible *Lectionary* so that it will have a balanced use of horizontal inclusive language. I have attended meetings in Rome relative to this matter and I am happy to report biblical experts are applying norms received from the Congregation for the Doctrine of the Faith to the *Lectionary*. This work is detailed and intense but it is moving ahead in a positive fashion.

Last year, I reported to you some of the difficulties that the Committee on the Liturgy and I were experiencing in regard to the approval of the *Sacramentary* and *Lectionary for Mass*. This year, I am happy to detail the progress that has been made on these two fronts.

Last November, the first two segments of the revised *Sacramentary* came before the bishops. After extensive discussions with the Doctrine Committee and its representatives, some 50 prayers were sent back to ICEL for further consideration. None of the texts was found to be unorthodox as some had claimed. The remaining texts were approved by large majorities. Most of the bishops recognize that the revised translation and new Original Prayers are a vast improvement over those presently in use, and look forward to the publication of the revised *Sacramentary*.

In June, the NCCB discussed and voted upon the third segment of the *Sacramentary* which contained the Order of Mass and the eucharistic prayers. The contents of Segment III were divided into a series of votes in order to simplify and to group related material together. It was also done to insure that if the bishops did not like one section, that section could be singled out and the whole document would not be rejected. The bishops were asked to vote on: the ICEL translation of the liturgical texts; the common ecumenical texts for the Gloria, Creed, Sanctus, etc.; the ICEL variations in the Order of Mass; the USA adaptations for the Order of Mass; the *Appendix to the General Instruction*; and the *Appendix to the General Introduction to the Liturgical Year and the Calendar*. Due to a lack of time, the bishops were unable to vote on the ICEL *Pastoral Introduction to the Order of Mass* and the corresponding USA adaptations for that document. The bishops spent more than a day discussing the various proposals presented by the Committee on the Liturgy. Most of the time was taken up by bishops whose amendments were rejected and who asked the NCCB to reverse the decision of the Liturgy Committee. In the end, the NCCB decided to accept the recommendations of the Liturgy Committee.

The Committee on the Liturgy withdrew its proposal regarding the posture of the congregation during the eucharistic prayer. It quickly became apparent that it was misunderstood, and rather than have all the other material in the *Appendix to the General Instruction* rejected, it seemed better to withdraw the proposal. I would note that the Committee was not changing the posture, but only attempting to provide a sign of reverence when, for legitimate reasons, it was not possible for the people to kneel. This means that there will be no change in the present discipline.

The bishops voted on the various items by written ballot, but because there were not a sufficient number of bishops present, it was necessary to send ballots by mail to the absent bishops. When the voting was completed, it was announced that all the liturgical items had ben approved by the required two-thirds affirmative vote of all the [de iure] Latin Rite members of the NCCB. A booklet has been sent to all the bishops incorporating all changes in the ICEL Order of Mass approved by the bishops and the various adaptations for the dioceses of the United States also approved by the bishops.

In November, the NCCB will consider the ICEL *Pastoral Introduction to the Order of Mass* and the USA adaptations of the *Pastoral Introduction*. The Committee on the Liturgy received a very large number of amendments on this document and made a significant number of changes which have made it a much better text. The bishops will also be asked to approve Segment IV: Order of Mass II, containing the prefaces, solemn blessings, prayers over the people and the sample general intercessions given in the appendix of the *Sacramentary*.

The bishops will shortly receive Segment V containing the Proper of Saints and Segment VI containing Holy Week, the Antiphonal of Volume I, and other miscellaneous texts of Volume I of the *Sacramentary* that have not yet been considered. The Liturgy Committee will also be sending the bishops a number of adaptations for the Holy Week rites as well as the texts of Masses proper to the United States, that is, the American saints and blessed and the Masses for the Fourth of July and Thanksgiving. These materials will all be considered by the bishops in June. The remaining two segments of the *Sacramentary*, Segments VII and VIII will be presented to the bishops for approval in November of 1996.

As you can see, the approval process for the *Sacramentary* is now moving along and should be completed by the end of next year. ICEL must still respond to the texts that the NCCB has returned for further consideration and must also consult with the other [English-speaking] episcopal conferences about them. Once all the texts for Volume I are approved, they will be sent to the Congregation for Divine Worship and Discipline of the Sacraments for confirmation. It may be optimistic to hope that we will have the confirmation of the Sunday volume of the *Sacramentary* before the beginning of the Third Millennium. This would be a marvelous way to begin the new millennium -- with a new book of beautiful and inspiring prayers for the celebration of the eucharist -- a book vastly superior to the present *Sacramentary*.

Although I cannot go into the details about the *Lectionary for Mass*, I can tell you that the discussions with the Congregation for the Doctrine of the Faith are progressing and that I and several other bishops with degrees in biblical studies are carefully going through the text and will be proposing some revisions to the Congregation. I hope that this work for the Sunday volume of the *Lectionary* will be completed by the end of this year.

As we prepare for the introduction of a new *Sacramentary* and a new *Lectionary for Mass* in the remaining years of this century, we need now to plan how we are going to introduce them. Catechesis of the clergy and the people is an absolute essential. The Federation of Diocesan Liturgical Commissions will have to take an active role in the preparation and implementation of such catechesis. I notice that several of the position statements for your consideration at this meeting address the issues of preparing our people for the liturgical changes and the revised texts. I have no specific ideas on how this catechesis should be carried out. But I do know that, in your discussions at the regional and national level, you will help to provide the bishops with creative and effective options for this very important task.

I am sure you realize that the Secretariat in Washington daily receives calls from individuals who are concerned about liturgical matters. Often they are distressed by something that is going on in their own parish. It is the policy of the Secretariat to encourage these people to call their diocesan liturgy office or to write to their bishops. It often happens that they do not receive an answer that they find acceptable from the diocesan office and so call Washington. In some cases, they are given incorrect information at the local level which represents the personal desires of the individual in the liturgy office, but does not correspond to the decisions of the NCCB or the current liturgical law. I mention this because catechesis is not just for the clergy and the people "out there." It is also necessary for us who are to give advice and answer questions. We must be pastoral, but we do no one a favor when we do not give clear and correct answers or when we limit legitimate options and diversity. My challenge to you in the days ahead is to continue to develop your knowledge of the Church's liturgy, to catechize yourselves so that you can effectively catechize others as the new books are introduced. We have great opportunities before us in the last days of the twentieth century. At the risk of using an ancient Latin phrase, *carpe diem* -- we must "seize the day" for a renewed effort to make the liturgy the source of our faith and its highest expression.

In addition to the major task of the revision of the *Sacramentary*, the Committee on the Liturgy and the Secretariat staff are engaged in a variety of projects, including a position paper on cremation, guidelines for televised Masses, the approval of an Hispanic *Lectionary,* and the formation of a task force to study art, architecture, and liturgical environment. If you have any specific questions about the work of the Secretariat or the projects currently in process, I would refer you to the written report presented by the staff.

Again, I thank you for your support and assistance over the past twelve months and wish to assure you of the commitment of the Committee on the Liturgy and my own personal commitment to the on-going liturgical reform.

In our various ministries we can become at times disappointed and discouraged, disillusioned and dejected. As we look to our world, our Church, our places of ministry, there may be a thousand reasons for frustration, a thousand reasons for pessimism, but there is always one reason for perseverance, one reason for optimism and that is, the Risen Lord is with us. The cross is not just a sign of pain and death, it is also a sign of hope and victory. May the Risen Lord continue to motivate us in fulfilling Josef Jungmann's words: "Liturgy, actively celebrated, is the most important form of pastoral care." That is our goal, that is our agenda, that is our mission statement. Thank you.

Resolutions of the 1995 National Meeting of Diocesan Liturgical Commissions

The following are some of the position statements and resolutions of immediate concern that were adopted by the delegates to the 1995 National Meeting of Diocesan Liturgical Commissions held in Providence, RI, October 5-8, 1995. The remaining position statements will be published in the November 1995 issue of the Newsletter. *The degree of commitment to each statement is indicated in parentheses. The voting scale is graded from +3 (highest degree of commitment) to -3 (complete opposition to the statement). A commitment of +1.5 is required for acceptance of position statements. These resolutions will be reviewed by the Committee on the Liturgy for appropriate action.*

PS 1995 A
Gesture and Posture at Eucharist

It is the position of the delegates to the 1995 National Meeting of Diocesan Liturgical Commissions that the Board of Directors of the Federation of Diocesan Liturgical Commissions commission bulletin inserts on the topics of gesture and posture of the assembly at Eucharistic celebrations giving special attention to standing, bowing, and genuflecting as well as appropriate signs of reverence in receiving communion. (Passed +2.00)

PS 1995 B
Support for *Environment and Art in Catholic Worship*

It is the position of the delegates to the 1995 National Meeting of Diocesan Liturgical Commissions that the Federation of Diocesan Liturgical Commissions' Board of Directors express to the Bishops' Committee on the Liturgy the Federation's support and endorsement of the document, *Environment and Art in Catholic Worship,* and urge that any revision of or sequel to this document preserve the vision of the original and its faithful adherence to the universal law of the Church. We further urge that references be cited more completely to clarify that relationship between the principles of *Environment and Art in Catholic Worship* and their primary sources in universal Roman documents. (Passed +2.90)

PS 1995 C
Sunday Celebrations in the Absence of a Priest

It is the position of the delegates to the 1995 National Meeting of Diocesan Liturgical Commissions that the Board of Directors of the Federation of Diocesan Liturgical Commissions communicate to the Bishops' Committee on the Liturgy that the practice of Sunday celebrations in the absence of a priest as a substitute for Sunday eucharist is not acceptable and that it is urgent that they take action to ensure that the celebration of the Holy Sacrifice of the Mass is provided on every Sunday to all parish communities, whose very identity and Catholic life is constituted in the celebration of the holy eucharist. (Passed +2.545)

(To be continued in the next issue.)

COMMITTEE ON THE LITURGY
NEWSLETTER

1995
VOLUME XXXI
NOVEMBER

November Meeting of the Committee on the Liturgy

The Committee on Liturgy met in Washington, D.C. on Sunday, November 12, 1995 in conjunction with the Plenary Meeting of the National Conference of Catholic Bishops The major portion of the meeting was devoted to discussion of the amendments submitted on Segment IV of the *Sacramentary* which contains the prefaces, solemn blessings, prayers over the people, and sample general intercessions. The Committee remanded thirteen texts to ICEL for further consideration and added an explanatory rubric to a new preface intended for use only at Sunday daytime Masses. In addition to the consideration of the amendments, the Committee prepared a response to a bishop who had suggested an alternative method for approving segments of the *Sacramentary*. The Committee also received reports on the work of the Hispanic Liturgy Subcommittee and its progress on the Spanish translation of the *Sacramentary* and the second edition of the marriage rite.

November Plenary Assembly of the NCCB

The National Conference of Catholic Bishops met in plenary assembly from November 13-16, 1995 at the Omni Shoreham Hotel in Washington, D.C. During the course of the meeting, the bishops approved two action items presented by the Committee on the Liturgy.

The first action item, consideration of the *Pastoral Introduction to the Order of Mass*, had been scheduled for consideration at the June 1995 Chicago meeting, but there was insufficient time to consider the text. At the November meeting, the *Pastoral Introduction* with the American adaptations was approved by the required two-thirds of the *de iure* Latin rite members of the Conference. At the time, 176 affirmative votes were needed for approval. The *Pastoral Introduction* received 198 affirmative and 28 negative votes. The American adaptations to the *Pastoral Introduction* incorporate the changes in Segment III approved at the June 1995 meeting. This section received 197 affirmative votes and 30 negative votes. The text now requires the confirmation of the Apostolic See. The *Pastoral Introduction* clarifies information in the *General Instruction of the Roman Missal* and supplements it with material taken from other liturgical documents. The *Pastoral Introduction to the Order of Mass* will appear at the beginning of the revised *Sacramentary* immediately following the *General Instruction of the Roman Missal*.

The second action item was a request for the approval of Segment IV of the *Sacramentary* which contains the prefaces, solemn blessings, prayers over the people, and sample general intercessions. This item also required a two-thirds affirmative vote of the *de iure* Latin rite bishops. Segment Four was approved with 182 affirmative votes and 39 negative votes. Confirmation of the *Pastoral Introduction* and Segment IV will be requested from the Congregation for Divine Worship and the Discipline of the Sacraments when the remaining segments of Volume I of the *Sacramentary* have been completed.

In other action, the Most Reverend Jerome G. Hanus, OSB, Archbishop of Dubuque, was elected chairman-elect of the Committee on the Liturgy. He will succeed the present chairman, the Most Reverend Donald W. Trautman, Bishop of Erie, at the conclusion of the November 1996 Plenary Meeting of the NCCB.

3211 FOURTH STREET NE • WASHINGTON, DC 20017

Pope John Paul II's Reflection on *Sacrosanctum Concilium*

On Sunday, November 12, before praying the Angelus, the Holy Father continued his recent reflections on the documents of the Second Vatican Council:

"We still have vivid memories of the great impression caused by the liturgical changes introduced by the Council. Christians and non-Christians alike first felt the impact of the Council's updating precisely through the reform of the rites.

"The Constitution *Sacrosanctum Concilium* on the Liturgy, approved on December 4, 1963, was in a certain sense the 'first fruits' of the Second Vatican Council. More than providing for a merely external reform of worship, it wished to imbue the Christian community with a new awareness of the liturgy as 'the summit toward which the activity of the Church is directed' and 'the fount from which all her power flows' (no. 10).

"Certainly -- as the Council itself recalled -- the liturgy is not everything (cf. n. 9). It belongs among the numerous dimensions of ecclesial life, while in Christians it presupposes and requires a constant process of conversion, formation, consistency, and witness. However, within these individual and community coordinates, we cannot fail to recognize that the liturgy has a truly central value.

"The reason for this centrality is clearly explained by the Constitution, which places it within the framework of the history of salvation. Liturgical prayer, in comparison with the many other forms of prayer, has a status all its own, not only because it is the public prayer of the Church, but above all because it is a true actualization, and in a certain sense continuation, by means of signs, of the marvels wrought by God for man's salvation. This is particularly true in the sacraments, and most especially in the eucharist, where Christ himself becomes present as high priest and victim of the new covenant. What happened once and for all in his death and resurrection is sacramentally represented and relived in the rite. In this way the celebrating Church becomes the recipient of grace as well as its vehicle, and all those who approach the sacraments with the proper dispositions receive from them the fruits of sanctification and salvation.

"The Council's directives to make the liturgy ever more meaningful and effective were truly wise. It made the rites correspond to their doctrinal meaning, imbuing the proclamation of God's word with renewed vigor, encouraging a more active participation by the faithful and promoting those different forms of ministry which, while expressing the richness of charisms and ecclesial services, eloquently show how the liturgy is at the same time an action of Christ and of the Church. Moreover, the impetus given to adapting the rites to the various languages and cultures, so that in the liturgy too the Church could give complete expression to her universal character, was decisive. With these innovations, the Church did not cut herself off from her tradition, but on the contrary fully interpreted its riches and its demands."

Eucharistic Prayer for Masses for Various Needs and Occasions

The new eucharistic prayer, based on a revised Latin version of the Swiss Synod eucharistic prayer, was approved by members of the NCCB in 1994 for use in the United States. Confirmation was given by the Congregation for Divine Worship and the Discipline of the Sacraments on May 9, 1995. At this time the prayer is being prepared for publication and should be available for purchase in early January from The Liturgical Press (Telephone: 612-363-2326) and Catholic Book Publishing Company (Telephone: 201-890-2400).

Resolutions of the 1995 National Meeting of Diocesan Liturgical Commissions (continued)

The following are the remaining position statements and resolutions of immediate concern that were adopted by the delegates to the 1995 National Meeting of Diocesan Liturgical Commissions held in Providence, RI, October 5-8, 1995. (The first three position statements appeared in the October 1995 issue of the Newsletter. The degree of commitment to each statement is indicated in parentheses. The voting scale is graded from +3 (highest degree of commitment) to -3 (complete opposition to the statement). A commitment of +1.5 is required for acceptance of position statements. These resolutions will be reviewed by the Committee on the Liturgy for appropriate action.

PS 1995 D
Implementation of the *Lectionary* and *Sacramentary*

It is the position of the delegates to the 1995 National Meeting of Diocesan Liturgical Commissions that the Federation of Diocesan Liturgical Commissions in conjunction with the Secretariat of the Bishops' Committee on the Liturgy develop and make available resource materials to facilitate effective implementation of the revised *Lectionary* and *Sacramentary*:

a) these resources should include, but not be limited to, commentaries, study guides, parish bulletin inserts and video presentations;

b) these resources may be developed by the Federation of Diocesan Liturgical Commissions in conjunction with the Bishops' Committee on the Liturgy or in cooperation with publishers;

c) these resources should be made available to bishops, pastors, worship offices and commissions throughout the United States as far as possible in advance of implementation. (Passed +2.497)

PS 1995 E
Publication of Liturgical Texts

It is the position of the delegates to the 1995 National Meeting of Diocesan Liturgical Commissions that the Federation of Diocesan Liturgical Commissions' Board of Directors request the Bishops' Committee on the Liturgy to require that liturgical publishers in the United States follow the layout presented by the International Commission on English in the Liturgy especially in the following areas: location of page breaks at a natural point in the text, location of options in a place that will facilitate their use, and similar aspects of layout and design, and to test the layout of these texts with priests, deacons, and other leaders of prayer to ensure the ease of use of future publications and new editions of current texts. (Passed +1.90)

RIC 1995 F
Norms for the Use of *Mustum* and Low-Gluten Hosts

Whereas the medical condition of persons suffering from Celiac disease, alcoholism, or another condition which prevents the ingestion of even the smallest quantity of alcohol has been a serious pastoral concern of the Latin Church during the past decade;

Whereas the presence of even a minute amount of gluten in altar breads or alcohol in wine can be extremely harmful to such persons;

Whereas the June 19, 1995, circular letter of Joseph Cardinal Ratzinger, Prefect of the Congregation for the Doctrine of the Faith, to presidents of episcopal conferences provides new norms concerning permission to use low-gluten altar bread and mustum for such persons;

Whereas norm III D of the circular letter states that "candidates for the priesthood who are affected by Celiac disease or suffer from alcoholism or similar conditions may not be admitted to Holy Orders";

The delegates to the 1995 National Meeting of Diocesan Liturgical Commissions are resolved that the insufficiency of the new norms in addressing the medical conditions of the above-named sufferers is a matter of significant and immediate concern to them; they urge the National Conference of Catholic Bishops after further study to communicate to the Congregation for the Doctrine of the Faith their desire that

a) the norm concerning low-gluten altar breads be changed to no-gluten breads, and the addition of a binding agent such as xanthum gum be permitted in the preparation of gluten-free altar breads, and

b) the prescription of norm III D of the circular letter of the Congregation for the Doctrine of the Faith be abrogated. (Passed +2.711)

RIC 1995 G
Posture During the Eucharistic Prayer

Whereas the 1969 edition of the Roman Missal for the first time included directives concerning postures and gestures of the congregation;

Whereas that missal prescribes standing during the eucharistic prayer except at the consecration, when kneeling is prescribed "unless prevented by the lack of space, the number of people present, or some other good reason;"

Whereas the present U.S. discipline regarding posture during the eucharistic prayer approved by the National Conference of Catholic Bishops in November 1969 departs from the universal norm by continuing the practice that was generally observed prior to the promulgation of the revised missal, namely, kneeling during the eucharistic prayer from the conclusion of the Sanctus to the Great Amen;

Whereas the responses of the National Conference of Catholic Bishops members to a January 1992 survey were evenly divided on the question of standing or kneeling as the posture for the eucharistic prayer;

Whereas in the U.S. there is now diversity in the posture of the assembly during the eucharistic prayer owing to different interpretations of number 21 of the *General Instruction of the Roman Missal*;

Whereas there has never been a thorough review and/or study of posture during the eucharistic prayer by the National Conference of Catholic Bishops nor an examination of the theological and liturgical implications of this for our understanding of the eucharist;

The delegates to the 1995 National Meeting of Diocesan Liturgical Commissions are resolved that the withdrawal of the new wording of no. 21 of the *Appendix to the General Instruction of the Roman Missal for the Dioceses of the United States of America*, proposed for the approval of the National Conference of Catholic Bishops in June 1995, is a matter of significant and immediate concern to them; they urge the Bishops' Committee on the Liturgy to provide a mechanism along with appropriate documentation by which the National Conference of Catholic Bishops may discuss the issue of posture during the eucharistic prayer, for the purpose of a reexamination of their 1969 decision or, at the very least, the reintroduction of the text withdrawn by the Bishops' Committee on the Liturgy in June. (Passed +2.727)

In Memoriam

Reverend James B. Dunning

Reverend James B. Dunning, founder of the North American Forum on the Catechumenate, died suddenly in Washington, D.C. on September 16, 1995. Father Dunning, a priest of the Archdiocese of Seattle, was a former pastor and chaplain as well as a seminary professor in the Archdiocese. As Coordinator of the Forum, Father Dunning was a presenter at national and international workshops and seminars on Christian Initiation, wrote extensively on the catechumenate, and taught as visiting professor in the area of initiation and the catechumenate in various universities and colleges around the country.

> God of mercy and love,
> grant to James, your servant and priest,
> a glorious place at your heavenly table,
> for you made him here on earth
> a faithful minister of your word and sacrament.
> (*Order of Christian Funerals*, 398.17)

COMMITTEE ON THE LITURGY

NEWSLETTER

1995
VOLUME XXXI
DECEMBER

November 2, 1996

November 2nd, the commemoration of All Souls, will fall on a Saturday in 1996. The *General Instruction of the Roman Missal,* no. 330, states: "Ritual Masses are prohibited on the Sundays of Advent, Lent, and the Easter season, on solemnities, on days within the octave of Easter, on All Souls, on Ash Wednesday, and during Holy Week. In addition, the norms in the ritual books or in the Masses themselves also apply."

The words "on days within the octave of Easter, on All Souls" did not appear in the 1970 edition of the *GIRM*, which was included in the USA editions of the *Sacramentary* published in 1974. However, those words did appear in the 1975 *editio typica altera* of the *Missale Romanum* and in the 1985 USA edition of the *Sacramentary.*

Since most marriages are celebrated on Saturdays in the United States, pastors should take care to respect the Church's liturgical calendar and to avoid scheduling wedding Masses on this day. In a 1985 letter to Father John Gurrieri, then Executive Director of the Liturgy Secretariat, Archbishop Virgil Noè, Secretary of the Congregation for Divine Worship, explained the prohibition:

"The directives already given in the liturgical books make it clear that the Ritual Mass may not be celebrated on this day and that the local bishop cannot grant permission for its use on the grounds of pastoral discretion." The rubric given in the *Sacramentary* on November 2 which refers to the occurrence of the celebration on a Sunday states: "Even when November 2 falls on a Sunday, All Souls Day is celebrated, with the following Masses." Archbishop Noè went on to state: "Given that the Sunday Mass gives place to this celebration, it follows that it (the Commemoration of the Faithful Departed on November 2) cannot give place to a Ritual Mass."

Given the difficulties in scheduling weddings, pastors should make couples aware of this prohibition as early as possible to avoid complications and consternation. Should scheduling conflicts exist, it should be noted that it is the Ritual Mass for Marriage that is prohibited on November 2, and that the Rite of Marriage outside of Mass is not prohibited on that day.

Hispanic Liturgy Subcommittee

The Hispanic Liturgy Subcommittee, chaired by Bishop Roberto Gonzales, O.F.M., is charged with advising the Committee on the Liturgy about matters relating to the celebration of the liturgy in the Spanish language in the United States. The Subcommittee met in Corpus Christi in October to prepare documentation for the *Ritual de Exequias Cristianas.* The Spanish translation of the Order of Christian Funerals was approved at the November 1993 Plenary Session of the NCCB and submitted for confirmation to the Congregation for Divine Worship and the Discipline of the Sacraments. The Congregation has requested clarification on several matters relating to the *Ritual.* This information is being sent to the Congregation.

3211 FOURTH STREET NE • WASHINGTON, DC 20017

The major work of the Subcommittee continues to be the preparation of the U.S. version of the *Sacramentary* in Spanish. The American Adaptations for the Order of Mass and its Pastoral Introduction are being translated at this time. The subcommittee has also begun work on the translation of the second edition of the *Rite of Marriage* and is completing a Spanish translation of the American blessings contained in the *Book of Blessings* for use in the dioceses of the United States.

New Associate Director for Liturgy Secretariat

Reverend James P. Moroney, a priest of the Diocese of Worcester, MA, has been named Associate Director of the National Conference of Catholic Bishops' Secretariat for the Liturgy. Father Moroney holds a bachelor's degree in sacred theology from the Pontifical Gregorian University in Rome and a licentiate in sacred theology from the Catholic University of America. He was ordained in 1980 and currently is pastor of Mary, Queen of the Rosary Parish in Spencer, MA.

Father Moroney has served on and chaired the Diocesan Liturgical Commission in Worcester and has been an active member of the Federation of Diocesan Liturgical Commissions. He is the current Chairperson of the FDLC Board of Directors. The Committee on the Liturgy is pleased to welcome Father Moroney as the new Associate Director of the Liturgy Secretariat. Father Moroney will begin his term of service on February 1, 1996.

With the appointment of Father Moroney, the Liturgy Secretariat is now fully staffed. Monsignor Alan F. Detscher serves as Executive Director of the Secretariat. Assisting him are Sister Ann Rehrauer and Father Moroney as Associate Directors, Mary Elizabeth Sperry, Staff Assistant and Seán T. Murphy, Administrative Secretary.

Eucharistic Congress - 1997

Wrocław, Poland is the setting for the forty-sixth International Eucharistic Congress to be celebrated May 27-June 1, 1997. The city of Wrocław is situated on the Oder River in the center of the region of lower Silesia which borders Germany on the west and the Czech Republic on the south. Today Wrocław is the fourth largest city in Poland with a population of over 640,000.

The celebration of international eucharistic congresses dates back to 1881 in Lille, France. The motto of the early congresses was "The salvation of society through the Eucharist". In their initial stages, the congresses were concerned with eucharistic works: adoration, communion -- especially for children, processions, various associations and movements. After the Second Vatican Council the congresses took on a new image reflected in the expression "Statio Orbis" -- the gathering of the particular churches, in a city, with the Holy Father or his legate, around Christ present in the eucharist. Participation in the eucharist is the center of the modern Congress which also includes study sessions, discussion panels, the Liturgy of the Hours, eucharistic adoration and devotions.

Preparation for a eucharistic congress takes place on many levels. It is catechetical, liturgical and pastoral, taking into account the history, tradition, and culture of each of the nations participating. It usually includes a study of the theme, catechesis on the eucharist, a more active participation in the eucharist and a deepened sense of adoration and prayer that transforms all of life.

At the close of the forty-fifth Eucharistic Congress in Seville, Spain, our Holy Father announced the reason for his choice of the site for the 1997 Congress: "Thanking God that such a significant ecclesial event can once again be celebrated in that part of Europe which after difficult trials has regained its freedom, I entrust to the motherly intercession of Our Lady of Czestochowa the preparations for and development of that future encounter around Jesus in the Blessed Sacrament, which we hope will give renewed impulse to the Church's activity, particularly in the countries of Central Europe."

The 1997 Congress theme, *Eucharist and Freedom* and its motto "For freedom, Christ has set us free," is based on a section of Paul's letter to the Galatians: "It was for liberty that Christ freed us: so stand firm and do not take on yourself the yoke of slavery a second time" (Gal. 5:1). In commenting on the theme, the Holy Father noted that for nations that have never known outside domination and for nations recently freed from oppression, the eucharist should give light for the future, as an affirmation of true freedom. He expressed a hope that the Congress would help bring a fuller understanding of the central place of the eucharist in the life of the Church and show the solidarity between the eucharistic table and sharing with the poor, announcing a more just world as we await the coming of the Lord.

International congresses are organized and coordinated by the Pontifical Committee for International Eucharistic Congresses, first established in 1879. The Committee works with local committees and with National Delegates appointed as liaisons with the Committee. These delegates also serve as coordinators in their own countries. The national delegates for the Wrocław Congress met in Rome in May of 1995 to begin planning for the 1997 Congress. Monsignor Alan Detscher, Executive Director of the NCCB Secretariat for Liturgy serves as the National Delegate to coordinate participation in the United States and to represent the United States at the Congress. It is hoped that more detailed information on the 1997 Congress will be available in the next several months.

1996 Pastoral Liturgy Conference

The Notre Dame Center for Pastoral Liturgy will hold its annual liturgy conference June 17-20, 1996. This year's conference theme "Traditions and Transitions: Culture, Church and Worship" addresses the increasing pressure for change on our culture, our church and our worship. Conference presenters will address topics of assessing and evaluating change, resistance to change, and holding tradition and transition in balance.

Presenters for this year's conference include Scott Appleby, Catherine Dooley, Edward Foley, John Hibbard, Alan Hommerding, Michael Joncas, Aidan Kavanagh, John Melloh, Kathleen Norris, James Schellman, Victoria Tufano, Richard Vosko, and Georgette Zalewska.

For further information contact the Notre Dame Center for Pastoral Liturgy at the following address: Box 81, Notre Dame, IN 46556 phone (219) 631-5435 or FAX (219) 631-6968. E-mail at ndcpl.l@nd.edu.

Thirty Years of the *Newsletter*

With the publication of the September 1995 issue of the *Newsletter*, we mark the completion of thirty years of the Bishops' Committee on the Liturgy *Newsletter*. The first volume of the *Newsletter* contained the issues for the months of September -- December 1965. Volume II began with the January 1966 issue.

In the past, bound volumes of the *Newsletter* have been published by the United States Catholic Conference. The bound volume of the *Newsletter* for 1986-1990 was published by Liturgy Training Publications (LTP) of Chicago (1800 North Hermitage Avenue, Chicago, IL 60622; 1-800-933-1800). LTP will soon publish the bound volume of the *Newsletter* from 1991-1995.

1996 Newsletter Subscription

The renewal forms for the 1996 edition of the Bishops' Committee on the Liturgy *Newsletter* were mailed to current subscribers in November. Subscribers are asked to return the completed renewal form with their payment by January 30, 1996 to insure continuing service. Subscriptions not renewed by January 30, 1996 will be placed on inactive status.

To insure proper credit, subscribers should follow the directions which accompanied the renewal notice. Anyone who has not received a renewal notice should contact the Liturgy Secretariat at (202) 541-3060.

If you are aware of anyone who is interested in subscribing to the *Newsletter*, please have them contact the Secretariat at 3211 Fourth Street NE, Washington, D.C. 20017-1194. The cost of an individual subscription is $10. Back issues of the *Newsletter* are available at $1 per issue. Special prices for bulk orders are available for orders of 20 copies or more. Contact the Secretariat for more information.

Resources

Roman Catholic Worship: Trent to Today by James F. White. James White, whose earlier publications include *Introduction to Christian Worship* and *Protestant Worship: Traditions in Transition*, is professor of Liturgical Studies at the University of Notre Dame and a past president of the North American Academy of Liturgy. In the preface to *Roman Catholic Worship*, Professor White notes that people recognize that a great deal has happened in Roman Catholic worship since the Second Vatican Council. However, the myth still persists that very little happened in the four centuries between the end of the Council of Trent in 1563 and Vatican II. He then proceeds to dispel that myth with six chapters of historical survey and a final section on the future. White follows the same structure in each chapter, considering the liturgical environment, liturgical events and persons, time and devotions, the Mass, key events in society, church music, preaching, and the Liturgy of the Hours during each time period. Written in a more popular style, Professor White's work is a useful overview of the period from Trent to the Second Vatican Council. The book is available from Paulist Press (997 Macarthur Boulevard, Mahwah, NJ 07430; 201-825-7300) for $11.95.

From Breviary to Liturgy of the Hours is Stanislaus Campbell's expanded version of his doctoral dissertation at the University of Notre Dame. In this clear and focused study, the author presents a detailed description of the reform of the Liturgy of the Hours from 1964-1971. At first one might wonder at someone's ability to generate more than three hundred pages on a topic within such a confined time frame -- especially when the author sets the context by summarizing the sixth to the twentieth centuries within the first fifteen pages. The remaining three hundred or so pages provide a detailed yet interesting account of the process of the reform, as well as offering a structural analysis of the reformed texts and an evaluation of both the process of reform and the structure of the final product. As one would expect, this scholarly study is carefully nuanced and well documented. Students of liturgy will find the footnotes especially helpful. The text is available from The Liturgical Press (Saint John's Abbey, Collegeville, MN 56321; 612-363-2326) for $34.95.

INDEX

provisional liturgical texts for Mary, Star of the Sea, 137, 143, 153, 174, 183, 225–227

Mass
biblical renewal of, 28
catechesis, 86
development of English usage, 34
examples of defects in liturgical renewal, 27
languages of the people, 34
Latin rites; vernacular, 33
Mass in Thanksgiving for Human Life, 22
obligation pertains to the entire celebration, 36
participation: reception of communion, 35
reforms not fully appropriated, 27
as sacrifice or banquet, 19, 20
silence and reflection in, 20
true participation in, 20
two parts forming one act of worship, 36
see also Concelebration; Order of Mass; Vernacular

Mass Intentions, Collective
catechesis of the faithful, 14, 16
celebration for individual intentions, 14
combining intentions and offerings, 13
commentary on the Decree, 15–17
as form of almsgiving, 14, 17
frequency of use of collective intentions, 16
fruits of the Eucharistic sacrifice, 15
great number of offerings (All Souls and other special occasions), 14
material needs of priests, 16
modest offerings in poor regions, 15
norms to be made known by bishops, 14
offering amount established by diocese, 14
places of pilgrimage, 14
prayer for the deceased, 16
priests' moral responsibility, 14

priests who do not accept particular intentions, 16
satisfying obligations of justice, 13, 15
separate Masses (canon 948), 14, 15
shrines, 14, 16
support of clergy, of Church works, 16
terms: stipend or offering, 15
use of money derived from ecclesiastical offices, 17

Masses with Children
Lectionary; translations, 11–12
Roman directory; adaptation, 37

Mauck, Marchita, 21

McLoughlin, Ellen, 132, 149, 163

McManus, Reverend Monsignor Frederick R., 22, 145, 149, 155, 179, 224, 229

Memorial Acclamation, 197, 219

Mexican American Cultural Center (San Antonio), 7

Middle Ages
spirituality, 81

Milwaukee Symposium for Church Composers
ten-year report, 128

Ministerial Roles
Resolution concerning expansion of, 44

Missal (the *Roman Missal*), 229, 233, 235
addition of new canons, prefaces, etc., 20
American adaptations of, 201, 203–204, 206–208, 209–211, 218–219, 237
approval by other English-speaking conferences, 212
approval of American adaptations to the Order of Mass, 219–220
approval of *Pastoral Introduction to the Order of Mass*, 202, 233

approval of Segments One and Two, 191
approval of Segment Three, 201, 202, 219–220, 230
approval of Segment Four, 233
catechesis, 37, 86, 87, 134
contact with Doctrine Committee, 149, 150, 153, 160, 174–175, 187, 202, 230
contents of Segment Three, 194–199
FDLC resolution encouraging approval, 183
guidelines for revision of ecumenical texts, 195
guidelines for revision of Order of Mass, 194
ICEL translation, 34
inclusive language in, 135
informational materials for revision; resolution, 87
involvement of Diocesan Liturgical Commissions in revision, 134
ministerial chants in, 128
NCCB Procedure for Approving the Revised Roman Missal, 133, 137, 141, 149–151, 174
original texts, 195–196
Pastoral Introduction to the Order of Mass, 176, 198–199, 208, 210–211, 218–219
possible third typical edition, 31
preparation of revised edition, 110, 153
process for approval in England and Wales, 152
reform, 20, 86
revision of, 117–118, 137, 141–142, 153, 174–175, 186–187, 189, 190
survey on the *Sacramentary*, 207–208
Task Group on American Adaptation, 69, 118, 174, 175, 201, 207
theme of Diocesan Liturgical Commissions meeting, 76
third progress report on revision, 57
use of ecumenical prayer texts, 130, 194, 195, 202, 210
variations in the Order of Mass, 196–198, 210